Illustrated History of the American Civil War

Oct. 1861

Illustrated History of the American Civil War

Edited by
Henry Steele Commager

with
Marcus Cunliffe
Maldwyn A. Jones

Orbis Publishing
London

THE EDITORS: Henry Steele Commager has taught history at
Columbia, Cambridge, Oxford, and other universities, and at
Amherst College, for over forty years. He is the coauthor
(with S. E. Morison) of *The Growth of the American
Republic*, and author of *Theodore Parker, The American
Mind, Majority Rule and Minority Rights,* and many other
books. He is the editor of *Documents of American History*
and, with Richard B. Morris, of the fifty-volume *New
American Nation Series.* Professor Commager was recently
awarded the Gold Medal of the American Academy of Arts
and Letters for his historical writings.

Marcus Cunliffe is Professor of American Studies at the
University of Sussex. He has been a Commonwealth Fellow
at Yale and has taught at Harvard and other American
universities. Professor Cunliffe's books include *The
Literature of the United States, The Nation Takes Shape,
Soldiers and Civilians,* and *The American Presidency.*

Maldwyn A. Jones is Commonwealth Fund Professor of
American History at the University of London. He has been
a visiting professor at Harvard and at the universities of
Chicago and Pennsylvania. Professor Jones has written
extensively on American ethnic groups and is the author of
American Immigration, a volume in the *Chicago History of
American Civilization.*

© 1976 by Grolier Enterprises Inc.
This edition published by Orbis Publishing Ltd., London.

Reprinted 1982, 1984

Printed in Singapore

ISBN: 0 85613 211 X.

Introduction

"This people is one of the happiest in the world," wrote Alexis de Tocqueville of American society in 1832. Impressed by the absence of poverty and by the general equality of condition he painted a picture of a proud, expanding, self-confident democracy. Yet Tocqueville was doubtful whether the Union could hold together permanently. It was menaced particularly, he believed, by the vast changes taking place in the relative strength of its constituent sections. The northern states were increasing in population and wealth much more rapidly than the southern states. Hence southerners, seeing their influence decline, were beginning to consider whether their interests would not be better served outside the Union than within it. The events of the succeeding thirty years showed that Tocqueville's misgivings had been well-founded.

Sectionalism was not of course a new phenomenon. It had been a problem at the Constitutional Convention of 1787. Only by skillfully reconciling competing sectional aspirations had the Founding Fathers been able to frame an acceptable Constitution. But sectional antagonisms persisted, despite Washington's warning against them in his Farewell Address. Indeed between 1796 and 1814 the integrity of the Union was to be briefly threatened on two occasions, first by the discontents of the trans-Allegheny West, then by those of New England. But the sectionalism of the South, developing after 1820, turned out to be of a more tenacious variety. It finally grew into a self-conscious southern nationalism. By mid-century many southerners had accustomed themselves to the notion that the South had a geographical, economic, and social unity, that it possessed a distinctive past and that it ought to have an independent future.

One ought not to exaggerate either the unity or the distinctiveness of the Old South. It was not just one huge cotton-field, but a region of great variety. In many respects, too, the South was very like the rest of the United States. Nevertheless there was one fundamental difference: whereas in the North blacks constituted an insignificant fraction of the population, in the South they were more than half as numerous as whites. The growth of cotton cultivation in the early nineteenth century and the consequent spread of plantation agriculture and of Negro slavery accentuated the South's special character and engendered attitudes and ideals that set the region further apart from the rest of the nation.

Southern sectionalism was in part economic. As a predominantly agricultural section the South resented the tariff and the other federal policies designed to benefit northern industry and commerce. Southerners complained that their section was nothing more than an exploited colony of the North. The South, they argued, produced most of the nation's wealth, but most of it ended up in northern pockets. Further, southerners contributed more than their share of federal revenues, but received proportionately less in return. But although hostility to federal tariff policies prompted South Carolina to threaten secession in 1832–33, the economic grievances of the South were not the basic source of sectional conflict. That a menacing shadow hung over the young Republic during these years was due rather to the development of divergent attitudes toward slavery.

At the time of the Revolution many leading southerners had had a bad conscience about slavery; they had apologized for its existence and had looked forward to its ultimate disappearance. Half a century later southerners took a different view. Although slavery was in glaring contradiction to the ideals of the Declaration of Independence, they became increasingly outspoken in defending it. Meanwhile, after about 1830, militant abolitionism made its appearance in the North. The abolitionists did not succeed in converting northern opinion to their cause; they were at first an unpopular and persecuted minority. But in time their propaganda persuaded a majority of northerners that slavery and American democracy were incompatible.

For more than a quarter of a century after the Missouri controversy of 1820–21 politicians, concerned for the future of the Union, succeeded in excluding slavery from national politics. But after the huge territorial gains of the Mexican War, that proved no longer possible. Whether slavery should be permitted in the unsettled West now became the dominant issue in American politics. The Compromise of 1850 proved to be a mere palliative, not a final settlement of the differences between North and South. Thus in 1860–61, after a decade of mounting sectional strife, the nation drifted finally into disunion and civil war.

In 1860–61 the southern Confederacy was prepared to fight in order to uphold the right of one or more states to leave the Union and form a new, separate national federalism. The immediate problem, first for James Buchanan's Democratic administration and then for President Lincoln's Republican one, was how to combat the secession movement. Lincoln's answer, in response to the South, was to meet force with force. He and the North might have hesitated if they could have known that the resultant war would last four years, and claim more lives than any other American conflict before or since. But then, President Jefferson Davis's Confederacy might have hesitated too if they could have anticipated the outcome.

In the second place, the struggle tested whether the Union could defeat the South by the test of arms. Compared with Europe's professionalism, the United States was militarily a nation of rank amateurs. Innate military talent was thought to be confined mainly to the South. Could the North create armies, men to lead them, strategies to invade and subjugate defiant Dixieland? Could the South, borne up by its special brand of martial ardor, prove on the battlefield that its spirit was superior? Would the Union be able to blockade southern ports? Would the need of Europe's textile industry for "King Cotton" impel Britain and France to back the Confederacy?

In the third place, the Civil War compelled the Union to face the problem of slavery. Secession was a way of dealing with the question, by splitting America into two nations, one of free states and the other of slave states. But since the Union would not accept this drastic solution, Lincoln's administration was driven toward the only other alternative: emancipation by decree.

None of these grave matters was easily or speedily decided. In his first inaugural address, for example, Lincoln insisted that secession was impossible because the Union was a kind of solemn contract between the member states. Contracts could only be broken with the consent of all parties. But then, slaveholding was recognized and protected by the highest law of the land. By what right could this form of contract be set aside?

The conduct of the war proved enormously difficult, for both sides. Until the summer of 1863, when Lee was turned back at Gettysburg and Grant captured Vicksburg, most of the battles and campaigns had gone badly for the North. Both sides had to resort to conscription. Both were troubled with dissension and war weariness. The South suffered serious shortages of war material—in fact commodities of all sorts. As late as November 1864, with Grant failing to break Lee's front around Richmond, disappointment was so acute in the North that Lincoln feared he would lose the presidential election to his opponent George B. McClellan. His premonitions of violent death were to be fulfilled when he died from an assassin's bullet in April 1865.

Wars generate terrible ironies. A contributory factor in the collapse of the South was the attempt to build a nation on the theory of states' rights. Davis's administration lacked authority in consequence. Its weakness served to underline the practical as well as the theoretical case for a strong, indivisible Union. In a way that problem was settled forever. The Union's conduct of the war, apart from revealing the national capacity to improvise and organize, showed the great latent powers of the presidency. But in the next generation these capacities and powers were largely denied: every man for himself was to be the general rule. The war was fought to preserve the Union, to end slavery, and to make a better place for the ordinary citizen. But the postwar Union appeared to some to be dominated by northern big business, so that neither the average white American nor the freed slaves could be certain that all the slaughter and turmoil had been worth the effort. The war healed some wounds: had it, though, created fresh ones?

Contents

Chapter 1

THE PECULIAR INSTITUTION

By the midnineteenth century the American South was the only region in the New World where slavery survived as a thriving institution. Its healthy state was due in the main to the spiralling overseas demand for cotton—a demand that, after the cotton gin had been invented, southern planters raced to meet. Cotton production and slave labor were linked in harness, and the bondage of black men in the service of whites became even more entrenched as the cornerstone of southern society. Hard labor and force were essential ingredients of slavery. But although some slaves rose in revolt and many escaped to freedom, there were important factors which discouraged any challenge to the system.

Slavery in America

When southerners referred to slavery as the "peculiar institution" they did not have in mind that it was odd or unusual. Slavery in the middle of the nineteenth century was indeed unusual, but what southerners meant was that slavery was the institution that identified them. It was what set them apart from other Americans. Generally, they were proud of that distinction. After all, in the end they went to war to defend their peculiar institution.

In 1850 slavery existed in the New World only in Cuba, Puerto Rico, Brazil, and the United States. But if slavery was unusual, it had not always been so. For over 300 years it had been a principal form of labor. Soon after the Spanish came to South America they enslaved the Indians, especially those in Mexico and Peru where the settled, urban civilizations of the Aztecs and the Incas made this easy and profitable. In time, however, enslavement of Indians was outlawed for religious reasons by the Spanish Crown. In place of Indian labor, the Spanish and the Portuguese in Brazil imported black people from Africa in ever-increasing numbers.

By the time the first English colonies were settled in North America in the early seventeenth century, black slavery was widespread throughout the Spanish and Portuguese possessions in the New World. It is not surprising, therefore, that the English colonists soon followed their example. The first slaves in Virginia and New England, as in the Spanish and Portuguese colonies, were Indians. But the importation of Africans did not lag far behind. In fact, the first Negroes were imported into Virginia in 1619, a year before the *Mayflower* dropped anchor in Massachusetts Bay. The large-scale importation and use of black slaves in the English colonies, however, did not occur until late in the seventeenth century. By then Indians were no longer held in slavery. When the Revolution broke out each of the thirteen colonies, though proclaiming their independence in the name of freedom, permitted slavery in law. They also counted slaves among their populations. Some colonies, it is true—Maryland, Virginia, North Carolina, South Carolina, and Georgia—made greater use of slave labor than the more northern ones. Indeed, in South Carolina slaves outnumbered the free white population. It was not until after the Revolution, however, that slavery began to wane in any of the English colonies. By the close of the eighteenth century the states north of Delaware had ended slavery, either at one stroke, as in Massachusetts, or gradually, as in New York, New Jersey, and Pennsylvania.

This outline of the history of slavery before 1800 raises two questions. First, why was slavery introduced into the New World on such a wide scale when it was virtually extinct in the Europe from which the settlers came? The answer is that the newness of the land and the sparseness of the Indian population meant that the labor needed to make a quick and substantial profit from the land was lacking. For if a planter (or a company) brought free people with him to work his land in America, these workers would not stay with him when they could quite easily obtain land for themselves. Land was cheap compared with labor. If a landowner was to work his acres he needed a supply of labor that could not desert him for independent employment. The answer arrived at by the English, as by the Spanish and Portuguese before them, was the enslavement of non-Europeans. It would have been difficult to enslave Spaniards or Portuguese or Englishmen. After all they were not slaves at home—and their freedom was protected by law. But it was not difficult to enslave strangers like Indians or Africans, who were also physically distinct from whites. By the same token, as the New World populations grew through emigration from Europe, the need for slave labor in some places fell or failed to grow. Thus in New England and New York, where agriculture was not as well suited to large-scale plantations as in Virginia and Maryland, slave labor was not widely employed. As a result, when anti-slavery sentiment arose after the Revolution, it was fairly easy to abolish slavery in those places where it was not important to the economy.

Why Slavery Lingered On

The second question about the beginnings of slavery arises from the answer to the first. Why did slavery persist in the South while it was being abolished in the North? The answer involves more than the fact that tobacco made good use of slaves, though that is part of the answer. For by the end of the eighteenth century tobacco was no longer a highly profitable crop. Its market was stagnant and its return low. Indeed, many planters in Virginia and Maryland were already abandoning tobacco growing for wheat. Slaves, however, were not well suited to growing wheat. Grain crops did not have a long growing season, nor did they require the kind of close, if tedious, labor that made tobacco well suited to slavery—a form of labor that must have employment all year round if it is to be profitable. The fundamental reason why slavery persisted in the South into the nineteenth century was the development of a new crop that was more profitable and better suited to slave labor than tobacco.

That new crop was cotton. Its expansion in the South was the result not only of the presence of slaves, but of distant as well as local events. Cotton had been grown in America before 1800, but only in small amounts and in the coastal regions of South Carolina and Georgia. Until the last quarter of the eighteenth century there was little demand for the white fiber. Then a series of mechanical

Slavery was a social as well as an economic system. Above: A daguerreotype of Caesar, said to have been the last slave held in New York, who died in 1852. Below: Eli Whitney's gin opened the way for a massive boom in cotton production. With the invention came the spread of the crop—and the spread of slavery.

inventions in England made it possible to speed up and cheapen the cost of manufacturing cotton thread and textiles. The demand for raw cotton skyrocketed to such an extent that southerners raced to grow more cotton. There was one great difficulty, however. The only kind of cotton that could be grown in the inland or upland areas of the South was one in which the fiber clung tenaciously to the seeds. The separation process was time consuming and therefore costly. Even with slave labor, the American crop could not compete in price with some foreign sources of cotton which did not have this drawback. It was to meet this competition that Eli Whitney, a visiting Yankee, was begged by Georgia planters to put his brains to work to construct a machine that would cheaply remove the seeds from the fiber of upland cotton. In 1793 he produced a workable cotton gin and the cotton kingdom was born. Within thirty years cotton, the plantation, and black slavery had spread from the seaboard over the Appalachian Mountains, across the Mississippi River, and as far west as Texas.

Cotton, of course, was not the only crop cultivated by slave labor. Tobacco continued to be raised by slaves, as did rice, which had been grown in southern coastal areas even before the Revolution. When Louisiana was added to the Union in 1803, a sugar-growing industry developed there, making extensive use of slaves. And there were many other tasks to which slaves were put in the South. But the important thing is that it was the gin, cotton, and the English textile industry that made slavery the important institution in the South that it was by 1830.

The very fact that slavery was abolished in the North

and in most of the remainder of the New World before 1850 suggests that it was not necessarily a profitable, much less a desirable, institution. Many men in the nineteenth century, as well as many historians since, have argued that slavery had become quite unprofitable and ought to have been abolished for economic as well as for moral reasons. Indeed, some historians have argued that because it was uneconomical, slavery would have died out naturally, without the intervention of the Civil War. The question of whether slavery was a profitable form of labor is thus most important in thinking about the significance of the conflict. For if slavery was unprofitable and therefore on the way to extinction, then the war must be viewed as an event without need or purpose and its loss of life and expenditure of treasure an unjustifiable calamity. It is worth looking then at slavery, first as an economic institution and a little later as a social institution.

Perhaps the single most important fact about southern slave society is that most white people did not own slaves. Moreover, slaves constituted no more than one-third of the total population of the region. Only about one-quarter of whites in the South owned slaves or were members of slave-owning families. This meant that most of the work was performed by white people. In some areas of the South, particularly in the Deep South, slaves outnumbered whites, but this was more the exception than the rule for the region as a whole. Only three states in 1860, for example, counted a slave majority and in none of those was the proportion above 60 per cent.

This pattern of population distribution was in marked contrast with that in other slave societies in the New World. In Brazil, Cuba, and Jamaica, for example, slaves outnumbered whites. The United States also differed from those other slave societies in that the number of slaves held by individual planters were, on the average, considerably smaller. In fact, in 1850 over half the slaveholders owned fewer than five slaves. Less than 1 per cent of slaveholders possessed 100 or more slaves. The romantic picture of an antebellum South in which there were dozens of plantations with thousands of slaves on them was simply not true. Fewer than half a dozen slave-owners held as many as a thousand slaves at the height of southern slave society.

Put in such terms, the distribution of slaveholdings seems to make slavery of minor importance to the economy of the South. But to draw that conclusion would be quite wrong. For if most slaveowners were only small holders, most of the slaves were actually held in groups more than adequate for plantation agriculture. More than half of all slaves were held in groups of twenty or more, a number well suited to a good-sized plantation. It was on the plantations, moreover, that the bulk of the cotton, rice, and sugar was grown, and these were the crops that earned

The wealth of the South derived from the plantations which grew cotton, rice, and tobacco. Below: Slaves working on a rice plantation near Montgomery, Alabama.

the southern economy its profits and accumulated its capital.

Despite the acknowledged economic importance of the plantation, a sizable proportion of slaves was employed outside the plantation. Many were used on small farms, just like a hired man on a northern farm, often working side by side with the master in the fields, planting tobacco or a little cotton as well as corn, potatoes, and other vegetables. These small farms with a few slaves were to be found all over the South, but particularly in areas where cotton was not easily grown, such as in parts of North Carolina, Tennessee, Kentucky, and Arkansas. On such farms slaves performed a variety of tasks and sometimes ate with, as well as worked with, their owners.

Slaves were not confined to farming or unskilled work by any means. The large plantations, for example, often had highly skilled slaves to maintain the farm and other equipment, to make casks, construct houses, lay bricks, to carpenter and to perform the myriad of other jobs a large economic enterprise demanded. In the cities and towns of the South skilled slaves were common. They could be found in virtually every trade and craft, some very highly skilled. Slaves, for example, not only constructed the railroad lines in the South; they were also well represented among the engineers who drove the trains when the lines were completed. Richmond's flourishing tobacco manufacturing industry, the biggest in the nation, was largely manned by slaves. Similarly, the largest iron works in the South, the Tredegar Works

Above: Negro cabins on a rice plantation. Although the accommodation provided for slaves was humble and frequently ill kept, it did not prevent the growth of a strong community spirit.

Brown Brothers

Mansell Collection

Above: Workers in a tobacco warehouse at Richmond, Virginia. Slaves were used in a wide range of jobs outside the plantation.

(also in Richmond), was staffed by slaves. In coal mines and textile factories slaves were sometimes found working side by side with white workers. Occasionally a trusted slave would have free white workers under his command, as happened at one rather exceptional plantation in Mississippi, where the master's business was lumbering.

Was Slavery Profitable?

The variety of occupations filled by slaves shows not only the importance of slavery in the southern economy. It helps to answer the question raised earlier, namely, was slavery a paying proposition? The traditional conception of slavery is that it was inefficient, mainly because it was coerced labor. In the nineteenth century that was the most common argument raised against it. Yet, as already mentioned, slave labor was quite capable of being used in a variety of tasks in competition with free white labor. Moreover, even on a plantation and in agricultural work there were ways of persuading the slave to work without always having recourse to the whip. Setting tasks for slaves on the understanding that when the job was completed the remaining time was their own, introduced an incentive into the system. Other rewards, too, were at the disposal of the overseer or master to induce slaves to work without resorting to physical punishment.

Another common argument against the efficiency of slavery was that it was inflexible. Once a master bought a slave the costs of maintenance became a drain on resources unless the master could find sufficient work for him to do the year round. Slaves could not be laid off, as a free worker might be, when the work slackened. Chronically poor workers or recalcitrant slaves could be sold, of course, but probably only at a loss. Actually, though, slavery was more flexible in practice than in theory. Slave-hiring was an important way by which slaveowners could receive a monetary return from a temporarily redundant slave without the costs of maintenance. At the same time, a man who wanted the labor of a slave for a limited period but did not want to use his capital to buy a slave— a young, strong field hand cost between $1,500 and $2,000 —could hire another man's slave for six months or a year. Maintenance was then a charge against the hirer and not the owner, while the owner received a payment of $100 or so as a return on his capital invested in the slave. Many of the railroads of the South were constructed by hired slaves, rented by the railroad companies from the planters

Slave auctions publicly displayed the callousness of slavery, and equated human beings with animals. There was a constant demand for strong, healthy workers to provide the plantation owner with a cheap form of labor.

RAFFLE

Mr. Joseph Jennings respectfully informs his friends and the public that, at the request of many acquaintances, he has been induced to purchase from Mr. Osborne, of Missouri, the celebrated

DARK BAY HORSE, "STAR,"

Aged five years, square trotter and warranted sound; with a new light Trotting Buggy and Harness; also, the dark, stout

MULATTO GIRL, "SARAH,"

Aged about twenty years, general house servant, valued at

Will be Raf

At 4 o'clock P. M., February first, at the selection hotel of th
and those persons who may wish to engage in the usual pract
fectly satisfied with their destiny in this affair.
The whole is valued at its just worth, fifteen hundred d

CHANCES AT ONE

The Raffle will be conducted by gentlemen selected by the i
will be allowed to complete the Raffle. BOTH OF THE A
AT MY STORE, No. 78 Common St., second d or from
Highest throw to take the first choice; the lowest thr
winners will pay twenty dollars each for the refreshments
N. B. No chances recognized unless paid f r previous

JOSE

$1200 TO 1250 DOLLARS! FOR NEGROES!!

THE undersigned wishes to purchase a large lot of NEGROES for the New Orleans market. I will pay $1200 to $1250 for No. 1 young men, and $850 to $1000 for No. 1 young women. In fact I will pay more for likely

NEGROES,

Than any other trader in Kentucky. My office is adjoining the Broadway Hotel, on Broadway, Lexington, Ky., where I or my Agent can always be found.

WM. F. TALBOTT.

LEXINGTON, JULY 2, 1853.

Slaves were primarily regarded as pieces of property which could be bought or sold as the need arose. Occasionally, a planter might be lucky and win a girl in a raffle (left). Much more usual was the market purchase. Traders such as the Kentucky businessman featured in the broadside below bought slaves, then took them to the Deep South where the demand—and price—was greatest.

Above: This bill of sale, dated October 1859, records the sale of a slave for $800 in Louisiana. The slave is declared to be "free of mortgages."

along the right of way. Most of the slaves who worked in the Richmond tobacco factories were hired slaves.

The costs of maintaining less-productive slaves like children and old people ought not to be seen as an uneconomic burden on the economy of the South. In the North, employers supported the young and the old, too, but only indirectly—by paying their workers sufficient wages to support their parents and children.

Although it is possible to show that slavery was more flexible in practice than it might seem in theory, that fact does not quite answer the question of whether slavery was profitable to the planters or the southern economy in general. It is still necessary to know whether the planters made sufficiently careful use of the slaves to gain a cash return commensurate with what they would have received if they had invested their capital in forms of economic activity other than the slave plantation. Some of the most informed historians on slavery have contended that slaveowners were not realizing an adequate return. The evidence was that on the eve of the Civil War the price of slaves was so high compared with the price of cotton that a planter could not expect to make a profit. It was this argument, or variants of it, that made popular the view that the Civil War was an unnecessary blood-letting. If the North had simply waited and not agitated against slavery, so the argument ran, slavery would have simply ended of its own accord, killed off by its lack of profits.

More recently, however, other historians have advanced new evidence to suggest that the returns on slave labor were much better. For example, one historian calculated that the value of property in the South doubled between 1850 and 1860 while general prices remained about the same. Obviously, if slavery was not producing a profit it would be difficult to account for the doubling of land values in so short a period. Nor should the rising price of slaves be interpreted as a measure of the difficulty of producing a profit by using slaves to grow cotton, when cotton prices were failing to rise as rapidly. The high price of slaves was, rather, a measure of planters' expectations that if they bought more slaves they would be able to make even more money in the future. For if they did not expect to make a profit from slave labor they would not have bid up the price for slaves; without that demand for slaves the price would fall. Indeed, it has been shown that the return to the average planter in the South was about what he would have received on his capital if he had bought bonds in northern railroads or some other nonsouthern enterprise. One important element that was introduced into the discussion was the gain the planters obtained from the slaves' reproducing themselves. As every planter or slaveholder knew, slave children were worth $100 at birth and each year increased their value. The cost of rearing slaves to maturity was relatively small.

The inclusion of the value of slave children as a gain to the planters was important in calculating profitableness. It helped to explain why slavery was profitable even in areas that were declining in agricultural fertility, such as Virginia and South Carolina. At the time and since, many commentators noted that the new lands of Mississippi and Texas could produce cotton at less cost than the worn-out lands of the old seaboard states. In fact, a good part of the income of slaveholders in Virginia and Maryland came from selling slaves to the new states of the Deep South, where cotton production was expanding and flourishing. All the states of the South reared slaves to maturity, but because the upper South had a surplus the internal trade in slaves ran principally from those states to the Deep South. This movement of slaves within the South was a vital part of the system. It permitted the peculiar institution to survive, for after 1808 no more slaves could legally be imported from outside the United States. This dependence upon an *internal* supply of slaves for an expanding economy was unique among slave societies in the New World. As a result, the ending of importations did not threaten the continuation of slavery in the United States as it did in Brazil and Cuba. Slavery in the United States flourished, as never before, *after* the African slave trade was halted.

It may be thought that dependence upon rearing young slaves on the plantations would result in systematic breeding of slaves for the market. The facts, however, seem to be otherwise. Planters might point out, as some did when selling a female slave, that she had borne children, but there was a general reluctance on the part of planters to sell children away from their mother. It happened, to be sure, but the typical practice was for mothers to be sold with their children. Stories of slave-breeding plantations on which women far outnumbered men, who acted as studs, much as would occur on a stock-breeding ranch, have little basis in fact. The standard practice, instead, was to allow the slaves to pair off and live together as man and wife and simply await the natural consequences. Both the practice and the results were succinctly stated by a Virginia planter at the time. "No man is so inhuman as to breed and raise slaves, to sell off a certain proportion regularly, as a western drover does with his herds of cattle," he wrote. "But sooner or later the general result is the same. Sales may be made voluntarily, or by the sheriff—they may be made by the first owner, or delayed until the succession of heirs—or the

misfortunes of being sold may fall on one parcel of slaves, instead of another: but all of these are but different ways of arriving at the same general and inevitable result. With plenty of wholesome though coarse food, and under such mild treatment as our slaves usually experience, they have every inducement and facility to increase their numbers with all possible rapidity, without any opposing check, either prudential, moral, or physical."

When all elements are considered, it seems clear that slavery was producing profits for slaveowners. Moreover, it also seems evident that the southern economy as a whole, so dependent upon slave labor, was an expanding one. Profits from cotton were being steadily plowed back into more slaves and more land, not because that was simply the old habit of southerners, but because that was the best use that could be made of their capital and profits. Indeed, it was this prosperous character that caused non-slaveholders to support the institution, even in the middle of the nineteenth century when world morality was shifting away from bondage as a way of exacting labor from men and women. To look at slavery only as an economic institution is not enough. It was always much more than that. It shaped the lives of white people, whether they owned slaves or not, just as it controlled and ordered the lives of black people.

Slaves and the Law

Slavery was indisputably a matter of economics, but it was equally a relationship between human beings. This was particularly true in the antebellum South where virtually all slaves were native born and in daily personal contact with masters and their families. But the way slavery functioned as a social relationship often came into conflict with its economic aspect.

Perhaps this was most evident in the law. A slave was defined in law as chattel property, which meant personal property as distinguished from real estate or land. (Chairs, tables, horses, and clothing are examples of chattels under the law.) Those abolitionists who charged southerners with considering a black slave as merely a piece of property certainly had that part of the law to support them. But in both the law and in everyday practice, slaves were also viewed as human beings. They were held responsible for any crimes they might commit. They were tried in courts and punished for crimes like robbery, assault, and murder. Obviously no other kind of chattel property was held legally responsible for its acts. In their trials slaves were entitled to certain protections of the law, including the right to be represented by counsel in capital cases. In at least one case in Georgia, the conviction of a slave for murder was rejected by the appeal court because the slave's owner had not provided the slave with the services of a defense attorney.

Courts of the southern states clearly recognized that in law the slave was at once a person and a piece of property. As a court in Tennessee pointed out in 1846, "a slave is not in the condition of a horse or an ox. His liberty is restrained, it is true, and his owner controls his actions and claims his services. But he is made after the image of the Creator. He has mental capacities, and an immortal principle in his nature that constitutes him equal to his owner but for the accidental position in which fortune has placed him. The owner has acquired conventional rights to him, but the laws under which he is held as a slave have not and cannot extinguish his high-born nature nor deprive him of many rights which are inherent in man."

A Mississippi court went even further in emphasizing that slaves were human beings. In a case in 1821, in which a white defendant contended that killing a slave was not murder, the judge asserted that the life of a slave could not be taken with impunity. He may lack freedom, the judge conceded, but he is "still a human being and possesses all those rights, of which he is not deprived by the positive provisions of the law. By the provisions of our law, a slave may commit murder, and be punished with death," the judge pointed out. "Why then is it not murder to kill a slave? Can a mere chattel commit murder, and be subjected to punishment?" he rhetorically asked. "Is not the slave a reasonable creature, is he not a human being, [and since] even the killing of a lunatic, an idiot, or even a child unborn, is murder, as much as the killing of a philosopher, . . . has not the slave as much reason as a lunatic, an idiot, or an unborn child?" The judge then answered his question in the affirmative, sentencing the white slayer of the black slave to death.

As these quotations from court decisions suggest, southern courts constantly wrestled with a contradiction: how to reconcile the slave's recognized humanity with his being at the same time the property of another. In fact, the more slavery came under attack from the North and from the spirit of the age, the more many southern jurists became concerned to ensure that the law protected black people from the enormous power of the master. In the eighteenth century the law had done little to hedge the slave about with the legal protections that have just been quoted. Laws requiring masters to feed their slaves properly, to house and clothe them adequately, and to refrain from brutal or cruel punishments were nineteenth century innovations. The growth of legal protections for slaves in the nineteenth century reflected the South's effort to keep slavery and yet make it fit the age's standard of humane behavior.

Southern appeal courts were anxious, too, that no Negro be held in slavery if there was any doubt about the legality of his or her status. It is true that the law presumed that a black was a slave unless proof in court or personal documents established his or her freedom. Yet hundreds of cases were brought before southern courts by Negro slaves protesting their illegal enslavement. Of the 675 such cases that reached the courts of appeal, almost half of the appellants were later declared to be legally free. (These cases highlighted a tendency for blacks to be pushed into slavery, for those slaves declared free by the courts must have been unjustly enslaved in the first place.)

Since in 1850 there were about 3.2 million slaves, the few hundred who won their freedom as a result of suits for freedom were insignificant. Generally the opportunities for a slave to escape his bondage through legal means were meager indeed. Some thousands did, of course. Each year, for example, hundreds of slaves were freed by their masters, for one reason or another. Sometimes it was because of a meritorious act, such as reporting a slave insurrection or for faithful service of a distinguished kind. Or sometimes simply because the master did not believe in slavery. Not infrequently a master might have an intensely personal reason to free a slave. The fact that there were more mulattoes proportionately among the free Negroes in the South than among the slaves suggests strongly that many planters were freeing their own offspring among the slaves, for under the law a child of a slave mother, regardless of the status of the father, was also a slave.

Slaves also obtained their freedom by purchase. What records exist on this means of escape indicate that perhaps several thousand black people obtained their freedom in this way. Denmark Vesey, who gave his name to one of the important slave conspiracies of the nineteenth century, purchased his freedom after winning a large sum of money in a lottery. Technically, under the law, all money acquired by a slave, whether earned or won, was the property of his owner. But most owners did not deprive their slaves of money they may have acquired. And many owners were prepared even to set a freedom price if the slaves could scrape it together. There are cases, too, of masters who set a price for freedom, took the money when the slave had accumulated it, only to refuse to live up to the agreement. Against this cruelty the slave had no recourse in the law.

Thousands of slaves may have managed to use the law in one fashion or another to escape from slavery. But on the whole the law and white society did not look favorably upon manumission. In fact, as the antebellum years wore on, southern states narrowed more and more the opportunities for freedom, usually out of fear that freed Negroes incited the slaves to revolt. The restrictions on manumission usually meant that masters could not free their slaves without an act of the legislature or under special circumstances. And even when manumission was finally accomplished the freed Negro was usually required to leave the state. Under such circumstances some slaves

Above: Slaves picking cotton, with an overseer nearby. Left: Bales of cotton being chuted down to the water's edge for loading on a paddle steamer. The working day usually lasted twelve hours. Right: Slaves Escaping Through a Swamp by Thomas Moran. Slaves had few opportunities to win their freedom by purchase or through the courts. Thus, in spite of the terrible risks they faced by running away— the constant struggle to stay alive en route to freedom and the punishment inflicted if they were recaptured—many slaves did attempt flight.

may well have preferred not to be freed, since it would mean leaving behind wife and children as well as friends and familiar surroundings. Considering the general unfriendliness of the law toward freedom, it is not surprising that in 1860, after over two centuries of slavery, there were only a quarter of a million free blacks in the South as against 4 million slaves. On the other hand, in Brazil, which began as a society in which slaves outnumbered whites, the number of free blacks in 1870 was about twice the number of slaves. Brazilian law and social attitudes were much more hospitable to freedom for blacks. Manumission was easy to achieve if the master desired to bestow it; few legal obstacles stood in his way as many often did in the United States.

How Slavery Worked

The law of slavery, however, constituted only the bare "skeleton" of the system. The "flesh" on the institution was the day-to-day activities of masters and slaves. And here the character of the master could be controlling, whatever the law might say. The law might prohibit

excessive whipping or prescribe a minimum diet for slaves, but there were no government officers to police legal infractions. The isolation of the plantation, if nothing else, made such policing unrealistic. Consequently the lot of individual slaves varied greatly, depending upon the region in which they worked, or the crop, the season of the year, and the kind of master. Wealthy masters in established planting areas usually treated their slaves better than those who were opening new lands in Louisiana or Texas. For in virgin areas the slaves were often driven to get the land cleared, buildings constructed, crops planted, and profits made as soon as possible. Similarly, a master whose crop had failed the year before would not be able to feed and clothe his slaves as well as one whose crop had been sold at a good price. Other kinds of care, like medical service, would also vary according to the planter's disposition, income, or size of his slaveholding.

The degree of severity of labor required from slaves depended not only upon a particular master, or the newness of the land, but upon the crop as well. Slaves who worked in the rice areas of coastal Georgia and South Carolina, for example, undoubtedly worked harder at certain times of the year than slaves on cotton plantations in the same states. Growing rice involved heavy work,

clearing the swampy land and keeping the draining ditches open. Moreover, the rice region was unhealthy for both blacks and whites because of malaria and yellow fever. Similarly, slaves working on the sugar plantations of Louisiana were regularly subjected to brutally long hours of hard work during the grinding season. At this time, the operation of the sugar mill could not be interrupted and the crushing of the cane and the boiling of the juice required constant attention. It also subjected the slaves to discomfort from the heat of the fires.

The character of the slaves' labor may have varied in different circumstances and places, but in the end it was always and everywhere the same. The purpose of a slave was work and no matter where or when a slave lived, his or her life was primarily taken up with labor. In the nineteenth century the standard work day for a free white worker in a northern city was between ten and twelve hours in a working week of six days. Most slaves worked twelve hours a day most of the year, with a somewhat longer day in the summer. It was not uncommon, however, for a master to give his slaves half a day off on Saturday as well as the whole day on Sunday. The half day on Saturday was largely consumed in taking care of the small plots that planters often provided their slaves for growing vegetables and other table items for themselves. Sometimes particularly enlightened planters would purchase their own slaves' produce for the table in the big house. Southern planters, it is worth noting, did not expect

their slaves to grow their own food, as the more demanding slave masters in Jamaica did. Both the law and the common practice of the South expected the master to feed, clothe, and house his slaves. Whatever the slave grew on his own was supplementary, not basic to his diet.

Generally masters were careful to instruct their overseers or managers to see that slaves were properly cared for. "The manager will frequently inspect the meals as they are brought by the cook," wrote one planter to his overseer in Louisiana, "to see that they have been properly prepared, and that vegetables be at all times served with the meat and bread. The manager will, every Sunday morning after breakfast, visit and inspect every quarter; see that the house and yards are kept clean and in order, and that families are dressed in clean clothes."

The clothes and food, as well as the housing provided for the slaves, were usually, even on the most favored plantations, of a simple or crude kind. Slaves might well be provided with meat, but it would be of poor quality, though they often supplemented it with game they trapped or shot, and with fish they caught on their own. Similarly, the corn meal or sweet potatoes and other vegetables supplied by the master would be varied by food from the slaves' gardens. Clothes were of the coarsest wool or cotton. Indeed, textile manufacturers in the North specialized in producing cheap "Negro cloth." Cheap shoes were also specially produced in the North for the slaves. The houses of slaves could vary from simple wooden shacks without anything but the ground for a floor and without windows, to rather comfortable, if small, cabins with windows, but no glass, and a wooden floor and fireplace. They were generally not large enough to have more than two rooms. Slave quarters were usually set in rows, behind the big house.

Although all slaves were alike in the eyes of the law, in practice they differed greatly, as masters quickly recognized. On the large plantation the most obvious division was between house slaves and field hands. But on most farms the number of slaves was rarely large enough to make that a significant distinction. Some were recognized for special skills, or for their high intelligence, or easy deference. Where there were house servants, they usually enjoyed a somewhat better standard of living than the field hands if only because their close association with the whites demanded that they present a more attractive appearance. They were also in a position to help themselves or simply steal some of the food and other supplies of the masters. They brought back to the slave quarters, too, stories of life among the whites and of activities beyond the plantation. Masters often gave the impression to visitors that their black servants understood nothing and were without resentments or feelings. But the more intelligent masters knew full well that their every activity was witnessed by impassive eyes and almost their every word overheard by the ever-present servants.

Some domestics were integral parts of the master's household. This was especially true of black women who might act as wet nurses of white children at birth and then continue to rear them in subsequent years. The warmth of intimate human contact over the years could not help but forge a connection that, at times at least, transcended the barriers of status and color. One Alabama mistress wrote at the death of a black slave who had been her children's nurse, "when I saw that Death had the mastery, I laid my hands over her eyes, and in tears and fervor prayed that God would cause us to meet in happiness in another world. I knew, at that solemn moment, that Color made no difference, but that her life would have been as precious, if I could have saved it, as if she had been white as snow." But relations of such warmth could

Although hard and basic, slave life had its lighter side. A dance was among the most popular forms of relaxation for the plantation community.

The Virginia Museum of Fine Arts, Richmond, Virginia

Left: Outsiders were often surprised at the intimacy that developed between house slaves and the planter's family. In this ca. 1790 painting, a Negro nurse looks after the master's young sons.

be encountered side by side with the coldness usually associated with the relationship between master and slave. James H. Hammond, a large planter in South Carolina, could mourn the death of his black gardener as a "patriarch" and "one of the best of men," but the deaths of two other slaves in the same year brought forth the comment: "Neither a serious loss. One valuable mule has also died."

Among the white and black children in particular it was possible for the human side to override the economic—at least for a while. Frederick Douglass, who was not only a runaway slave, but a major figure in the antislavery movement, wrote that as a child "it was a long time before I knew myself to be a *slave*. . . . The first seven or eight years of a slave-boy's life," he went on, "are about as full of sweet content as those of the most favored and petted *white* children of the slaveholder. . . ." But the awakening could be abrupt and cruel. Another slave narrative described the moment of truth. "When I began to work, I discovered the difference between myself and my master's white children," wrote Lunsford Lane. "They began to order me about, and were told to do so by my master and mistress. . . . Indeed all things now made me *feel*, what I had before known only in words, that *I was a slave*."

Northerners were often struck by the intimacy between blacks and whites under slavery. Frederick L. Olmsted, a northern traveler in the antebellum South, tells of being both surprised and disgusted to see a master's son, returning home from college, being greeted with a kiss from a black domestic as he stepped off the steamboat. Northerners generally lacked that intimate association and familiarity with blacks that made it possible for southern whites to see them as living human beings as well as slaves. It is not without significance, either, that most masters preferred to refer to their slaves as "Negroes" or "our people." Sometimes a slave could play upon this intimacy between slave and master to secure a favor or prevent his family from being broken up.

A System Based on Force

For all the potential and actual paternalism in slavery, however, at bottom it was a system of power. At its root lay force. The most common form that coercion took was whipping. It was usually done by either white overseer or black driver, using a three-foot-long piece of rawhide, one inch thick at the butt and tapering to a point. (In Brazil a wooden paddle with holes drilled through the surface was often used, too; the holes increased the sting and with enough application could draw blood.) Planters often specified the maximum number of permissible lashes,

The Bettmann Archive

twenty to thirty being usual and fifty not rare. Some planters tried to avoid whipping their slaves, but few succeeded, if only because an overseer often demanded it to maintain his authority. "Had to whip my Man Willis for insolence to the overseer," wrote one Tennessee slave-owner. "This I done [*sic*] with much regret as he was never whipped before." For those slaveowners too squeamish to whip their own slaves, or who did not have an overseer or driver to do it for them, the town might provide a public whipping place—a measure in itself of the importance the society placed upon the proper subordination of slaves. "Slavebreakers" were also available. They were men whose job it was to subdue recalcitrant slaves by main force. In his autobiography Douglass tells of his encounter with a slavebreaker. In this case the breaker failed, but Douglass was no more a typical slave than he was a typical man. Whippings were usually carried out in the presence of the other slaves, for the purpose was not only to punish a particular slave, but to deter others from the same behavior. The system could not function if force had to be

Coercion was at the heart of every slave system.
Above: An erring American Negro suffers the
additional indignity of having his punishment
administered by one of his colleagues.
Right: Sketch of a Cuban slavemaster.

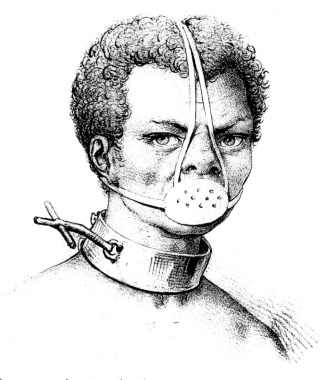

When measured against other slave regimes in the New World, the American institution was comparatively humane. This illustration shows the type of punishment inflicted on troublesome slaves in Brazil.

applied continuously so the aim was always to instill the master's will in the slaves.

Whipping may have been the most common form of punishment, but it was certainly not the only form nor the most severe. Theodore Weld compiled an abolitionist tract, *Slavery As It Is*, in which were reprinted over a thousand examples of extreme violence against slaves. Extraordinary as the instances of deliberate malnutrition, hanging, maiming, mutilation, and torture may have been, their validity is hardly in question for they were all copied from southern newspapers.

At the time and since, the argument has been made that examples of burning slaves, of burying them alive, or starving them could not have been other than rare because slaves were, after all, valuable property. And to a certain extent that check on the violence of the master or the overseer was effective. But even in modern society it has been necessary to enact laws against the abuse by parents of their own children and against the abuse of animals by their owners. Slavery, after all, was a system wherein the power of the master was almost unlimited, at least in moments of excitement or passion, regardless of the controls that the law or public opinion sought to impose. In fact, the very existence of laws limiting the kinds and degree of punishments that could be inflicted on a slave suggests that masters were in the habit of exceeding

reasonable limits. "To manage negroes without the exercise of too much passion," wrote one master to his sons, "is next to an impossibility. I would therefore put you on your guard, less their provocations should on such occasions transport you beyond the limits of decency and Christian morality." Even a kindhearted mistress could lose control. "I feel badly," wrote a woman in her diary, "got very angry and whipped Lavinia. O! for government over my temper." In the end, the principal check on the master was the opinion of his neighbors and friends, which usually frowned on mistreatment, but public opinion rarely did more than that to protect the mistreated slave. Fortunately, brutality and cruelty were not the rule.

Although slavery was hardly a moral institution, the masters did have an interest in the existence of the slave family. From the pairing off of the sexes came new slaves. Slaves themselves were well aware of the advantages that accrued to the master. Fanny Kemble, the English actress who was married to a Georgia planter, tells of Negroes pointing to slave children and exclaiming: "Look missus! little niggers for you and massa; plenty little niggers for you and little missus." Some masters even went so far as to impose their morality on their slaves. One planter instructed his overseer that "stealing, lying, adultery, fornication, profane language, fighting and quarrelling must be invariably punished." Another master tried to regulate the marital life of his slaves by holding divorce and marriage courts. "Had a trial of Divorce and Adultery cases," wrote a planter in his diary in 1840. "Flogged Joe Goodwyn and ordered him to go back to his wife. Ditto Gabriel and Molly and ordered them to come together again. Separated Moses and Anny finally and flogged Tom Kollock . . . [for] interfering with Maggy Campbell, Sullivan's wife." From this pairing off of the sexes, masters obtained more than merely the salving of their Christian consciences. Marriage between slaves and the subsequent offspring gave the male slave a stake in the plantation. He was less likely to run away or even to resist the system since he had given hostages to docility by taking a wife and producing children. It is not accidental that runaway slaves were most often male—that is, less attached to children than a mother would be—and usually young—not yet paired off with a woman or the father of children.

Since the relationship of master to slave was between a person with power and one without, it is not surprising that sexual exploitation of slave women by white men was a recognized abuse under slavery. Neither the black husband nor the woman herself could effectively stand against a determined planter, his son, or an overseer who sought her sexual favors. That the census of 1860 counted half a million mulattoes in the South was a concrete measure of the sexual liaisons that slavery permitted without actually encouraging.

It would not be accurate to see all sexual relations between black slaves and free whites as the result of

A Civilized View of Slavery

Frances Butler's dilemma troubled her deeply. Born into the Kemble family, widely celebrated in English theatrical circles, she had had a brief but successful acting career before retiring from the stage during an American tour in 1834. That year, aged twenty-four, she had married well-to-do Pierce Butler of Philadelphia. Then she learned that her husband was heir to prosperous slave plantations in Georgia—and "Fanny" was a staunch opponent of slavery.

Shortly after the marriage, Butler assumed ownership of the two plantations, growing rice and cotton, on Butler and St Simons islands at the mouth of the Altamaha River. And in December 1838, the couple arrived for a stay that lasted fifteen weeks. During this period Fanny kept a journal of her experiences.

She now found herself residing in the big house attended by six black servants, her life of leisure made possible by the sweat of 700 slaves. "The more I hear, and see, and learn, and ponder the whole of this system of slavery," she wrote, "the more impossible I find it to conceive how its practicers and upholders are to justify their deeds before the tribunal of their own conscience or God's law . . . it is too intolerable to find myself an involuntary accomplice to it."

Fanny's Christian principles were offended by slavery. She took an intelligent interest in social matters and admired William Elley Channing, the Unitarian preacher who urged Christians to try and convince slaveowners that the system was sinful and should be ended.

In her journal, Fanny Butler wrote about the wretchedness of dirty, crowded slave quarters; the high rate of infant mortality; and the cruelty of a system that forced a woman back to work in the fields three weeks after childbirth. She was appalled by the lack of slave cleanliness and gave a penny to each child that had a well-washed face and hands. She deplored the fact that field hands on the rice plantation worked from dawn to dusk on two meals a day. And increasingly slaves came to her for redress of grievances, for clothes and food.

Fanny was frustrated by the limits to what she could accomplish—and her husband forbade her to raise grievances with him. Although she improved conditions in the infirmary and agreed to a slave's request for reading lessons, she was trapped by the system. She bemoaned "the weight of horror and

The Brooklyn Museum, (Gift of Charles A. Schieren

Above: A portrait of Fanny Kemble by Henry Inman. Left: Title page of Fanny's book, first published in 1863.

JOURNAL

OF

A RESIDENCE ON A

GEORGIAN PLANTATION

IN 1838—1839.

BY FRANCES ANNE KEMBLE.

SLAVERY THE CHIEF CORNER STONE.

'This stone (Slavery), which was rejected by the first builders, is become the chief-stone of the corner in our new edifice.'—Speech of ALEXANDER H. STEPHENS, Vice-President of the Confederate States; delivered March 21, 1861.

NEW YORK:
HARPER & BROTHERS, PUBLISHERS,
FRANKLIN SQUARE.
1863.

Schromburg Collection, New York Public Library

depression which I am beginning to feel daily more and more, surrounded by all this misery and degradation, that I can neither help nor hinder."

The Butlers' marriage ended in divorce in 1849. Only in 1863—twenty-five years after the sojourn in the South—did Frances Anne Kemble's *Journal of a Residence on a Georgian Plantation in 1838–1839* appear on both sides of the Atlantic. She probably sought publication when she did because of English newspaper hostility to Lincoln's plans for Negro emancipation. And although the book appeared too late to influence the debate over slavery, it has remained a useful account of plantation life as seen by an English observer.

violence and coercion. Not all of these relationships across the color line were between white men and black women. A white man's divorce petition in Virginia in 1835, for example, complained that his wife had "lived for the last six or seven years and continues to live in open adultery with a negro man." Moreover, there are too many examples in court records of white men leaving money or other property to beloved black women to describe the relationships as always violent or coercive. Furthermore, as often happens outside slavery, and unrelated to the question of blacks and whites, some slave women undoubtedly found sexual relations with the master a means of improving status or self-esteem. Power, in short, corrupts not only its wielders, but those who lack it as well.

Comparisons With Harsher Regimes

The sexual exploitation of slave women was a favorite indictment of slavery by abolitionists, and raises the question of the harshness of American slavery compared with other slave systems. On one level, of course, it is fatuous to talk about different degrees of harshness. All slavery was harsh, subjecting people to the almost unlimited power of others. Yet it is worth making comparisons between slave practices in the United States and other areas of the New World if only because contemporaries and more recent historians have done so. Moreover, it provides a historical measure of the character of slavery in the United States. One comparison has already been made in looking at the opportunities for manumission.

In comparing the physical burden of slavery it is perhaps worth noting that some forms of ill-treatment in Brazil were very rare or entirely absent in the United States. It was a common practice for masters in Brazil to turn out old and sick slaves to fend for themselves since they were incapable of working any longer. This practice, against which laws were passed and complaints were lodged, was almost unknown in the United States. Even the abolitionists, who understandably sought out every evil that slavery produced, did not levy this charge against southerners. Brazilian slaveholders also widely used slave women as prostitutes. This was not simply the sexual exploitation of a female slave by a master or another white man; rather it was the deliberate employment by an owner of a female slave as a full-time prostitute. It was a means of obtaining income from her. Again, there is only a rare case or two of this in the United States. Finally, the third class of cruel practice in Brazilian slavery for which there is no evidence of comparable behavior among southern slaveholders, is that of requiring slaves to wear metallic masks to keep them from drinking liquor or eating clay. Pictures of slaves wearing masks appeared quite commonly in travel accounts of Brazil.

Perhaps the most convincing evidence that the physical treatment of slaves in the United States was the mildest in the New World is that only in the United States was it possible to maintain and augment the slave population by natural increase. In all the other areas of the New World, fresh importations from Africa were necessary to keep up, much less increase, the slave population. In the United States, as noted already, the slave trade from Africa was closed quite effectively in 1808. The very fact that Brazilian and other slave societies could not maintain their slave populations by natural increase suggests that they were subjecting them to more rigorous and harsh conditions than slave masters in the United States. Brazilians, for example, thought that Africans simply did not reproduce in captivity, so low was the birth rate among slaves in Brazil. Probably the principal reason southern slaveholders treated their slaves less harshly than Brazilians or Jamaicans did is not that they were more moral, but because they had to do so if the slaves were to reproduce themselves and thus provide a sufficient number to keep the system going.

Native Culture Destroyed

The psychological and social impact of slavery upon black people began early; it began in Africa with the destruction of the slaves' African culture. There was nothing necessarily deliberate about that destruction, but that did not make it any less shattering. Nor should it be forgotten that the enslavement of millions of Africans was a product of African as well as European cupidity. White men had little direct access to potential slaves in Africa. It was always necessary for them to trade with Africans for the slaves that the New World's exploitation required. Once the economic relationship between European and African had been established, African traders were wedded to the nefarious practice by their increasing dependence upon goods from Europe. Hence they continued to seek out in wars and raids their fellow Africans to satisfy the unending demand for labor in the New World. The most recent estimates place the number of Africans ripped from their homeland and transplanted to the New World at around 9.5 million. Most of this number went to Brazil and the Caribbean; less than 5 per cent were actually imported into the continental English colonies that became the United States. (Today about 31 per cent of the colored people in the Western Hemisphere live in the United States.)

The great majority of the slaves that were carried to the English colonies in North America came from West Africa. Yet despite the limited area of Africa from which they came, their culture and character differed greatly. Thus the erosion of the Africans' native culture began as soon as they were placed in the hold of the slave ship that

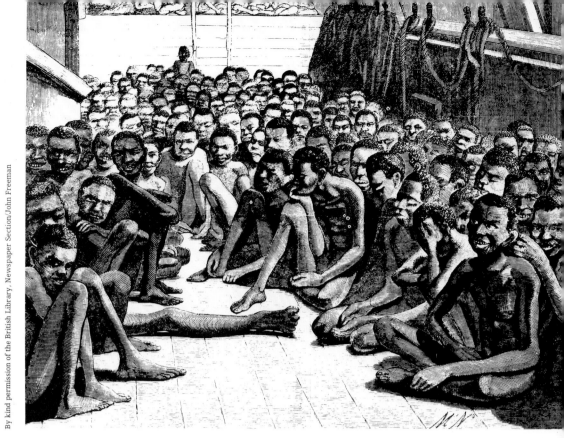

The slave trade originated in Africa. The long voyage out in the vile, cramped holds of slave ships began the process of cultural destruction. Deaths were common, and survivors were often little more than skin and bone by the time they were unloaded.

Although slave marriages were not recognized in law, the family unit was an enduring institution. This photograph shows several generations of a family born on the same plantation.

would take them to the New World. For the slave was thrown among a great variety of other Africans who neither spoke his language nor knew his customs. This mixing of Africans continued once the ship landed, sometimes by deliberate design of masters who sought to prevent conspiracies by making it difficult for slaves to communicate with one another.

The mixing of African nations, however, was a relatively minor cause for the slaves' loss of their native culture. More important was the fact that the society into which the blacks came was overwhelmingly European. The English colonies, unlike those in Brazil or the Caribbean islands, were relatively thickly settled by white families. Thus when the slaves were introduced they found themselves surrounded by English culture, and under the compulsion of slavery they had no choice but to learn the new language, abandon their old customs, and take up the white Englishman's ways. This submersion of Africans in a sea of white Europeans did not occur in Brazil, Jamaica, Cuba, or the other important slave societies in the New World. There blacks usually outnumbered the whites, thus permitting Africans to continue in some fashion their African culture. This difference was reinforced by the fact that importations from Africa were stopped in the

United States in 1808 while in Brazil and Cuba Africans continued to arrive until the middle of the century. In short, Africans, fresh from their homeland, came into Brazil and Cuba not only in greater proportion than into English America—they also continued to come for a longer time. It is not surprising, therefore, that in Brazil, Cuba, and Jamaica (the last of which was also an English colony) African dances, songs, religious customs, and even African languages persisted much longer than in the United States. It is true that modern scholars have discovered by diligent searches in the coastal areas of South Carolina, where slaves made up as much as 80 per cent of the antebellum population, African words and certain burial and artistic customs that seem to be indisputably African in origin. But in Brazil the search does not have to be diligent at all. Even inexperienced visitors can detect the institutional, artistic, and linguistic Africanisms still present in the life of black Brazilians, particularly in the northeast, where the slaves were concentrated. Indeed, black people moved across the South Atlantic between Bahia in Brazil and West Africa in both directions as late as the early twentieth century, some twenty years after the abolition of Brazilian slavery.

More striking evidence of the slaves' African influence on America can be seen in the ways in which Negroes have affected American culture. Jazz music is well recognized as not only one of the Negro's contributions to American culture, but as being also of African derivation. Musicologists generally agree that jazz goes back to Africa for its rhythm and syncopation. The food of the southern states also seems to have been strongly influenced by African slaves. The emphasis upon frying and the use of okra, yams, and rice all point to the influence of African cooks on the cuisine of Englishmen in America. At least one Brazilian scholar has commented on the similarity between the cuisine of northeastern Brazil, where black slaves predominated, and that of South Carolina, where the predominance of blacks stretches back to the colonial era. Yet when measured against the African survivals in places like Brazil or Jamaica, the Africanisms still to be found in the United States pale into insignificance. That insignificance is testimony once again to the basic fact that in the United States the first measure of the impact of slavery upon Negroes was that they were effectively stripped of their African culture.

Black Community Life

Africans may have lost their cultural heritage under American slavery, but that did not mean they failed to develop their own communities. Some historians, it is true, have argued that one of the consequences of slavery in North America was that blacks became irresponsible, even infantile "Sambos," and that this development was perhaps the most striking and devastating consequence of chattel slavery in the United States. And it is true that some slaves often identified with the will of the master, as the master intended. It was not unusual, for example, for slaves in speaking to other slaves to take pride in their master's wealth and status, or even more grotesque, to take pride in the fact that one slave commanded a higher price than another. Slaves spoke, too, of "po' white trash" or "po' buckra" in referring to nonslaveholding whites, thus taking pride in being part of their master's property. Perhaps the most dramatic example of slaves' adopting the sanctions of slavery was when a slave revealed to his master the plot of a revolt or warned a mistress of another slave's plan to run away. In fact, a significant number of slave revolts were nipped in the bud because faithful slaves gave them away. At least one slave, after he had escaped to freedom, revealed how much his thinking had been conditioned by his status. After describing how he decided to run away, he went on to tell how he looked

The music of the Negro continues to reflect its African origins. This painting, The Old Plantation, *shows South Carolina slaves dancing to the music and rhythms of African-style instruments about 1800.*

back from afar toward the plantation; he saw his mistress calling after him. "I hid in the woods, I could not realize it," he recollected. "I sat down on a stump and said to myself, 'isn't this a dream?' I could not realize that *I* had done such a thing as to run away—it seemed so *low*. I—that had always been trusted, and had served faithfully—to be a *runaway* at last."

Masters may have sought to instill their interests in the slave, but the great majority of slaves were far from incomplete human beings or compliant creatures of their masters, whatever they might have seemed to be when playing their assigned roles in the presence of white people. Even the slave who was astonished that he could finally run away, did in fact make the break. Outside the orbit of the master, slaves could be themselves and create for themselves a community life that, among other things, enabled them to survive. It was the endurance of the Negro people under the weight of slavery that is the central achievement.

The slave community on a large plantation was a complex system of relationships. It was made up of a variety of black folk, young and old, wise and foolish, reckless and cautious, active and somnolent, just like any other community. There were natural leaders like the conjure woman, who could work cures for illness or break up

Eastman Johnson's 1859 painting, The Old Kentucky Home, *conveys the image, prevalent then as now, of southern slavery. This rose-tinted view flattered the South's peculiar institution by focusing on the spirited black community life that developed despite the inhumanity of the system.*

33

love affairs through magic. There was the preacher, who knew his Bible and could use it to soften the rigors of slavery for his flock, or, as in the case of the preacher and rebel Nat Turner, use it to arouse his people to discontent and rebellion. The cook in the big house often served as the figure who linked white and black and thus stood as a preeminent adviser on all kinds of matters in the community of the slave quarters. Then there were the special occasions around which much black life surged: Christmas, New Year, funerals, and weddings. On these occasions presents were often dispensed by the master and the slaves carried on their own celebrations with music, dancing, gambling, and games. Along with fishing, hunting served as recreation as well as a way of supplementing diet. Marriages might not be binding in law, but on many plantations the marriage of slaves called for a celebration by both slaves and white folks.

Probably no aspect of slave life, however, was more fundamental to the black community than religion. Technically Christian, the religion of the slaves was suffused with their own purposes and with touches from Africa. The "ring shout"—a form of singing, clapping, and dancing that was an integral part of worship on many plantations—seems to have had strong connections with West African customs. The reminiscences of former slaves, long after emancipation, also make evident that their religion was their own and a community-building thing as well as a way of worshipping God. "Us niggers used to have a prayin' ground down in the hollow," recalled one former slave, "and sometimes we come out of the field, between eleven and twelve at night, scorchin' and burnin' up with nothin' to eat, and we wants to ask the good Lawd to have mercy. We put grease in a snuff pan or bottle and make a lamp. We takes a pine torch, too, and goes down to the hollow to pray. Some gits so joyous they starts to holler loud and we has to stop up they mouth. I see niggers get so full of the Lawd and so happy they draps unconscious."

The life of the slave, in short, was not limited to labor or to being under the watchful eye of whites. In fact, one can surmise that it was the opportunity to escape the white eye that made it possible for Negroes to endure. For in the quarters they could be themselves, make fun of the whites, construct their own lives and relationships, worship in their own ways, and replenish their sense of humor and zest for life.

Perhaps the best witness to the truth that slavery did not make Sambos or dependent people out of slaves is to observe the independent and often self-confident way slaves behaved once the legal bonds of slavery were dropped. Such a historic moment can be glimpsed in an excerpt from the diary of a Mississippian who commented on his father's slaves as they made the transition to freedom. At the end of 1865, soon after slavery was ended by the Union Army, the Reverend Samuel Agnew wrote in his diary of the arrangements that his father tried to make with his former slaves. The elder Agnew was trying to sign them up to work on his plantation for the coming year. The equality of the bargaining between black and white is noteworthy. On Christmas Day, Agnew wrote, "the negroes came up this morning for their annual settlement. Pa paid them their part of the tenth of the proceeds of the cotton. . . . The negroes talked of the plans for another year. Pa told them whoever he hired would have to work the whole year and do whatever he told them. The negroes were willing to work in the crop, but no more. They are disinclined to hire their whole time at all —and went away without making a trade. They have exalted ideas," Agnew concluded. By the beginning of January, his father had failed to make any arrangements that were mutually satisfactory to former owner and former slaves. "Time changes plans and opinions," commented the son. "Our negroes are all gone now. The negro yard is silent and dark."

The Disastrous Effects of the System

To point out that few slaves were Sambos is not the same as saying that slavery had no effect upon blacks. The effect was particularly noticeable after emancipation, for the peculiar institution had provided no preparation for life in freedom. Moreover it was a severe handicap in that the association between race and slavery made an indelible impression on whites. Accustomed to seeing blacks only as slaves, and often as fawning and irresponsible dependents at that, whites continued to view Negroes after emancipation in the same way and with the same low expectations for them. Whatever the deep historical and psychological causes for racial prejudice may be, surely they were reinforced by the simple but portentous fact that only Negroes were held in the degraded status of slaves.

White southerners in the nineteenth century and some historians since have called slavery a school for conditioning Africans to American civilization. If it was a school it was one from which few slaves graduated and none as a matter of course. Therefore, from the standpoint of Negroes as free people in American society, slavery was disastrous. It did nothing to prepare blacks for their future in America and did much to burden them. In a society in which work was prized and looked to as the way in which men created their own identities, slavery effectively discouraged blacks from working by giving the fruits of their work to someone else. In a society in which private property was highly valued, slaves learned to ignore that value because they themselves were property under the law and stealing property from a master seemed only a way of counterbalancing the larger injustice. In a society in which independence of spirit and constant

Joseph Cinque (above) led a mutiny of African captives on board the slave ship Amistad *in 1839. Most members of the crew were killed, and Cinque later stood trial in the United States for murder. He was successfully defended by John Quincy Adams.*

activity were measures of a true American, slavery inculcated the very opposite values in Negroes. They were expected to be docile, dependent, unaggressive, and satisfied with routine and established ways of doing things. Some planters may have tried to create families in the Victorian model among their slaves, but the majority did little about it. The sanctity of the family, so highly prized by white Victorians, received no support from slavery. Slave families could be, and were, disrupted by the sale of one or more partners. Marriage between slaves had no legal basis, though if sanctified by a minister or priest it was viewed as a fully Christian marriage, as a marriage between whites would have been. Most slaves, however, were not married by any religious ceremony. As one slave recalled many years later, "When I got married I jumped a broomstick. To git unmarried, all you had to do was to jump backwards over the same broomstick."

Although the whole thrust of slavery was contrary to the values that white Americans identified with, slaves managed to overcome this drawback to an amazing degree.

Among slaves, the family was more firmly rooted than the weak supports from the system would lead one to expect. For when slavery ended, the ties of family caused many a slave to seek out relatives who had been sold away or who had been separated by the war. Many years after emancipation old slaves could still clearly recall the network of relationships and kin during slavery. Thousands of slave couples came to the Freedman's Bureau after the Civil War for marriage certificates, testifying that their relationship within slavery may have been without legal sanction, but it was nonetheless enduring. Certainly the slave family was more common in the American South than it was in Brazil. There, most slaves had no mates at all because a disproportionate number of males were brought in each year, leaving the majority of them without mates. To that extent, at least, the slave family was more firmly based in the United States than in Brazil. But even with that qualification, it is fair to say that the American slave family was a fragile institution. It made no place for the father at all, since the institutional father was the master, who provided housing and food, not the black man who was the biological father of the slave children and the mate of the black mother. What is remarkable about the slave family is that it persisted even though the system failed to acknowledge the father as breadwinner. When newly freed blacks signed contracts for work with their former masters, it was the father who signed for the whole family, it being recognized that he was the head.

Slave Attitudes to Slavery

Implicit in what has been said up to now is that blacks endured slavery, but were hardly content with it. Certainly this is the conclusion that emerges from the few sources from blacks themselves, principally the narratives written by runaway slaves or the reminiscences of Negroes many years after emancipation. But the response during slavery of the majority of slaves to their lot is not easy to ascertain if only because slaves necessarily leave few records. Nor do the number of runaways or slave revolts reveal much about their feelings towards slavery. It is true that the white South was very anxious about the encouragement to running away given by the so-called Underground Railroad and the agitation of northern abolitionists. But the truth of the matter is that very few slaves actually ran away. The highest number estimated is about 60,000 over a period of thirty years. But this number must be seen against a total of 4 million slaves in 1860. In that context the figure is small indeed. The same point can be made about slave revolts, the number of which has been placed at 250 in the course of two centuries. The area of the South, however, is enormous and the definition of a revolt is only ten slaves. Moreover, many of these

Nat Turner's Rebellion

Nat Turner was born in October 1800, the property of a wealthy farmer in Southampton County, Virginia. As a boy he had a keen, inquisitive mind and soon learned to read and write. He had a practical bent too, and experimented in making paper and gunpowder. But from the first Nat Turner believed himself to be special, set apart from others for a later mission in life. His seeming uniqueness and his childhood recollection of things that his mother said had happened before his birth quickly earned him a reputation and influence among his fellow slaves. In his 5,000-word confession, written up by Thomas R. Gray, a court-appointed white lawyer, after Turner's capture, Nat said that as he grew older he "studiously avoided mixing in society and wrapped myself in mystery devoting myself to fasting and prayer." He also attended religious meetings and even preached.

Then he began to hear voices and see visions. When he was twenty-five he saw black and white spirits "engaged in battle, and the sun was darkened, the thunder rolled in the heavens, and blood flowed in streams." While working in the fields he saw drops of blood on the corn and found strange writing and numbers drawn in blood on leaves in the wood. On May 12, 1828, "the Spirit" appeared to him and told him that the day of judgment was near, when the first would be last and the last first. The sign for him to rise and slay his enemies would be an eclipse of the sun, and in February 1831 such an event took place. But Turner hesitated. Only when he witnessed the unusual atmospheric conditions of August 13 did he know for sure that his hour had come. That day the sun went through a variety of hues, from yellow to green to blue and finally silver. A black spot could be seen on its surface.

Turner had reported these recent visions to four trusted slaves, and along with these and two others he finalized his plans on Sunday, August 21. They would begin their work that night at the home of their master, Joseph Travis who, Turner acknowledged, had been kind and considerate. Under cover of darkness they entered the house and murdered Travis and his family as they lay sleeping. Two of the slaves later went back to kill a baby in a cradle that they had overlooked at the time.

Their killing had begun and for the next two days it was to continue in like vein—sudden, bloody, and merciless. They had set out on foot armed with axes, swords, and hatchets. As they went from property to property they gathered recruits, guns, ammunition, and horses, and sometimes money and valuables. "It was my object," Turner said, "to carry terror and devastation wherever we went." Each house was approached at galloping speed by a mounted advance

Nat Turner's rebellion was the most bloody slave revolt in America. Fifty-five whites were butchered, and Turner and sixteen others were hanged. Below: Turner tells a few trusted colleagues of his plans to liberate the Negro. Right: This contemporary woodcut depicts the beginnings of the massacre. Turner's owner, Joseph Travis, is portrayed on his knees at center. Although Turner conceded that Travis was "a kind master" and that he had "no cause to complain of his treatment," Travis and his family were the first victims. Lower right: Turner is apprehended. He evaded capture for ten weeks.

group while Turner and the rest followed some way behind. This also made escape much more difficult for the intended victims. Turner's own attempts at killing were conspicuously unsuccessful. They continued their massacre through Monday and into Tuesday, by which time troops and armed locals were on their trail. At Mr Parker's property the slaves, now numbering between fifty and sixty and all mounted, suffered a reverse. Some were scattered and others wounded by white fire. Turner was hoping to reach

Jerusalem (now Courtland) about two miles away to gather more arms before taking refuge in the Great Dismal Swamp. He managed to regroup some followers but then faced another attack from a mounted force which left him with twenty men. He now backtracked and suffered further defections until he alone remained. Turner's men had killed fifty-five people, all whites, including fourteen women and twenty-eight children.

For ten weeks he evaded his captors until, on October 30, his hideout—"a

little hole I had dug out with my sword . . . under the top of a fallen tree"—was discovered by Benjamin Phipps. "On Mr Phipps discovering the place of my concealment," said Turner, "he cocked his gun and aimed at me. I requested him not to shoot, and I would give up, upon which he demanded my sword. I delivered it to him, and he brought me to prison."

Turner was totally unrepentant in his confession. Lawyer Gray was so struck by Turner's calm recital of such cold-blooded killing, his "helpless innocence" and undaunted spirit that, he said, "my blood curdled in my veins." On November 4, Turner was charged with insurrection and plotting to kill free white persons. Although he had confessed, he pleaded not guilty because, he said, he didn't *feel* guilty. The confession was read to the court and he was promptly found guilty. A week later he was hanged. In all, fifty-two Negroes faced charges arising from the revolt: twenty-four were acquitted, seventeen hanged, and eleven transported south. The rebellion terrified the state. Properties were temporarily abandoned in the county and rumors of uprisings in neighboring areas were rife. Overnight the abolition movement lost most of its support in the South, and slave codes were soon tightened in many states. In Virginia, for example, slaves were barred from attending religious teachings or meetings conducted by whites without their masters' written consent, and it was made illegal to write or print anything likely to incite slave revolt.

The immediate consequences were more drastic; the white backlash was terrible. No one knows how many Negro lives were taken as avenging bands of armed men swept through the county. Estimates vary from 40 to 200, and this is but one of several points of contention in the controversy over the most significant slave revolt in American history. Some at the time believed the plot was part of a wider rebellion involving several states, which Turner denied. In 1900, William S. Drewry alleged that the Negroes tortured some of their victims to death. But forty years before, Thomas Higginson, an abolitionist, maintained "there was no gratuitous outrage beyond the death-blow itself, no insult, no mutilation." This was the view of novelist William Styron a century later. Nat Turner saw himself as a prophet; he was certainly a religious fanatic. But Drewry, wedded to the old ways of the South, likened him to "a spoiled child who, having been allowed too many privileges in youth, soon thinks he ought to be master of all he surveys."

so-called revolts were no more than plots that never matured into outbreaks. Indeed, of the three best-known slave revolts in the nineteenth century, that of Gabriel Prosser in 1800, Denmark Vesey in 1822, and Nat Turner in 1831, only the last was an actual revolt. The other two were plots that never came to a head. The Stono revolt of 1739 in colonial South Carolina was no more successful than Turner's, for it, too, was suppressed with much bloodshed.

Neither runaways nor uprisings are an adequate measure of how blacks felt about slavery. For one thing, successfully running away or organizing an uprising was extremely difficult to accomplish in the United States. In places like Jamaica or Brazil the number of successful runaways was much greater, it is true. In Jamaica, for example, escaped slaves established themselves permanently as a separate community, signing a treaty with the British and promising, in return, to send back any new fugitive slaves that might reach them in the future. In Brazil the most famous *quilombo* or community of escaped slaves was that of Palmares. It endured for two generations in the depths of the Pernambuco country and at its height contained 20,000 inhabitants, all escaped slaves or the descendants of such. It is significant, however, that both Brazil and Jamaica are semi-tropical in climate, a fact that permitted escaped slaves to live more easily off the country and to escape detection. In North America it was difficult to survive in the woods, undetected, through winters, even in Alabama or Georgia. Moreover, in the United States white settlement was much denser, and the possibility of being able to find a hideaway without running into whites or coming under attack from them was much more difficult.

Some historians have emphasized the greater number of slave revolts that occurred in Brazil compared with the United States. But a close comparison shows that the number of revolts in Brazil was not much more significant than it was in the United States. For one thing, what is often spoken of as slave rebellions in Brazil turn out to be *quilombos* like that of Palmares. And even the series of quite large slave rebellions that broke out in the city of Bahia between 1800 and 1835 were quite unusual. There is no other such series of revolts in the almost 400-year history of slavery in Brazil. Those revolts, instead, seem to be closely related to rather special circumstances. In Bahia during those thirty-five years there seems to have been a concentration of slaves from warlike, aggressive African nations like the Yoruba and Hausa. These Africans were not only aggressive; they had leaders who were exceptional in that they were united by a common religion, Islam, and were able to communicate since they were literate. The spectacular revolts in Bahia were the product of circumstances that had not occurred before and would not again. They do not support the contention that in other slave societies revolts were characteristically more frequent than in the United States.

What is learned from the paucity of slave rebellions is not how the blacks felt about slavery, but rather how whites have felt about it. Liberal historians have sought out examples of rebellion and runaways in order to show that blacks were opposed to their enslavement. One reason they have felt compelled to do so is because historians who argued that slavery was in fact benign have used the absence of slave revolts as a measure of black contentment under slavery. Both interpretations of the facts miss the main point. Slave revolts everywhere, whether in nineteenth-century United States with black slaves or in ancient Rome with white slaves, were rare. And one reason they were rare is that they were everywhere repressed, usually with violence and bloodshed. (Only in Haiti were the slaves able to rise up and overthrow their white rulers.) Given the nature of American society in the nineteenth century, with a predominantly white population fortified with enormous military power, a slave uprising came close to mass suicide. And in fact that is what virtually every revolt turned out to be. It is highly unrealistic and romantic to seek out revolts among slaves as a measure of black discontent. Rather, such revolts reflect the foolhardiness of the rebels, hardly the characteristic of a people who managed to survive the rigors of three centuries of slavery.

The force of the argument that slave revolts, or even runaways, are not a good measure of Negro reaction to slavery is brought home when consideration is given to what slaves did when resistance to the system was no longer fraught with impossible odds. During the Civil War, as the Union armies penetrated the southern states, slaves flocked to the Union lines, seeking their freedom. Before the war was over, almost 200,000 former slaves had enlisted in the armed forces to help end slavery.

The hostility of Negroes toward their bondage can also be seen in other ways. One is the universal admiration of Lincoln by blacks, even before Lincoln's martyr's death, because he had already earned his place as the Emancipator. The slave songs that often spoke forcefully of dissatisfaction with slavery are another. Frederick Douglass reported one that went:

> We raise de wheat,
> Dey gib us de corn;
> We bake de bread,
> Dey gib us de cruss, . . .
> We peal de meat
> Dey giv us de skin
> And dat's de way
> Dey takes us in.

Whatever limitations slavery may have placed upon the aspirations of blacks, on the eve of the Civil War it was a flourishing institution. One undoubted measure of its success was that it took a Civil War to abolish it. Nowhere else in the New World was that necessary.

Chapter 2

THE OLD SOUTH

The antebellum South remained wedded to the old way of doing things. Slavery gave southern society its uniqueness, although the vast majority of whites owned no slaves at all. But the region did derive its wealth almost exclusively from the land. Cotton, tobacco, sugar, and rice were the sources of this well-to-do planter aristocracy who gave the South an air of social refinement. More numerous, however, were the self-sufficient yeoman farmers whose contribution to the wealth of the region was far more modest. In time, southerners developed a fierce pride in the society they had created—and a determination to resist outside interference in their affairs.

A Distinctive Society

The tourist in the South today often comes upon the remains of the Old South. Here and there along the great rivers or in the old towns he finds stately mansions that have been carefully and lovingly renovated and opened to the public. Garrulous guides lead him through spacious rooms furnished with the finest appointments and decorated by artists from all over the world. He can wander over expansive lawns, walk through carefully managed gardens, and pause to admire the magnificent groves of live oaks. And he can glance into the little cabins clustered at the edge of the mansion's grounds, the cabins that once housed the slaves who worked the lands and supported the luxury of the life in the big house. In other places, like an archaeologist in an ancient land, he comes upon the ruins of old mansions, long vacated and allowed to weather the elements virtually untended. Here his imagination takes over from the guide and the renovator. In his mind's eye he can see the lives of the great planters who once lived in these mansions that have fallen prey to time, the weather, and the ever-present thieves.

What the tourist hears and sees and imagines is a legend of the Old South that lives on in novels and the movies and in romantic memory. It is the South of white columned mansions peopled by aristocrats, the men gallant and strong-willed, excelling as soldiers and statesmen, the women delicate and gentle, serving as mistresses and nurses to the plantation family. The "family" of legend was a big one including not only children and maiden aunts and a perpetual hoard of welcome visitors, but also the blacks who worked in the cotton fields and in the big house. The best known of the slaves were the house servants—patient, eager to please, intensely loyal to massa and missus, yet childlike, often providing amusement by their antics and always requiring firm "parental" discipline. In addition to the great planters and their black and white families, there were others in the Old South of romantic legend. These were the poor whites—or "white trash" as they were often called. Lazy and dirty, these people lived on the margins of society earning their bread by occasional work and more regular theft. Most of their days were spent drinking, fighting, or squatting contentedly in the sun spitting massive streams of tobacco juice at the dusty ground in front of the ramshackle hovels in which they lived.

Familiar as it is, this picture of the Old South is erroneous and profoundly misleading because it ignores the complexity of antebellum civilization. In reality, there were many Souths in the years before the Civil War. There was the South of agriculture—of cotton farms and plantations along the rich river bottoms and delta lands; of tobacco farms in Carolina, Virginia, and Tennessee; of sugar plantations in lower Louisiana; of rice farms in the lowland areas of South Carolina. Some of the owners of the cotton, tobacco, sugar, and rice plantations were very rich, owned many slaves, and lived in the haughty splendor of the big house. Others, often equally rich, lived much more modestly. These were relative newcomers to the rich soils of western Georgia, central Alabama and Mississippi, and northern Louisiana. They were parvenus who had not yet acquired the polish and the gentility of the older, more established aristocrats. Their efforts were bent on establishing plantations in the wilderness and, although their wealth in land and slaves brought them political and economic power, they lived in circumstances quite modest compared to the older, more established planter aristocrats. Most of the planters, however, lived modestly because they lacked the wealth necessary to support the luxurious life of their wealthier neighbors. Only about 12 per cent of the South's slave-owning families in 1860 owned at least twenty slaves and while that number might give their owners influence and prestige in the community as well as an ample living, it would not support the style of life that the truly large slaveowners enjoyed.

And so the Old South of reality, in marked contrast to the Old South of legend, had few families of aristocratic lineage with genteel manners living in great mansions and owning hundreds of slaves. Here instead was the South of the small farmer who owned no slaves or at most a few. He operated a largely self-sufficient farm, usually in the back country, and managed an adequate but simple living. He might grow some cotton or tobacco—never rice or sugar because these crops required an investment in land, slaves, and machinery which he could not afford— but his major crop was corn which served as food for his family and livestock.

These were not the poor whites of the romantic legend. Southerners at the time carefully distinguished between the "po' white trash," that miserable class of people who eked out a marginal living in the pine barrens and isolated hill country, and the small farmers, often termed "sturdy yeomen," who made up the vast majority of the southern white agricultural population. Fiercely independent and somewhat suspicious of outsiders, the small farmer owned his own land and agricultural tools. In addition to his basic food source—corn—he grew vegetables such as peas, beans, and sweet potatoes. He raised some livestock to provide meat and milk, and chickens to provide meat and eggs. When possible he supplemented this diet with fish and game.

The agricultural South, then, was extremely varied in

White columned mansions standing in well-kept lawns are a lingering reminder of just one level of white society that existed in the antebellum South. This stately plantation house is near Wilmington, North Carolina.

the wealth and station in life of its farmers and planters and in its crops. But not all southerners were farmers. There was also an urban South in the ports of New Orleans, Mobile, Savannah, Charleston, and Baltimore and in inland towns such as Memphis, Louisville, Augusta, and Natchez. Here, like their northern counterparts, an urban population of factors, storekeepers, innkeepers, and merchants of every description along with draymen, warehousemen, artisans, and common laborers provided the goods and services of a commercial society.

The diversity of the South's population was matched by the diversity of its terrain. The South stretched from the temperate zone to the tropics. Its land was rich, black, and flat; it was rolling and red-soiled; and it was rugged and mountainous.

Bonds of Unity

Of course geography and climate influenced life in the Old South. The southern climate and soil were particularly well suited to the growing of cotton, rice, tobacco, and sugar while northerners found their lands better suited to wheat and other grains. These differences were very important because they encouraged specialization. When each region concentrated on the production of agricultural commodities congenial to its climate and soil conditions, the result was a general overall increase in the nation's agricultural productivity. Specialization in turn encouraged interregional trade. Thus, increasing specialization was a sign of the nation's economic progress. An experience shared by people North and South specialization helped to unite the country.

Similarly, the South shared with the North the experience of the westward movement. The existence of thousands of square miles of fertile land in the West attracted thousands upon thousands of settlers. Driving the Indians before them, they tore farms and plantations from the wilderness, formed new states, and founded towns and cities. Their common needs and common problems united westerners, North and South. They favored land policies that would make the western lands available at low prices. They looked to their governments—federal and state—for aid when they needed it to build or help build canals, roads, and railroads, to charter banks and corporations, to protect them from Indians, to dredge rivers and improve harbors, and to do a multitude of things that they could not do alone.

Geography also played an important part in uniting westerners, North and South. The great river systems of the Missouri, Mississippi, and Ohio drained southward into the Gulf of Mexico. Whatever their ultimate destina-

Sugar levee, New Orleans, in 1853 by Hyppolyte Sebron. By midcentury the "queen city of the Mississippi" was a sprawling metropolis of over 100,000 and the South's major port.

tion, western commodities began their movement to market via the rivers. New Orleans became the entrepôt for the Southwest's cotton and sugar and the Northwest's grain and meat. The rafts and steamboats that plied the western waters were the commercial links that bound North and South in mutual economic self-interest.

There were other bonds of unity. One was religion. Most Americans in the early nineteenth century were Protestants and, if they were divided into many different denominations, these divisions cut across North-South boundaries. More important was the prevailing religious toleration, born of religious diversity and a growing secular mood. Doctrinal differences did not disappear but they did not divide people into opposing forces ready to do battle for religious purity.

Party politics was another unifying institution. Of course, Americans did not always agree with each other. They divided into parties and factions, and political struggles were sharp and often bitter. But party divisions did not correspond to sectional divisions. Political differences in the South paralleled those in the North: the issues were essentially alike in both sections and each boasted active political organizations representing all parties. Moreover universal white manhood suffrage made it necessary for political leaders to appeal to all sections of the white electorate in order to win office. Early nineteenth-century politicians were well aware of this need. Andrew Jackson, Henry Clay, John C. Calhoun, and all the other aspirants for national office, successful and unsuccessful alike, ran on platforms which they hoped would have the broadest appeal, North and South. The result, then, was that political differences helped to cement unity between the sections.

Having so much in common with their fellow citizens in the North it is no wonder that southerners joined in the general celebration of American nationality in the early decades of the nineteenth century. They could extol the nation's free institutions and proclaim that it was their "manifest destiny" to bring these institutions to the unenlightened everywhere. Seeing themselves culturally as well as politically unique, all Americans could applaud Ralph Waldo Emerson's call for American literary and intellectual independence. America had turned its back on an evil and corrupt Europe—and it was a success.

And yet, despite its internal diversity, despite its shared political, economic, and religious outlook with the North, the South gradually began to see itself as having a unity and a distinctiveness that set it apart. This sense of a distinct identity derived from the South's unique historical experience, the root cause of which was its peculiar institution—slavery.

As it existed in the South in the nineteenth century slavery was much more than a barbaric means to organize labor. Rather, its historical importance lies in the peculiar social and economic system it engendered. This peculiar slave system, like all other systems of political economy, created a configuration of cultural, social, and political ideas and practices—in short, an ideology and a set of institutions—that made the South distinctive and led in turn to the development of southern nationalism.

Creation of the Cotton Kingdom

While Americans were winning their revolutionary war and establishing their new independent government, profound economic changes were taking place in England. That country was undergoing what has become known as her Industrial Revolution, and at its heart was the massive expansion of textile manufacturing. To the older, more established woolen industry was added the growing cotton textile enterprises. Technological changes, along with the ability to use steam power to run machinery, increased production and created what seemed to be an insatiable demand for raw cotton to feed the growing mills. English sources of supply proved inadequate to meet the spiraling demand and prices for raw cotton moved sharply upward.

Americans were familiar with cotton. They had been growing small amounts for over 150 years. Southern farm families had been using it, often along with other fibers, in the production of clothing on the farm. Now, for the first time there was a commercial demand for the crop. Lands on the coast of South Carolina and Georgia and on the islands just off the coast produced a long staple cotton that was superior to that grown in the West Indies and other areas that had been supplying the British, and planters in those areas moved quickly into cotton production. But the opportunities for commercial production seemed limited because the short-stapled interior or upland variety of cotton had seeds which clung to the fiber. The problem was overcome when Whitney perfected his cotton gin, which mechanically separated the seeds from the staple of upland cotton.

The results were truly revolutionary. Commercial cotton production spread quickly into the interior of South Carolina and exports rose sharply. In 1790 fewer than 9,000 bales were produced in the United States of which only 10 per cent were exported. By 1800, the United States produced over 200,000 bales and exported about 40 per cent of the crop. Production continued to rise at a rapid rate, reaching over 2 million bales by the end of the 1830s. By the 1850s production exceeded 3 million bales and on the eve of the Civil War almost 5 million bales of cotton were harvested in the South.

Cotton is king, proclaimed southerners as they watched his kingdom spread to the west. As the lands in western Georgia and South Carolina were taken up, cotton farmers moved further west into Alabama, Mississippi, and

Louisiana and then into Arkansas and eastern Texas. But the influence of King Cotton reached far beyond his southern kingdom. In the North settlers flocked into the western lands partly in response to the growing demand for grain and meat products from the South. The South provided virtually all of the cotton needed by the growing textile mills in the Northeast, and American cotton nearly monopolized the European cotton markets. More than half the value of all American exports in the three decades before the Civil War came from cotton. To move the crop and supply the cotton plantations required an army of middlemen. Merchants, bankers, brokers, shipowners, storekeepers in the South, the North, and abroad owed their livelihood to King Cotton.

The cotton kingdom was also a slave kingdom, for the expansion of cotton production meant also the expansion of slavery. At the time of the Revolution, many southerners doubted that there was much of a future for slavery. Indigo production had virtually ceased with the end of the English subsidy and tobacco was a glut on the world market. But the growth of the cotton kingdom ended all talk about the end of slavery. Cotton and slavery became inextricably intertwined. A visitor to the South noted the obvious connection: "To sell cotton in order to buy negroes—to make more cotton to buy more negroes, 'ad infinitum,' is the aim and direct tendency of all the opera-

tions of the thorough going cotton planter; his whole soul is wrapped up in the pursuit. It is apparently, the principle by which he 'lives, moves, and has his being.'"

Cotton was not the South's only commercial crop using slave labor in its production. In Maryland, Kentucky, North Carolina, and Tennessee farmers and planters continued to grow tobacco; some rice was grown in the lowland areas of South Carolina and Georgia; and southern Louisiana was dotted with huge sugar plantations. But when measured in terms of land used, slaves employed, and value of the crops, these were minor endeavors when compared to cotton production.

The dominance of cotton was obvious to the most casual observer. Cotton seemed to monopolize the South's thoughts, conversation, and activity. Travelers told of plantations where gangs of slaves worked the cotton fields, in the spring and early summer planting, and then hoeing out the weeds. In the fall and early winter came picking, ginning, and baling the cotton to make it ready for its journey to market. In the early winter the market towns and cities were virtually inundated by cotton.

Harvest time on a cotton plantation could be any period between August and January, depending on the climate. This Currier and Ives lithograph shows a scene on the Mississippi.

"Look which way you will you see it; and see it moving," wrote a visitor to Mobile. "Keel boats, ships, brigs, schooners, wharves, stores, and press-houses, all appeared to be full." And the people seemed to talk of little else: "I believe that in the three days that I was there . . . I must have heard the word cotton pronounced more than 3000 times."

However, King Cotton's dominance may not have been as complete as appeared on the surface. A glance at production figures in the Old South shows that corn, not cotton, was the region's chief crop in acreage and value. The Middle West is often thought of as the corn belt, yet the South produced far more corn. With about one-third of the country's land area and population, the South in the two decades before the Civil War produced well over half the nation's corn. "Corn," historian Paul Gates concludes, "is as basic to southern history as were Thomas Jefferson and John C. Calhoun."

Farming Patterns and Social Divisions

If only one-quarter of the South's families owned slaves and if corn, rather than cotton, was the South's chief crop, why the emphasis on cotton and slaves? What

The Bettmann Archive

appears to be a paradox is immediately resolved when the consumption rather than the production of the two crops is compared. Cotton and the other staple crops, tobacco, rice, and sugar, were produced for sale on the foreign and domestic markets while corn was consumed by the producers themselves or in their immediate neighborhood. A closer analysis of this situation will reveal much about the class structure of the Old South.

Fully three-quarters of the South's farm families owned no slaves and most of these grew little or no cotton. The great majority of these families were the so-called sturdy yeomen or plain folk of the Old South. They were largely self-sufficient, growing food and fiber for their own use on the farm and producing little surplus for sale on the market. Their principal crop was corn, which they ate in a variety of forms such as corn bread or grits or fed to their livestock which supplied them with milk and meat. Sweet potatoes, peas, beans, and other vegetables along with game and fish supplemented their ordinary diet of corn and pork. Those farmers who had sons to help them in the fields and those who could afford a slave or two might also have a few acres in cotton which, when sold, would give them some cash to buy a few items from the local store or the traveling peddler that they could not produce themselves. They might also realize some cash if their lands were close enough to a plantation to enable them to sell some corn and meat to the planter.

But this market was extremely limited because planters made every effort to grow their own food. Although planters concentrated on cotton production they had adequate land and labor time after the cotton had been planted to put in an ample corn crop. They could not increase the land devoted to cotton beyond the ability of their labor force to pick all the crop in the fall before bad weather set in and injured the ripened bolls. But they could allow their corn crop to stand in the fields until all the cotton was safely harvested and then put their slaves to work harvesting the corn. This kept the planter's labor force busy throughout most of the year and provided the plantation with food for man and animal, thereby diminishing its demand for grain and meat.

But even when the planters did not produce all the food they needed they often did not buy from southern corn growers. Because of transportation costs, corn that had to be hauled overland fifty or a hundred miles was often more expensive than that which came from much further away in the North by way of the Ohio and Mississippi river systems. Even if improved transportation facilities linked land in the interior South to southern markets, corn growers in the newly opened areas quickly moved to cotton production or sold out to planters who moved in with their slaves.

In short, then, cotton and corn were both vital to the South but in vastly different ways. Cotton (along with the other staple crops, tobacco, rice, and sugar) was the commercial crop. Its production and sale provided the wealth of the planter class and the economic impetus for the perpetuation of slavery. Corn was the predominant food crop, but it rarely entered the commercial market. Its production was the major economic activity of southern farmers and as such was the basis for the self-sufficient economy in which the majority of southern farmers lived. Thus, the Old South really had two agricultural economies —one, dominated by the slave-owning planters engaged in commercial production; the other, comprised of the majority of the white population engaged mainly in subsistence production.

In part, this division between self-sufficient and commercial sectors of the economy was the result of the rapid westward movement into virgin lands, and therefore it was an experience that the South shared with the North. The first task of settlers on the frontier was to clear the land, build shelter, and plant a food crop. Only after these tasks were completed could farmers consider producing a surplus for sale on the market. The ability to do so, however, was not enough to turn him into a commercial farmer. He required also adequate transportation facilities to move his surplus to market.

Nature provided the initial means of transportation;

Corn, not cotton, was the South's major crop. It was grown by the self-sufficient, small farmer who made up the vast majority of southern agriculturalists before the Civil War. Cornhusking is depicted in this painting by Eastman Johnson.

Songs for the Millions

Stephen Foster wrote almost 200 songs and many instrumental pieces. For nearly thirty years, "Old Folks at Home" was published in Christy's name. The daguerreotype of Foster dates from 1859.

Stephen Foster was born in Pittsburgh on July 4, 1826. By the age of thirty he was America's most popular composer. From 1849 to 1860 he earned about $15,000 in royalties, but at his death in 1864 he had under $1 to his name.

Foster's knowledge of the South was minimal, yet many of his most widely sung songs were in praise of the region's tranquil, old-world charm. They conveyed an idealized view of southern society and frequently expressed a yearning for bygone days.

As a youngster Stephen Foster played the guitar, drums, and the flageolet (similar to a recorder). At fifteen he is said to have written a waltz, but not until late 1844 was his first music published. This was "Open Thy Lattice, Love," with words by George P. Morris and melody by the young Foster. He had had no formal musical training.

Minstrel shows were now becoming popular: touring groups performed so-called Negro songs with whites dressed up as blacks imitating the Negro dialect. Stephen absorbed this influence and by the mid-1840s had penned "Louisiana Belle" and "Old Uncle Ned."

He spent two years as a bookkeeper and then, in 1848, one event changed the course of his life. "Oh! Susanna" was accepted for publication; Foster was paid $100 for it. This ditty found its way into the repertoire of E. P. Christy's minstrels and within a year it had become the theme song of the Forty-Niners bound for California. Foster decided to devote himself full-time to music.

He exploited the popularity of minstrel songs, and wrote to Christy: "I wish to unite with you in every effort to encourage a taste for this style of music so cried down by opera mongers." Accordingly, the title pages of many songs stated that they were performed by Christy's minstrels, and Christy himself did much to popularize Foster's music.

Publishing delays led Foster to sell Christy the performing rights to a batch of songs for $10 each. In 1851 he received $15 for "Old Folks at Home." For the extra $5 Christy was named as composer, but the royalties still went to Foster. This song, also known as "Swanee River," was a stunning success. In three years the publishers were boasting sales of 130,000 copies of the sheet music. Despite several triumphs, Foster kept running short of money. To pay off his debts he sold all rights to sixty-eight songs for $3,600.

In 1860 Foster shifted from Pittsburgh to New York. It was a fateful decision. For the second time he separated from his wife and daughter whom he was unable to support. He degenerated into almost a hack composer, dashing off a stream of songs and arrangements for whoever would pay. His creative powers were in decline and he took refuge in drink.

In January 1864 Foster fainted and gashed his head. He entered Bellevue Hospital where he died on the thirteenth. In his purse were just thirty-five cents in scrip, three pennies, and a piece of paper with the words: "Dear friends and gentle hearts." Stephen Foster had valued the simple things in life. In his music it took the form of an innocent charm that exerted a strong appeal to a nation wracked by doubts about the future.

lands along the rivers were the first to support commercial production. Beginning in the 1820s, canals and later railroads supplemented the natural transportation network, opening vast areas of the nation to commercial production. But in this, the southern experience differed markedly from that in the North. Southern canal and railroad construction lagged far behind that of the North and as a result large parts of the interior lands in the South remained isolated from the market and the economic benefits it fostered. Thus, in the North there was a tendency for family farmers producing grain and livestock to be incorporated into the market economy. But in the South, only that relatively small portion of the population engaged in staple crop production with slave labor became part of the market economy. Most small family farmers remained in a state of self-sufficient production.

It would be a mistake to conclude from this that the South's self-sufficient family farmers were poor, that they were the poverty stricken "white trash." On the contrary, their "income" as measured in terms of the value of the commodities they produced and consumed was often as high as that of their northern counterparts. But it was not money income, as it was in the North, and this had important effects on the lives of the farmers and on the economy and society of the Old South.

A Largely Static Society

Commercial production requires an army of middlemen to market the crops and supply the needs of the producers. Merchants and brokers assemble the crops, warehousemen grade and store them, and buyers gather in market towns to dicker with sellers. Bankers provide credit and transfer funds from buyer to seller. Waggoners, laborers, and transportation workers move the crops from farm to farm, in and out of warehouses, and on to distant markets. Storekeepers stock their shelves with goods for farmers with cash to spend after their crops are sold. The middlemen themselves become a market for food, shelter, and clothing as they assemble in villages and towns, thus attracting others to supply these needs. The population becomes denser and more varied, opening new opportunities to the surrounding people and attracting energetic and enterprising outsiders.

This dynamism is absent in a society of self-sufficient producers. Farmers who had little to sell obviously lacked the money income to become buyers. The need for middlemen was sharply diminished; towns and cities were smaller and scarcer in the South than in the North. The South boasted far fewer country stores and those that did exist were smaller with far less merchandise on their shelves. Economic self-sufficiency thus created and perpetuated a primitive and relatively static society. A

perceptive English traveler was struck by this during a visit to the South in 1856: "Every step one takes in the South, one is struck with the rough look of the whole face of civilization. The country is nowhere well cleared; towns and villages are few and far between, and even those which you see have an unfinished look. . . . Notwithstanding the rapid prosperity of the South, and especially of the Gulf States, during the last twenty years, they have, on the whole a very wild appearance."

The commercial sector of the southern economy was far more dynamic. The production and sale of the staple crops provided the wealth of the planter class, supported the merchants and bankers necessary for trade, and were the economic basis for the wealth and prosperity of great markets such as New Orleans. But slavery robbed even the commercial sector of much of the dynamism commercial production had in the North. Most of the actual producers of the staple crops were slaves, but the money income from their efforts went to their owners, the planters. Slaves, of course, were consumers, but like the self-sufficient white farmers they grew most, if not all, of their food. Their consumption of manufactured goods such as clothing and tools was limited by their masters' desire to keep costs down. The results were cogently summarized by the Kentucky antislavery editor, Cassius M. Clay, in his Lexington newspaper, the *True American*: "Lawyers, merchants, mechanics, laborers, who are your consumers; Robert Wickliffe's two hundred slaves? How many clients do you find, how many goods do you sell, how many hats, coats, saddles, and trunks, do you make for these two hundred slaves? Does Mr. Wickliffe lay out as much for himself and his two hundred slaves, as two hundred freemen do?"

Clay correctly noted that slavery, like self-sufficient farming, created what economists call a shallow market and this stifled economic development. He went on to observe that slavery helped to perpetuate self-sufficiency by blocking avenues to change: "Under the free system the towns would grow and furnish a home market to the farmers, which in turn would employ more labor; which would consume the manufactures of the towns; and we could then find our business continually increasing, so that our children might settle down among us and make industrious, honest citizens."

The South's self-sufficiency in food production did not extend to manufacturing. During the two or three decades before the Civil War the United States began the revolution that would transform it from an agrarian to an industrial nation. Factories and mills producing textiles, boots and shoes, leather goods, iron, machinery, and other manufactured goods were centered mainly in New England and the Middle Atlantic states of New York, New Jersey, and Pennsylvania. But there were also sizable manufacturing centers in the middle western states. The South, however, lagged far behind, hardly participating

Compared with the North's highly developed urban society, southern life was predominantly rural in character. Southern cities and towns—more service centers than industrial conurbations—were smaller and life proceeded at a leisurely pace. The region as a whole lacked the progressive dynamism that characterized the North. Above: A view of Greenville, South Carolina, painted by Joshua Tucker. Below: A lithograph of Natchez, Mississippi, in 1847.

in the nation's industrial revolution. Its most important manufacturing was the simple processing of locally produced raw materials—lumber, tobacco, and flour. There were a few cotton textile mills in the South but despite the fact that the region produced all the nation's raw cotton, it accounted for less than 10 per cent of the nation's cotton manufacturing output on the eve of the Civil War. Its iron mills and other manufacturing establishments were few in number and small in size. Not only did the South lag far behind the highly industrialized Northeast in 1860, it also failed to come close to the manufacturing development in the still largely agrarian Middle West. Southern mills and factories were fewer in number and smaller, averaging less capital invested per establishment and employing fewer workers per establishment than both the Northwest and the West.

The lack of manufacturing development robbed the South of the industrial vitality evident elsewhere in the nation, just as self-sufficient and slave-based agriculture robbed the South of commercial vitality. As a result, the South remained overwhelmingly agricultural: about 85 per cent of its labor force in 1860 was employed in farming compared with 40 per cent in the North and West. And the South remained overwhelmingly rural: less than 10 per cent of its population was urban in 1860 compared with over 25 per cent in the North and West.

The South, of course, had some large cities. Some such as New Orleans, Charleston, and Savannah were beautiful, even exotic, and boasted a sophisticated society. But, as David Donald has noted, the South's "principal cities were on the periphery of the region." Baltimore, Louisville, and St Louis were located in the slave states but they faced north and were in reality part of the northern economy. The great ports of New Orleans, Savannah, Mobile, and Charleston were based primarily on the staple crop trade and, except for New Orleans whose commercial hinterland stretched northward into the great Mississippi Valley, were small compared with large northern cities such as Boston, New York, Philadelphia and even Chicago, Cincinnati, and Buffalo. In the interior, towns were sparse and tiny. Except for the flurry of activity in the markets during the brief harvest season, most southern towns were sleepy hamlets, as a Yankee school teacher in search of a job in the South reported: "The usual hum of business one does not hear in these southern towns; they are more quiet than ours. No whirling mills—no whining machinery—no clang of anvils—no ringing of factory bells—no din and bustle of the crowded mart. They have no wheat to grind, no manufacturing, and but little 'smithing,' to do; hence their trade and traffic have no strife and commotion. From the quiet appearance of their towns the stranger would think that the energies of trade were hushed—that business had gone into a pause, or was taking a siesta."

Below: Charleston, South Carolina, in 1831. Surrounded by a wealthy rice-growing region, Charleston mirrored the refinement of aristocratic ways. Inset: St Louis in the late 1850s was a major transportation and distribution center.

Above: Harvesting sugar cane in Louisiana in the 1850s. The crop was introduced to the present state of Louisiana about 1750, and by the 1830s half the nation's supply came from this state.

The rural, agricultural South turned to the North or to Europe for its manufactured goods and for much of its commercial needs such as shipping and insurance. To some southerners this reliance on outsiders created a dangerous dependency. It arose from "habit and indolence," said an angry Mississippi planter, and made the South little more than a colony of the North. "By mere supineness, the people of the South have permitted the Yankees to monopolize the carrying trade, with its immense profits," railed the *Vicksburg Daily Whig* on the eve of the Civil War. "We have yielded to them the manufacturing business. . . . We have acquiesced in the claims of the North to do all the importing, and most of the exporting business, for the whole Union. . . . Meantime, the South remains passive—in a state of torpidity—making cotton bales for the North to manufacture, and constantly exerting ourselves to increase the production as much as possible."

Those who decried southern dependency organized a series of conventions in an effort to bring reform. They urged direct trade with Europe so that southern cities instead of New York, Boston, and Philadelphia would become importing centers for the South. They advocated diversification of the southern economy, calling on planters to divert some of their resources to manufacturing and commerce. But these and other proposals produced little more than stirring resolutions and a few supporting editorials in the local press.

The failure of reform was not due to habit or indolence or supineness. There were powerful economic factors hindering southern industrial and commercial development. The shallow market limited demand in the South. Therefore, if southern manufacturing were to succeed it would have to be able to compete with northern manufacturers for a part of the national market. This the South was unable to do. Its wealth and money income—and hence its source of savings for investment—were in the hands of a small planter class which reinvested its surplus in more land and more slaves to produce more of the staple crops. It was a process that the planters found socially advantageous and economically rewarding. The southern transportation system, admirably suited to bringing staple crops to market, was inadequate when it came to reaching the national market which would add to the cost of marketing southern manufactures and thereby lessen their ability to compete with the North. The South's potential labor supply was also a hindering factor.

The purchase of slaves as factory workers would entail huge start-up costs which meant that southern industry, in order to compete with the North, would require a heavier capital investment and higher overhead costs. Free labor was in short supply. To induce the self-sufficient white farmers to leave their land and give up their independent life-styles would require economic inducements in the form of high wages that would lessen the South's ability to compete.

Resistance to Change

But there were more than purely economic reasons that hindered the South's industrial and commercial development. The planter class was, on the whole, hostile to industrial and commercial expansion—and with good reason. Should manufacturing become extensive, it would create a powerful class of urban industrialists whose interests in many ways would clash with those of the planters. In the end, a wealthy class of urban industrialists would undermine the power and prestige of the rural planter class. The process seemed clear enough.

Their need for cheap labor would make industrialists hostile to costly slave labor and favorable to measures to attract immigrants and free workers to the factories. As industrializing cities grew so too would the political power of the urban population. Like their northern counterparts, industrial leaders in the South would favor measures such as tariffs, bounties, and improved transportation facilities to protect and advance their interests—measures that the planters resisted because they increased their operating costs. But southern manufacturers would more than likely make common cause with their northern counterparts and this, along with support from the growing numbers of urban workers (who in this case would have interests identical to their employers), would weaken the planters' political influence and eventually overwhelm their opposition.

Even if slaves were hired or purchased for factory work, there was danger to the slave-owning interest. Slaves in city factories would be free of many of the strict controls that were exercised over them in the plantation setting. James Hammond expressed the fears of the planters: "Whenever a slave is made a mechanic he is more than half freed, and soon becomes, as we too well know, and all history attests, with rare exceptions, the most corrupt and turbulent of his class."

These fears were not mere conjecture on the part of the

Below: Unloading rice barges. Georgia and the Carolinas were the major rice-growing regions before the Civil War. The work was done by slaves, and the long hours spent in malaria-infested waters led to many deaths.

planter leaders. They saw in their own cities how urban life loosened the bonds of slavery. More important was what they saw in the North—political turmoil, labor unrest, a powerful and growing industrial class, abolitionism, and many other things they deemed menacing to their interests. Progress, at least as measured by the changes taking place in the North, was more to be feared than welcomed. An Alabaman cogently expressed this view to a British visitor: "We are an agricultural people; we are a primitive but a civilized people. We have no cities—we don't want them. . . . We have no commercial marine—no navy—we don't want them. We are better without them. Your ships carry our produce, and you can protect your own vessels. We want no manufactures; we desire no trading, no mechanical or manufacturing classes. As long as we have our rice, our sugar, our tobacco, and our cotton, we can command wealth to purchase all we want from those nations with which we are in amity, and to lay up money besides."

There was a certain bravado in the Alabaman's words. The Civil War had just begun when he spoke and he, like most southerners, was convinced that the South would succeed in its quest for independence. He denied the contentions of those who said the South was dependent upon the North and Europe. The dependency ran the other way. So dependent were the people of the Western world on the South's staple crops, that they would not countenance a blockade and a long war.

But in other respects there was less bravado and more accurate appraisal in the Alabaman's description. The South was indeed agricultural; it was in the countryside that most of the South's people lived and earned their living. But it was, of course, the planter class that owned the slaves who produced the rice, sugar, tobacco, and cotton and it was the planter class that found it possible to "lay up money." Southern wealth and power resided in the countryside where the planter ruled his lands and slaves and ultimately the entire section.

The Alabaman was correct also when he called the South "primitive," by which he seems to have meant that its social and economic structure was simple and static relative to that of the North. Of course, southerners, like Americans everywhere, lived in the midst of change. They were a mobile people, steadily moving westward turning virgin forests into farms, plantations, and towns. Some also experienced social mobility: the small farmer could and sometimes did become the respected planter.

Yet, at the same time, there was much that was steady and unchanging about the South. The thousands of immigrants who entered the United States avoided the South, where opportunities seemed limited. As a result the white population of the region remained homogeneous. The introduction of machinery on northern farms which made labor easier and increased productivity was not paralleled in the South, where production methods remained

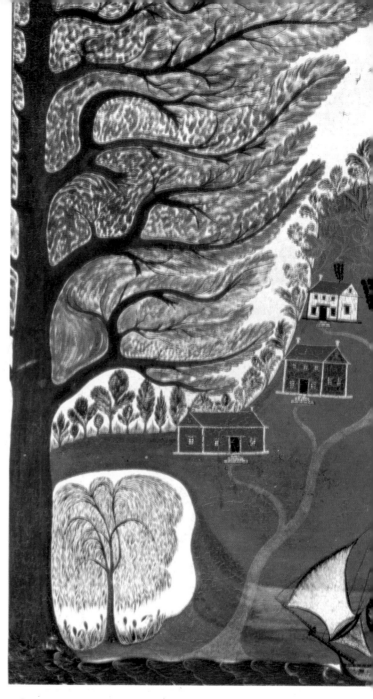

relatively unchanged over the decades. The lack of industrial and urban growth also helped to perpetuate the static and rural social and economic organization.

Class, Violence, and Fear

Also unchanging was the southern class structure. Undisturbed by expanding and varied economic activities, it remained relatively stable and rigid—a rigidity that was further hardened by a parallel caste structure based on race. It must be remembered that not all blacks were slaves. Some 250,000 southern blacks, half of whom lived in the eastern states, were legally free. But this small group—about 6 per cent of the total black population in the South—was locked into an inferior status by both

An unknown artist created this impression of a southern estate. Entitled The Plantation, *this striking painting captures the carefully structured nature of plantation life.*

custom and law. In the minds of most white southerners race and slavery were inextricably combined; the "proper" status of the black was in slavery. The free black was therefore an anomaly. His freedom was restricted, his opportunities limited. Since he was presumed because of his race to be a slave, he had to be able to prove he was free, an often difficult and sometimes impossible thing to do before hostile police, courts, and juries. Although a few free blacks managed to carve out a niche for themselves in southern society, most lived a difficult and marginal existence.

A primitive, static, and rural society bred a white population that was independent and self-reliant. These are characteristics of the frontier where they are required for simple survival. Left unrefined these frontier characteristics breed in turn a ready acceptance of personal violence to settle disputes and a mistrust of legal institutions which seem alien, slow moving, and ineffective. The frontier experience, of course, was common to both North and South and therefore the South had no monopoly on violence. But the South, with its sparse and scattered rural population, retained many of its frontier characteristics far longer than did the North. "Where such conditions existed," historian John Hope Franklin has written, "they produced, not a civilized, refined society, characterized by restraint and order, but a positive, aggressive reckless one where disorder and irresponsibility were outstanding features."

There were other features which gave rise to violence.

The real and imagined dangers from nearby Indians led southerners to stand ready to fight to defend their homes and families. The persistence of poorly policed and isolated areas attracted fugitives and criminals of various descriptions, people who were often quick to use violence and, because of the dangers they often posed, were quick to feel violence from those they endangered. But the most important source of violence in southern life was slavery.

Slavery, of course, was based on violence. The whip, rather than discharge, fine, or imprisonment, was used to ensure obedience. The planter, living in relative isolation on his plantation, was the source and the interpreter of the laws regulating his slaves. He expected to be obeyed and used or threatened violence when he was not. The slave, with scant protection by legal agencies, faced physical punishment not only from his owner, but also from other whites as well. And, because he sometimes returned violence with violence of his own, he posed a danger to whites who saw physical intimidation as the surest means of protection.

Because slavery was based on race and was justified as a means to control a dangerous and inferior people, those who questioned it posed a danger not merely to the economic well-being of the slaveowners, but to all whites. They feared that the end of slavery would mean that they would be engulfed and menaced by a dangerous and inferior race. Abolitionists, therefore, were seen as agitators who would destroy race controls and turn slaves into raging, pillaging, and murderous mobs. Such agitators did not deserve the right of free speech and assembly or the niceties of legal protection. Survival required that they be driven out, denied their rights, and violently dealt with if found.

Slavery also affected the relationships between the sexes which served to promote tension often leading to violence. The violence slave women or their men could use to protect themselves against the sexual advances of whites could be, and often was, answered by far greater violence by their attackers. On the other hand, white women were seen as the potential victims of vicious, oversexed black men who lusted after them. Violence, quick and aggressive, was seen as the only way to protect the defenseless white women.

Southerners were quick to take offense at real or imagined wrongs and quick to settle matters by resort to violence. Class relations affected the manner in which matters were settled. Among the planter aristocracy, the duel became the socially accepted, if often illegal, means to settle disputes. Among the lower classes, there was the no-holds-barred fight, bloody affairs in which combatants sometimes gouged eyes and bit off pieces of ears and noses. A gentleman used his cane or a horsewhip to punish social inferiors, reserving the duel for redress with his social equals. White southerners of every class regularly went about armed with daggers or pistols and were ready to use them to punish wrongdoing or to protect themselves.

The readiness to use violence, the ability with which weapons were used, and the felt need for protection created a tradition of militarism in the South. The accurate marksman, the fearless duelist, the successful fighter gained fame and prestige. But, while they applauded individual prowess, southerners recognized also that there was a need for direction and discipline. This produced an emphasis on military school education and the militia musterings, an emphasis that grew as tensions between North and South increased. Southerners were proud of their military skills, and with good reason. They made good soldiers and fine officers as their conduct in the Civil War would amply demonstrate.

The Threat from the North

A rural, sparsely settled population gave little support to formal education. While public education was expanding rapidly in the North during the early nineteenth century, expenditures for education in the South grew slowly and haltingly. For the planters and others who could afford it, private tutors, local military academies, or northern and European schools provided education for their children. But for the great majority of the white population, formal schooling was limited or nonexistent. J. D. B. De Bow, the southern editor and superintendent of the census, reported that in 1850 illiteracy among the adult native white population in the South was over 20 per cent compared with 3 per cent in the Middle Atlantic states and less than one-half of 1 per cent in New England. Although conditions improved in the 1850s, the Old South never reached northern standards of education.

Many southerners with a distrust of "book larning" considered formal education an expensive and unnecessary luxury. It could also be dangerous because it was suspected the northern teachers and northern books often promoted ideas subversive to the South. Indeed, the increase in expenditures for education in the 1850s was part of an effort to counteract the menace of northern education. Legislatures encouraged the writing of southern texts and the employment of southern teachers who could be trusted not to infect their students with alien ideas.

Formal education became part of a massive campaign to defend the South. At the heart of this campaign was a defense of the South's peculiar institution, for critics and defenders alike were aware that slavery was the source of southern distinctiveness and therefore the source of sectional conflict. This had not always been so. From its beginning, there had always been critics of slavery who had variously condemned it as vicious, un-Christian, barbaric, or unprofitable. At the time of the Revolution, it seemed to many to be in blatant contradiction to the ideas that motivated the revolutionaries. But the criticism had always been of slavery, not of the South. Indeed, many of the critics were southerners who openly opposed slavery on both moral and economic grounds.

Gradually, however, both the nature and the source of the criticisms changed. By the 1830s the attack on slavery came exclusively from the North and increasingly the criticism became an attack not simply on slavery, but on the South itself. In response, southern publicists mounted a campaign to defend slavery, to defend the South and its institutions, and to attack the North. Critics of slavery were enemies to be opposed when they appeared in the North and to be silenced or driven out when they appeared in the South. However much southerners were divided on a variety of national and local issues in their often bitter political campaigns, the issue of slavery was not up for discussion. Southern abolitionists found it wiser and safer either to remain silent or to leave.

To many of its defenders at the time of the American Revolution, slavery was a dying institution. Planters such as George Washington questioned the value of their slaves who produced tobacco for a glutted market on lands which had lost much of their fertility. The first president predicted in 1794 that slaves will be "found to be a very troublesome species of property 'ere many years pass over our heads." But even those who agreed with this pessimistic assessment found reason to defend the institution. Slavery, they argued, maintained control over an alien and inferior race that could not be absorbed into the white population. And those who did advocate emancipation coupled their advocacy with plans to return the freed blacks to Africa.

By the third decade of the nineteenth century, the defenders of slavery had considerably expanded their argument. Slavery, they maintained, was far more than a means to control an alien race; it was a positive good—to the slave, to the South, to the nation, and to the world. "No fact is plainer than that the blacks have been elevated and improved by their servitude in this country," wrote Albert Taylor Bledsoe. "We cannot possibly conceive, indeed, how Divine Providence could have placed them in a better school of correction." Slavery rescued the blacks from the barbarism of their African homeland and turned them into civilized, productive workers, wrote William J. Grayson, using heroic couplets to make his point:

> Instructed thus, and in the only school
> Barbarians ever know—a master's rule,
> The Negro learns each civilizing art
> That softens and subdues the savage heart,
> Assumes the tone of those with whom he lives,
> Acquires the habit that refinement gives,
> And slowly learns, but surely, while a slave
> The lessons that his country never gave.

Productive slave labor under the wise direction of the master class, the argument continued, provided the mills of the world with cotton and gave the country its most important export.

Growth of Southern Nationalism

The proslavery argument sometimes went far beyond a mere defense of black slavery in the South. In the hands of men such as Grayson and George Fitzhugh it became a blistering attack on northern capitalism in general and on free labor in particular. Grayson's long poem in defense of slavery, *The Hireling and the Slave*, was really a comparison between the lives of the hireling or free worker and the slave, a comparison in which the life of the free wage worker was found lacking. The slave, he wrote, is

> Guarded from want, from beggary secure,
> He never feels what hireling crowds endure,
> Nor knows, like them, in hopeless want to crave,
> For wife and child, the comforts of the slave,
> Or the sad thought that, when about to die,
> He leaves them to the cold world's charity,
> And sees them slowly seek the poor-house door—
> The last, vile, hated refuge of the poor.

The logic of the next step was obvious enough—miserable wage slaves would be better off if enslaved—and Fitzhugh was bold enough to suggest it. "The world will only fall back on domestic slavery when all other social forms have failed and been exhausted," he wrote, and from his analysis of the free labor system he concluded, "That hour may not be far off."

But most proslavery advocates had no intention of pursuing the logic of their argument to that point. Their goal was to defend their own system of black slavery and to strengthen support for it in the South. This could be best done by showing how all whites, not just slaveowners, benefited from it. Slavery freed all white men from the menial and backbreaking tasks which were the lot of their brothers in the North, said editor De Bow. Southern white workers were not forced to work in unhealthy shops; they did not face the competition of "foreign pauper labor." "No white man at the South serves another as a body servant, to clean his boots, wait on his table, and perform the menial services of his household." And most important of all, De Bow concluded, every white man in the South has the opportunity to become a slaveholder himself—and many have seized that opportunity to their benefit. Every white man becomes an aristocrat in the South argued a Kentuckian: "When it is said that slavery is calculated to produce aristocracy, there is more truth in the remark than persons generally allow. But it is a general aristocracy—an aristocracy of the whole white race."

Thus, the proslavery argument was far more than a

defense of the practice of holding blacks as chattel: it was a defense of the entire southern social system. True, part of the argument was a simple denial of abolitionist attacks. Southern publicists denied that slaves were badly treated and underfed or that slave families were regularly broken up. But very often the proslavery writers turned northern attacks back on themselves, accepting some of the charges but finding them good, not bad, and sources of strength, not weaknesses. Slavery was not only generally benign; it was good for the slave. Slaveowners' profits might be lower than those of northern industrialists, but that was, as Fitzhugh put it, "because the master allows the slave to retain a larger share of the results of his own labor, than do the employers of free labor." Slavery might degrade menial work, but this was good for the southern white man who did not have to do it. Slavery might slow industrial development and urbanization, but this was beneficial because it safeguarded the South from the turmoil and conflict that plagued the North.

The South, then, was different—and it was better. As historian T. Harry Williams has put it: "Other peoples have looked forward or backward to a golden age, but those of the antebellum South proclaimed that they lived in one." This was not merely the cynical view of apologists or propogandists—although there was some of that involved —nor was it just the self-serving view of those who would protect their valuable investments in slaves—although

this too was not entirely absent. It was a view that transcended immediate needs and selfish interest. It was a view that reflected a consensus, a basic unity in the Old South. It built pride in that which was southern and provoked antagonism towards those who would criticize. As John Hope Franklin has written: "Southern pride in its institutions and ways of life was transformed into a fierce intolerance of everything outside of and the most slavish acceptance of everything within the sectional sanctuary."

By the eve of the Civil War, the South, despite all it had in common with the rest of the country, had become different. It had a distinctive society and economy based on slavery and a distinctive ruling class, the slaveowning aristocracy, that gave the South its tone, its goals, and its

At the outset, northern criticism of the South had centered on slavery, but later it broadened into a wide-ranging denunciation of southern life and attitudes. To this the South responded positively. Many whites who had previously regarded slavery as a necessary evil—a legacy from the past—now began to eulogize it as a beneficial method of social organization. And upon it they had, in their view, built an orderly and gracious way of life. Right: Oakland House and Race Course, Louisville, an 1840 oil by Brammer and Von Smith. Below: A Louisiana plantation.

general ideology. This was a landed aristocracy but a peculiar one in that it was an aristocracy without a long aristocratic tradition. Few southern planters could trace their ancestry back to the great noble families of England. Indeed, most could not trace their aristocratic lineage back very far in American history. This was a new aristocracy, peopled by self-made men or the sons and grandsons of self-made men. It relied for its existence not on birth or blood, but on the ownership of land and slaves. Therefore, although it was small, it was open-ended; the energetic and the lucky could dream of entering its ranks— and many did. This was a landed aristocracy that lived in the midst of a bourgeois-capitalist world of the market-place with which it had a paradoxical relationship: it responded to it and participated in it while at the same time it rejected it by repudiating bourgeois goals and the free labor system.

Southerners developed a unity under the aegis of this ruling class, a unity which accepted and glorified southern distinctiveness. This became more than sectionalism or local pride; it was the stuff of nationalism. It became the ideology that would propel the South into secession, into an effort to achieve its national independence.

The southern historian David Potter has pointed out that historians often mistakenly see nationalism as the result of unity arising from cultural affinities among people. He argues that nationalism also arises out of the unity of common material interests which are felt to be under attack. In the last decades before the Civil War, both common culture and common interests worked to create southern nationalism. Many southerners felt that they had developed a distinct—and superior—culture. "There can be no question that the supposititious Line of Mason and Dixon separated two people as dissimilar in thought and feeling, in habit and in need, as were the Saxons and the knights of Rollo the Norman," wrote a South Carolinian. Buttressing the idea that the South was culturally distinctive was the idea that the South was under attack from abolitionists, hostile northern politicians, and an antagonistic northern population—all of whom were bent on destroying the southern way of life.

The effort by proslavery advocates to defend the South from without and to squelch opposition from within became in reality, if not always in aim, an effort to create and sustain national consciousness in the South. The quest for independence in 1861 was the successful outcome of this effort. The failure to achieve independence was not proof that the South had not become a nation; it signalled merely that the South lacked the military and economic power to win independence. That southern nationalism died so quickly and so completely after failure in war is a sign, not that it did not exist, but rather that its material, cultural, and class basis vanished with the destruction of slavery and the planter aristocracy.

Chapter 3

"I WILL BE HEARD"

Of all the voices calling for the abolition of slavery in the United States, the loudest and most passionate was that of William Lloyd Garrison. He rebelled against gradual reform by persuasion and urged instead a head-on attack seeking immediate freedom for slaves. Like other prominent reformers, Garrison stirred up strong opposition: meetings were disrupted, property was destroyed, and people were injured and even killed—but then the abolition cry was itself often strident and disruptive. The movement was rarely a unified campaign and the many groups in the field were frequently at odds with each other over tactics. Nevertheless, abolitionists managed to stir the conscience of the nation and strengthen the political commitment to ending slavery.

The Abolition Campaign

Urge me not to use moderation in a cause like the present. I am in earnest—I will not equivocate—I will not excuse—I will not retreat a single inch— AND I WILL BE HEARD. The apathy of the people is enough to make every statue leap from its pedestal, and to hasten the resurrection of the dead.

William Lloyd Garrison swore that he would be heard. He put the promise and prophecy in capital letters in his little newspaper's first issue so that his readers would not miss them. The *Liberator* had few readers, however, and most of them were Afro-Americans who could be expected to agree with Garrison's attack upon slavery but who had very little power. This fact should have allowed his words to evaporate harmlessly. But they did not. Ignored by most people at first, Garrison's words frightened a few southerners who feared they would incite slave rebellions. They invited a few white persons who shared their vision to speak out. They encouraged many black persons to hope for liberation. Within a few years, Garrison's words were at the center of a national debate which filled the press, lecture halls, churches, and Congress. The issues were human equality, American freedom, moral responsibility, and the immediate abolition of slavery. By 1838 the abolition movement was an important fact of American life—William Lloyd Garrison had been heard.

Abolitionists' accomplishments can be understood only against the background of religious and intellectual developments in the seventeenth and eighteenth centuries

By kind permission of the British Library/John Freeman

Friends Historical Library, Swarthmore College

William Lloyd Garrison (above) provided much of the impetus for the abolition crusade. On the speaker's platform and in his newspaper (below) he campaigned strenuously for the immediate freeing of slaves.

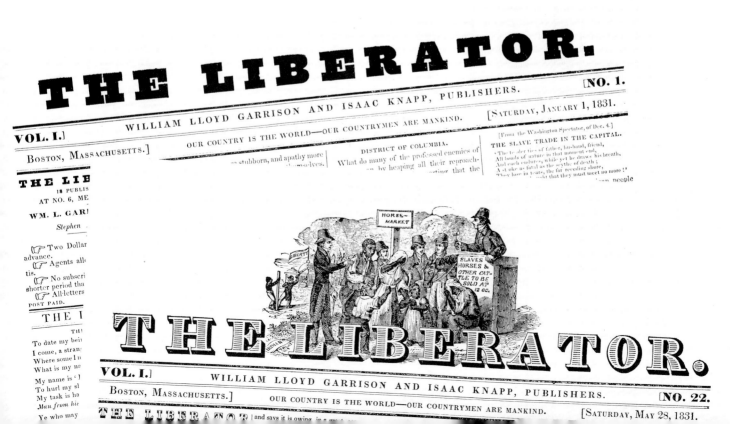

which combined with the American Revolution to create an antislavery tradition in the United States. In other words, what Garrison and his allies could achieve was made possible by changes that preceded them, and which they sometimes only dimly understood.

The contradiction of slavery and Christianity—a significant part of abolitionist criticism—had not been sufficiently powerful to abolish slavery. The institution slowly died out in Christian Europe for economic reasons, leaving little moral revulsion against it to pass on to the people who reestablished it in the New World. There, the need for laborers and the availability of Africans resurrected slavery in a new and complicated form even as events were taking place to make possible the development of antislavery ideas. Momentous social changes in fifteenth- and sixteenth-century Europe forced men to slough off allegiance to traditional authority and declare a reformation of church and society. The turmoil of questioning helped to place all institutions under scrutiny, but the process of criticism and change was very slow. Not until the eighteenth century, when there was a renewed interest in man's sin and a new identification of sin with slavery, did a few dissidents transform scrutiny into condemnation.

From nonreligious sources, too, the stream of antislavery thought was fed. The Enlightenment, with its emphasis on testing all institutions by the standards of natural law, the application of reason, and the criterion of usefulness allowed astute and sensitive rationalists to consider slavery unnatural, irrational, and useless. Cool, rational analysis and impassioned condemnation were beginning to converge by the end of the eighteenth century to provide American abolitionists with a sense of being part of the most progressive, enlightened tradition in Western culture.

Even more important, abolitionists could identify with specific groups, men, and events, as well as vast trends. The most important group was the Society of Friends whose members eventually transformed their repudiation of worldly authority and their intense concern with creating a perfect community into a "witness" against slaveholding. The process of this change was neither smooth nor easy, but required hard work on the part of men like John Woolman. In 1746 this young, pious New Jersey tailor returned from a visit with fellow Quakers in the southern colonies deeply troubled by the slaveholding among Quakers there. He wrote down his dismay and anguish in *Some Considerations on the Keeping of Negroes* which he did not publish until 1754. Before that time, however, Woolman's smoldering sense of guilt was enflamed by persistent personal reminders of the evil of slavery until he finally persuaded the Philadelphia yearly meeting to publish a statement he had written favoring gradual emancipation. Thereafter he traveled almost continually from Quaker meeting to meeting, urging, contesting, appealing to Friends to purge themselves of

Methodists were in the forefront of the fight against slavery, and spoke out against the system at religious meetings like the one above.

slaveholding. Woolman was not alone. Other Quakers were writing pamphlets against slavery as if it were the epitome of sin itself. Within a generation this barrage of the printed word, combined with Woolman's activities, made membership in the Society of Friends synonymous with opposition to slavery.

The impulse to create a perfect Christian nonslaveholding community was not the property of Quakers alone. Other Protestant groups such as Methodists, with the Quaker example in mind, began to make pronouncements against slavery as early as 1780. Emboldened by the actions of a small number of Methodists who emancipated their slaves, Wesleyan conferences attempted to identify Methodism with emancipationism in 1785 by excommunicating slaveholders. Although essentially unsuccessful, such actions as these helped to spread antislavery sentiments. Throughout the last twenty years of the eighteenth century, members of Baptist, Presbyterian, and Congregational churches joined their Methodist and Quaker brethren in making statements against slavery, working in local antislavery societies, or emancipating their slaves. Antislavery evangelism was a nondenominational effort. Methodists, for example, printed antislavery tracts of a Presbyterian clergyman, David Rice. His ideas were becoming familiar in 1792 when he published them under the title *Slavery Inconsistent with Justice and Good Policy*. His basic assumption was that all men were created equal "with respect to liberty" including black slaves who had been denied their natural rights. Among these were the love and sanctity of family life, the right to protection of the law, the right to improve oneself through education and labor. Rice also emphasized the impractical aspects of slavery as uneconomical and dangerous since potential rebels who worked only reluctantly were a threat to the Republic. Rice's solution was that each state—his was Kentucky—should import no more slaves, but promise to emancipate all children of slaves born after 1792, educate all people held in bondage, and free them at a time established at once by the law.

Slavery Abolished in the North

Rice's emphasis on equality, liberty, and natural rights was given special force by the American Revolution. That event was to become signally important to later abolitionists like Garrison, because it identified the birth of American nationality with the concept of universal equality and basic human rights. It did so by creating a climate of opinion that made possible the scattering of antislavery ideas, the abolition of slavery in the North, and the development of an American antislavery tradition. In justifying their secession from the British empire,

In their propaganda, abolitionists indulged unashamedly in an appeal to the emotions. This colored engraving appeared in a German-language publication and has the fair maiden of abolition rushing to protect the youthful, praying slave.

revolutionary writers argued that Crown and Parliament conspired to cast Americans into abject slavery by depriving them of the right to direct their own lives. Such a claim could carry weight, observed some Americans, only if their own domestic enslavement of Africans were abolished. And soon the inconsistency of freedom-loving Americans holding Africans in bondage became the theme of pamphlets, sermons, tracts, political declarations, and private arguments.

Public action resulting from the "contagion" of antislavery ideas came slowly in the North, although the Continental Congress in the heat of revolutionary ardor banned the importation of slaves in December 1774. After that, the process of rooting out northern slavery took thirty years beginning in Vermont and New Hampshire, which had few if any slaves at all. In Massachusetts, where 3 per cent of the population were slaves, a series of court cases had established the illegality of slavery by 1790. By 1784 both Rhode Island and Connecticut had easily passed laws abolishing slavery. The major conflicts over northern abolition were in Pennsylvania, New York, and New Jersey where slaves made up between 8 and 12 per cent of the population. Pennsylvania Quakers were primarily responsible for passing the first general abolition act in 1780, only to discover that it required constant surveillance. New York antislavery forces fought for over a generation to get a general abolition law finally in 1799. And New Jersey tagged along after the rest of the northern states in 1804.

The process of abolition had been long and difficult. Far from fizzling out as an uneconomic use of labor, slavery was abolished through hard work on the part of pressure groups and legislators who believed it unjust on the one hand and harmful to moral and economic development on the other. The persistence of state abolition societies after gradual emancipation laws were passed reveals the continuing interest of a few white reformers in the education, well-being, and just treatment of blacks. The laws had not made all blacks free—only those born after a legally prescribed date for which they had to wait as long as twenty-eight years. In the meantime, there were many loopholes for masters to wriggle through. Abolition societies had to try to plug them up as best they could

Above: Slaves were freed in Philadelphia before 1800 but emancipation by no means implied social equality. Pavel Svinin's painting depicts wealthy whites and Negro chimney sweeps.

through legal battles, education, and constant surveillance. Although emancipationists were victorious in the North only after years of hard work, they did not have so strong an enemy as their counterparts in the South. There, unlike the North, slaveholders were in power in state legislatures where they could ignore antislavery petitions, and make emancipation increasingly more difficult for whites and less pleasant for blacks. Gradually, North and South were becoming different because of the way in which revolutionary ideas about slavery could be applied in the two regions.

Despite the regional differences established by northern abolition, a national antislavery tradition developed. Even slaveholders were a part of it and the most prominent of these was Thomas Jefferson of Virginia, author of the Declaration of Independence. He was so tormented by slavery that he won restrictions keeping it out of the western territories in the Northwest Ordinance of 1787. He was also one of the leading opponents of the foreign slave trade which, as president, he was instrumental in abolishing on January 1, 1808. Thus, Jefferson, with southern as well as northern allies, limited slavery to one section of the country and tried to curtail its growth even there by cutting off importation of new slaves. In doing so, he made it possible to claim that American values were essentially opposed to slavery.

Reforming Zeal Slackens

Real as was the American antislavery tradition, it had weakened by the nineteenth century. Abolition societies met spasmodically in the North and the border states of the South until the later 1820s with members expressing themselves in much the same language as David Rice's pamphlet of 1792. But although angry people demanded the excommunication of slaveholders from their churches, they were few in number and isolated from the spirit of accommodation that permeated American life. Antislavery churches gradually repealed or ignored their earlier rules against slaveholding. Antislavery southerners left their native states for free territory or retreated into silent antagonism that sometimes erupted in anonymous letters to one or two antislavery newspapers. Thus frustrated, those who clung to the tradition did so in a kind of defeated, if defiant, manner that expressed their hope in "gradualism."

As children of the eighteenth century they believed in the inexorable if slow progress of history towards ulti-

Although the abolition cry was muted in the early 1800s, a trickle of publications kept interest alive. Left: An author takes notes from freeborn Negroes who had been kidnapped and enslaved.

mate freedom and equality. The laws which they had passed were "gradual" emancipation laws that presumably eased the transition from slavery to freedom for both masters and slaves over a period of about a generation. Even evangelists who wished to throw slaveholders out of the churches would have been satisfied with such laws in the South. But opposition and defeat slowly reshaped the idea of gradualism from a plan of action to an attitude. The idea began to mean that moral influence would eventually change the minds of people who supported slavery.

The institution which embodied gradualism and revealed its weaknesses as well as its good intentions was the American Colonization Society. Founded at the end of 1816 by a curious combination of slaveholders, reformers, and politicians, the society was designed to provide a way for black people to emigrate to West Africa to set up a Christian republic. (In this way, Liberia was founded.) Its members agreed to provide a haven from white American racism for blacks. They also believed that the haven could demonstrate the political and moral sophistication of blacks once they were allowed full participation in a social system. Reformers also hoped that the society would encourage individual acts of emancipation which would eventually accustom southerners to the idea of freedom for blacks even in the South. Less idealistic members wished merely to rid the country of a free black population whose existence demonstrated that blacks need not be enslaved, and who therefore were a constant source of trouble. This latter view, rather than that of the reformists, seemed to many black leaders to characterize the movement and so they opposed it as a threat. They were impressed not so much by the reformists' good intentions as by their knuckling under to racial prejudice and the danger which this surrender posed to the claims of blacks for justice.

By the mid-1820s the American antislavery tradition was becalmed. The radical onslaught of the postrevolutionary era had lapsed into a few isolated curses or a diluted gradualism. The debates over the admission of Missouri to the Union as a slave state alarmed the South and had more the effect of frightening slaveholders than arousing emancipationists. The explosion of abolitionism awaited the conjunction of four important changes in northern society in the middle 1830s. These were the development of new institutions which demanded a reexamination of traditional roles and responsibilities; the emergence of a younger generation to influence and power through professional reform; the emergence of a self-conscious black community that addressed itself to public issues; and the communication revolution.

Social change was accelerating in the North during the 1820s and 1830s. Politically, the old party system of choosing leadership on the basis of family and status was being challenged by a new system that was an

The Underground Railroad

The Underground Railroad was the name given to a system by which fleeing slaves were helped to freedom by sympathizers in the North. The Reverend John Rankin of Ripley, Ohio, who was active in the movement, wrote that the Underground Railroad was so called "because they who took passage on it disappeared from public view as really as if they had gone into the ground." It was formed "without any general concert, there were no secret oaths taken, nor promises of secrecy extorted. And yet there were no betrayals."

By aiding escapers the Railroad contravened the laws of the land. The first fugitive slave law had been passed by Congress in 1793. This remained in force until 1850 when a tougher statute made refusal to help in the recapture of fugitives a crime punishable by a $1,000 fine or six months jail. Accordingly, the Underground Railroad worked quietly.

The Railroad extended from Kentucky and Virginia to Indiana and Ohio, from Maryland across Pennsylvania, New York, and New England. The preferred destination was Canada, for the free states were an uncertain zone from which fugitives could be taken back to the South. Levi Coffin, a prominent Railroader, wrote that fugitives "sometimes came to our door frightened and panting and in a destitute condition, having fled in such haste and fear that they had no time to bring any clothing except what they had on, and that was often very scant." Every mode of travel was used to ferry slaves from one hideout to another along the "road." They were taken on foot, in carriages or wagons (often under a pile of goods or in a load of hay), by rail, river steamers, and oceangoing ships. They were hidden in houses and sheds. But for the journey through the South to the free states it was the wood and swamp which most often gave sanctuary to the fugitive.

Prominent workers in the movement, apart from Coffin, included Harriet Tubman, a former Maryland field hand who returned frequently to the South to bring out slaves, Isaac Hopper, one of many Quakers active in Pennsylvania, and Thomas Garrett, who is said to have helped some 3,000 slaves to freedom.

John Fairfield differed from most Railroaders by receiving payment from Negroes in Canada and the North to spirit away friends and relatives. Coffin described Fairfield's dangerous methods. "He would go south into the neighborhood where the slaves were whom he intended to conduct away, and, under an assumed name and a false pretence of business, engage boarding, perhaps at the house of the master whose stock of valuable property he intended to decrease. He would proclaim himself to be a Virginian, and profess to be strongly proslavery in his sentiments, thus lulling the suspicions of the slaveholders while he established a secret understanding with the slaves. . . . Then he would suddenly disappear from the neighborhood and several slaves would be missing at the same time."

Estimates of the number of slaves who escaped to freedom range from 25,000 to 100,000. Whatever the figure, it was only a tiny fraction of the total slave population. After the Civil War, when the fight for emancipation had been won, the Underground Railroad passed into history, its services no longer required.

Top left: Tired and ragged fugitives are unloaded from a wagon at Levi Coffin's farm in western Indiana in this painting by Charles T. Webber. Right: In northern states, free Negroes played an important role in the work of the Railroad. William Whipper was an escort at Columbia, Pennsylvania. Above: Eastman Johnson's A Ride for Liberty portrays a family riding north on a stolen horse. Far right: Various ruses were employed on the Underground Railroad to lessen the risk of the fugitive being tracked down by his owner. Some, like the woman shown here, were dressed in clothes of the opposite sex.

uneven mixture of party loyalty, personal merit, and cunning manipulation. Economically, northerners were diverting their capital from commercial to industrial enterprise, creating a factory system that in its turn created new opportunities and new problems. As political parties sought to organize voters, so factories sought to organize workers, and in both cases organization led to a manipulative attitude on the part of people in power. This attitude placed a high value on orderliness, submissiveness to the organization, the production of results. Individuals counted for little. The confusion thus created was compounded by the increasingly transient character of the population as people moved from place to place in a feverish search for improved opportunities.

One of the most significant changes of the period was the development of a series of reform movements that by the 1830s were engaging energetic young men and women in various schemes of moral and social improvement. Missionary and benevolent societies had been a part of the institutional landscape in America since the 1790s, but as northern society began to change, the resulting confusion sent many idealistic young people in search of a "meaningful" way to deal with ignorance, poverty, and the increasing manipulation of human beings. Most had been converted to evangelical Christianity during the revivals of the early nineteenth century. This did not make them reformers, but it did give them a deep sense of sin, belief in the redeeming qualities of self-sacrifice, a commitment to God's work, and an optimistic hope in a new and better world which they could create. Sharing in part the new values of organizing to achieve a specific goal, and even of manipulating people (for their own good of course), these reformers tried to build a better world through education, Bible, and temperance groups among many others. They approached their society as if it were in their power to remake it. Past failures to do so did not daunt them.

In their utopian search, white reformers discovered the black community which had been using the evangelical churches as a basis for organizing their common life since the 1770s. From then until 1820 they gradually moved away from the control of white evangelicals whose racial prejudice severely limited black autonomy. Once men like Richard Allen led their fellow blacks out of the white churches they were free within the limits of their poverty and low status to develop a sense of solidarity that enabled them to take stands on public issues. Allen, first bishop of the African Methodist Episcopal Church, led his people in attacking the American Colonization Society as anti-Negro. He also helped start a Negro Convention movement which helped blacks to coordinate activities and develop a sense of solidarity through periodic conventions that discussed their problems. Soon a few Afro-American journals began to be published, and as blacks began to increase the tempo and vigor of their public statements, they encountered white reformers who were willing to listen. It is not surprising, therefore, that most of Garrison's early support came almost entirely from the black community.

The convergence of black self-determination and white reform zeal came at a time when communication in the United States was becoming much more rapid and general. Cheaper newsprint and more effective printing presses made possible the vast distribution of tracts after 1834. Newspapers and journals proliferated in number and circulation over the succeeding decades and were carried to all parts of the country by an ever-expanding system of canals and railroads. The resulting explosion of information informed previously isolated hamlets not only about politics in the nation's capital, but also about how people lived and thought in the rest of the country. The exotic habits and institutions of southerners could become a topic of discussion at first out of curiosity, and then, perhaps, out of moral indignation. The transformation from curiosity to indignation was the accomplishment of those reformers who chose to become abolitionists.

Spreading the Militant Message

The abolition movement began with the disillusionment of restless reformers with the American Colonization Society and gradualism. Garrison's own pilgrimage was symbolic of that taken by many of his fellow militants. Driven by a compulsive ambition to do something important with his life, he early discovered that poverty and a self-righteous devotion to principle would keep him from influential positions in either business or politics. He finally settled upon journalism as his means of access to the public, but a reckless intensity and taste for unpopular causes made his first editorial venture a failure. Undismayed, he continued to seek his place in a crusade which could combine moral commitment with just enough income to keep body and soul together. He found what he was looking for with the help of Benjamin Lundy.

Lundy was a Quaker and former saddle maker whose profound opposition to slavery had begun as soon as he became acquainted with it in Wheeling, Virginia, in 1809. After a few years in Ohio working against race prejudice in his spare time, Lundy finally sold his business to devote all his energy to publishing an antislavery paper, *The Genius of Universal Emancipation* (1821), and organizing abolition societies. Although always on the edge of poverty and without consistent support of an organization, Lundy used his paper to publicize activities of the Convention for Promoting the Abolition of Slavery and other groups. Lundy's primary purpose was to discuss the questions of race prejudice and slavery as thoroughly as possible. Through the years, he discussed

Above: Negro Methodists hold a meeting in a Philadelphia street in this watercolor by Pavel Svinin. Right: Bishops of the African Methodist Episcopal Church. Having found a convenient meeting place in the church, northern Negroes proceeded to break away from the dominance of white preachers and establish their own churches. Leaders like Richard Allen attacked the American Colonization Society for its equivocal stand on slavery. The society wanted to ship slaves abroad rather than press for their right to be free citizens in America.

Quaker Benjamin Lundy devoted years of effort to
the abolition cause, and in 1821 founded a paper
to publicize his views. He favored resettling
Negroes in colonies in Mexico.

ways to get rid of slavery including federal action against
the domestic slave trade, the admission of slave states to
the Union, and the persistence of slavery in the federal
territories. States should support programs of voluntary
gradual emancipation, he suggested in 1822. But soon he
began to urge a scheme of compulsory apprenticeship and
education which would prepare slaves for freedom. In his
search for a solution to slavery, Lundy had settled upon
the idea of colonization when Garrison met him in 1828.

The little Quaker had come to Boston seeking public
support but succeeded in influencing only Garrison. The
impression was deep. Lundy gave the intense young man
the kind of cause which he needed to make his life
significant. Thereafter, the tireless Garrison studied
English antislavery writers as he attacked slavery in his
short-lived *Journal of the Times*, and, when the paper
ceased publication, eagerly accepted an opportunity to
help Lundy with *The Genius of Universal Emancipation*
in Baltimore. The association was doomed, for Lundy and
Garrison were already diverging onto two different paths,
the former advocating schemes for colonizing blacks in
Mexico, the latter seeking a downright repudiation of
colonization. Garrison's friendship with blacks who
opposed the American Colonization Society undoubtedly
confirmed his own opposition, and he agreed to Lundy's
suggestion that they sign their articles with initials so that

neither would be accused of inconsistency. The result was
a series of anticolonization articles which was to become
the basis of Garrison's important *Thoughts on African
Colonization*, published in 1832.

The tract was a blunt, angry, partisan attack that
emphasized three important differences between the
gradualist, genteel reformers of the American Colonization
Society and a new breed of militants. The first was the
society's attempt to achieve its goals in cooperation with
slaveholders. This alliance, based upon the belief that
moral influence for emancipation would be effective only
without confrontation, was doomed, Garrison charged.
It seduced colonizationists into apologizing for their slaveholding friends and therefore slavery itself. This tendency, he insisted, was consistent with their fear of
blacks as potential revolutionaries or moral misfits who
threatened the survival of the Republic. The society's
inconsistency of expecting people thus demeaned and
despised to create a viable republic in Africa seemed to
Garrison to reveal an inability to face facts. By trying to
remove black people from their native land, colonizationists betrayed an eagerness to surrender to racial
fears and prejudices that brought their sincerity into
question. Rather than fight evil or provide means by
which blacks could freely engage in American life on the
basis of equality, they merely attempted to lull the consciences of white Americans.

Garrison offered another approach—immediate emancipation. It was not so much a plan as a view of moral
responsibility and a call to action. The major fault of
colonizationists, he wrote, was that they did not say
slavery was a sin which required immediate repentance.
That was the crux of the matter, and the major departure
from gradualism. Colonizationists did not, Garrison
emphasized, "*identify the criminals.*" The words expressed his frustration with reformers who pretended to act
for the good of mankind without facing up to the problem
of moral responsibility. Slaveholders were responsible for
maintaining slavery, he said, but they would not act
unless confronted with the enormity of their sin. He
would have been unfair to slaveholders who had already
freed their slaves as an act of conscience, he confessed, if
he did not expect others to be convicted of sin.

At this point Garrison was following a way of thinking
provided by British reformers and American evangelicals.
British antislavery writers of the 1820s, some of whom he
cited in his *Thoughts*, had called for immediate abolition
of West Indian slavery in a clear, authoritative way that
persuaded Garrison to do the same for his own country.
His experience as a religious person who had heard the
best of evangelical preaching shaped his view that sin
could not be repented of gradually. Immediate repentance
and commitment to an active life of discipleship, although
an important religious ritual, was also an affirmation of
men's ability to change the direction of their own lives

and those of others as well. Garrison knew that many people in both North and South spoke the evangelical language of moral responsibility and to them he preached the doctrine that gradualism was capitulation to slavery. What are we waiting for, he demanded? Slavery will not go away by itself, and the longer we wait, the more slave children are born. Let masters therefore repent and free their slaves, giving them payment for the work they have done, jobs for the support of their families, and education for the enjoyment of life.

Garrison's third emphasis was his demand for racial equality in the United States, an important difference between abolitionists and colonizationists. The latter in their best moments had sought to help the "poor degraded blacks" escape to Africa, to get away from race prejudice. Justice within the United States, they believed, was impossible. Such pessimism in reformers, charged Garrison, was a self-fulfilling prophecy. Far better that men should fight evil than submit to it, he wrote. Far better, too, to listen to what northern blacks—or at least most of them—thought about colonization than to consort with slaveholders and adopt their viewpoint. To make his point, he printed page upon page of Afro-American attacks upon colonization. Garrison and his white friends had yet much more to learn from blacks, for they could not slough off all of their own racial assumptions, concerns, and illusions. Nevertheless, they, among all the millions of white Americans, were the only group willing to maintain communication with blacks and to respond to their claims upon the Republic. The communication did not establish a perfect relationship, but it did change American reform.

Garrison's pamphlet represented an intellectual process shared with an ever-increasing number of men and women. Like him they were seeking a way to put into practice American pretensions to egalitarianism and Christian affirmations of human brotherhood. Like him they read British reformers and came to wrestle with the problems of race prejudice and slavery, only to find the American Colonization Society inadequate. When he wrote his pamphlet, therefore, Garrison had a small public which was now ready to organize a crusade against slavery.

The Movement's New Lease on Life

In 1831 a group of New York reformers led by two wealthy merchants, Arthur and Lewis Tappan, called a meeting to discuss the abolition of slavery. The result was a decision to create some sort of national antislavery society as soon as possible. In Massachusetts the same year, Garrison began to print his *Liberator* with the support of the black community, and persuaded some associates to form the New England Anti-Slavery Society.

The Tappan brothers, Lewis (top) and Arthur, were the driving force in establishing the American Anti-Slavery Society in 1833. Its aim was immediate freedom for slaves and within five years the body had about 250,000 members.

Persistent and intense discussions carried on by the New York and Massachusetts reformers increased the number of people interested in slavery, until Garrison's *Thoughts* jarred them into a rejection of colonization and a commitment to immediate emancipation. Even more dramatic, however, was the victory of British antislavery reformers in 1833 when Parliament passed an act abolishing slavery in the British West Indies. Now was the time, announced the Tappans, to form a national antislavery society.

In response, sixty-three people met in Philadelphia, December 4, 1833, to form the American Anti-Slavery Society. They were middle-class white men for the most part, although four were women and three were black men; and they shared the intense morality of Protestant evangelicalism as well as the determination to destroy slavery through a great moral crusade. They rested their case on the contrast between the Declaration of Independence—"all men are created equal"—and the fact that "at least one-sixth part of [their] countrymen" were treated as "brute beasts" and marketable property. To end this shameful discrepancy, they proposed immediate emancipation without compensation to the masters or expatriation of the blacks. With this proposal they set themselves clearly against a majority of their fellow citizens who feared, disliked, or distrusted blacks and

71

Massachusetts Historical Society

THIS IS THE LORD'S DOING.

SLAVERY ABOLISHED IN THE BRITISH WEST-INDIES

AUGUST 1st 1834.

LAUS DEO.

*The morale of abolitionists in the United
States received a boost in 1834 with the ending
of slavery in the British West Indies. Banners such
as this were used in the propaganda war
waged against southern slavery.*

With organization went an almost volcanic explosion of printed matter. Taking advantage of the communications revolution, antislavery societies printed thousands of pamphlets against slavery after 1834. They took the form of didactic or evocative sermons, poems, short stories, biblical exposition, and detailed analyses of southern society. Only information could persuade Americans to repudiate slavery, abolitionists thought, and so they printed *Emancipation in the West Indies, The Power of Congress over the District of Columbia*, the *Bible Argument*, and the most popular tract of all, Weld's *American Slavery as it is: The Testimony of a Thousand Witnesses*. With the pamphlets came also the weekly journals in such great quantities that by 1838 the annual production of the national society alone exceeded 647,000 copies of abolitionist tracts, pamphlets, and papers. After Garrison launched his *Liberator* in 1831, between thirty and forty antislavery newspapers were founded. The American Anti-Slavery Society sponsored the *Emancipator* and then the *National Anti-Slavery Standard*. James G. Birney, a former slaveholder from Kentucky and Alabama, published the *Philanthropist* in Cincinnati. La Roy Sunderland shook the Methodist Episcopal Church to its foundations with *Zion's Watchmen*. The list was long, for it seemed that almost every abolitionist was, like Garrison, eager to be heard.

The Tactics of Confrontation

One of the most important methods for enticing people into the movement was the petition campaign which served three very important functions. First, it used the almost mystical identification of a person with his name to seal commitment to the cause. Once he signed the petition, a convert had committed himself irrevocably, defending the cause as he defended his name. Second, it informed the public men to whom it was addressed that thousands of Americans were counting on them to do something about slavery. The propaganda, however, not only flowed from the society to potential converts and from them to legislators, but also to the public at large. As millions of Americans watched their fellow citizens peacefully petitioning the House of Representatives, they could not possibly ignore the dramatic character of the forces in conflict. To be sure, antislavery petitions had trickled into the House ever since 1790, and since 1825 had been sent to each session. After 1834, however, the tactic of petitioning became a vital part of antislavery activity through enthusiastic but unorganized campaigns conducted by local and state societies. Distressed by the inefficient use of what they thought was an excellent weapon, the national society in 1837 took over all projects, coordinated activities, and pushed their agents to herculean

valued property rights above all others. Only vast optimism and a disregard for facts could have lent conviction to the statement that "the prospect before us is full of encouragement."

And yet, during the next few years, the antislavery movement burst out of the confinement of a few isolated societies into the public life of the entire North. By 1837 there were 145 societies in Massachusetts, 274 in New York, and 213 in Ohio. The next year the North boasted a total of 1,350 societies with a membership of perhaps 250,000. This remarkable achievement resulted from a process of organization, propaganda, and dramatic confrontational tactics. The task of developing an organizational base for abolitionism fell to agents of the national and state societies who traveled about assigned districts, speaking about the sin of slavery, the necessity for repentance, and the promise of emancipation. Theodore Dwight Weld was perhaps the most effective of these agents. A protégé of the Tappan brothers who had become engaged in temperance and educational reforms, Weld had been converted to immediate abolition by friends who had read Garrison's *Thoughts*. The eloquent Presbyterian became in effect a revivalist for abolition. Ranging throughout Ohio, Pennsylvania, and New York, he preached a new kind of Gospel which summed up all good works in one mighty work: the abolition of slavery. By 1838 over sixty agents had joined Weld in the exhilarating process of organization.

*The printed word carried the message of emancipation
throughout the United States and abroad.
The profusion of material published from the
1830s stressed slavery's denial of human rights
and the irony of its continued existence in
a nation which, above all others, proclaimed
a belief in liberty and equality.*

efforts with spectacular results. During the 1837–38 session, Congress received petitions with over 414,000 signatures, most of them in support of abolishing slavery in the nation's capital (130,000) and against the annexation of Texas (182,000). Other prayers, supported by between 20,000 and 30,000 people, sought abolition of slavery in the territories and the outlawing of the interstate slave trade. Others opposed the admission of new slave states to the Union and the attempt to keep antislavery petitions from being considered by the House.

The petitions were obviously more than attempts to communicate ideas and solicit support. They were also a very important part of the tactics of confrontation. The abolitionists' primary assumption was that if people were confronted with the enormity of their sins they would be filled with a sense of moral revulsion that would lead to a radical change of mind. The manner was boldly provocative, and permeated almost everything that abolitionists said and did. To a rather easy-going or genteel person, abolitionists must have seemed obsessed with arousing emotions and creating dissension. They spoke of the *crime* of slaveholding, the *corruption* of American life, the *cowardice* of keeping silent. And they settled on ideas that could not nestle easily in men's minds: for example, if compensation were ever paid in the process of abolition, it should go to slaves instead of slaveholders.

This attitude shaped action as well as words. Almost from the beginning of their movement, abolitionists tried to get local, district, state, and national religious and reform organizations to cooperate with antislavery societies in condemning slavery and ostracizing slaveholders. If antislavery resolutions were passed by a group, abolitionists of course were encouraged to repeat their victory. If a body refused to speak out against slavery, however, abolitionists would make an issue of it, accusing the organization of hypocrisy and a "cowardly groveling" before authority. This last charge was meant to exploit latent resentment toward authority by members who sided with abolition. The minority sentiment on any abolitionist resolution could with persistent pressure, abolitionists believed, become the majority view. But even if it did not, continued agitation might create such alienation within the institution that men would finally have to decide issues on the basis of division over abolition. This process split the Presbyterian church in 1837 and the Methodist Episcopal church twice—once in 1842 when abolitionists formed the Wesleyan Methodist church and once in 1844 when southerners left because northerners seemed to be trying to mollify abolitionists. Baptists divided between North and South in 1845.

All major evangelical Protestant denominations, missionary societies, and benevolent organizations were afflicted in some way by abolitionist agitation. The leaders were presented with an unhappy dilemma. If they yielded to pressure they would alienate slaveholders. If they did not, they would lose many people who for one reason or the other resented the deference to southern sensitivities. The process was to affect political parties. It is not surprising that the tactics of confrontation (with consequent disruption of institutions) should have made abolitionists' opponents accuse them of anarchism.

Although the charge was true for some abolitionists, it was not for most of them. And far from opposing institutions as such, they tried to build new organizations which would combine man's need for order with a commitment to racial equality and the abolition of slavery. Abolitionist attempts at institution building began in New Haven, Connecticut, where the Tappans and the Reverend Simeon Jocelyn hoped to build a college for blacks in 1831. But the college was never begun because a worried town council and mayor called a mass meeting which condemned the scheme and warned its proponents not to try to carry it out. Two years later in Canterbury, Connecticut, a Quaker teacher by the name of Prudence Crandall tried to establish a school for both white and black girls. The townspeople got the state legislature to outlaw the school. But abolitionists persisted until they finally found help in building a college.

When Prudence Crandall tried to establish a multiracial school in Connecticut in 1833, a restrictive law was passed. Although arrested, she was later released on technical grounds.

Cornell University Archives

The train of events began with debates on slavery at Lane Theological school in Cincinnati during the winter of 1834. Through eighteen February nights in the emotion-laden atmosphere of a revival testimony meeting, seminarians from both North and South discussed slavery and abolition until, at the end, they unanimously organized an antislavery society. The result was not merely the passage of resolutions but the creation of evening and sabbath schools for the free blacks of Cincinnati. With the schools came social and benevolent societies and an employment agency for blacks. Frightened by rumors of violence and expectations of more trouble if such "madness" persisted, Lane's board of trustees voted to abolish the society and silence the students. In response, almost all of the students resigned. The Reverend John Shippherd, who was trying without success to begin a college in northern Ohio, approached the rebels to see if they would become the student body he so desperately needed. Only if Negroes are admitted, they said; only if we are free to preach our beliefs. After negotiations in which both demands were eventually met, the college acquired both finances and a student body and the abolitionists acquired a college.

An antislavery society was formed at Lane Theological school (below) in Cincinnati in 1834. An important consequence of this event was the establishment of classes for the city's free blacks.

Opposing the Abolition Campaign

Opposition to abolition took many forms, but fell into three general categories: governmental action, institutional discipline, and collective violence. Action by southern state governments ranged from the symbolic act of Georgia's legislature in offering a $5,000 reward for the conviction of Garrison as a fugitive from justice, to the outlawing of antislavery ideas whether expressed privately or publicly in oral or printed form. Those caught disobeying these laws were imprisoned, fined, or even whipped, although Francis Scott Key, the author of "The Star Spangled Banner," observed that one person at least deserved capital punishment. Many prominent abolitionists had prices on their heads, but none higher than Arthur Tappan whom the Louisiana legislature believed was worth $50,000. The universal southern fear of slave insurrection which had been rekindled by Virginia's Nat Turner rebellion in August 1831 not only required repression south of Pennsylvania but in the North as well. Governors received appeals from their Dixie counterparts to do something about the "incendiary" literature which originated there, and although northern legislatures considered taking such action, they never did so. Constitutional scruples and a dislike of being called upon to defend slavery where it did

not exist apparently prevented northern action. The South had no doubts about curtailing free speech, however; for its reading of the Constitution was affected by its domestic institutions. Northern reticence in Congress to breach the Constitution by forbidding abolitionists to use the federal mails made no difference to southerners, who simply passed laws allowing officials to seize "incendiary" materials with impunity.

By far the greatest effort within the federal government to silence abolitionists came as a result of the militants' petition campaign which began in 1834. In response, the Senate voted to receive but reject such petitions, despite the demands of John C. Calhoun and his allies that it follow the rule laid down by the House in 1836 that all petitions on slavery be laid on the table without being printed or considered. The result of the House action was precisely what its Senate opponents had predicted: a debate on slavery and the creation of an issue which aided the abolition movement. Former President John Quincy Adams, a representative from Massachusetts, led the attack upon the "gag rule" with all the wit and cunning at his command. He argued that freedom of petition guaranteed by the Constitution included consideration and not mere reception of appeals from the people. In the long discussions which ensued, Adams taunted the southerners into exaggerated defenses of slavery and the damaging admission that they believed the right of petition was a restricted one to which persons of "low moral character" were not entitled. Adams observed that

Whether antislavery petitions should be discussed in Congress was hotly contested. This engraving shows a scene in the House with the petitioning tactic being denounced. For a decade until 1845, the House barred discussion of these petitions.

Americans' liberties were threatened by such belief, a conclusion which an increasing number of northerners were also drawing. In their haste to win a short-term victory of silencing abolitionist propaganda in the House, southerners had lost the long-term battle for northern sympathy, and in 1845 they lost the "gag" as well.

Institutional discipline, too, was used by antiabolitionists to quash antislavery activity. The unlucky southern teacher who was so imprudent as even to hint at antislavery bias was soon sent packing to the North, but even there his words and actions together with those of his students would be carefully scrutinized. Some colleges were more open to antislavery ideas than others. The Amherst Anti-Slavery Society was ordered to disband within a year of its founding, but college students in Illinois, Ohio, and Indiana often organized abolition groups with no interference whatsoever. The churches as particular targets of abolitionist agitation provided arenas of conflict with the hierarchy of every denomination trying unsuccessfully to avoid an open discussion of slavery. Radical demands that slaveholders be excommunicated were especially resented in churches with large southern constituencies such as the Methodist Epis-

THE FRIENDS OF HUMANITY LAYING THE AXE TO THE UPAS TREE OF SLAVERY: WHICH IS EVER LOADED WITH THE SUM OF ALL VILLANIES.

copal, Baptist, and Presbyterian churches. Authorities at the local, state, and national levels refused to put antislavery resolutions to a vote, tried abolitionists before ecclesiastical tribunals for being disorderly or heretical, and even expelled some of the more vociferous militants.

The most dramatic opposition, however, came in the form of collective violence. Between 1833 and 1838, the period of most intense public reaction to abolitionism, there were 165 riots aimed at abolitionists. As one newspaper editor put it: ''A few thousand crazy headed blockheads have actually frightened fifteen million people out of their senses.'' To be sure, it seemed as if abolitionist agitation were not possible without attracting crowds throwing rotten eggs, rocks, and tomatoes, and playing drums, blowing horns, and heckling. The occupational hazard of being an antislavery lecturer was so great that many speakers carried an old suit of clothes to wear on the platform in case of physical attack. Gentlemen of ''property and standing'' as well as skilled workers joined to drive antislavery conventions out of their churches or lecture halls. Abolitionists' homes were attacked, their furniture burned, their persons assaulted, and their presses destroyed. Birney had to leave Kentucky because no one would print his antislavery paper, the *Philanthropist*, and when he arrived at Cincinnati he was warned by a series of public meetings to leave well enough alone for his own good. Undaunted, he persisted in publishing his periodical to the disgust of the mob which on July 30, 1836, made a shambles of his printer's

The abolitionist message seemed to many to threaten the existing social order, and gave rise to a violent response. Above: Engraving from an antislavery pamphlet. Below: James Birney, publisher of the antislavery Philanthropist. *His printing shop was sacked by an angry mob in 1836.*

shop before it rampaged through the Negro quarters of the city. Almost exactly a year earlier, mobs had attacked abolitionists in New York City simply for meeting in Chatham Street chapel.

Many of the riots seemed to have been well planned by self-appointed defenders of the public honor. And even mobs which were not organized and directed by community leaders had an unerring sense about their targets. Abolitionist meetings and Negro neighborhoods were carefully isolated as objects of antiabolitionist fury. But the abolitionist press could be particularly galling, and because of this a special object of collective violence. Garrison was mobbed in Boston in October 1835, but he merely landed in jail for his own protection. Elijah Lovejoy suffered a much more grisly fate but earned thereby a special place in the abolitionist pantheon. Lovejoy, a native of Maine who published a paper in St Louis, moved to Alton, Illinois, in 1836 to escape the violence of Missourians who bitterly resented his attack on a mob that had lynched a black man. Almost immediately an Alton mob wrecked his press. A second and third time mobs destroyed his replacements until in November 1837 he placed his fourth press in a warehouse guarded by friends with loaded rifles. When the mob came to destroy it, he fought back. The warehouse was burned, the press was thrown in the Ohio River, and Lovejoy was killed with five bullets in his body. Abolitionism had a martyr.

The reasons for taking extreme measures in so many different ways were a mixture of anxiety, fear, and calculated self-interest. Southerners feared that persistent agitation against slavery would lead to slave insurrections and a possible division of white solidarity in the South. They also feared that an abolitionized North would exert pressure upon the South to give up a system of labor and social control which was basic to its way of life. Northerners had different reasons of course. Throughout the 1830s and 1840s Americans had witnessed such great changes that they labored to maintain the unity and integrity of institutions such as churches and political parties which provided stability and order in a period of rapid social change. Abolitionists threatened to split these institutions, and worse yet, to split the nation just at the time when American nationalism was becoming so important. It was a fragile nationalism, to be sure, because it was made possible only so long as slavery did not become a public issue. The compromises which enticed southern states into ratifying the Constitution included guarantees about slavery. And the Missouri Compromise of 1820 (which preserved the balance between free and slave states in the Union and prohibited slavery in the Louisiana Purchase above latitude 36°30') reaffirmed them for a new generation. But abolitionists so hotly condemned compromise that they were condemned as subversives.

They were even accused of being under the influence of foreign enemies who wished the American experiment to fail, since they had praised British West Indian emancipation as if it were even more important than the American Revolution. More damaging, perhaps, was their admission of foreign connections when they sent British antislavery lecturers throughout the North. Allied with foreigners, and therefore under suspicion of being un-American, abolitionists were also charged with anarchism for reputedly indiscriminate attacks upon traditional authority. With this charge in mind, it is not surprising that so many rioters were community leaders, aspiring politicians, and leading professional men who feared that abolitionists were attempting to take from them their prerogative of leadership. By appealing, as they did, for the support of women and black people, abolitionists seemed to be dangerously repudiating traditional leadership, and attempting to create a new political base.

But the most radical of abolitionists' beliefs, and one for which all of their opponents attacked them, was an emphasis on racial equality. Race prejudice in the North had limited the access of blacks to the rights of citizenship, for in most northern states they could not vote in elections nor testify against white people in court. While they lived they did not have equal educational or employment opportunities, and when they died they were buried in segregated sections of the cemetery. Simply to be seen with a black person was in many cases to degrade the position of the white. So when abolitionists held conventions with blacks, walked with them into the hall, and sat side by side with them passing resolutions on behalf of racial equality, they had broken one of the most strict taboos of their culture. In a highly mobile society in which men improved their social position through marriage to women of higher status, the elevation of black men was thought to be possible only through interracial marriage (amalgamation). The sexual fantasies and aggressions which accompanied race prejudice also shaped the views of most whites, so it is not surprising that antiabolitionists accused radicals of favoring amalgamation, or that mobs attacked Negro neighborhoods after disrupting abolition meetings. Abolitionists had simply assaulted the last refuge of frightened white people, their race.

Far from silencing abolitionists, opposition made them more articulate and strong. The South's success in limiting free expression emphasized that section's disregard for the Bill of Rights which southerners, ironically enough, had written into the Constitution. Southern insistence that freedoms be curtailed also in the North made citizens there apprehensive about surrendering too much to slaveholders' sensitivities: Adams had become a folk hero by sounding the alarm. In churches as well as government, opposition to abolition made "repression" seem a greater danger than free speech. A majority of northerners were never converted into ardent civil libertarians, but the more antiabolitionists insisted on silencing militants, the more friends the latter acquired and the

Above: William Lloyd Garrison's uncompromising stand for immediate abolition of slavery attracted intense opposition in some quarters. This cartoon appeared in 1835 after the thirty-year-old crusader had been set upon by a Boston crowd.

Below: The tide of violence against leading abolitionists reached a peak with the killing of Elijah Lovejoy at Alton, Illinois, in 1837. Lovejoy, who printed an antislavery newspaper, was shot and his warehouse burned down.

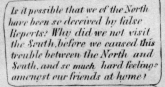

SLAVERY AS IT EXISTS IN AMERICA.

PUBLISHED BY J. HAVEN. 86 STATE ST. BOSTON. 1850.

SLAVERY AS IT EXISTS IN ENGLAND.
(See Bulwers' England   and the English)

THOMPSON
THE ENGLISH ANTI-SLAVERY AGITATOR.
"I am proud to boast that Slavery does not breathe in England."
(See his speech at the African Church in Belknap St.)

more devoted to their cause they became. Opposition had an effect exactly opposite to what it was designed to accomplish. Mobs dramatized abolitionists, transformed them into defenders of American freedom, and provided martyrs to capture the popular imagination.

Disagreement and Division

Success created dissension in abolitionist ranks. Each person who joined the movement did so for private as well as public reasons. The resulting diversity of personal needs and loyalties created differences so great that they could be reconciled only through the division of the antislavery crusade into four "parties": radical, ecclesiastical, political, and Afro-American. Each party had its own internal disputes and shared concerns with other abolitionists, but each also had a common interest or view which separated it from others. Differences began to afflict the movement almost from the beginning. Leading western abolitionists believed that Garrison's vicious harangues were detrimental to the cause, and others quibbled about his statement of immediate abolition. But rhetorical style did not seriously divide abolitionists. The issues were essentially over tactics: whether or not to limit abolitionists to the support of only one reform; whether or not to support women's rights, to remain associated with antiabolitionist institutions, or to engage in elective politics. Also at issue was how to define the role of black people in the movement.

Radicals, largely associated with Garrison and the eloquent Wendell Phillips, had developed their probing of slavery into criticism of a wide range of institutions and values. Limited by their respect for property, and angered by working-class opposition to abolition, they did not attack business per se except insofar as it was in league with slaveholders. They did, however, support women in their fight for equal rights; and they discussed the problems of power and coercion to the point of entertaining both pacifist and anarchist principles. In continuously questioning the authority by which men acted, and in being constantly under attack themselves from churchmen, they began to challenge the legitimacy of organized Christianity and finally to slough off their reverence for the Bible as the infallible word of God. Anything that tended to religious or philosophic authoritarianism, abolitionists repudiated as a restriction of inquiry and advocacy. And as a corollary of this attitude, they were unwilling to put themselves and the truth of their position at the mercy of electoral politics. This did not mean that they rejected out of hand the responsibility of abolitionists to vote, although their opponents claimed they did so. Rather, they feared that making abolition a political movement would involve it in the kind of compromises neces-

New York Public Library

Above: Some abolitionists working within the churches found their task hampered by a reaction against radical tactics. Orange Scott broke away from the Methodists and formed his own church.

sary for political survival which would mean that the cause of black people would be diluted or lost. Far better, they argued, was the course of confrontational tactics, or what they might have called nonelectoral politics, which required constant propaganda, pressure, and polarization by radicals until opinions were shaped to produce the ultimate political act of abolition.

Ecclesiastical abolitionists might well agree with Garrison on a few points, but their loyalty to institutional Christianity was sure and their belief in biblical authority unshaken. They were shocked by Garrison's accelerating departure from orthodox principles which they feared would alienate many pious northerners, and attempted to demonstrate that churchmen could be good abolitionists, too. The task was difficult, however, and not a few men like Orange Scott, leader of Methodist abolitionists, had to secede from their churches to form new ones. Others managed to carry on the fight through nonchurch societies such as the American Missionary Association. Founded in 1846 by Congregationalists, the AMA served the freedmen well after the Civil War because of its educational activities in the South. Ecclesiastical abolitionists were part of every religious denomination in the North and although they never determined policy, they often influenced it by constant criticism. The result was not a mass conversion to abolition, but a growing distaste for "proslavery" principles.

Left: This cartoon defends American slavery against northern critics and visiting reformers from England—which had grave social problems of its own.

Political abolitionists were largely identified with men like Birney, the former Kentucky slaveholder and a frustrated Whig politician. Many of the New York group were responsible for founding the Liberty party which nominated Birney for president at a convention in April 1840 in Albany, New York. The differences between this group and the radicals had already been formalized by a schism in the American Anti-Slavery Society in January 1840. Trouble had been brewing for two years over the issue of whether or not abolitionists should engage in a variety of reform activities. Cautious abolitionists, fearing the public's identification of abolitionism with utopianism and religious heresy, wanted to restrict the antislavery movement to one reform only. They were especially perturbed by Garrison's tendency to repudiate political action as a viable tactic as well as his refusal to make the movement essentially a male affair. Many conservatives could not accept the idea of female equality, but even abolitionists who could do so did not wish to have their movement associated with women's rights for fear of losing converts. The bid for public acceptance was so strong in this group that they left the parent society to form the weak American and Foreign Anti-Slavery Society. But the organization which best represented their views was the Liberty party.

The party resulted from the belief that direct political action was required to abolish slavery; Garrison's tactics were thought to be utopian. Radicals could agree with political acts such as petitioning and voting for antislavery men in the two major parties, but Birney and his allies could not leave the matter there. They wanted to engage in politics as a party because they assumed that neither the Whigs nor the Democrats could ever free themselves from the domination of slaveholders. A new party committed only to abolition would presumably avoid the compromises that had crippled the early American antislavery impulse. Just what political action they would have had the federal government take was not at first discussed. They simply offered committed antislavery people to the voting public. In 1840 Birney received 7,000 votes to his combined opposition's 2,300,000, and four years later managed to attract 62,300 in contrast to 2,600,000. While losing at the polls Liberty men were also losing their pristine commitment to one idea, because the political process required them to have opinions on various public issues that interested voters. This led them to deviate from their original motivation. Attempts to broaden the party's appeal meant that men committed to the nonextension rather than the eradication of slavery came to dominate its national ticket by 1848.

Black abolitionists belonged to all three other groups. Yet, by their distinct experience and peculiar contributions to the antislavery movement, they constituted a separate faction. They had helped to define issues within the abolition movement since before 1831 by attacking coloniza-

tion and supporting Garrison with ideas, money, and agents. They had also been present at the founding of the American Anti-Slavery Society as well as numerous local auxiliaries because the antislavery movement provided the only organizations where white and black could meet on relatively equal terms. Furthermore, blacks knew that if they were ever to break the chains of prejudice, segregation, and slavery, they would have to have white help, and when it was offered they accepted. But their efforts were not merely cooperative enterprises. Before the Civil War, blacks printed seventeen periodicals including *Freedom's Journal, The Colored American,* and *Frederick Douglass' Paper.* They also created a network of organizations that were important for a sense of black solidarity.

Solidarity and the confidence it inspired were vital to the entire movement, for blacks offered something unique to abolitionism—their own experience. Fugitive slaves appeared as lecturers, at first as curiosities, and then as articulate spokesmen for their brothers and sisters. They wrote autobiographies packed with real and fictional stories of suffering, cruelty, and heroism designed to win sympathy and converts. But slavery was not the only

Sojourner Truth (Isabella Van Wagener) was a frequent and powerful speaker at abolitionist meetings. She escaped from enslavement in 1827 and soon after became active in the reform movement. An evangelist and civil rights pioneer, she took a particular interest in women's rights.

82

enemy. Abolitionists of both races also attacked race prejudice, the extent and nature of which blacks understood much better than whites. Thus, the role of black abolitionists was clearly to educate, cajole, push, and shame their white colleagues into acts and public stands consistent with their professed commitment to racial equality. After the first enthusiasm of the early 1830s, black abolitionists began to complain of their "underling position" in the movement, the patronizing attitude of whites, the suspicion that blacks could not measure up to standards of excellence. This "overseer" attitude made blacks take independent action which led some even to threaten violence in order to gain their goals. Douglass, an ex-slave from Maryland who became one of the foremost leaders of black abolitionism, annoyed Garrison with an independence which led him to support political action in 1851. He did not by this act become beholden to white political abolitionists, however, for only he and blacks like him could emphasize with authority that the black man was not an "Uncle Tom," as Douglass said, but a fighter.

To fight laws that expressed northern racism, black and white abolitionists fought to abolish segregated transportation facilities and the insulting laws which forbade interracial marriage. They desegregated most New England schools and attacked the myths of racial inferiority taught there. These and other efforts received a great impetus during the Civil War when the North's need for an ideology of freedom made politicians susceptible to abolitionist pressure. By that time, the abolition movement was prodding white Americans to grant blacks a better chance in national life. But the most authentic statements about racial justice and equality came from those blacks who insisted upon racial equality without compromise.

The abolitionist movement thus went through four cycles from 1830 to 1870. The first lasted from 1831 to 1838

when immediate emancipation became a public issue and attracted support. The second included the years 1838–50 when abolitionists divided into factions while acquainting Americans with the issue of slavery and freedom. From 1850 to 1861 a new generation of reformers entered the ranks through fear of southern aggressiveness as much as a commitment to racial equality. Subsequently receptive to pressure from blacks and radicals, they supported political and constitutional reforms during and after the Civil War. In each period, abolitionist factions worked together seeking to persuade Americans to resist slavery if not race prejudice. Indeed, the citadel of white race prejudice remained almost intact; but not quite. The outward, legal expressions of racial antagonism suffered severe damage from years of abolitionist agitation. The political and constitutional accomplishments were real even if they fell far short of the abolitionists' goal of a just society purged of racism and oppression.

Negro workers in the antislavery cause often brought to the movement a firsthand experience of slavery which could not be disputed. Frederick Douglass (right) was one of the best-known former slaves and lectured widely to reform groups. His paper (below) appeared between 1847 and 1860. It was first known as the North Star.

Library of Congress. Bottom: By kind permission of the British Library/John Freeman

Chapter 4

The Great Issue of the Age

Slavery had long been a contentious political issue, but the heated debates over the admission of Missouri threatened to split the nation and many men feared for the future. Then in the 1840s the issue of territorial expansion came to the fore and at its heart was concern over slavery. Not until the following decade, however, did political dissension lead to armed conflict as advocates of "free soil" battled proslavery forces in Kansas. Despite the fact that in 1820 and again thirty years later a formula had been found to still the argument, the basic quarrel remained unsolved. As the 1850s unfolded, the spirit of compromise subsided, opinions became polarized, and local warfare erupted.

Slavery and Politics

From the very beginning of the American Republic, the question of slavery was an obstacle to political unity, a threat to the very existence of the Union. Even at the Constitutional Convention of 1787, James Madison remarked that "the great danger to our general government" was the dispute between "the great southern and northern interests of the continent." On too many issues, "the institution of slavery and its consequences" was the main "line of discrimination" among the delegates. Realizing the danger this explosive issue posed to the formation of a national community, the Founding Fathers acted to place the peculiar institution outside the arena of national politics. Aside from the African slave trade, Congress was given no power to regulate slavery in any way. The intention was simply to exclude slavery from national political debate.

Although differences of opinion about slavery could not be completely silenced, and New England Federalists grumbled about southern political power and Virginia's domination of the presidency, the first full-scale intrusion of the slavery issue into national politics occurred in 1819. In February of that year, Representative James Tallmadge of New York introduced an amendment to an act authorizing the territory of Missouri to form a constitution, before admission as a state. Tallmadge's proposal prohibited the further introduction of slaves into Missouri, and provided for the gradual emancipation of slaves already there. The amendment shattered party lines in the House—virtually every northern Representative voted with Tallmadge, and almost every southerner against. It was adopted by a vote of 79 to 67. The Senate refused to go along, however, and Congress adjourned with neither house willing to break the stalemate.

Not until early 1820 was a settlement reached. This, the Missouri Compromise, would defuse the slavery question for over two decades. The House agreed to withdraw from the Tallmadge amendment and allow Missouri to

The debates over the Missouri Compromise in 1820 raised the specter of disunion. Then, ten years later, Robert Hayne of South Carolina made a powerful speech in the Senate attacking greater federal powers and urging instead the primacy of states' rights. He was opposed in the debate by Daniel Webster of Massachusetts, who replied that the federal government's claims to sovereignty were superior to those of individual states. His address, one of the most eloquent ever delivered in Congress, ended with the cry: "Liberty and Union, now and forever, one and inseparable!" They were words which captured the imagination of northerners in later years when the concept of Union, to which the South seemed increasingly hostile, assumed an almost sacred character. This painting of Webster making his speech is by G. P. A. Healy.

enter the Union as a slave state. In exchange, Maine was admitted to maintain the sectional balance, and slavery was prohibited from the great bulk of the territory obtained from France in the Louisiana Purchase—all the land above latitude 36°30'.

The Missouri debates were important because they raised for the first time the fatal issue of the expansion of slavery, and demonstrated the power of that issue to disrupt normal party alignments. It was not surprising that northern Federalists would seek to use the issue of slavery in Missouri to weaken the Republican administration of James Monroe. What was unexpected was that northern Republicans would side with them on this issue. Moreover, the debates revealed the latent hostility to slavery and to southern power—two very different things—which existed in the North. Virtually every argument against slavery which would be used in the debates of the 1840s and 1850s from the idea that slavery was immoral and uneconomical, to the widely voiced resentment of southern domination of the federal government, was heard in Congress in 1819 and 1820. For their part most southerners were still tentative in their defenses of slavery. Most defended the peculiar institution as a "necessary evil." Thus, Governor Randolph of Virginia could comment during the debates on "the deplorable error of our ancestors in copying a civil institution from savage Africa" and passing "a depressing burden" on to the nineteenth century. But a few southerners began to insist that it was a positive good, beneficial to both whites and blacks. And many southerners warned that if northerners interfered with the institution of slavery, disunion would result.

The most perceptive political leaders in 1820 were filled with dismay by the Missouri debates. "This momentous question," wrote Jefferson from Monticello, "like a firebell in the night, awakened and filled me with terror. I considered it at once as the knell of the union. It is hushed, indeed, for the moment, but this is only a reprieve, not a final sentence." And John Quincy Adams noted that the debate "disclosed a secret: it revealed the basis for a new organization of parties. . . . Here was a new party really formed, terrible to the whole Union, but portentously terrible to the South—threatening in its progress the emancipation of all their slaves, threatening in its immediate effect that southern domination which has swayed the Union for the last twenty years."

Adams was right. But it would take another thirty years for the "new organization of parties" along sectional lines fully to emerge. In the meantime, political leaders recognized the need to strengthen the national party system to prevent a repetition of the Missouri controversy. No one recognized the implications of the sectional debate more clearly than Martin Van Buren of New York, the architect of the Democratic party, the new political coalition which would sweep Andrew

Library of Congress

When John Calhoun of South Carolina became secretary of state in 1844 he began to push for the annexation of Texas. This issue soon involved the nation in divisive debate. Northern interests hotly opposed the annexation of any territory where the South's peculiar institution would be likely to flourish.

Jackson into the presidency in 1828. In a well-known letter to a southern associate, Van Buren called for a strengthening of party organization to prevent a repetition of sectional division. "Party attachment," he wrote, "in former times furnished a complete antidote for sectional prejudices by producing counteracting feelings. It was not until that defense had been broken down that the clamor against Southern Influence and African Slavery could be made effectual in the North." Van Buren, in other words, saw national two-party competition as an alternative to sectional conflict, and by the 1830s his Democratic party and the new Whig organization had reached an unspoken but well-understood agreement. The slavery issue was simply too divisive to be introduced into national politics. If parties were forced to take a stand on slavery, national political organization would be impossible. Meanwhile, political radicals in both sections—northern antislavery men and southern fire-eaters—struggled to break the conspiracy of silence and force the major parties to confront the issue of slavery.

Significance of Annexation

Congressional debates over the "gag rule" and the right of abolitionists to send their pamphlets and newspapers in the mails prevented slavery from being totally ignored by politicians in the 1830s. But it was not until the next decade that sectional conflict once again came to the center of the political stage. As in the case of Missouri, the issue was not the existence of slavery, but its expansion. And it is significant that the two men most involved, Calhoun and President Tyler, were political outsiders, tied to neither of the major parties. Tyler had acceded to the presidency on the death of William Henry Harrison, and had soon broken with the Whigs. Calhoun, as a spokesman for the interests of South Carolina and the South, had long given up hope of achieving the presidency through the national Democratic party. The careers of both men, in other words, were blocked by the major parties, but might be advanced if tied to the slavery question.

In February 1844, Tyler's secretary of state, Abel Upshur, was killed in an explosion aboard a US Navy vessel. Calhoun was brought in as his successor, and quickly concluded negotiations for the annexation of Texas, which had existed as an independent republic since winning independence from Mexico in the 1830s. In April, Calhoun sent to the Senate a treaty of annexation. At the same time a letter written by him to the British ambassador was made public. It justified annexation on the ground that it was necessary to protect and expand the institution of slavery. Annexation thus became a sectional issue, and many northerners reacted harshly. Ex-president Van Buren, who seemed assured of the Democratic presidential nomination, came out against annexation, as did the prospective Whig candidate, Henry Clay. Clay's position did not endanger his nomination, but at the Democratic convention in May 1844, a coalition of southerners and proexpansionist westerners succeeded in blocking Van Buren from achieving the two-thirds vote necessary for nomination. In the end, the delegates turned to a "dark horse," James K. Polk of Tennessee, who pledged not simply the annexation of Texas, but the occupation of Oregon, whose boundary was disputed with Great Britain.

In the election of 1844, Polk won a narrow victory over Clay (made possible by the large vote in New York State for the abolitionist Liberty party, which threw the state to Polk). The annexation of Texas followed in due course, but the seeds of sectional antagonism had been sowed in the Democratic party. Van Buren's followers never quite got over his rebuff in 1844. Four years later the ex-president would run as the candidate of the antislavery Free-Soil party, and in the 1850s many of his followers, although not Van Buren himself, would abandon the Democratic party for the Republican.

On the eve of Polk's inauguration, Van Buren expressed his political fears to a close friend. He was willing and anxious to support the new president, but he had one solemn warning. "Too much care cannot be taken," Van Buren declared, "to save us from a war, in respect to which the opposition shall be able to charge . . . that it is waged for the extension of slavery." In such a war, northern Democrats would be faced with the choice of breaking with their southern allies or supporting the war and running the risk of political annihilation in the North. Yet within two years such a war, and such a choice, confronted the nation. In the summer of 1846, the United States found itself at war with Mexico. Whichever side began the hostilities, the impact on the slavery question was clear. Thousands of northerners were instantly convinced that the sole purpose of the war was to acquire territory for the further expansion of slavery.

The Mexican War was not the only issue which fed northern resentment against the Polk administration.

Martin Van Buren's opposition to the annexation of Texas cost him the 1844 Democratic nomination and the chance to return to the White House. Expansionist James K. Polk was endorsed instead.

Brown Brothers

Congressman David Wilmot of Pennsylvania wanted to bar slavery from any territory won from Mexico. Although his measure was passed in the House, it was defeated in the Senate.

After annexing Texas, Polk had concluded an agreement with Britain dividing the Oregon territory between the two countries. Westerners who had supported Polk on Texas believed that their part of the "bargain of 1844" had been gone back on. Other northerners were annoyed at the administration's low tariff policies, and at Polk's veto of an internal improvements bill in 1846.

Party Lines Shattered

All these groups and resentments were united by a measure introduced in August 1846 by David Wilmot, an obscure Pennsylvania Democratic congressman. Wilmot simply proposed that slavery be barred from any territory acquired from Mexico. As a Van Buren supporter his aim was, in part, to express the group's resentment against southern domination of the Polk administration. He also wanted to enable northern Democrats to combat Whig arguments that the war was being waged to extend slavery. Northern Whigs, who opposed the war altogether, joined in support of Wilmot, as did other Democrats who had their own reasons for disliking Polk. As a result, just as in 1819, party lines were suddenly replaced by sectional ones. The Wilmot Proviso passed the House by a purely sectional vote, but the Senate adjourned without taking action. By 1847, enough northern Democrats had second thoughts about the measure to defeat it in the Senate. But by then the damage had been done. The issue of "free soil" had been born.

As the presidential election of 1848 approached, it was clear that the debate over slavery extension would not be silenced. Within both parties, strong groups of northerners had emerged, committed to the Wilmot Proviso. The Democratic group, centered around the aggrieved supporters of Van Buren, were known as the "Barnburners." Their Whig counterparts, mainly a rebellious group of young Massachusetts politicians, were known as the "Conscience Whigs." Both major parties frantically searched for a way to win back the allegiance of these groups and defuse the slavery issue.

The problem was simpler for the Whigs. Since most of them opposed the Mexican War altogether, Whigs North and South could unite on the simple demand for "no territory." If the war ended without territorial acquisitions from Mexico, the question of the extension of slavery would not arise.

For Democrats, the problem was infinitely more complex. Most were avid expansionists who did not want to abandon the possibility of large territorial gains from Mexico. But how could differences within the party over slavery be compromised? Southerners were increasingly adopting the position outlined by Calhoun, which denied the right of Congress to prohibit slavery in the territories. Some were even voicing a demand for direct federal protection of slavery in the West. And a majority of northern Democrats still clung to the Wilmot Proviso.

By late 1847, Democratic leaders had developed a plan to settle the dispute over slavery extension. First announced by Vice President Dallas, it was endorsed by Lewis Cass of Michigan in December. Cass was widely expected to be the presidential candidate for 1848. His position was variously defined as "popular sovereignty," "squatter sovereignty," or "non-intervention." Essentially it would leave the question of slavery up to the inhabitants of each individual state or territory. By taking the issue out of Congress it would reestablish sectional harmony and the unity of the Democratic party. Deceptively simple and appealing in principle, squatter sovereignty did leave some basic questions unanswered. At what point could the people of the territory make their decision? Could the first few hundred settlers take a vote and bind incoming thousands? If not, what was the status of slavery until a large population had been reached? Northerners, expecting the first settlers to be from the North, insisted that the vote on slavery be taken early. Southerners replied that slavery should exist until the territory was ready to be admitted as a state; only then could settlers vote to exclude the peculiar institution. But whatever its ambiguities, squatter sovereignty was accepted for the time being as the Democratic solution to the question of slavery in the territories.

Early in 1848, the Polk administration concluded a treaty ending the Mexican War and acquiring a vast amount of territory for the United States. When the war began, Emerson had predicted: "The United States will conquer Mexico, but it will be as the man who swallows the dose of arsenic which brings him down in turn. Mexico will poison us." And as sectional antagonism reached new heights in the election campaign, Emerson's forecast appeared all too accurate. Neither the Whig nor Democratic national conventions chose candidates who satisfied northern antislavery men. Cass, the Democratic choice, seemed a classic "doughface"—a northerner who had abandoned the Wilmot Proviso and embraced squatter sovereignty to court the support of the South. The Whig

MARRIAGE OF THE FREE SOIL AND LIBERTY PARTIES.

convention, ''the slaughterhouse of Whig principles'' according to antislavery editor Horace Greeley, chose the military hero of the Mexican War, Zachary Taylor, and adopted no platform at all. Taylor's popularity was assumed to be enough to unify the party and carry the election. Taylor was a southerner, so his running mate had to come from the North. Eventually Millard Fillmore, a relatively undistinguished New Yorker, was nominated.

In response to the major party nominations, antislavery men moved to organize a third party. At the end of June 1848, the Barnburner Democrats met at Utica, New York. Against Van Buren's better judgment, they nominated him for the presidency on a Wilmot Proviso platform. At the same time, Conscience Whigs, meeting at Worcester, Massachusetts, repudiated Taylor and heard Charles Sumner deliver a fiery speech denouncing the alliance of ''the lords of the loom and the lords of the lash''—the cotton manufacturers of Massachusetts and slaveholders of the South. And in Ohio at the Free Territory Convention, Liberty party members, led by Salmon P. Chase of Ohio, were joined by antislavery men from the major parties. They called for a meeting of northern Free-Soilers at Buffalo in August.

The three major antislavery groups convened at Buffalo in one of the most enthusiastic gatherings in American political history. Some 15,000 delegates and spectators heard speaker after speaker denounce slavery, the South,

The Wilmot Proviso raised the issue of ''free soil,'' and in 1848 a Free-Soil ticket appeared on the ballot paper. This cartoon depicts the Liberty party, an abolitionist group which joined the Free-Soilers, as the party of the Negro.

and the ''Slave Power'' for a whole series of transgressions dating back to the origins of the Republic. Men would long remember the gathering as one in which principles triumphed and old political allegiances were forgotten. But behind the scenes, some hard-nosed bargaining was going on. The Barnburners insisted on maintaining Van Buren's candidacy, while Conscience Whigs were understandably unhappy about supporting a man whose entire career had been devoted to opposition to the Whig party. Finally, the Whigs were appeased by the choice of Charles Francis Adams as Van Buren's running mate. And in exchange for merging into the new Free-Soil party, Liberty men were given the right to draft the platform. As written by Chase, it called not only for the restriction of slavery to its present boundaries and firm adherence to the Wilmot Proviso, but also for free homesteads for western settlers and government aid to internal improvements. The platform was a major step in linking the idealistic antislavery of abolitionists with the pragmatic economic interests of many northerners.

Almost as important as what the platform contained

Confound this Wilmot Proviso, I'm afraid it will lead to something bad

Clear the track! or I'll ham you both!

If I had stood on the Whig platform firmly, this would not have happened.

CALF RIVER

THE BUFFALO HUNT.

The Free-Soil party vigorously contested the 1848 election. Contrary to the fears echoed in this cartoon that Cass (left) and Taylor (right) would suffer, Van Buren won only 10 per cent of the vote.

was what it omitted. Abolitionists and Liberty party men had always insisted that the struggle against slavery was inextricably intertwined with the fight for the rights of free blacks in the North. Yet the politicians at Buffalo recognized that no party aspiring to mass support in the North could flout the intense racial prejudices which permeated free states as well as slave. Moreover, the Barnburners had long opposed suffrage for free blacks in New York and were unwilling to acquiesce in any problack planks in the platform.

Whatever the reason, Free-Soilers were the first major antislavery group to divorce antislavery from concern for the rights of free blacks. It was a step which was necessary to make the party acceptable to a broad spectrum of northern opinion, but one which had profound implications for the future course of the slavery issue. It enabled antislavery men to draw support from a large number of northern racists. These people opposed the extension of slavery not out of any love for the slave,

but because they did not want to be associated with blacks, free or slave, if they moved to the West. Even Wilmot could describe his measure as "the White Man's Proviso," insisting "I plead the cause and rights of the free white man," and disclaiming any "squeamish sensitiveness upon the subject of slavery, or morbid sympathy for the slave."

Slavery the Central Issue

The story of the campaign of 1848 is quickly told. Although the Free-Soilers brought enthusiasm and dedication to the contest, they were no match for the disciplined organizations of the two major parties. In the North, both Whigs and Democrats appealed to antislavery voters in an effort to minimize the Free-Soil vote. The tactic made antislavery sentiment more respectable, even as it reduced Free-Soil support. In the end, the Free-Soilers received 10 per cent of the total vote, and outpolled Cass in New York. Taylor, meanwhile, appealing to southern sectional prejudice, won over significant numbers of southern Democrats and carried a majority of the slave states. He won a narrow overall victory, with a popular plurality of only 138,000 votes.

The election was one of the most momentous in the nation's history. Its significance was summed up by William Seward of New York: "Antislavery is at length a respectable element in politics." The slavery issue now occupied center stage, and it would be extremely difficult to relegate it once more to the wings. At the same time, antislavery as a political force had come to focus on the comparatively narrow issue of the expansion of slavery, abandoning any explicit concern for abolition, or the rights of free blacks. For this there were many reasons. For one thing, the expansion of slavery was a constitutionally "available" issue. Few believed that Congress could interfere directly with slavery in the states. But in the territories, congressional authority was unchallenged (or at least had been until the 1840s, when southerners began to question the constitutionality of the Wilmot Proviso). Secondly, the issue raised the question of southern political power which, as the Missouri debates had shown, struck deep resonances in the North. More slave territories meant more slave states, which meant stronger southern opposition to northern measures like homesteads and internal improvements. For southerners, the demand for free soil translated into a future in which the South was a steadily shrinking minority of the nation, increasingly beleaguered by the nonslaveholding states.

Finally, the demand for free soil raised the question of the existence of slavery itself. It was commonly believed in both North and South that slavery to live had to expand. Already in 1850, there were more slaves outside the original slave states than within them. Soil exhaustion, the pressure of an increasing black and white population, and the need to maintain a political balance between the sections all pointed to the necessity for continued expansion. Moreover, in discussing the reasons for restricting the expansion of slavery, northern politicians increasingly used quasi-abolitionist language condemning the peculiar institution in toto. As Charles Sumner wrote in 1848: "We are disposed to select this single point, because it has a peculiar practical issue at the present moment, while its discussion would, of course, raise the whole question of slavery." Free soil, in other words, enabled the politicians to garb themselves in the moral mantle of the abolitionists, while remaining firmly within the Constitution and the bounds of widely accepted political programs.

In the aftermath of the election, Congress met for a brief session, dominated by debates over slavery. One congressman complained: "From morning to night, day after day, and week after week, nothing can get a hearing that will not afford an opportunity to lug in something about Negro slavery. Sir, . . . a stranger, on listening to the debates on this floor, would consider that Congress was instituted mainly for the protection of Negroes." At the urging of Calhoun, southern congressmen met in caucus, and adopted the South Carolinian's Address of the Southern Delegates in Congress, calling for the unity of southerners, regardless of party affiliation, in defense of slavery and the right of the peculiar institution to expand into the territories. Meanwhile, northern radicals like Joshua Giddings of Ohio—and including a lame-duck congressman from Illinois, Abraham Lincoln—were pressing for the abolition of slavery in the District of Columbia, the nation's capital. Congress adjourned in March 1849, completely stymied by sectional antagonisms. No provision had been made for territorial governments for California, New Mexico, and other lands acquired in the Mexican War.

Deadlock in Washington

Taylor was inaugurated on March 4, 1849. His inaugural address, described by the press as "negative and general," called for sectional compromise but did not propose any specific measures. But it soon became apparent that, despite being a Louisiana slaveholder, Taylor was much more pronorthern than anyone had expected. Senator Seward, known to the South as an extreme antislavery spokesman, quickly became Taylor's right-hand man. Under Seward's influence, Taylor evolved a policy, if such it can be called, which ignored most of the outstanding sectional issues and insisted simply on the immediate admission of California as a free state, as the territory had requested.

When Congress met in December, it quickly became apparent that traditional party alignments had been all but shattered by the successive years of sectional conflict. Theoretically, the Democrats had a majority in the House. But in reality the balance of power was held by a shifting group of about a dozen Free-Soilers, who refused to support the nominee of either party for the Speakership. Only after sixty-three ballots was Howell Cobb of Georgia, a moderate Democrat, chosen as Speaker.

An air of crisis hung over Washington as 1850 dawned. Men from both sections recognized that if the outstanding sectional issues were not resolved, the dissolution of the Union was a distinct possibility. The status of California was only one of a host of such issues. Territorial governments had to be provided for the remainder of the Mexican Cession, and some decision made about the status of slavery in these territories. Another dispute involved the exact size and boundaries of the state of Texas, and the status of its debt, incurred during its period of independence. Then there were northern demands that slavery be abolished in the District of Columbia, where human beings were regularly auctioned within sight of the Capitol. And finally, there was the vexed question of fugitive slaves. The Constitution clearly provided that fugitives must be returned to slavery. But the Founders had neglected to make explicit whether state or federal authorities had the responsibility for taking action. The old fugitive slave law, dating from the 1790s, seemed to leave most of the responsibility to the states. But in 1842, the Supreme Court had decreed that the federal government was required to fulfill the constitutional obligation. As a result, several northern states passed personal liberty laws, barring state officials from taking part in the apprehension and return of fugitive slaves. Southerners now demanded a new and tougher federal law to reclaim escaped slaves.

Into the breach in January 1850 stepped the "Great Compromiser," Henry Clay of Kentucky. He had served in Congress since the days of the War of 1812, and had helped engineer both the Missouri Compromise and the settlement of the nullification dispute. Clay now proposed an omnibus measure which would become the basis for the eventual Compromise of 1850. His program was made up of the following points: the admission of California as a free state; the establishment of territorial governments in Utah and New Mexico with no reference to slavery (leaving the decision up to the settlers in accordance with squatter sovereignty); defining the boundaries of Texas and having the federal government take over responsibility for the Texas state debt (thereby satisfying the speculators and bondholders who had been pressuring Congress to guarantee their investment); the abolition of the slave trade in the District of Columbia, but the continuance of slavery there; and a new and effective fugitive slave law. Clay followed with an impassioned plea for compromise and Union. He appealed particularly to the North not to press for adoption of the

Wilmot Proviso, since climate and terrain almost certainly barred slavery from the southwestern territories without the need for congressional action.

There followed in February and March one of the great debates in the history of the United States Senate. The highlight, in the first two weeks of March, was a series of speeches by Calhoun, Daniel Webster, and Seward. On March 3, the dying Calhoun, too weak to deliver his last speech, sat in stony silence while it was read by Senator Mason of Virginia. A firm rejection of

Washington was the scene of feverish activity in 1849 and 1850 as legislators sought to avoid a split in the Union. Henry Clay's compromise package won wide approval and overcame the immediate crisis. Below: The Capitol in 1852. Right: Henry Clay, Lincoln's "beau ideal of a statesman."

compromise, it insisted on the right of southerners to take their slaves into all the territories, opposed the admission of California, and warned that disunion was the certain result if southern interests were ignored. Four days later, Webster delivered the great March 7 speech. Abandoning his previous support of the Wilmot Proviso, he pleaded for compromise. "I wish to speak today," he began, "not as a Massachusetts man, not as a northern man, but as an American. . . . I speak today for the preservation of the Union. Hear me for my cause." Like Clay, he addressed his appeal primarily to the North, and while antislavery men denounced him for a betrayal of his earlier beliefs, Webster, more than any other individual, rallied moderate northern sentiment in support of the compromise.

Webster, Clay, and Calhoun, all well past their prime, were the voices of the past. On March 11, the voice of the future spoke—William H. Seward, who would shortly become the leading light of the new Republican party. In a speech made famous by his statement that there existed a "higher law" than the Constitution, which should guide congressional actions, Seward rejected compromise and ridiculed Calhoun's demand for a continuing equilibrium between the sections. He laid down a challenge to the South—it would find it impossible to resist the onward march of the antislavery cause and eventual emancipation.

Seward may have spoken for the future, but for the present the forces of compromise were in the ascendant. During the summer of 1850, two major obstacles to the enactment of Clay's plan were removed. The first was the Nashville Convention, a gathering of delegates from the slave states, called by the Mississippi legislature, to consider disunion. But moderates held a majority, and the convention adjourned to await developments in Congress. Secondly, President Taylor died suddenly in July, and was succeeded by Fillmore. Until his death, Taylor had been a foe of compromise and, perhaps imagining himself in the position of Jackson twenty years earlier, had threatened to hang southern traitors if they took steps toward disunion. Fillmore, by contrast, threw his support behind the compromise measures.

In the end, the Compromise of 1850 was enacted in basically the same form as Clay had introduced it. There was, however, one difference. While Clay had proposed an omnibus measure embracing all the proposals, each provision was individually enacted, a strategy developed and carried through by Senator Stephen A. Douglas of Illinois. By the end of 1850, majorities in both sections seemed to acquiesce in the compromise. For the North, the main objection was the new fugitive slave law. This imposed heavy fines on those who aided escaped slaves or refused to help apprehend them, and denied the fugitive the right to a trial by jury. Many northern communities refused to enforce the act. Yet southerners were announcing that faithful execution of the fugitive slave law was a prime condition for their acceptance of the compromise

Millard Fillmore became president on the death of Zachary Taylor in 1850. The support he gave to the 1850 Compromise ensured its passage through Congress. This portrait is by G. P. A. Healy.

as a final settlement of the slavery question.

Clearly, grave dangers still lay ahead, but for the time being it appeared that the sectional conflict had been settled. In southern elections of 1850 and 1851, pro-compromise candidates were uniformly victorious, even in such radical states as Mississippi. Similarly, in the North, the Free-Soil party suffered a sharp decline as many voters returned to their original party allegiance.

The Compromise of 1850 reflected the recognition by political leaders of both sections that sectional controversy had developed to the point where it seriously threatened the Union. It sought to restore the old basis of political behavior—the tacit agreement that slavery be excluded from national politics. Ironically, few of the compromise provisions worked out as planned. California, admitted as a free state, remained under the control of proslavery Democrats during the 1850s. The slave trade was abolished in Washington, but the sale of slaves continued illegally. Few fugitive slaves were actually brought back from the North under the operation of the new law. Yet

In the 1852 election slavery was not a contentious issue as both main parties supported the 1850 Compromise. Right: A Democratic campaign banner.

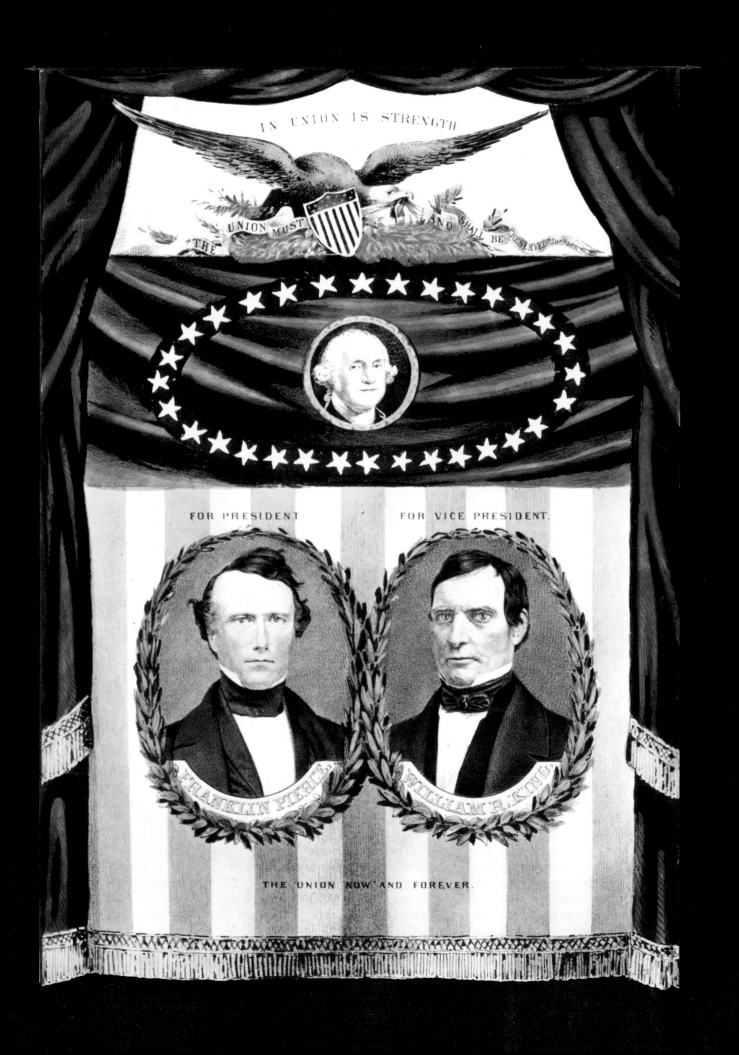

the compromise did succeed in meeting the first real threat of secession, and the debates of 1850 marked the emergence of a new generation of political leaders, men like Seward and Douglas, whose national reputations were based on their stand on the slavery question. The old-style career for the Union, represented by Clay and Webster, would no longer be possible in the 1850s.

A Cooler Political Climate

National politics in 1851 and 1852 seemed remarkably tranquil compared with the heated controversies of the previous years. A few antislavery radicals in the Senate—Chase and Sumner, who had been elected by coalitions of Free-Soilers and Democrats, and Seward—tried to continue the antislavery agitation, but their efforts received little support. Yet it soon became apparent that one key element of the compromise, the fugitive slave law, was simply not enforceable in some areas of the North. This fact was highlighted by a series of dramatic rescues of fugitive slaves. In Boston, in February 1851, the slave Shadrach was liberated by a crowd of free blacks who entered the courthouse, overpowered federal marshalls, and sent the fugitive on his way to Canada and freedom. In Lancaster, Pennsylvania, a master who attempted to recapture a fugitive was killed. And in

The 1852 contenders for the presidency: Franklin Pierce (left) and Winfield Scott. Pierce, the youngest leader to be elected up to that time, made little impact on domestic affairs.

upstate New York, a large mob, including leading abolitionists, rescued the fugitive slave Jerry from prison and spirited him off to Canada. By 1854, when Anthony Burns was apprehended in Boston, it would take a sizable force of federal troops to ensure his return to the South. The spectacle of the manacled Burns being led to the ship surrounded by soldiers outraged many Bostonians who had hitherto been indifferent to the antislavery cause. The plight of the fugitive slave brought the slavery issue home to many northern communities with an impact which speeches and pamphlets could never achieve.

But the written word could also move men. In 1851, there appeared in an obscure antislavery newspaper, the *National Era*, a serialized novel about slavery entitled "Life Among The Lowly." When reprinted in book form as *Uncle Tom's Cabin* it became one of America's great best sellers, and probably the single most effective piece of propaganda in the history of antislavery agitation.

Despite continuation of the antislavery campaign in many areas of the North, the presidential election of 1852 was the last until 1880 in which slavery and its aftermath would not be the central issue. On the other hand, there was clear evidence that the political system

Above: A fugitive slave is retaken. Such incidents hardened northern opinion against slavery. Left: This broadside appeared in Boston after the capture and return south of an escaped slave.

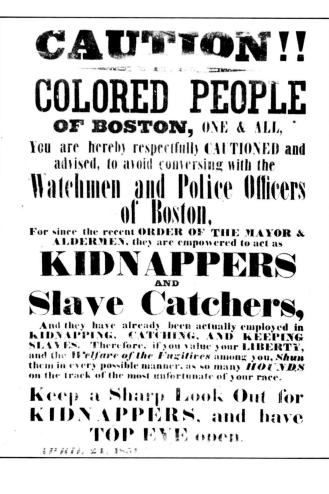

CAUTION!!
COLORED PEOPLE
OF BOSTON, ONE & ALL,

You are hereby respectfully CAUTIONED and advised, to avoid conversing with the

Watchmen and Police Officers of Boston,

For since the recent ORDER OF THE MAYOR & ALDERMEN, they are empowered to act as

KIDNAPPERS
AND
Slave Catchers,

And they have already been actually employed in KIDNAPPING, CATCHING, AND KEEPING SLAVES. Therefore, if you value your LIBERTY, and the *Welfare of the Fugitives* among you, *Shun* them in every possible manner, as so many *HOUNDS* on the track of the most unfortunate of your race.

Keep a Sharp Look Out for KIDNAPPERS, and have TOP EYE open.

APRIL 24, 1851.

had not fully recovered from the disorganization of the crisis years. Only after forty-nine ballots were the Democrats able to agree on the colorless Franklin Pierce of New Hampshire as their candidate, while the Whigs took fifty-three ballots to choose Winfield Scott. Both parties endorsed the Compromise of 1850, and in this seemed to reflect the national mood. The Free-Soil party received only about one-half the votes it had garnered in 1848, and most Barnburners returned to the Democratic fold. In November, Pierce won an overwhelming victory, limiting Scott to four states. Southern Whigs, fearing that Scott would be controlled by Seward and other antislavery Whigs, deserted their party in droves.

The result left the Whig party demoralized and disorganized. One southern newspaper declared, "the Whig party of the South, as a party, is as dead as a mackerel." The party's deterioration continued on the local level during 1853 as new issues suddenly emerged in state elections. Temperance and nativist candidates made deep inroads on the Whig vote, especially in the North and thousands of Whigs flocked into nativist Know-Nothing lodges. The party was disintegrating, and in 1854 came the final blow.

Uncle Tom's Cabin

Serialized first in a small-circulation anti-slavery newspaper, *Uncle Tom's Cabin* was reprinted in book form a year later in 1852. The reception it received was the most remarkable of any novel in American history. It immediately became a best seller; the first printing was sold out in a couple of days, and almost overnight the name of Harriet Beecher Stowe was known throughout the land.

The story related the trials and adventures of Uncle Tom, a middle-aged and religious Kentucky slave who is sold down the river to a new owner, Augustine St Clair. After St Clair's death he becomes the property of Simon Legree, a cruel plantation overseer on the Red River. Tom's death results from a flogging given by Legree because the slave refused to reveal the whereabouts of two fugitives. Other characters include St Clair's child Eva, whom Tom saves from drowning, and the mulatto girl Eliza who, rather than be sold apart from her baby, escapes to freedom across the frozen Ohio.

Uncle Tom's Cabin was a melodrama with striking portrayals of good and evil. It exaggerated the worst aspects of slavery and, in its central character, painted a picture of a fawning and overly polite Negro that later resulted in the term ''Uncle Tom'' being regarded by blacks as a term of abuse.

Although the novel cannot be classed as a great piece of literature, its influence as a piece of propaganda against slavery was profound not only in America but throughout the world. In the first year 300,000 copies were sold in the United States alone, and in England sales exceeded 1 million in the first twelve months. It was later translated into many languages including German, Danish, Portuguese, Welsh, and Russian. It was praised by leading men of letters, among them Thomas Macaulay, Leo Tolstoy, and Heinrich Heine. Numerous stage versions of the book were produced, and played to packed houses for over half a century.

From the South came angry denunciation of the work. Abolitionist William Lloyd Garrison, a prime target for southern venom, wrote to Mrs Stowe: ''I estimate the value of anti-slavery writing by the abuse it brings. Now all the defenders of slavery have let me alone and are abusing you.'' There soon appeared a number of books portraying slavery as southerners saw it. For her part, Mrs Stowe responded to the criticism by writing in 1853 *A Key to Uncle Tom's Cabin*, which claimed to document every incident described in the novel.

She traveled in Europe and was widely feted. She met Charles Dickens, had an audience with Queen Victoria, and during the Civil War met President Lincoln at the White House. He greeted her with a gleam in his eye: ''So you're the little woman who wrote the book that made this great war!''

Uncle Tom's Cabin was Mrs Stowe's first novel. She had had some short stories published in magazines since the 1830s but none had touched the subject of slavery. Indeed, her first-hand knowledge of the institution was minimal. What direct insight she did gain into slavery derived from two decades spent living in Ohio, during which time she occasionally visited Kentucky. The passage of a new and stringent fugitive slave law in 1850 —''a nightmare abomination'' she called it—finally provoked in her a sense of quiet outrage which resulted in her story highlighting the sufferings of the Negro under slavery. ''God wrote it,'' she said much later. ''I merely did His dictation.''

Religious and humanitarian concerns were a powerful force in Mrs Stowe's life. Born in Litchfield, Connecticut, in 1811, she was the daughter, sister, and wife of clergymen. Her father was the influential Lyman Beecher and in 1836 she married a theological teacher, the Reverend Calvin E. Stowe. She began writing to supplement her husband's meager salary. For the magazine serialization of *Uncle Tom's Cabin* she was paid $300; after its publication as a book she received $10,000 in royalties in the first four months alone. Although Mrs Stowe wrote many other books—novels, short stories, poems, and nonfiction works—before her death in 1896, none approached the popularity her first book achieved.

A preface to the work spelt out the author's credo. ''The scenes of this story . . . lie among a race hitherto ignored by the associations of polite and refined society; an exotic race, whose ancestors, born beneath a tropic sun, brought with them, and perpetuated to their descendants, a character so essentially unlike the hard and dominant Anglo-Saxon race, as for many years to have won from it only misunderstanding and contempt. But, another and better day is dawning; every influence of literature, of poetry and of art, in our times, is becoming more and more in unison with the great master chord of Christianity, 'good will to man.'''

Uncle Tom's Cabin hastened that dawn of a better day for the Negro. It did not cause the Civil War but it did, more than any other single factor, rally northern opinion against slavery and the South.

Both pictures Stowe-Day Foundation

Far left top: An 1853 portrait of Harriet Beecher Stowe. Although she wrote many books after Uncle Tom's Cabin, *none came near to it in popularity.*
Above: This lithograph depicts a scene from the book: Eliza and her baby flee to freedom across the frozen Ohio.
Left: Uncle Tom dies after being flogged by his overseer, Simon Legree, portrayed at left. Far left bottom: Stage versions of the novel were popular for well over fifty years.

The Kansas-Nebraska Act

Looking back on the dramatic events of 1854 from the 1870s, Vice President Henry Wilson observed: "No event in the progress of the great conflict stands out more prominently than the abrogation of the Compromise of 1820. . . . No single act of the slave power ever spread greater consternation, produced more lasting results upon the popular mind, or did so much to arouse the North." Wilson was referring to the Kansas-Nebraska Act. In its final form, it repealed the Missouri Compromise, and applied the doctrine of popular sovereignty to the territories of Kansas and Nebraska from which slavery had previously been barred. The act's supporters, led by Senator Douglas, insisted the measure was a logical extension of the Compromise of 1850, which had adopted popular sovereignty as the national policy for western territories. Its opponents charged that it was a conspiracy to spread slavery over lands which had long been reserved as free territory.

Why Douglas introduced the measure in January 1854 is not entirely clear. Certainly he had long been interested in speedy western development, and had supported such policies as homestead legislation, railroad development, and territorial expansion. As early as 1844, he had proposed the organization of the Territory of the Platte, a vast area which included the present states of Nebraska and Kansas. Douglas was chairman of the Senate Committee on the Territories, and he had seen a bill to provide territorial governments for Nebraska defeated in 1853 because some southerners opposed organizing additional free states. He knew their support was essential if a similar bill was to be enacted in 1854.

Douglas, moreover, was an energetic and ambitious politician. His role in the passage of the Compromise of 1850 had given him a national reputation, and in 1852, while still aged only thirty-nine, he had tried for the Democratic presidential nomination. Many observers in 1854 viewed the Kansas-Nebraska bill as an attempt to woo southern support for another presidential bid in 1856. But more importantly, Douglas realized that the weak-willed President Pierce was simply not providing leadership for the Democratic party. Factionalism over patronage and other matters was weakening the party, and Douglas decided that the time was ripe for a new leader, with a new and dynamic policy. Finally, Douglas sincerely believed that popular sovereignty was the only equitable solution to the slavery question, and that applying the principle to the Louisiana Purchase territory would settle the slavery question once and for all. As a middle ground between prosouthern and pronorthern measures, popular sovereignty was a principle on which all Democrats could unite. And privately, Douglas

Courtesy of Chicago Historical Society

Senator Stephen Douglas, the "Little Giant," sparked off renewed sectional strife with his bill for the organization of Kansas and Nebraska. The bill as passed shattered the consensus Henry Clay had established four years before and raised the controversy over slavery to a new fever pitch.

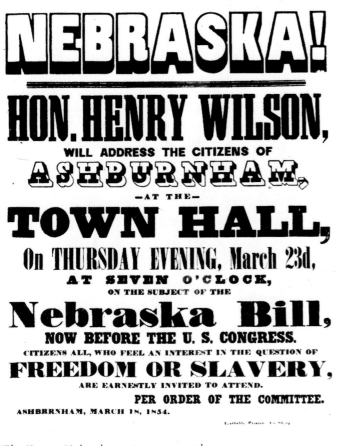

The Kansas-Nebraska controversy was the dominant issue in Congress in 1854. Throughout the land, the merits and drawbacks of Douglas's bill were discussed.

expressed his conviction that, given the climate and soil of Kansas and Nebraska, it was almost certain that they would end up as free states.

So, on January 4, 1854, Douglas reported from the Committee on the Territories a measure for the organization of the Nebraska territory. In language copied from the Compromise of 1850, the bill declared that when Nebraska was ready for statehood it would be accepted into the Union with or without slavery, as the inhabitants had decided. There followed a complicated series of political maneuvers, culminating in an amendment introduced by Senator Dixon of Kentucky explicitly repealing the Missouri Compromise. Douglas had wished to avoid so direct a statement, but he reluctantly accepted Dixon's measure, and pressured Pierce into backing it as well. On January 24, 1854, the *Washington Union*, spokesman for the administration, declared the measure as amended "a test of Democratic orthodoxy."

But already storm clouds were gathering. On the same day there appeared one of the most effective pieces of political propaganda in American history, the Appeal of the Independent Democrats. Written primarily by Chase,

it arraigned Douglas's measure as "a criminal betrayal of precious rights . . . part and parcel of an atrocious plot" to spread slavery into all the territories. The appeal was reprinted in newspapers throughout the North, and was instrumental in rousing public sentiment against the bill. No longer did the sectional conflict focus on northern attacks on the institution of slavery. Now it seemed that slavery was on the offensive, threatening land which northerners had assumed since 1820 would be guaranteed to free settlers. The reaction was summed up by an Ohio politician: "We have submitted to slavery long enough, and must not stand it any longer. I am done catching Negroes for the South."

That the measure would pass the Senate was never in doubt. There southern influence was strongest, and a majority of northern senators were Democrats, susceptible to pressure from the administration. After an acrimonious debate, the Senate approved the Kansas-Nebraska bill by a majority of 37 to 14 early in March. In the House, the bill faced much rougher going. But finally, in May, it was approved by the narrow margin of 113 to 100. The division showed how party alignments had been shattered. Of eighty-seven northern Democrats voting in the House, forty-three opposed the measure and forty-four voted in favor. All forty-five northern Whigs voted against, while thirteen of the twenty southern Whigs supported the bill, providing the margin of passage. The Whig party had been presented with a golden opportunity to revive its fortunes. Had it united in opposition to the bill on the simple basis of avoiding a revival of the slavery agitation, the party could have reestablished its stature as the defender of the Union. When southern Whigs decided to support Douglas's bill they sealed the death of the Whig party.

Northern fears that the South was bent on spreading slavery at all costs were intensified by the activities in 1853 and 1854 of the colorful adventurer, William Walker. When Walker launched filibustering expeditions against Lower California and then Nicaragua, southerners gave him enthusiastic support, and the Pierce administration did little to stop him. More serious were the administration's efforts to acquire Cuba from Spain. Secretary of State Marcy secretly offered to purchase the island, but when his efforts were turned aside he was directed to employ any means necessary to annex Cuba. Marcy directed the American ministers to Britain, France, and Spain to confer on the best policy to pursue. They met at the Belgian town of Ostend in October 1854 and issued a statement of policy stressing America's right to purchase Cuba, or seize it by force if Spain refused to sell. When news of the proposal leaked to the press, the embarrassed administration was forced to repudiate it, but not before northerners were once again convinced that southerners would stop at nothing in their effort to extend the boundaries of slavery.

But the Ostend Manifesto was in truth a diversion from the nation's main concern—the impact of the Kansas-Nebraska Act. On the night the Senate passed the bill, as bells tolled in celebration, Chase had remarked to Sumner, "they celebrate a present victory, but the echoes they awake shall never rest until slavery itself has died." And the echoes of the measure continued to roll across the country. So great were the protest meetings that Douglas declared he could travel from Washington to Chicago by the light of his own burning effigies. When the Illinois senator attempted to explain his measure in a Chicago speech, the crowd shouted him down for two hours, until Douglas stormed out in disgust.

Formation of the Republican Party

These protest meetings, most of which seemed virtually spontaneous, quickly turned toward the arena of politics. Disregarding former party loyalties, they called for the union of all opponents of the Kansas-Nebraska Act. Various names were tried—People's Party, Anti-Nebraska —but by 1856, these new groups had united under the name coined by a meeting in Ripon, Wisconsin, in February 1854—Republican. The process of creating the new Republican party was a complex one, which varied from state to state. In the most antislavery areas, such as Wisconsin, Michigan, Vermont, and Maine, the party was fully organized during 1854, and swept to impressive victories in the fall election of that year. In New York, the Whig organization survived into 1855, and it was not until the end of that year that men like Seward and Greeley unequivocally identified themselves with the new party. In Illinois, Whig leaders like Lincoln held aloof from a "Republican" organization created by abolitionists and Free-Soilers in 1854. It was only in 1856 that a broadly based Republican party finally emerged.

Further complicating the political scene was the striking success of the Know-Nothing party in 1854 and 1855 in certain northern states. Moving into the vacuum created by the collapse of Whiggery, the Know-Nothings swept to an unprecedented victory in Massachusetts in 1854, winning almost every seat in the legislature, and all the state's congressional seats. In Pennsylvania and New York, the party held the balance of power in 1855. And in the West, large numbers of Know-Nothings entered the fledgling Republican party and helped give it a nativist tinge. But by 1856 it was clear that, like the Whigs, the Know-Nothings could not exist as a national party. Its northern and southern wings disagreed on the slavery issue, and most northern Know-Nothings silently merged into the Republican ranks.

The Republican party was a new thing in American politics—a sectional, ideological party. Unlike the Democratic and Whig parties of the Jacksonian period,

Former Whigs, Know-Nothings, and antislavery Democrats made up the ranks of the fledgling Republican party. Support for the new coalition was confined to the North, for the party took a firm line against slavery. Left: Charles Sumner was one of the Senate's most trenchant critics of slavery. A former Conscience Whig and Free-Soil supporter, he was among the Republicans' founding members. Right: The new party entered the national political arena in 1856 when John C. Frémont ran for president. This cartoon appeared before the election.

THE GREAT REPUBLICAN REFORM PARTY,
Calling on their Candidate.

it was geographically confined, having virtually no support in the southern states. And equally unlike its predecessors, its internal unity was provided not simply by the struggle for office and spoils, but by a coherent ideology—a consistent perception of American society, and of what that society should become in the future. At the core of the Republican outlook was the concept of "free labor." To Republicans, what differentiated northern from southern society was not simply the existence of slavery in the South, but the fact that in the free states labor was afforded opportunity for economic advancement. "Our paupers of today," said the *New York Times*, "thanks to free labor are our yeomen and merchants of tomorrow." Every man in northern life had the opportunity to achieve middle-class status, to establish himself as an independent farmer or entrepreneur. The Republicans glorified their section's middle class as the backbone of the nation, looking down on those who were permanently poor (because, it was thought, of their own failings of character), and distrusting

the aristocratic and wealthy. Their social outlook reflected the dynamic, expanding capitalism of the North, particularly of the rural areas and small towns where Republican strength was greatest. (The large cities, with their concentrations of immigrant voters, tended to vote Democratic.)

The Republican critique of slavery flowed naturally from their self-image of northern society. In contrast to democracy, the South represented aristocracy. In place of economic development and expansion, the South seemed stagnant and backward. And in place of a society which afforded dignity and advancement to the laborer, the South seemed to look down on labor, white as well as black. Poor whites of the South had no hope of social advancement, because their society was so tightly controlled by an aristocracy of slaveholders. It is only within the context of this belief in the South as a totally alien society that the struggle over the expansion of slavery can be fully understood. The question, simply put, amounted to this: would northern or southern society come

103

to dominate the West? Would white labor there be degraded or dignified? Would democracy or aristocracy control these territories? "Shall," asked one Republican senator, "thriving villages and cities spring up all over the face of Nebraska, or shall unthrift and sparseness, stand still and decay, ever characterize that state?"

The Republicans had thus added to the abolitionists' moral assault on slavery a sophisticated political and economic critique of southern society. Slavery was not simply immoral, it was an essential element of weakness in the nation, stunting the growth of a large part of the country, preventing full economic development and opportunities for social advancement. And now the South was attempting to spread this social system into lands where northern men and women or their children would someday wish to settle.

Closely linked to the issue of slavery expansion was the Republican conception of the Slave Power. Like the idea of free labor, it was an ideological glue which united all elements of the party. The South, Republicans believed, had long been organized politically to control the federal government and expand the peculiar institution. Within the South, the Slave Power exercised total control—antislavery presses had been destroyed, and spokesmen driven to the free states. Poor whites, who were almost as oppressed by slavery as the slaves themselves, had little or no influence on the conduct of public affairs. And now the Slave Power was threatening to expand its influence into the West, and further entrench itself in the federal government. The only way for northerners to protect their own interests was to organize a political force capable of combating southern influence, and driving the Slave Power from control of the national government.

These then were the ideas Republicans held in common. Of course, as in any political party, there were divisions and factions. As a coalition of radicals and conservatives, former Democrats and former Whigs, the Republicans had more than their share of tensions. The radical Republicans, who included most of the old Conscience Whigs of Massachusetts and Liberty men, represented the most extreme antislavery position within the party. Long-time foes of the South, they were, in truth, political abolitionists, viewing free soil as simply the first step on a long road which would eventually lead to abolition. They stressed the moral argument against slavery rather than economic and political appeals. They insisted that a Republican administration would not simply bar slavery from the territories, but would prohibit it wherever the federal government had constitutional power to act—in the District of Columbia and on all federal property. Never a majority of the party, the radicals were the most articulate and consistent of antislavery spokesmen, the most persistent workers in organizing the Republican party and combating those who wished to compromise with the South. Their presence made it

certain that a Republican president would find it very difficult to go back on his preelection pledges to act against the Slave Power.

Then there were the ex-Democrats, who comprised less than one-quarter of the Republican party but also had a crucial role to play. Their presence provided the margin of victory in many northern states, and also prevented the Republicans from being simply a resurrection of Whiggery. Many Barnburner Democrats, who had never quite forgiven the South for the rejection of Van Buren in 1844, flocked to the Republican banner in 1856. Imbued with the staunch unionism of their political hero, Andrew Jackson, they would insist when the secession crisis occurred in 1860 that Republicans meet treason with resolution, and not give in to southern threats.

The largest segment was composed of former Whigs. Such men tended to be moderate on the slavery issue, but firmly committed to the principle of nonextension. Concerned with the future economic development of the nation, they were the group to whom the economic critique of slavery appealed the most. Unlike the radicals, they were not interested in launching a crusade against the South once the Slave Power was defeated in national politics. But neither were they willing to compromise on the principle of free soil, or allow the South to break up the Union. By 1860, one of these former Whigs would prove capable of uniting the Republican party and leading it to national victory. Lincoln would represent better than any other individual the paradoxical political stance of his party. He was moderate enough to carry every northern state in 1860, but radical enough for his election to signal the commencement of the secession movement.

Back in 1820, John Quincy Adams had observed that the votes on the Missouri Compromise, the alliance of northerners against the expansion of slavery, contained the seeds of a powerful new sectional party. It had taken over thirty years for Adams's prediction to be fulfilled. But by 1856, the national political system had been shattered. In place of two national parties, whose very presence helped hold an increasingly divided nation together, there existed an increasingly prosouthern Democratic party, a declining Know-Nothing party, and a sectional Republican party which was on its way to becoming the most formidable political force in the nation. By the mid-1850s, the bonds of Union seemed to have worn very thin. Churches had fragmented along sectional lines. Southerners had withdrawn in increasing numbers from northern educational institutions. In place of sectional good will, attacks and recriminations filled the air. The one remaining major national institution, the Democratic party, was increasingly subjected to sectional pressures. If this last bond between the sections shattered, could the Union survive it for very long?

To the Brink of the Abyss

Senator Seward of New York earned a somewhat unde-served reputation as a radical in the 1850s as a result of his talent for manufacturing provocative phrases. His reference to a ''higher law'' than the Constitution, and his later prophecy that sectional conflict was ''irrepressible,'' both greatly alarmed the South. In like vein, he issued a challenge during the debates over the Kansas-Nebraska bill which had the effect of sharpening northern sentiment against the South. ''Come on, then, gentlemen of the Slave States,'' he cried. ''Since there is no escaping your chal-lenge, I accept it in behalf of the cause of freedom. We will engage in competition for the virgin soil of Kansas, and God give the victory to the side that is strong in num-bers as it is in right.''

Assisted by such organizations as the New England Emigrant Aid Society, settlers from the eastern states made their way to Kansas and established the town of Lawrence. Even more settlers poured in from the old Northwest, from Missouri, and from other parts of the upper South. Those who came from the free states were determined to hold the line against a further expansion of slavery while those from the slave states sought to estab-lish slavery in the new territory. Yet these were not their only, nor even their dominant, motives. Much of the old Northwest was suffering from drought and the fertile lands of Kansas offered welcome relief. Kansas had the same attractions as any other virgin territory and from wherever they came the settlers exhibited the same characteristics to be found in any frontier settlements. They included in their number farmers, lawyers, store-keepers, speculators, and the usual riffraff. The New England Emigrant Aid Society was a joint-stock enterprise as concerned about profits as it was about freedom. But few were untouched by sectional squabbles and hostilities. The emigrant aid societies appeared to Missourians and others to be corporate attempts to win the West for northern business. Free-state settlers saw the influx of Missourians, with their proslavery attitudes and an undue proportion of frontier riffraff among them, as a threat to free labor and orderly government. Rumors of intended and actual aggression emanated from all sides and a com-petitive and hostile spirit soon manifested itself as between proslavery and free-state settlers, with each group calling for reinforcements.

Whether Kansas was to enter the Union as a free or a slave state was bitterly disputed by settlers. This broadside advertises elections to a free-state convention that met in October 1855.

FREE STATE CONVENTION!

All persons who are favorable to a union of effort, and a permanent organization of all the Free State elements of Kansas Territory, and who wish to secure upon the broadest platform the co-operation of all who agree upon this point, are re-quested to meet at their several places of holding elections, in their respective districts on the 25th of August, instant, at one o'clock, P. M., and appoint five del-egates to each representative to which they were entitled in the Legislative Assembly, who shall meet in general Convention at

Big Springs, Wednesday, Sept. 5th '55,

at 10 o'clock A. M., for the purpose of adopting a Platform upon which all may act harmoniously who prefer Freedom to Slavery.

The nomination of a Delegate to Congress, will also come up before the General Convention.

Let no sectional or party issues distract or prevent the perfect co-operation of Free State men. Union and harmony are absolutely necessary to success. The pro-slavery party are fully and effectually organized. No jars nor minor issues divide them. And to contend against them successfully, we also must be united.— Without prudence and harmony of action we are certain to fail. Let every man then do his duty and we are certain of victory.

All Free State men, without distinction, are earnestly requested to take immediate and effective steps to insure a full and correct representation for every Dis-trict in the Territory. "United we stand; divided we fall."

By order of the Executive Committee of the Free State Party of the Territory of Kansas, as per resolution of the Mass Convention in session at Lawrence, Aug 15th and 16th, 1855.

J. K. GOODIN, Sec'y.   **C. ROBINSON, Chairman.**

Herald of Freedom, Print.

Above: In response to the proslavery constitution drawn up in Kansas, free-state settlers formulated their own document. This engraving shows delegates at the free-state convention in Topeka.

Missourians harassed free-state settlers. They crossed the border in large numbers to vote illegally in the March 1855 elections for a territorial legislature, and generally boasted of their intentions to make Kansas a slave state. Militant free-state settlers, men like John Brown's sons, sent inflammatory reports back east and requested reinforcements and arms. Their concern was further heightened when the fraudulently elected proslavery legislature enacted a slave code which discriminated against non-slaveholders and proscribed the expression of antislavery sentiments. Violent language was the order of the day and the contending forces each called rival conventions for the autumn. The territory seethed with excitement and in early December very nearly erupted in civil war following the murder of a free-state settler by a proslavery man. The incident reveals only too clearly the tendency for all issues to be overlaid by that of slavery. The murder was the culmination of a quarrel over land and timber rights, the sort of quarrel which was the curse of the frontier everywhere. But observers were not concerned with the merits or demerits of the argument. What interested them were the allegiances of the protagonists—were they for or against slavery?

In October the free-state convention had met at Topeka and had drawn up a constitution which, on December 15, was put to the people and ratified. However, in the elec-

tions that followed in January 1856 there was considerable violence, and in the same month President Pierce declared the Topeka convention and constitution illegal. He expressed his determination to crush all resistance to the legally constituted, if illegally elected, proslavery government in the territory. His action convinced Free-Soilers everywhere that there really was a Slave Power conspiracy to win the West for slavery. When migration to Kansas picked up again in the spring, settlers tended to go armed for battle as well as for settlement. Their influx was in turn seen by the proslavery camp as an abolitionist plot, and armed bands crossed into Kansas from the South to harass free-state settlers.

Major violence was precipitated by the attempt of the proslavery faction to secure the arrest of members of the illegal Topeka government and to destroy the free-state press. In the spring of 1856 a mob converged on Lawrence, where some of those under indictment were allegedly hiding, and proceeded to sack the town. The outnumbered free-state settlers put up only token resistance. Also in May, news reached the territory of a savage assault upon Senator Sumner of Massachusetts on the floor of the Senate. Sumner had spoken for two days about what he called the ''Crime against Kansas'' and had criticized many for their alleged involvement. One who received the sharp edge of his very sharp tongue was Senator Andrew P. Butler of South Carolina. Enraged by this attack on his uncle, Representative Preston S. Brooks beat Sumner almost to death.

It was these events which appear to have provoked John Brown to launch his murderous assault upon pro-slavery settlers at Pottawotomie. That atrocity incited the territorial militia, supported by Missourians, to plunder southeast Kansas where the Browns lived. The area fell quickly into a state of anarchy with Brown and others leading guerrilla bands of free-state men from the brush. In August free-state settlers in Lawrence sallied out to attack proslavery settlements round about and provoked retaliatory raids, including the burning of the settlement of Osawotomie. The territory had succumbed to a state of civil war. Not until August 1856 did Pierce appoint as governor a man with the qualities needed to govern turbulent Kansas. In time Governor Geary, a Pennsylvanian

Below: The bloodshed in Kansas was repeated on the Senate floor in Washington when Senator Sumner was beaten nearly to death by Congressman Preston Brooks in 1856. This lithograph was published soon after the incident.

veteran of the Mexican War, was largely to pacify the territory. But in the summer of 1856, on the eve of a presidential election, Kansas was characterized by violence and bloodshed.

There were many reasons why the civil war in Kansas came to dominate the electoral campaign of 1856. It was a year of almost unprecedented prosperity. Expansion and speculation, particularly over the question of a Pacific railroad, were almost universal. Traditional political differences over economic issues such as the tariff and federal sponsorship of internal improvements were temporarily engulfed. Meanwhile, the continuous excitement over Kansas had prolonged the life of the various anti-Nebraska parties and alliances created in the summer and autumn of 1854. By the summer of 1856 they had given way in many places to formal new organizations calling themselves Republican. Holding its first national convention that year the new party was sufficiently powerful to nominate a presidential candidate who had a distinct chance of winning. The diverse origins of the party's followers made the creation of a party platform rather difficult. But all had in common a determined opposition to the expansion of slavery: ''liberty'' and ''free soil'' proved to be slogans with a powerful appeal. In John C. Frémont they found a standard-bearer who was a western hero, an undoubted nationalist, and a fervent believer in an American destiny to spread free institutions across the face of the continent.

SOUTHERN CHIVALRY — ARGUMENT versus CLUB'S.

The Democratic party found it more difficult to speak with a single voice. In the turbulent months following the Kansas-Nebraska Act it had suffered many defections to the cause of free soil. In some respects those defections were a blessing in disguise in that they left behind a more united party. But that unity was precarious. It was clear the party could not choose the ground upon which the election would be fought. It had to meet the Republican challenge to its territorial policies and therefore had to defend the idea of popular sovereignty embodied in the Kansas-Nebraska Act. But popular sovereignty proved to be a unifying concept only because it was so ambiguous and so capable of widely divergent interpretations. Some southern extremists applied to it a pragmatic test: did it permit the actual expansion of slavery? For others in the party the issue was one of timing: when did the settlers in a territory become sovereign?

The party had to find a presidential candidate who would satisfy both factions. Pierce had proved too weak in office and Douglas was too closely associated with the

The Union was gravely imperiled by events in Kansas in the mid-1850s. The Kansas-Nebraska Act, intended to settle the issue of slavery in the territories, merely intensified sectionalism. Fighting resulted as free-soilers battled pro-slavery forces in Kansas. Above: A free-state battery near Topeka. Above right: Cartoon criticizing Democratic handling of the Kansas question. Right: The Battle of Hickory Point, near Lawrence.

passage of the act and with a factional interest within the party. Under the circumstances the choice of James Buchanan of Pennsylvania seemed at first a wise one. He had behind him a life of public service; he represented a key state; and as he had been American minister in England at the time of the passage of the Kansas-Nebraska Act he was in no way tainted by it. He could be presented to the South as a conservative; to the North as a supporter of popular sovereignty; and to all factions as a unionist and nationalist. In the campaign, moreover, he supported differing interpretations of popular sovereignty.

LIBERTY, THE FAIR MAID OF KANSAS_IN THE HANDS OF THE "BORDER RUFFIANS".

Nevertheless, it was not inevitable that the election would revolve around the Kansas question. There had been other disruptive tendencies in American politics in preceding years and as late as the summer of 1856 it was by no means obvious that the Republicans would assume the mantle of the Whigs as chief opposition party to the Democrats. Ever since the end of the war with Mexico the expansion, industrialization, and urbanization of the nation had been rising to a crescendo. Traditional American values and group loyalties were being threatened in the process. In particular, one element caused great alarm: the change in the character of the American population through immigration. In California alarm rose over the influx of considerable numbers of Chinese; elsewhere it was Europeans who occasioned it. Following a series of disastrous harvests in Europe in the late 1840s the rate of immigration accelerated. Between 1846 and 1854 more than 3 million immigrants entered the country which itself had a population of no more than 20 million. A high proportion were from Ireland and southern Germany. Nearly all the Irish and about half of the Germans were Roman Catholics so that traditional Protestant fears of popery were aroused. Those fears were accentuated by an evangelical revivalist movement and Roman Catholic attempts to secure the use of public funds for Catholic schools. Irish and German drinking habits also caused offense and the vigorous prohibition movement of the time was tinged with a distinct hostility to foreigners. Many immigrants, and especially the Irish, congregated in the seaboard cities of New England, New York, Pennsylvania, and Maryland. Upon them was often heaped the responsibility for the evils brought about by an uncontrolled and rapid urbanization: the growth of slums, poor sanitation, drunkenness, crime, and prostitution. To some extent, too, they were made pawns in the game of American politics. Political parties hastened to register them and march them to the polls whether or not they were aware of the issues or even the meaning of voting.

Not surprisingly, a strong nativist movement was stimulated and pledged itself to control of immigration, to the maintenance of a Protestant America, and an end to political corruption. This nativist impulse, moreover, was strongest amongst Whigs, the very group which provided the Republican party with its major source of recruits. Always more favorable to the intervention of government in shaping society, the Whigs were also aggrieved by the fact that it was primarily the Democratic party which benefited from the immigrant vote. The movement rapidly evolved during the 1850s into an insurgent political party —the so-called Know-Nothings or American party. The nativist upsurge peaked in 1856 and for a time threatened to overwhelm traditional politics. In the northern states, however, nativists tended also to oppose the spread of slavery while in the southern states the reverse was true. When it came to write a national platform in 1856 the

The Maryland Historical Society, Baltimore.

party divided along sectional lines. Although they nominated ex-President Fillmore to carry their banner in the presidential election the party had collapsed almost at the moment of creation. Northern nativists swung behind the Republicans who frequently exploited nativism as vigorously as they exploited antislavery. In the South the party remained formidable but was essentially sectional in its appeal. Alarmed at the increasing numerical strength of the North and the West through immigration, southern nativists stressed southern rights and acted to ginger up the more extreme wing of the Democratic party.

Sectionalism and the Dred Scott Case

When the votes were finally counted the Democrats had won easily enough. Although Buchanan received only 45 per cent of the popular vote he comfortably defeated both his Republican and nativist rivals. And yet Democrats

The Know-Nothing party had a meteoric life in the 1850s and died as quickly as it had risen. Founded on a hatred of Catholics and immigrants, it became split over slavery once it entered the national political arena. Above: A Know-Nothing mob storms through Boston in 1856. Right: Former Whig Millard Fillmore contested the presidency for the Know-Nothings in 1856 but made little impact.

could draw only limited satisfaction from the result. Frémont had carried eleven of the sixteen free states; the voting in Indiana, Ohio, Illinois, New Jersey, and Pennsylvania had produced Democratic victories but the margins were unspectacular and this middle block of states was clearly vulnerable in the future. The Republicans needed only to have won Pennsylvania and either Illinois or Indiana to have won the election. Moreover, the election revealed the extent to which the Kansas-Nebraska question had generated and consolidated intense sectional animosities. The Republicans had drawn great

President Buchanan became enmeshed in the Kansas question soon after taking office. Although he hoped to restore national unity, he was unable to stem the tide of sectionalism.

strength from antisouthern sentiment and the South had played vigorously upon the theme of southern rights. The parties had all stressed positive and divisive programs in a reversal of the normal strategy of ignoring them during elections. The contest seemed to contemporaries to have spelled out the dangers of sectionalism rather than resolving them. One obscure Georgian spoke for many when he ventured to draw the lessons of the campaign. ''Buchanan and [John C.] Breckenridge are elected,'' he wrote, ''and owe their election to the South mainly; while the vote of the North with but few exceptions has been cast for Frémont. The next issue will doubtless be purely sectional in its character. The prospect is fearful, but everything indicates such a future condition of affairs. And when it does come, we of the South must and will be prepared to meet it bravely and without concession.''

As 1857 unfolded it became increasingly apparent to those who viewed the outcome of the election apprehensively that their forebodings were justified. By the end of the year Democratic hopes for a satisfactory solution to the Kansas problem had been blasted, and the party torn asunder. In the summer and early autumn, moreover, the bubble of prosperity burst and the nation was plunged into a financial panic, involving a run on the banks, followed by unemployment and hardship. Yet in the weeks surrounding his inauguration in March 1857, President Buchanan had felt optimistic.

After a great deal of intrigue and bargaining the new president had managed to put together a cabinet which was solidly conservative but which, despite a tendency to favor the South, was also representative of all sections. In his inaugural address he put forward a policy of quiet reform at home and a vigorous foreign policy abroad. The latter was designed to meet both his own inclination and the demand of the South for room to expand its institutions, perhaps into Cuba, Mexico, and Nicaragua. Buchanan hoped, moreover, that the problem of slavery in the territories was on the point of solution.

Prompted by the president, the Supreme Court undertook to bring the issue into its orbit and thereby, hopefully, to remove it from partisan politics. In the Dred Scott case the Court ruled that the Missouri Compromise, already superseded by the Kansas-Nebraska Act, had been unconstitutional and that Congress had no authority to outlaw slavery in the territories. In fact, the case concerned the freedom of Dred Scott, a slave. Since the issue of territorial legislation by Congress was not formally before the Court it can be argued that its ruling on the matter was not binding. But Buchanan and most southern Democrats regarded it as binding and hoped naively that all parties would adhere to it. That was not to be. Republicans refused to regard the decision as final and pledged themselves to secure its overthrow. Many northern and some southern Democrats declared that it was irrelevant, and argued that slavery needed the positive protection of favorable legislation in order to survive in a socially hostile environment: a territorial legislature had only to refuse to pass such legislation to outlaw the institution. The Dred Scott decision had no practical impact upon slavery but, emanating as it did from a southern-dominated Court, it enhanced sectional animosities. Northerners saw it as further evidence of a conspiracy to enlarge the power of the ''slavocracy'' while southerners regarded the northern response as evidence of lawlessness and aggression.

Political Maneuvers in Kansas

Buchanan's hopes of a workable solution to the Kansas problem were further undermined by events in Kansas itself. He had appointed as governor of the territory Robert J. Walker. Walker was a man of considerable prestige, still-smoldering political ambition, and committed Democratic allegiance. His appointment signaled the determination of the administration to win over Kansas to the Democratic party even if it could not be won over to slavery, for it seemed inevitable that Kansas would achieve statehood before the next presidential election. But Walker's own ambition and stature had made him reluctant to tackle the job, and when he eventually agreed he did so on his own terms. He made it clear, publicly,

The Dred Scott Case

In his inaugural speech of March 4, 1857, President James Buchanan announced that the slavery issue would soon be ''speedily and finally'' resolved by a forthcoming Supreme Court decision which he urged the nation to accept. It was an inauspicious start, for the Court's finding, revealed two days later, has gone down as among the most disputed in American legal history.

In the 1830s Dred Scott, a slave, was the servant of Dr John Emerson of St Louis, Missouri. When Emerson joined the army as a surgeon he was posted in 1834 to Illinois (where slavery was barred by the Ordinance of 1787) and later to Fort Snelling in Wisconsin Territory (where it had been outlawed by the 1820 Missouri Compromise). Both men later returned to Missouri. After his master's death, Scott sued for freedom on the grounds that he had lived for the best part of four years in free territory. The lower court in Missouri found in favor of Scott but this was reversed by the state supreme court. The case was contested next in the federal district court and finally in the Supreme Court.

The majority decision of the Court, five of whose nine members were southerners, went against Scott on three points. A slave was not a citizen of the United States, it said, and so could not sue in a federal court; because Scott was a resident of a slave state when the action was begun, the law of Illinois was irrelevant; and finally, residence in a territory where slavery had been barred did not make a slave free, for Congress could not deprive a citizen of property without due process of law. This last held the Missouri Compromise to be unconstitutional. (Only once before, in 1803, had an act of Congress been declared unconstitutional.)

The findings were legally dubious. In many northern states Negroes were viewed as citizens with access to the courts, and congressional power to legislate on the issue of slavery in the territories had been recognized for seventy years. Theoretically, slavery was now permitted in all territories and could not be barred until statehood was achieved.

The decision of the Court was later annulled by the Thirteenth and Fourteenth Amendments to the Constitution, but the immediate consequence was a new spur to bitter sectional debate.

A PUBLIC MEETING
WILL BE HELD ON
THURSDAY EVENING, 2D INSTANT,
at 7½ o'clock, in ISRAEL CHURCH, to consider the atrocious decision of the Supreme Court in the

DRED SCOTT CASE,
and other outrages to which the colored people are subject under the Constitution of the United States.

C. L. REMOND,
ROBERT PURVIS,
and others will be speakers on the occasion. Mrs. MOTT, Mr. M'KIM and R. S. JONES of Ohio, have also accepted invitations to be present. All persons are invited to attend. Admittance free.

Top: Dred Scott and his wife, Harriet. The couple met and were married during the period Scott spent in Wisconsin Territory. Although the case went against him, Scott was freed with his family on the death of his owner, ten weeks after the Supreme Court's decision. Above: A broadside for a Philadelphia meeting called to protest against the verdict. The Court's ruling inflamed sectional feeling in the North. Left: a caricature of President Buchanan. In a breach of legal ethics, two justices of the Court advised him in advance of the decision.

Robert J. Walker was governor of Kansas for a brief period in 1857. He resigned when the president endorsed the proslavery Lecompton constitution.

of courts operating on the basis of the Dred Scott decision. Southern pressure was applied to the delegates to bypass the people and submit the constitution direct to Congress along with an application for admission to the Union. Although it was far from universal practice to submit the constitutions of new states to the people for ratification, the administration realized that a failure to do so in this instance would be political dynamite. It persuaded the delegates to accept a compromise. Existing slavery was guaranteed in a constitution which was not to be submitted for popular ratification. However, the people would be asked to vote on the question of whether or not to permit any extension of the institution.

It was an unhappy compromise and won little approval. The president favored it, but he was under great political pressure owing to the financial panic and was inclined to clutch at straws. Southern Democrats were prepared to go along but northern Democrats were in a difficult position. While most southern states held their elections in odd years most of the northern states had elections in 1858 and it was clear that the Lecompton constitution, drawn up by a fraudulently elected and unrepresentative convention, was greatly unpopular. Buchanan thought that the admission of Kansas under the Lecompton constitution would take the issue of slavery expansion out of national politics and would kill the Republican party. Douglas and his supporters were convinced that acceptance of it by northern Democrats would virtually hand over power in the North to the Republicans. But the president was determined to have his way. Without consulting Douglas, although he was chairman of the Senate Committee on Territories, he declared himself in favor of admission under the Lecompton constitution.

The president endorsed the constitution in his annual address to Congress on December 8, 1857. Douglas counterattacked the following day by declaring the constitution fraudulent and a mockery of popular sovereignty. His attack was reinforced by the action of the recently elected, free-soil dominated legislature in Kansas which demanded a referendum on the measure and set aside a day in January for that purpose. Governor Walker resigned and attacked Buchanan's action. On December 21, 1857, voting took place on the referendum called by the Lecompton convention on the single issue of slavery extension. There was a proslavery majority of 6,143 to 569 votes. On January 4, 1858, the free-soil organized referendum showed a majority of 10,266 to 162 votes in favor of rejecting the Lecompton constitution outright. Southerners demanded that Buchanan accept the former

that Kansas was sufficiently near statehood for the people to decide the issue of slavery for themselves. And he was determined to ensure a fair referendum on the subject. In his inaugural address as governor, moreover, he alarmed much of the South when he indicated his belief that the boundaries of slavery were naturally determined by climate and geography and argued that the institution could never be viable in Kansas. On his arrival in the territory Walker managed to prevail upon the free-state settlers to acquiesce in the convention called by proslavery men to meet in Lecompton for the purpose of drafting a state constitution. It was too late for them to participate since many had refused to register, but he promised that the constitution would be submitted to the people for their approval. He also persuaded them to participate in the October elections for a territorial legislature. That was to be the first election in Kansas in which both proslavery and free-state settlers had participated fully.

The election passed peacefully but with such obvious frauds by proslavery Democrats that Walker refused to accept the returns from some districts. His action resulted in the failure of the Democrats to win control of the legislature and was met with outrage from most southern and some northern Democrats. Meanwhile, the constitutional convention met at Lecompton. It was composed of relatively low-calibre, proslavery men who would not listen to Walker's advice. He urged them to omit all mention of slavery and place the future of the institution in the hands

Right: Wall Street during the 1857 panic, set off by the failure of a major insurance company. Although the crisis was short lived, it added to the problems facing President Buchanan, already hard pressed over Kansas.

vote as legally binding; northern Democrats urged him to accept the latter as consistent with a policy of popular sovereignty. Douglas had behind him a solid block of anti-Lecompton Democrats and he cooperated fully with the Republicans in a campaign to defeat the administration and prevent the admission of Kansas without a submission of the constitution to the people.

The struggle lasted to the end of March. It was brought to a conclusion only by further compromise—the so-called English bill. (William English of Indiana was chairman of the conference committee which drew up the compromise.) Under it there would be an effective resubmission of the constitution to the people but not ostensibly on the question of slavery. The Lecompton delegates had demanded a land grant from the federal government some four times larger than was normal for new states. Under the terms of the English compromise the people would be able to vote to accept a normal land grant and immediate admission, or to postpone the whole question to a later day. The slavery issue was thus implicit rather than explicit. But it was to prove a costly measure for the Democratic party. Southern radicals opposed any action which would kill slavery in Kansas under whatever disguise the death blow was concealed. Many northern Democrats rejected the compromise outright: their antisouthern stand had proved very popular with the electorate from which they had shortly to seek endorsement. The Democratic party had been torn asunder.

Divisive Economic Issues

The final battle over Lecompton took place in Kansas in August 1858 when the referendum was held. The Lecompton constitution was rejected by a large majority which preferred to delay entry into the Union rather than accept slavery. But already by then it had become clear that the struggle had precipitated a crisis in the nation's sectional relationships. Two decades earlier antislavery men had proclaimed the existence of a Slave Power thirsting for control of the country's destiny. The Kansas-Nebraska Act and subsequent events had made that a popular theme throughout the eastern states and the northern parts of the middle and western states. In sloughing off its free-soil wing the Democratic party had achieved greater unity. But at the same time the dominance of the southern wing had become both greater and more obvious. Its determination to make the Democratic party its instrument and mouthpiece was viewed with alarm. The supercession of the Missouri Compromise in the Kansas-Nebraska Act, followed so soon by the Dred Scott decision and the attempt to force the unpopular Lecompton constitution upon an unwilling people, seemed to many to be convincing evidence of a determination in the South to make

the West in its own image and thereby to win control of the nation. There was real fear, moreover, that the South's intentions did not stop there. Might not the Supreme Court go on to rule that state legislatures had as little right to outlaw slavery as territorial legislatures?

Antisouthernism had become a powerful force and in the process it came to comprehend rather more than the slavery issue which gave it life. Increasingly the opposition to federally sponsored internal improvements was viewed in sectional terms as emanating from the South. Similarly, the South was castigated for its opposition to protective tariffs and cheap land policies. The panic of 1857 and the ensuing recession sharpened that hostility. Many manufacturing interests in the North and West demanded a protective tariff and urged that full employment could not be restored without it. Westerners argued for a program of internal improvements both to stimulate employment and to enrich the West by integrating it into the increasingly market-oriented economy of the nation. For similar reasons they declared in favor of free homesteads for western settlers. The South, on the other hand, was relatively untouched by the recession. Indeed, good cotton harvests had resulted in better than average prosperity. More and more southerners saw the prosperity of their section, and the distress of other sections, as evidence of the superiority of the southern economy and the southern way of life. They tended to compare the condition of their slaves favorably with those of northern wage earners who had no security. At precisely the moment that northern sentiment was hardening into an antisouthern mold it was confronted by a unified South extolling the virtues of slavery and an agricultural economy. The slavery issue, and the sectional bitterness that resulted, proved too strong to be eclipsed by the recession. Instead of dominating the political scene in their own right, economic issues merely sharpened the sectional animosities which already existed. The failure of the panic and recession to divert attention from slavery is indication enough that a crisis was fast approaching.

Lincoln Challenges Douglas

The theme of approaching crisis provided an important element of Abraham Lincoln's electoral campaign strategy in 1858. Along with many other important northern states, Illinois was in the throes of electioneering. Lincoln had failed to secure election to the Senate in 1854 but he now had high hopes of wresting Douglas's Senate seat from him. Buchanan had carried Illinois in 1856 by only the most narrow of margins, and on a minority vote. Douglas was in open conflict with the administration and seemed vulnerable. But the political situation was more confused than it appeared. Douglas's cooperation with Republicans in Washington during the previous winter, together with his own continued opposition to Lecompton and the English compromise, had endeared him to many eastern Republican leaders. Led by Horace Greeley, they urged Illinois Republicans to endorse Douglas and to refrain from putting up a rival candidate. It was largely as a reaction to pressure from out-of-state Republicans that a convention in Springfield took the unprecedented step of nominating Lincoln as the Republican candidate. The thinking behind this decision was largely Lincoln's own. It appeared to him that the move to recruit Douglas was evidence of a very real danger that the Republican party might destroy itself.

Douglas had adopted two positions in 1857–58 which threatened to erode Republican party support. In the summer of 1857 he denied that the Dred Scott decision repudiated both the free-soil policy of the Republicans and the popular sovereignty lauded by Douglas Democrats. Douglas responded by arguing that slavery depended for its survival upon positive law and that a territorial legislature might refuse to enact such legislation. Many southerners subscribed in practice to a similar belief. They thus played down the significance of the Dred Scott decision. In his opposition to Lecompton, Douglas further nibbled at Republican support for he was able to tap the same well of antisouthern sentiment which sustained his opponents. Indeed, he had often been tempted to mend his fences with the administration only to be restrained by evidence of the enormous popularity of his antiadministration and antisouthern stand. When he arrived in Chicago from Washington in July 1858 he left behind him concerted attempts to heal the breach in the Democratic ranks. But his journey to Illinois, and through the state, had convinced him that only a continued opposition to the southern-oriented administration would give him any hope of victory. As a consequence he renewed his assault upon Buchanan's Lecompton policy and thereby destroyed all hope of party unity. For Lincoln and his supporters, however, opposition to the administration was insufficient reason to endorse Douglas. They were alarmed at the call for Republicans to rally behind the Douglas banner for it implied that there was no essential difference between Republican free soilism and Douglas's popular sovereignty. The main thrust of Lincoln's campaign was to spell out what he conceived to be fundamental differences and thereby to define the essence of Republicanism.

The campaign was an unusual and significant one from the start. Interest naturally focused upon Douglas for he had been in the national limelight for a decade. His opponent was unknown beyond the boundaries of the state and he had held no public office since 1849. Illinois was a crucial state. In the first place, it was marginal and the way it voted in 1860 could well determine the outcome of the presidential election. But out-of-state Democrats were not at all sure that a party rebel, like Douglas, was more desirable than a Republican nonentity. Douglas's showing would be a clear indication of the degree of antiadministration feeling among northwestern Democrats. In the second place, Illinois was in some respects a microcosm of the nation. It was a rapidly growing state which doubled its population during the 1850s and became the fourth largest by 1860. The northern portion was settled largely by New Englanders and other northerners. It was experiencing great industrial and urban growth, and was intensely antislavery and antisouthern. The southern portion of the state was settled largely by southerners with southern sympathies. It was relatively backward and poor and was becoming proportionately less powerful. The middle counties were mixed and appeared similar in composition to the middle states of the Union. They were marginal in their political allegiance and held the balance in the state as a whole. What happened in Illinois in 1858 might prove a reliable pointer to what would happen in the nation at large in 1860.

Debating the Issues

Lincoln was nominated on June 16, 1858. He accepted the nomination the same evening in a speech which has achieved fame as the "House Divided speech." In it he argued that existing divisions threatened the very existence of the Union which, he declared, could not survive forever "half-slave and half-free." He expressed his belief that the Union would survive and that it would do so by becoming all one thing or all the other. He observed a present tendency toward the spread of slavery and pledged the Republican party to seek a solution which would reverse this tendency and which would ensure the "ultimate extinction" of slavery and the triumph of liberty within the United States. The precise meaning of some of his utterances was not fully clarified until later in the campaign, but his general purpose was clear from the outset. He sought to level Republican guns not merely at the administration but, more particularly, at Douglas's popular sovereignty. Over the next two years he was to be absolutely consistent in his argument that the issue was a moral one. Republicans believed slavery was wrong; believing it to be wrong they were committed to the prevention of its further expansion. While constrained by the Constitution to tolerate it in existing states they were confident that if its expansion was checked it must eventually suffocate under its own weight. Conversely, he argued that popular sovereignty was morally indifferent to slavery. As a result it offered an inadequate barrier to future expansion of the institution. In a speech delivered at the Cooper Institute, New York, in February 1860, Lincoln was to argue that popular sovereignty was insidious in its effects and that it posed a greater threat than southern radicalism. If it did nothing else the campaign of 1858 involved an attempt by Lincoln to define the nature of the Republican commitment and to prevent its erosion by Douglas Democrats.

The House Divided speech was a sharp challenge to Douglas and he accepted it as such. Challenged further to stump the state with Lincoln in a form of continuous debate he refused, but he did agree to a limited number of joint debates. It proved to be a fierce campaign which drew huge crowds, generated great warmth, and aroused considerable national interest. Douglas adopted a simple strategy. He attempted to brand Lincoln as a dangerous radical who preached sectional warfare and desired a national uniformity. He exploited the strong anti-Negro prejudice to be found throughout the state and accused Lincoln of desiring to establish full racial equality. He reasserted his own belief in popular sovereignty, in the irrelevance of the Dred Scott decision, in the inferiority of the Negro, and in the fundamental diversity of the American character and customs.

For his part, Lincoln denied he was a radical. He argued that in seeking to restrict the expansion of slavery he was reverting to the policy of the Founding Fathers who, in the Northwest Ordinance of 1787, had sought the same end. He accepted the constitutional right of the South to an effective fugitive slave law. He denied his intention or desire to interfere with slavery in existing states. The racial issue was a delicate one for the intensity of anti-Negro prejudice was too strong to ignore. Lincoln, to some extent, shared that prejudice. He denied that he favored racial equality—on the contrary, he supported discriminatory legislation—but he refused to succumb entirely to the prejudices of his time. He insisted that Negroes were entitled to those rights guaranteed in the Declaration of Independence: to freedom and the right to work for their own benefit and happiness. One theme recurred again and again: he emphasized the moral basis of Republican policy and the amorality of popular sovereignty. He sought to associate Douglas with the slave interest and argued that the recent aggressiveness of the "slavocracy" was the work of Pierce, Buchanan, Chief Justice Taney, and Douglas himself.

Although Douglas was opposed by the administration as well as by the Republicans he was in full control of his state Democratic party. Buchanan Democrats polled only 2 per cent of the votes cast. The Republicans won a plurality of the votes with a margin of some 5,000 over Douglas Democrats. Although this gave them the important state offices being contested it was insufficient to win the Senate seat for Lincoln. The legislature would pick the winner and not all the legislative seats were up for election: a majority of those not so up were occupied by Democrats. Coupled with an inequitable distribution this was enough to ensure Douglas his reelection. But it was a Pyrrhic victory. It was not that Douglas had said

Illinois State Historical Library

Abraham Lincoln is shown speaking at Charleston, Illinois, in September 1858 in this painting by Robert Marshall Root. Stephen A. Douglas sits on Lincoln's right. Lincoln, the Republican candidate for the Senate, had challenged the Democratic incumbent to a series of debates which were held throughout the state from August 21 to October 15. At Ottawa, Freeport, Jonesboro, Charleston, Galesburg, Quincy, and Alton the candidates spelled out their position on the issues of the day. Up to 12,000 people turned out each time. There were street parades with cheering supporters and blaring bands. Douglas, the polished professional, was

short and stocky, snappily dressed in the latest fashion. He exuded enthusiasm and vigor. Lincoln, by contrast, was tall and thin. His clothes were ill fitting and looked well worn. He seemed stiff and awkward and spoke slowly. Slavery dominated the debates. Lincoln hammered the moral aspect: the basic quarrel was between "men who think slavery a wrong and those who do not." For Douglas this was irrelevant: the nation could exist "forever divided into free and slave states, as our fathers made it." Lincoln said Congress had a right and a duty to prohibit slavery in the territories, but states could still decide whether or not to permit it. Whenever slavery had been limited to existing bounds, he said, there had been peace. "All the trouble and convulsion has proceeded from efforts to spread it over more territory." He did not favor social and political equality between the races. Like Douglas, he believed in the inherent superiority of whites. But, unlike his opponent, Lincoln saw no reason "why the negro is not entitled to all the natural rights enumerated in the Declaration of Independence." Lincoln failed to unseat Douglas, but he earned a national reputation. The result, he said later, was "a slip not a fall."

anything particularly new during the campaign but that he had insisted upon maintaining his feud with Buchanan. That feud had guaranteed him support in Illinois at the cost of alienating a large section of the party in Washington. When he returned to the capital in January 1859 he was stripped of his chairmanship of the Senate Committee on Territories and soundly berated by the southern wing of the party, led by Jefferson Davis. Lincoln, on the other hand, had lost another election and earned a national reputation. He had managed to hold the Republican line even against so formidable an opponent as Douglas despite the latter's exploitation of antisouthern feeling. It was not an inconsiderable achievement.

The Darkening Horizon

While Lincoln and Douglas had been fighting it out in Illinois, election campaigns had been in progress in other northern states. The Democrats came out of them badly. In the vulnerable states of the middle belt their performance was not encouraging. They lost ground in Ohio and Indiana and were routed in Pennsylvania and New York. Even when they won seats in those states it was often a Douglas Democrat who was returned. With a net loss of eighteen seats and the return of more anti-Lecompton men the administration had lost control of Congress. That loss of control was soon to be exacerbated by revolts within the Democratic ranks. Pennsylvania Democrats were acutely aware of the problems of campaigning in an area particularly hard hit by the economic recession and suffering extensive unemployment. They urged that the future loyalty of the state to the Democratic party depended upon the passage of a protective tariff in order to boost the ailing iron industry. They bolted the party and determined to remain in opposition until such a tariff was enacted. They were unable to carry the party with them. Western Democrats watched as Douglas was stripped of his committee chairmanship and his followers and supporters were denied federal patronage. They found themselves vigorously opposed by the southern wing of the party which was digging in against demands for internal improvements and homestead legislation. At the same time, the southerners made new demands for a federal slave code in the territories in order to meet the arguments of Douglas and others that slavery could survive only when protected by positive legislation.

The split between radical southerners and Douglas Democrats encouraged conservatives to work toward the creation of a Union party to contest the 1860 elections. In the face of this confused activity, and with a critical presidential election looming ever larger on the horizon, it is not surprising that that session of Congress should prove unfruitful. At the end of it some essential appropriation measures still remained unpassed. As the year wore on nominating conventions were chosen in northern states while southern states held their congressional elections. Political rhetoric grew ever more fierce. Sectional feeling grew in intensity almost daily. When, on the morning of October 16, 1859, news spread across the nation of a raid on the federal arsenal at Harpers Ferry, Virginia, by John Brown and a racially mixed band of abolitionists, emotions were already running high. The news raised those emotions to fever pitch.

It was not emotionalism, however, which had brought the United States to the brink of the abyss. That was the tip of the iceberg. The key to the conflict to come can be found in the growth of northern criticism of the South, the development of southern nationalism, and in the rapid transformation of both into political forms in the 1850s. Southern institutions and culture appeared increasingly to the growing ranks of Republicans to be un-American. Southerners might claim, with some legitimacy, that it was not they but others who had changed since the Revolution. But that was precisely the point. A belief in progress was a major element in mainstream American thought. Northern and western states had transformed their politics from the eighteenth-century republicanism of the Revolution into the democracy of Jackson and his successors. Their inhabitants had built canals, railroads, manufacturing industries, and had turned farming into an ever more business-oriented activity. They were launching wholesale reforms of their school systems, their penal and health institutions, and urban government. Moving daily further away from old-style Jeffersonian agrarianism, they were replacing the concept of equality with one which stressed equality of opportunity. As they transformed the face of the continent, and subtly altered the outlook of its inhabitants, they developed an ambition to spread their ideas, their free institutions, and their people from coast to coast—and perhaps beyond.

Nationalist expansion was not, of course, the preserve of the North and West. The South had driven the nation to war against Mexico and even now hankered after further acquisitions in the Caribbean and Central America. But to Republicans, southern expansionism appeared to be of a rather different character. It carried with it, or sought to embrace in such places as Cuba, not free institutions but slavery, not the American dream but the American nightmare. The future destiny of the nation seemed to hang upon who would control western expansion. It could fairly be argued that slavery would not be able in the Northwest to withstand the pressure of northern settlement, and that the Southwest was too arid for slavery to flourish there. But the annexation of Texas and the Mexican War had raised fundamental issues. The wish of the South to spread slavery westward said something about the health of the institution in existing states. The revolutionary generation had tended to believe that

MISTRESS COLUMBIA, WHO HAS BEEN TAKING A NAP, SUDDENLY WAKES UP AND CALLS HER NOISY SCHOLARS TO ORDER.

At the close of the 1850s the outlook for the Union was at best uncertain. True, a series of crises had been overcome, but the basic quarrel over slavery remained. This January 1860 cartoon comments on the uneasy peace.

slavery was uneconomic and would die a natural death; or that a future generation would be able to come up with a satisfactory solution to the problems it raised; or that somehow it might just go away. The naiveté of such beliefs had been exposed for some by the Missouri crisis of 1819–20; the Texan and Mexican crises had exposed it for others; the territorial problems of the 1850s drove it home to the great majority of northerners. Slavery would not die, nor would it be destroyed, if left in southern hands alone. Lincoln spoke for many when he rejected the vision of an America perpetually pledging itself to freedom and permanently containing within itself the most extensive slavery.

The territorial question had come to encompass rather more than slavery. It embraced hopes and fears for the nation's total future. As they looked to that future Republicans grew more hostile to the South. The South favored slavery. It sought to stifle initiative and opportunity by blocking a cheap land policy in the West that would encourage settlement and growth. Similarly it blocked federally sponsored internal improvements without which, it was argued, a fully integrated national market economy was impossible. Moreover, the South appeared increasingly undemocratic. Its political institutions might be democratic, but at the national level it opposed majority rule in favor of state and minority rights. Territorial expansion thus involved questions of progress, equality of opportunity, the free exercise of initiative, and the meaning of the nation's democratic destiny.

Slavery had provided the motive force toward the development of what Republicans saw to be deviant cultural values and institutions. Largely to protect slavery from northern interference, the South insisted upon a strict construction of the Constitution and thus opposed federal involvement in internal improvements. In defense of its export-oriented staple agriculture it rejected the idea of protective tariffs. But by 1860 the problem had grown even larger. Sectional animosities had developed to the point where an unremitting and mutual suspicion had become endemic. If a free nation depends ultimately for its existence upon a currency of trust and consent then the nation was already bankrupt.

John Brown's Raid

It was a cold, rainy Sunday night when eighteen men left a Maryland farmhouse and began a four-mile trek south. Their fifty-nine-year-old leader rode ahead on a wagon. His followers were armed with rifles which were barely disguised by the shawls that covered them. The date was October 16, 1859; John Brown's raid would soon begin.

For over a decade Brown had been actively involved in the antislavery crusade. Fired by a fanatical religious fervor, he inherited the commitment to abolition from his father. But it was in Kansas that Brown first came to prominence. The brutality of his raiding party's actions at Pottawatomie and his staunch defense of Osawatomie made him a hero to a small group of radical abolitionists.

From these men Brown obtained money for a conspiracy to liberate the Negro from the stranglehold of slavery. He rented a Maryland farm in the summer of 1859 and planned a raid on Harpers Ferry in Virginia, some four miles distant across the Potomac. This was to be the first step of an incredible, crazy plan. Brown aimed to establish a fortified base in the Virginia mountains and set about freeing slaves. This would provide popular support for an alternative government in the South which would then be able to force emancipation. When he set out with his followers, thirteen whites and five blacks, Brown did so as self-styled president and commander in chief of the "provisional government" he had drawn up on paper.

The invaders reached the railroad bridge that spanned the river, captured the sole watchman, and left behind two men as guards. They then slipped into the town. The federal arsenal was a natural objective, for Brown would need arms for the Negroes once they flocked to join his freedom army, as he was sure they would. Furthermore, the town's major industry was the manufacture of weapons and the arsenal, armory, and fire engine-house buildings were grouped together. Brown captured all three, then ordered his men to bring in hostages. Each could be ransomed, said Brown, if replaced by a "stout Negro," but the captives refused. And the hoped-for slave rebellion never took place.

Soon after midnight the Baltimore & Ohio express approached the town. Told that the arsenal was in hostile hands, the conductor refused to take the train any farther. A little later the station baggage master, Shephard Hayward, walked out on to the bridge. He was hit by a rifle shot and died twelve hours later. He was the first victim—and a free Negro.

Brown personally guaranteed the train safe passage and it resumed its eastward journey. From Monocacy the conductor informed Washington officials by telegraph of the situation at Harpers Ferry. President Buchanan then sent a detachment of Marines under Colonel Robert E. Lee who arrived just before Monday midnight. Much earlier in the day the alarm had been raised in the nearby county seat of Charles Town, and the militia and armed citizenry had driven the raiders from their separate strongholds into the enginehouse. Brown tried to bargain with Lee, but refused to surrender. Lee responded by ordering men to batter down the enginehouse door. This

they did and easily took the defenders. During the two-day siege Brown lost ten men, including two of his sons. On the other side, seven were killed.

With his remaining men, Brown was handed over to state authorities. He was indicted a week later on charges of treason, insurrection, and murder. The trial in Charles Town intensified the strong sectional feelings his futile raid had aroused. And throughout the court proceedings the old man played the role of wronged hero superbly well. He lay on a cot, feigning illness from superficial cuts sustained during the battle; he rejected the charges outright, claiming that his sole purpose had been to set slaves free; and from his cell he issued a stream of persuasive letters, many of which were published in the North, setting forth his case. But he was unable to explain away the weapons, the killing, and the political plans he had committed to paper. Furthermore, at the outset he repudiated the plea of insanity his lawyers advanced. It was therefore withdrawn. So, on November 1, after a recess of forty-five minutes, the foreman of the jury announced to a packed, hushed court that Brown was guilty on all counts.

The next day he was sentenced to death. A month later, December 2, he was led from the jail. On his way to the place of execution he handed a prophetic note to one of his guards: "I, John Brown, am now quite certain that the crimes of this guilty land will never be purged away but with Blood. . . ." The governor had ordered a security clampdown and troops ringed the town as the old man mounted the gallows. For fifteen minutes he had to wait while troops took up their positions. Then the trap door opened and he dropped to his death.

To many in the North, Brown became an instant martyr crucified by the evil of slavery; to southerners, he was an insane instrument of aggressive abolitionism. In the North his name would soon be immortalized in song, his soul keep marching on. But for the moment the Richmond *Inquirer* reflected southern feeling when it remarked: "The Harpers Ferry invasion has advanced the cause of Disunion more than any other event that has happened since the formation of the Government."

Left: Troops break into the Harpers Ferry enginehouse. Opposite: Brown was a martyr in northern eyes. This painting shows him leaving his cell for the gallows—as the North imagined it. No Negroes, in fact, were present.

Chapter 5

THE SOUTH SECEDES

Lincoln's victory in the 1860 election was the cue for the lower South to take the decisive steps toward secession from the Union. There had been crises before, but the victory of the Republican candidate—supported as he was by antislavery and antisouthern groups—represented a direct challenge to the South and its way of life. As the Mississippi convention later declared: "The people of the Northern states have assumed a revolutionary position towards the Southern states." Within three months, seven states had broken away, a constitution had been drawn up, and a president and cabinet selected. In a spirit of jubilation a new and confident nation had been formed in the South.

A Dash for Independence

As 1859 came to an end many Americans feared for the future. John Brown's raid on Harpers Ferry the previous autumn brought to the forefront all the bitterness between the sections over slavery. In Congress northern and southern politicians glowered at one another, the selection of a House Speaker took weeks to complete and reopened old wounds. In the press newspaper editors exchanged angry words over real and imagined injuries to their sections. Everywhere people were tense and uneasy.

Southerners were particularly apprehensive. Writing in his diary on the last day of the year, agricultural reformer Edmund Ruffin noted: "This year closes with appearances of awful portent to the Southern States & to the whole nation. The leading northern politicians have used the pretence of opposition to negro slavery solely for their own political gain, & selfish objects, until they [have] made fanatics of the majority of every northern state." Like Ruffin, other southerners were determined to resist northern aggression. In towns and villages from the Potomac to the Rio Grande meetings were held to urge a boycott of northern manufactured goods. Vigilance committees were formed to patrol the countryside and militia units were strengthened. In February 1860 the Alabama legislature instructed the governor to call a state convention to consider secession in the event of a Republican victory in the November presidential election. Newspaper editors in other slave states expressed support for Alabama's move and urged their own political leaders to take similar action.

In such an atmosphere of tension and uncertainty the Democratic party held its national nominating convention. As a concession to the southern wing, party leaders chose Charleston, South Carolina, for the 1860 convention. Events soon showed this to be an unfortunate decision. Charleston was the Mecca of southern ideals and traditions. It was, in the words of one historian, "the great cultural center of southernism." The atmosphere of the city was hostile not only to northern men and ideas but also to talk of compromise or conciliation. Charlestonians were determined that the party should choose a candidate and adopt a platform committed to defending slavery.

It was apparent that Stephen A. Douglas had a majority of delegates, mainly northerners, supporting him. Under Democratic rules, however, two-thirds was required for nomination. Opponents of the Illinois senator still hoped to prevent his selection; southern radicals were especially eager to block the "Little Giant." Four years earlier Douglas's candidacy was acceptable to southerners. But his failure to speak out more clearly on the issue of slave protection in the 1858 debates with Lincoln, and his break with President Buchanan over

Kansas, angered the South. When the convention adopted a pro-Douglas platform which was vague on the question of slavery in the territories, William L. Yancey of Alabama, leader of the southern fire-eaters, delivered a bitter speech denouncing the North and demanding new guarantees for the protection of slavery in the territories. Northern delegates were willing to make some concessions, but they were not prepared to accept an ultimatum. "Gentleman of the South," responded Senator George Pugh of Ohio, "you mistake us—you mistake us! We will not do it!"

Once it was clear that northerners would not concede on this issue, delegates from the cotton states withdrew from the hall. The next day the remaining delegates attempted to nominate a candidate, but the convention chairman, Caleb Cushing, ruled that two-thirds of all delegates chosen (rather than two-thirds of those remaining in the convention) was necessary. For two days the Democrats balloted. Douglas received $152\frac{1}{2}$ votes, a majority but not the 202 needed. After fifty-seven ballots the delegates agreed to adjourn and reassemble in Baltimore the following month.

When they did so many of those who had withdrawn at Charleston attempted to retake their seats but were refused. This led to another walkout, not only by the original bolters but also by delegates from the upper South. Several days later they were joined by Cushing, who was succeeded as convention chairman by David Tod of Ohio. The delegates remaining proceeded to nominate Douglas on the second ballot. Senator Benjamin Fitzpatrick, a moderate from Alabama, was chosen as his running mate but declined the nomination. His place on the ticket was given to another southern moderate, Senator Herschel V. Johnson of Georgia.

The southern bolters and a handful of northern sympathizers formed the Constitutional Democratic party. At their convention in Baltimore they selected Vice President John C. Breckinridge of Kentucky and Senator Joseph Lane of Oregon as their nominees for president and vice president. The adopted platform called for the protection of slavery in all the national territories.

The Republican Choice

In May the Republicans held their national convention in Chicago. In many ways the rapidly growing city on Lake Michigan was like the Republican party itself, new, enthusiastic, and little concerned about restraints or dignity. The delegates met in a building specially constructed for the occasion, a two-story affair of rough lumber called the Wigwam. Although raw and ugly, and something of a firetrap, the building was large, spacious, and had excellent acoustics. Ten thousand people, including hundreds of newspaper reporters, crowded in to follow the proceedings.

The split of the Democratic party at Charleston gave fresh hope to prospective Republican candidates. Of those seeking the nomination, Senator Seward of New York was clearly the best known and had the most pledged delegates. A former governor of his state, Seward had a long and distinguished career in public service. His support for a protective tariff, internal improvements, and rights for immigrants had won him many admirers. His campaign manager, the wily Thurlow Weed, had put together an able organization and appeared confident of victory. On the other hand, Seward as a leading opponent of slave expansion in the early 1850s had gained a reputation as an extremist on the slave question that was damaging in the eyes of party moderates.

Salmon P. Chase of Ohio was considered another front runner when the balloting began. Like Seward, a man of high intellect and character, Chase was a veteran leader in the struggle to contain slavery. But he too had made powerful enemies and was considered by many as too radical. Edward Bates of Missouri, Simon Cameron of Pennsylvania, John McLean of Ohio, in addition to

University of South Carolina Collection

Left: John C. Breckinridge was the candidate in 1860 for the breakaway southern Democrats. He took a firm stand on protecting slavery in the territories.

Below: This cartoon shows a cocky Douglas having secured the Democratic nomination despite Buchanan's opposition. Right: The humble background of "Honest Abe," the Republican candidate, is eulogized in this painting of the "rail splitter."

Nathaniel P. Banks of Massachusetts all had some support but mainly within their own state delegations.

Lincoln was clearly the convention "dark horse." The debates with Douglas had given him a national reputation as a serious statesman who understood the nation's most pressing problems. During 1859 Lincoln traveled some 4,000 miles throughout the Old Northwest making speeches and meeting local politicians, newspaper editors, and party leaders. In February 1860 he delivered an extremely important address at the Cooper Union in New York. There he spoke in terms of conciliation and nationalism while denouncing extremists in both North and South. "Even though the southern people will not listen to us," he remarked, "let us calmly consider their demands, and yield to them if, in our deliberate view of our duty, we possibly can." At the same time he reemphasized his opposition to the expansion of slavery.

Lincoln's campaign for the nomination was skillfully managed by an old political friend, Judge David Davis. Davis and his co-workers packed the galleries with supporters who stomped their feet and cheered lustily for the "rail splitter" while Lincoln's managers made arrangements with state delegations for additional support.

Seward led on the first ballot with $173\frac{1}{2}$ votes. Lincoln had 102, Chase 49, Cameron $50\frac{1}{2}$, and Bates 48. On the next ballot Seward picked up 11 votes, but Lincoln gained 79, mainly from Ohio and Pennsylvania. Lincoln's strength increased to $231\frac{1}{2}$ votes on the third ballot and before the roll could be called again enough delegates changed their votes to give him the nomination. Hannibal Hamlin, a political moderate from Maine and close friend of the defeated Seward, was chosen as Lincoln's running mate.

The Republican platform was cleverly written to appeal to northern and western voters. A homestead law providing free land was offered western farmers, and a protective tariff was promised eastern industrialists. The party pledged itself to work for a transcontinental railroad and other internal improvements. Opposition was expressed to the reopening of the African slave trade and to any efforts to legalize slavery.

By kind permission of the British Library/John Freeman

John Bell of Tennessee (left) and Edward Everett of Massachusetts (below) stood as Constitutional Unionist candidates in 1860. They denounced sectional extremists and warned the nation of the danger of disunion. Their platform was silent on slavery and they received most support in border states. Below left: A campaign banner used by the Republicans. Maine senator Hannibal Hamlin had been a Democrat until 1856, when he switched allegiance because of what he regarded as proslavery policies.

Republicans departed from Chicago with much enthusiasm and merrymaking. Murat Halstead, a newspaper reporter who covered the convention, noted that departing railroad passengers "were allowed no rest, but plagued by the thundering jar of cannon, the clamor of drums, the glare of bonfires, and the whooping of the boys, who were delighted with the idea of a candidate for the Presidency who thirty years ago split rails on the Sangamon River . . . and whose neighbors named him 'honest.'" Halstead himself was not impressed with Lincoln's nomination. He described it "the triumph of a presumption of availability over pre-eminence in intellect and unrivaled fame—a success of the ruder qualities of manhood and the more homely attributes of popularity over the arts of a consummate politician and the splendor of accomplished statesmanship."

A Momentous Campaign

Several days before Lincoln's nomination, a group of Whigs and Know-Nothings met in Baltimore to choose their candidates. Calling themselves Constitutional Unionists, they ignored the slavery issue and urged the nation to support the Union, the Constitution, and the laws of the

Dewitt Collection, University of Hartford

land. John Bell, sixty-four-year-old former Speaker of the House from Tennessee, and Edward Everett, sixty-seven-year-old former governor and senator from Massachusetts, were nominated for president and vice president. They were men of the highest character, experience, and intellect, but they evoked little enthusiasm. Their main appeal was in the border states where the other candidates were considered too extreme.

The 1860 campaign for the presidency was unique. Not only were there four major candidates and parties in the field, but emotions ran high and the consequences were enormous. Southerners knew little about Lincoln himself but were convinced that the election of any Republican would result in the destruction of their way of life. The *New Orleans Daily True Delta* declared that Lincoln's election would be "the death knell of the political and social prosperity of the South." The *Charleston Mercury* saw the election as not only the question of "a Democratic or Black Republican President, but union or disunion." Rumors of slave rebellions encouraged by Republican agitators spread throughout the South. A series of fires in Texas were attributed to abolitionists.

Of the four candidates, Douglas was the most active. Despite a recent illness and a sore throat, the "Little Giant" toured the country. During July and August he journeyed to New England, visiting his birthplace in

Vermont and speaking to gatherings of friends and supporters. In September he traveled through Maryland, Virginia, and North Carolina trying to convince voters that his was the voice of moderation and restraint. He swung through the Midwest in October, and in the last days of the campaign moved into the Deep South. He was in Mobile, Alabama, on election day.

Breckinridge, the youngest candidate, and Bell, the oldest, did limited traveling and campaigning. Although Breckinridge had the support of several prominent northerners including President Buchanan, the Kentuckian's main strength rested in the Deep South where R. Barnwell Rhett, Yancey, and other fire-eaters labored in his behalf. Bell's candidacy was also strongest in the South, especially in the border states where the spirit of compromise still prevailed. Bell hoped for a fusion with Douglas Democrats in the North but this never materialized.

Lincoln did no personal campaigning. He remained at his home in Springfield and allowed other Republicans to speak for him. Seward was particularly effective, making

Unlike his opponents, Lincoln did no traveling during the campaign. He chose instead to stay in Springfield, Illinois. This photograph shows the old court house (behind tree at center left) where Lincoln pleaded his clients' cases.

several major addresses during the summer and early autumn. Torchlight parades by young Republican enthusiasts called "Wide-Awakes," picnics, mass meetings and rallies, and laudatory campaign biographies called attention to Lincoln's humble origin, virtuous character, and moderation. The reprinting and circulating of Hinton Rowan Helper's *The Impending Crisis of the South* (an 1857 book written by a nonslaveholder from North Carolina) reminded voters of the evils of slavery. Republican campaigners stressed the economic aspects of their platform and the advantages of free labor in a free society.

By early autumn it was apparent that a Republican victory was imminent. Maine and Vermont voters chose Republican governors in September. Pennsylvania and Indiana voters did likewise in October. Any chances for a fusion between opponents of Lincoln were made impossible by the bitterness between the supporters of Douglas and Breckinridge. Some southerners still hoped that a stalemate might prevent any candidate from securing a majority, thus throwing the contest into the House. But by October this appeared unlikely.

Reaction to Lincoln's Victory

On election night, November 6, it was obvious that Lincoln was sweeping the key northern states and picking up sufficient electoral votes to win. Final results available several days later showed that although Lincoln had received only 39.9 per cent of the popular vote (1,866,452), he had carried every free state and received 180 electoral votes—a majority of 57. Douglas, who had campaigned longer than any other candidate, won only 12 electors, 9 in Missouri and 3 in New Jersey. Breckinridge carried 11 slave states and received 72 electoral votes, while Bell won Virginia, Kentucky, and Tennessee and 39 electoral votes.

Douglas, last in electoral votes, was second in the popular count with 1,376,957. Combining these with the 849,781 votes for Breckinridge, the Democrats together received over 2,200,000 votes, or 47 per cent of the total. Bell's 588,879 popular votes represented only 14 per cent of the overall vote, much less than the 22 per cent received by the Whig-Know-Nothing ticket in 1856.

Above left: Lincoln outsprints his rivals in this pro-Republican cartoon published two months before polling day. The Republicans benefited from the split in the southern vote. Left: The campaign generated great enthusiasm among Republicans, and young supporters staged "Wide-Awake" night rallies in northern cities. Above right: A member of the Wide-Awakes.

Floyd and Marion Rinhart Collection

It is easy to speculate that Lincoln, a minority president, was elected only because of a divided opposition. In fact, if the Douglas-Bell-Breckinridge votes had been combined within each state, Lincoln would still have received 169 electoral votes, a majority of 35.

Lincoln's greatest strength was in the small towns and farms of the North. Voters in the larger cities of the Northwest were more prone to support Douglas and the national Democrats. Although some individual businessmen gave financial support to the Republican cause, the majority were anti-Republican in 1860. And while some immigrants hesitated to endorse Lincoln because of the prominence of former Know-Nothings in the Republican party, most German and Scandinavian voters supported Lincoln.

A smooth and efficient party organization, unlike that in the Frémont campaign four years earlier, contributed to the Republican triumph. By emphasizing economic factors and opposition to the extension of slavery, Republicans convinced northern voters that Lincoln's election would promote freedom and economic growth without a violent upheaval or civil conflict. A vote for Lincoln, it was argued, was a vote for progress and moderation.

Even some southerners were willing to concede that Lincoln was not radical on the slave question. Alexander H. Stephens, a congressional leader from Georgia who knew Lincoln from earlier service in the Congress, argued that "he is not a bad man" and "will make as good a President as Fillmore did and better too in my opinion." Some pointed out that Lincoln was born in a slave state, had many personal contacts in the South, and had consistently stated that he did not intend to interfere with slavery in the states where it already existed.

Other southerners emphasized that the Republican party was dominated by abolitionists. They noted that the party included Sumner and that many of its supporters had lauded John Brown. Controlling influence in the new administration, they argued, would not be that of the moderates but of radicals such as Seward (who was still regarded as an extremist in the South) and Chase. Lincoln would be a mere figurehead. Even Stephens was forced to admit that Lincoln's party "may do mischief."

The reaction to Lincoln's election was strongest in South Carolina. The Palmetto State had long been a leader in the fight for southern rights. South Carolinians supported Calhoun and the doctrine of nullification in 1831–32. Twenty years later a state convention, studying the compromise proposals adopted by Congress in 1850, passed a series of resolutions supporting the right of a state to secede. Now in November 1860, South Carolinians were prepared to take their state out of the Union. The legislature had convened on the fifth for the purpose of choosing that state's presidential electors. It received a request from the governor to remain in session to await the outcome of the national election. He asked that a convention be called to consider action by the state should the Republicans be victorious. By November 7, South Carolinians knew that Lincoln had been elected. Six days later the legislature passed a bill calling for the election of delegates to a convention which would meet the third week in December.

Other states in the lower South quickly followed South Carolina's lead. The governor of Alabama announced that he would call elections for a convention immediately after the presidential electors formally selected Lincoln in early December. Special sessions of the Mississippi and Florida legislatures set convention elections for December 20 and 24. Conservatives in Georgia and Louisiana were able to gain brief delays but elections were held in these states on January 2 and 8. In Texas, Governor Sam Houston, the only unionist chief executive in the Deep South, refused to call a special session of the state legislature. Even so, An Address to the People written by leading Texas secessionists called for citizens to take action themselves by electing delegates to a convention in January.

Meanwhile, efforts were being made to calm southern fears. Douglas and other Democratic leaders urged southerners not to give way to hysteria and emotion. They noted that the party had gained sufficient seats in the congressional elections to prevent the Republicans from controlling Congress. Also, the Supreme Court headed by Chief Justice Taney of Maryland was still sympathetic to southern interests.

President Buchanan, in his seventieth year, rather feebly attempted to formulate policies that might delay secession. In his annual message to Congress on December 3, 1860 the president blamed the crisis upon "the long-continued and intemperate interference of the Northern people with the question of slavery in the Southern States." This interference, he argued, had created a sense of insecurity throughout the slave states. He called upon the American people to see that southerners were "let alone and permitted to manage their domestic institutions in their own way." At the same time, Buchanan insisted that secession was illegal: "Such a principle is wholly inconsistent with the history as well as the character of the Federal Constitution." Even so, he believed the federal government had no authority to resist secession. "The power to make war against a State is at variance with the whole spirit and intention of the Constitution," he noted. "The fact is that our Union rests upon public opinion, and can never be cemented by the blood of its citizens shed in civil war." He recommended that Congress adopt new legislation protecting slavery in the national territories and prohibiting any interference with the capture of fugitive slaves. Meanwhile, he intended to enforce all federal laws and protect all federal property.

The Breakaway Begins

Congressmen were divided as to what course should be followed. Those from the Deep South were disturbed at Buchanan's denial of the legality of secession. Many northerners were disappointed at his refusal to take any action to prevent secession. Republicans believed that little could be done until Lincoln took office in March. In their party caucus they agreed to shun all public debates over the controversy and await future developments. By mid-December, however, some of their more outspoken members, such as Ben Wade of Ohio, had departed from this position in order to answer southern fire-eaters.

Northern Democrats and border-state Whigs were anxious for compromise. The House leadership created a special Committee of Thirty-three, consisting of one member from each state, to consider conciliatory measures. In the Senate Vice President Breckinridge appointed a Committee of Thirteen, chaired by Senator Powell from Kentucky and including some of the most influential members of the upper house, to consider the crisis.

On the same day that the Committee of Thirteen was

PUNCH, OR THE LONDON CHARIVARI.—January 19, 1861.

An Ordinance,

To dissolve the Union between the State of South Carolina and other States united with her under the compact entitled, "The Constitution of the United States of America."

We, the People of the State of South Carolina, in Convention assembled, do declare and ordain, and it is hereby declared and ordained,

That the Ordinance adopted by us in Convention, on the twenty-third day of May, in the year of our Lord one thousand seven hundred and eighty-eight, whereby the Constitution of the United States of America was ratified, and also, all Acts and parts of Acts of the General Assembly of this State, ratifying amendments of the said Constitution, are hereby repealed; and that the union now subsisting between South Carolina and other States, under the name of "The United States of America," is hereby dissolved.

EVANS & COGSWELL, PRINTERS, CHARLESTON.

DIVORCE À VINCULO.

Mrs. Carolina Asserts her Right to "Larrup" her Nigger.

Lincoln's election win drew a swift response from the Deep South. A week after polling day, South Carolina began to arrange for a state convention and on December 20 a secession ordinance was carried. Left: South Carolina's ordinance. Above: Cartoon from the English Punch. *Top: A "flag of Independence" was flown in Savannah, Georgia, on November 8. Its legends included "southern rights" and "equality of the states."*

R. Barnwell Rhett was called the "father of secession." He earned the title as a result of his fiery campaign, waged over two decades, for southern independence.

appointed (December 20), the South Carolina convention adopted an ordinance of secession. Consisting of the state's most distinguished citizens, including former governors, senators, and congressmen, the convention had assembled three days earlier in the state capital, but then moved to Charleston because of a smallpox epidemic in Columbia. The ordinance formally dissolving the union between South Carolina and the other states was passed by a unanimous vote of 169–0. A Declaration of the Immediate Causes of Secession and an Address to the Slaveholding States were also approved. The first emphasized recent events that had led South Carolinians to withdraw. The second, written by the "father of secession," R. Barnwell Rhett, reviewed the struggle of the southern people for their rights since the inception of the Constitution. To Rhett and the more extreme members of the convention, the election of Lincoln was merely the last step in a struggle for self-government that the South had been urging for decades.

South Carolina's actions focused attention upon three federal forts in the Charleston area: Castle Pinckney, a small structure on an island near the city itself; Fort Moultrie, a larger but poorly designed fortification on Sullivan's Island; and Fort Sumter, begun years earlier but yet unfinished, on a man-made island at the entrance of the harbor. None of these were properly staffed. Pinckney was held by a caretaker sergeant; Moultrie had seventy-four regulars, but half of these were not available for combat duty; and Sumter was unoccupied except for laborers who were working to complete it. For weeks northern members of Buchanan's cabinet had pressed for reinforcements for the area. But the president had declined to make any moves, fearful that such gestures might lead to trouble. Now commissioners from South Carolina were demanding the surrender of the forts. Buchanan refused to accede to their demands but hoped that bloodshed could be prevented. Major Robert Anderson, a Kentuckian recently assigned to command of the Charleston area, was instructed to avoid acts that might

provoke aggression. He was authorized to transfer his troops to any of the forts if he so desired.

On December 26, Anderson moved his forces to Fort Sumter. Such action he reasoned would put federal forces in a stronger defensive position (since Moultrie could be taken from the rear) and at the same time prevent clashes between his troops and the civilians of Charleston. South Carolina authorities, however, interpreted the movement as an act of aggression. They angrily demanded that Buchanan order Anderson to abandon Sumter and return to Moultrie. Once again the president refused.

Meanwhile, elections held in December gave the secessionists control in the Mississippi, Florida, and Alabama conventions. In each there were futile efforts by conservatives to elect delegates who would either block or delay secession.

A secession ordinance was presented the first day the Mississippi convention met. Its sponsor argued that the Magnolia State should move quickly to join South Carolina in a southern confederacy. Opponents countered with a proposal supporting constitutional guarantees to protect slavery within the Union, but were defeated by a 71–28 vote. They then attempted to amend the secession ordinance by stipulating that the break should become effective only after Alabama, Georgia, Florida, and Louisiana had withdrawn from the Union. Such a proposal, conservatives argued, would lead to greater cooperation between the slave states. Secessionists again marshalled their forces to defeat the delay. A final effort to refer the ordinance to the people in a referendum was similarly rejected. On January 9, the Mississippi convention adopted the ordinance of secession by an 84–15 vote.

The Florida convention assembled four days before the Mississippi body. Conservatives used the same tactics to stall for time as were used in Mississippi, but again to no avail. Separate motions to delay Florida's secession until after Alabama and Georgia had acted and until approved by the state's voters were defeated by comfortable margins. The ordinance of secession was then adopted 62–7 on January 10.

The Alabama convention was in session at the same time. Here, the opponents of immediate secession were stronger than in Mississippi or Florida. Elected from counties in northern Alabama where the spirit of nationalism was strong, these conservatives hoped to refer the question of secession to the voters in a popular referendum. Failing by eight votes, they moved in favor of consultation with the other slave states before withdrawing from the Union. Once again proponents of delay were defeated, so that an ordinance of secession was adopted by a 61–39 vote on January 11. The doors of the convention, closed earlier because of excessive applause for secessionist speakers, were thrown open and a vast crowd poured onto the floor. Patriotic demonstrations continued into the early hours of the following morning.

John J. Crittenden of Kentucky drew up a compromise plan to save the Union. Republican hostility prevented it from coming before the full Senate for consideration.

While residents of Mississippi, Florida, and Alabama determined their course of action, members of Congress considered ways to stem the tide of secession. The Senate Committee of Thirteen began its work in late December. A motion by Senator Jefferson Davis of Mississippi that no proposals be reported to the full Senate unless supported by a majority of both Democratic and Republican committee members was adopted with little difficulty. The committee then began to consider proposals from various senators. The only ones to receive serious support came from John J. Crittenden of Kentucky.

Crittenden proposed six amendments to the federal Constitution. Slavery was to be prohibited in all national territory, now held "or hereafter acquired," north of the line 36°30', and recognized and protected in all territory south of the line. Congress was prohibited from abolishing slavery in places within national jurisdiction which were surrounded by slave states. Slavery was not to be abolished in the District of Columbia. Congress was denied authority to interfere with the interstate slave trade. Slaveholders prevented from recovering fugitive slaves by violence were to be compensated by the federal government. No future amendment to the Constitution was to affect the five preceding articles, or give Congress the right to abolish slavery in the states. Crittenden also recommended repeal of the personal liberty laws and rigid enforcement of the fugitive slave laws.

The proposals received much public support. Letters, petitions, and memorials praised the Kentuckian's efforts. Prominent border state and northern Democrats endorsed his plan. Ex-President Van Buren declared that the six amendments could easily gain ratification. Even northern editor Horace Greeley admitted that a large majority of people favored the recommendations.

Republican leaders were unwilling to endorse the Crittenden proposals. The clause "hereafter acquired" in the first point of the plan they considered particularly objectionable. They believed that such a proviso would subject the nation to numerous filibustering activities in the Caribbean in attempts to add slave territory. Lincoln was especially adamant. Writing to a friend in early December, the president-elect declared: "Let there be no compromise on the question of extending slavery." Later in the month he wrote similarly to another supporter: "There is no political compromise upon it [slavery extension] but which puts us under again, and leaves all our work to do again."

Lincoln was willing to make concessions on other issues. He repeated his belief that states be allowed to maintain slavery, and assured southerners he would not interfere with slavery where it already existed. He agreed with Crittenden and others that the fugitive slave law should be rigidly enforced.

All five Republicans on the Committee of Thirteen voted against the Crittenden proposals. They were joined by Robert Toombs and Jefferson Davis, Democrats from the lower South who had previously announced they would vote for the measures only if a majority of Republicans did. Three northern Democrats and three border-state Democrats voted for the plan. Thus the committee rejected Crittenden's proposals, 7–6. On December 28 it reported to the Senate that it could not agree upon a plan of reconciliation.

Crittenden did not give up. On January 3 he proposed to the Senate that his compromise be submitted to the people in a referendum. Although this suggestion received much praise in the press, neither northern radicals nor southern extremists favored the scheme. Border-state senators worked for modifications that might placate both sides, but to no avail. Both Toombs and Seward denounced Crittenden's efforts. A resolution by Crittenden that the Senate vote on his proposals was defeated when a meaningless substitute was adopted, 25–23. All twenty-five votes for the substitute came from Republicans, who were aided by the abstention of six southern Democrats.

Efforts at conciliation were no more successful in the House. The Committee of Thirty-three was deeply divided. Southern Democrats favored extending the old Missouri Compromise line, with slavery prohibited above and protected below, but were defeated 17–14. Republicans were willing to admit New Mexico as either a free or slave state, but southerners, increasingly aware that climatic factors precluded a large slave population in New Mexico, argued that this was a meaningless gesture. By the middle of January it was obvious that agreement on any serious proposal was impossible. The committee finally agreed to submit several propositions to the full House without any recommendation. Three of these—faithful execution of the fugitive slave law, a constitutional amendment guaranteeing no interference with slavery where it already existed, and jury trial of fugitive slaves in the state from which they fled—were adopted by the House. A fourth proposal, immediate admission of New Mexico, was defeated. Both southern Democrats and northern Republicans agreed that the adopted measures would satisfy no one.

While Congress worked unsuccessfully for compromise, the president worried about Fort Sumter. Repeated demands by the South Carolina commissioners for the surrender of the fort were rejected by Buchanan. In late December several southern members of the cabinet resigned as their states left the Union. They were replaced by northern unionists who urged the president to maintain a firm position in the sectional controversy. The new attorney general, Edwin M. Stanton of Pennsylvania, was particularly determined to preserve the Union and protect federal property. He advised Buchanan to be unyielding and even questioned the propriety of talking with the Carolina commissioners.

Buchanan's increased resolve was illustrated by two events in early January: a stern message to Congress on January 8 in which he again denied the legality of secession, and an attempt to reinforce Major Anderson's beleaguered garrison in Charleston Harbor.

The decision to reinforce Sumter was made by Buchanan and cabinet leaders in consultation with Winfield Scott, the aged commanding general of the army. Although a Virginian, General Scott was a dedicated unionist who opposed secession. Like President Buchanan, he had difficulty in deciding whether coercion or conciliation would be the most effective weapon in maintaining the Union. For the moment, he agreed that efforts should be made to reinforce the Sumter garrison.

The *Brooklyn*, a 2,000-ton, propeller-driven, heavily armed vessel laying off Hampton Roads, Virginia, was assigned the task of carrying reinforcements. Two hundred fully armed and equipped regulars stationed at nearby Fort Monroe would make up the relief force. Plans were laid and all seemed in readiness.

At the last moment General Scott changed the arrangements. The *Brooklyn* was a deep-draft ship that might have trouble crossing the bar at the entrance of Charleston Harbor. And the sailing of 200 regulars would be quickly noticed. With the president's reluctant consent, Scott canceled the *Brooklyn*'s orders and made other plans. A private merchantman, the side-wheeler *Star of the West*, was chartered in New York for $1,250 a day. Extraordinary precautions were taken to maintain secrecy. False papers were taken out showing New Orleans as the destination. Food, supplies, and 200 recruits from Governor's Island were taken aboard under cover of darkness. Late on the night of January 5 the *Star of the West* slipped out of New York Harbor and headed south.

At the same time, a message was sent instructing Major

Below: Southern guns fire on the Star of the West *in Charleston Harbor in January 1860 and repel federal attempts to reinforce Fort Sumter. To the South it was a legitimate response to interference; to the North it was an act of aggression.*

THE "SECESSION MOVEMENT".

Anderson to open fire if the relief ship was attacked. Unfortunately the dispatch, sent by the regular mails, did not reach Anderson who knew nothing about the government's plan. In fact, the War Department received a message from Anderson at this time reporting that his garrison was in fair condition and could hold out for some weeks. Anderson's message caused General Scott to telegraph New York to have the vessel held in port, but Scott's telegram was received too late. The *Star of the West* had already sailed.

Major Anderson did not know that relief was on the way. Nevertheless, several northern newspapers published rumors that the *Star of the West* was being sent to Charleston. On the morning of January 8 Governor Francis Pickens of South Carolina received a telegram from friends in Washington stating that troops had sailed. When the *Star of the West* entered Charleston Harbor the next morning South Carolina guns opened fire from Morris Island and Fort Moultrie. The captain hoisted a large United States flag as if to signal Fort Sumter for assistance. It was expected that Anderson would open fire on the Carolinians. Union artillerists stood ready at their guns, confident that at any moment the order to fire would be given. But Anderson held back, uncertain what course to follow. The *Star of the West*, now under a murderous crossfire, swung around and headed back for

A sizable number of moderates in the Georgia convention urged that a final attempt be made to wring concessions from the North. This cartoon magnified the extent of the state's "deviation."

open water and safety. The South Carolina batteries ceased their fire and Anderson ordered his men back to their quarters. The effort to reinforce Sumter, too little and too late, had failed.

An exchange of charges and counter-charges followed. Major Anderson protested to Governor Pickens, threatening to close the harbor. Southern extremists applauded South Carolina's actions and charged the federal government with being the aggressor. Northern newspapers praised the administration's attempts to reinforce Sumter but voiced disappointment that the efforts failed. Both Anderson and Pickens sent emissaries to President Buchanan defending their positions. For the moment an uneasy truce prevailed.

The Georgia secession convention met one week after the firing on the *Star of the West*. Former congressmen, senators, and governors, and a former secretary of war were among the 301 delegates who assembled in Milledgeville on January 16, 1861. Present were men of national reputation such as Toombs, Herschel V. Johnson, and

137

Alexander H. Stephens. State political leaders included T. R. R. Cobb, Eugenius Nisbet, and Linton Stephens. All in all, the convention was one of the most distinguished gatherings in the state's history.

The importance of Georgia's actions was not lost on contemporaries. The most heavily populated and wealthiest state in the lower South, Georgia had long occupied a position of leadership. Her refusal to break with the Union following the Compromise of 1850 had been a serious blow to the abortive secession movement of the early fifties. The other slave states, and the nation, watched anxiously to see what action Georgia would take.

The convention was divided between immediate secessionists and "cooperationists" who favored some form of delay. Few Georgians debated the legality of secession, but the cooperationists questioned the need for immediate or separate state action. Johnson and Alexander H. Stephens, leaders of the cooperationists, proposed that Georgia and the other slave states present a series of demands to the northern states. These would guarantee protection for slavery in the territories and the interstate slave trade as well as enforcement of the fugitive slave law. Johnson and Stephens argued that if these conditions were not met then the southern states should secede. Toombs and Cobb, speaking for the secessionists, argued that such a proposal was a meaningless gesture and would delay Georgia's entry into the proposed con-

federacy of slave states. After a heated debate, the cooperationist measure was defeated by thirty-one votes. Nisbet, another of the secessionist leaders, now moved for adoption of an ordinance calling for immediate secession. His resolution passed by a 208–89 vote.

Most Georgians greeted the convention's action enthusiastically. Parades, cannon salutes, fireworks, and bonfires marked the occasion. Speakers reminded Georgians of their proud heritage and predicted a glorious future in the confederacy. One delegate who had voted against secession was more fearful of the consequences. Writing his autobiography later, Herschel V. Johnson expressed his feelings: "And so the Rubicon was crossed and the State of Georgia was launched upon a dark, uncertain, dangerous sea. Peals of cannon announced the fact, in a token of exultation. The secessionists were jubilant. I never felt so sad before. The clustering glories of the past thronged my memory, but they were darkened by the gathering gloom of the lowering future."

This painting records the scene in the convention hall at Baton Rouge during the signing of the Louisiana secession ordinance. As in Georgia, a significant number of delegates did not want an immediate break from the Union. But the wave in favor of secession then sweeping the South finally carried the day.

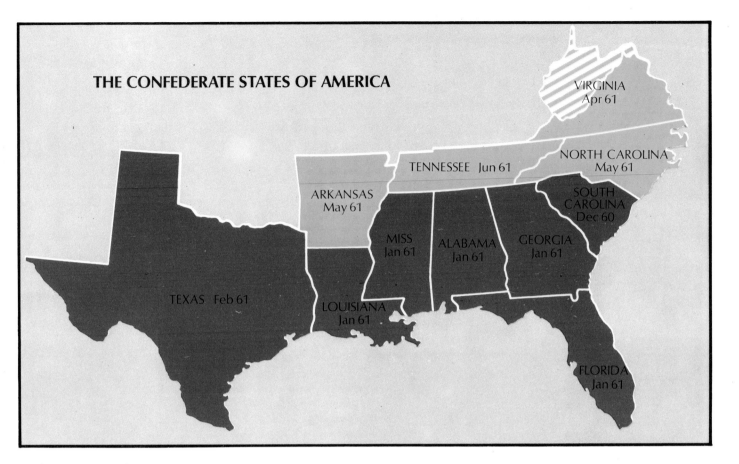

THE CONFEDERATE STATES OF AMERICA

VIRGINIA
Apr 61

TENNESSEE Jun 61

NORTH CAROLINA
May 61

ARKANSAS
May 61

SOUTH
CAROLINA
Dec 60

MISS
Jan 61

ALABAMA
Jan 61

GEORGIA
Jan 61

TEXAS Feb 61

LOUISIANA
Jan 61

FLORIDA
Jan 61

Map showing the states of the Confederacy and the months they voted to break from the Union. The Deep South seceded before the surrender of Fort Sumter on April 14, 1861, and Lincoln's call for volunteers to deal with the "insurrection." In April and May, Virginia, Arkansas, and North Carolina broke away. But West Virginia remained loyal to the Union and was admitted as a separate state in June 1863.

Four days after the passage of the secession ordinance in Georgia, the Louisiana convention assembled in Baton Rouge. As in the other slave states, the membership included former governors, senators, congressmen, and state legislators. One delegate, Richard Taylor, was the son of a president. Of the 130 delegates, 107 were slaveholders, 55 of these owning 20 or more slaves in 1860.

Opposition to immediate secession in Louisiana came from wealthy sugar planters who feared the loss of the protective tariff. Like the Georgia cooperationists, the Louisiana conservatives played for time. They first proposed a series of constitutional guarantees which they would present to the North. Then they urged consultation with the other slave states before secession was attempted. Finally, they moved to refer the work of the convention to the people for ratification. In each case they were defeated by 30 to 40 votes.

Once the delaying tactics of the conservatives were defeated, the secessionists urged that Louisianians rally together in the spirit of harmony. The ordinance of secession was adopted 113–17. Convention president Alexander Mouton then declared "the connection between the State of Louisiana and the Federal Union is dissolved," and that Louisiana was "a free, sovereign, and independent power." The governor and other high-ranking officials marched into the hall bearing the state flag. A prayer for divine guidance was offered. Outside the convention hall bells tolled and bands played. Louisiana's ties with the Union were broken.

Texas was the last state in the lower South to secede. Governor Houston was bitterly opposed to secession. An ardent unionist, Houston at first refused to convene the legislature or call a special convention of the people. Secessionist leaders in the state took matters into their own hands and called upon the people to elect delegates to a convention, with or without the governor's approval. In a desperate effort to forestall the secessionists, Houston called the legislature into special session and recommended that legislators refuse to recognize the proposed state convention. Instead, the legislature endorsed the convention, requiring only that its actions be subject to final approval by the people.

Delegates to the hastily called convention assembled in Austin on January 28, 1861. After listening to addresses delivered by commissioners from South Carolina and Georgia, the convention moved quickly to approve an ordinance of secession by a 166–8 vote. This ordinance was endorsed by the state's voters, 44,317 to 13,020, on February 23.

Texas's action completed the secession of the lower South. In six weeks, seven states had held conventions which cut the ties of their state with the federal Union. In only one state, Texas, were the people given an opportunity to vote directly upon secession. In all states the election contest for convention delegates had been hurried, with the voters subjected to pressure from the secessionists to act quickly before Lincoln was inaugurated. In some states, particularly Louisiana, there was much suspicion that fraud and manipulation occurred in counting the ballots. Even so, the movement for secession in the lower South seems to have had the approval of a majority of the white citizenry. Contemporary newspaper accounts from both secessionist and unionist sources testify to the joyful reception that the news of secession was given in every town and hamlet. For good or bad, citizens of the region believed that their hopes lay outside the Union.

Formation of the Confederacy

A last desperate effort at reconciliation was made in February. At the invitation of the Virginia legislature, twenty-one states sent representatives to a Peace Convention which met in Washington. One hundred and thirty-two delegates participated in the meeting, referred to contemptuously by Greeley as the "Old Gentleman's Convention" because of the advanced age of many of its members. Chairman of the meeting was the seventy-one-year-old former president John Tyler. Included in the membership were many former office holders, including cabinet officers, governors, senators, congressmen, and ambassadors. Notably absent were representatives from the states of the lower South.

For three weeks, members of the Peace Convention considered various schemes for saving the Union. On February 27 it submitted seven proposed constitutional amendments to Congress for consideration. In general they followed the old Crittenden proposals: extension of the Missouri Compromise line to the Pacific, no congressional interference with existing slavery, and compensation to owners prevented from recovering fugitive slaves.

Neither southern fire-eaters nor northern extremists were pleased with the work of the "Old Gentleman's Convention." Leaders of both factions privately advised their friends in Congress to reject the suggested amendments. The House of Representatives refused to suspend its rules to receive the proposals; in the Senate extremists voted down an effort to substitute the work of the convention for Crittenden's plan. Once again the forces of moderation were defeated.

On February 4, the same day the Peace Convention assembled, delegates from the states of the lower South convened in Montgomery, Alabama, for the purpose of creating the Confederate States of America. In contrast to the gloom prevalent in Washington, a spirit of optimism and excitement prevailed. Delegates were confident that a new era of prosperity was beginning for the South.

Within four days the delegates had drafted a new constitution. Then they selected Jefferson Davis of Mississippi as the provisional president of the new confederacy. One of the southern leaders in the Senate during the 1850s, Davis was a political moderate, a factor that would appeal to the states of the upper South still considering secession. A graduate of West Point, veteran of the Mexican War, and former secretary of war, he had extensive military experience. Indeed, he had expected to serve the Confederacy in a military rather than in a political capacity.

Alexander H. Stephens, a veteran member of the House of Representatives, was chosen as vice president. As a member of his state's convention Stephens had opposed immediate secession, but, like many former unionists, was now ready to support the new government. A delegate to the Montgomery convention, Stephens took the oath of office on February 11. Davis received word of his selection at his plantation home, Brierfield, on the Mississippi River. He arrived in Montgomery on Saturday evening, February 16. To the large crowd that greeted him at the railway station he spoke briefly. "Our separation from the Union is complete," he stated. "No compromise and no reconstruction can now be entertained."

The following Monday morning Davis was formally installed as president of the Confederate States of America. In his inaugural message, he emphasized the continuity between the new nation and the old Constitution. "We have changed the constituent parts, but not the system of our government," he declared. "The Constitution formed by our fathers is that of these Confederate States."

The new nation was thus born. A constitution had been written, leaders chosen, and a government organized. Eyes now turned northward to see what course the incoming administration of Abraham Lincoln would pursue and whether the new Confederacy would live in peace or war.

"All we ask is to be left alone": Jefferson Davis makes his inaugural speech as president of the Confederacy. The Deep South embarked on its new course in a spirit of jubilation and optimism.

Chapter 6

BROTHER AGAINST BROTHER

The shelling of Fort Sumter in April 1861 touched off the most traumatic experience in American history. Was the Civil War an inevitable consequence of injustice, misunderstanding, and fear? Was it about slavery or about sovereignty? Was it a laudable crusade or an avoidable catastrophe? Whatever the answers to these questions, as Americans rushed to take up arms against their fellows, few in either camp anticipated a long war of attrition. As is usual at the outbreak of war, each side tried to believe that it was bound to win—and win quickly.

The Struggle in Prospect

A balance sheet of the strengths and weaknesses of the two sides in the Civil War customarily leans heavily in favor of the North. The 1860 national census recorded a population of 22 million in the twenty-three states that were to remain loyal to the Union (including Kansas, which was admitted to the Union in January 1861). The eleven states that formed the Confederacy contained 9 million people. Of these only 5.5 million were white; the other 3.5 million were nearly all Negro slaves. Of the 30,000 miles of railroad track, over 21,000 were in the free states. So were four-fifths of the nation's factories. There was the same imbalance in raw materials: coal, iron, and the new oil industry. Shipbuilding was almost entirely a Northern skill. By every index of wealth, size, and sophistication the North far outstripped the South, and that gap was widening all the time.

On the Southern side of the ledger, there was the fact that even though the four border slave states never joined the Confederacy, a good many of their inhabitants enlisted in its army. Many sympathizers were to be found in the free states, while loyal Northerners living in the far western and northwestern territories were too remote from the physical conflict to play a part. And the Union war effort was weakened by the need to send troops into the West to fight the Indians. There were other factors that involved emotions and traditions rather than statistics but were none the less important.

Northerners as well as Southerners tended to believe at the outset that the slave states produced the best soldiers. Planters and farmers, it was said, knew from boyhood how to ride and shoot. The Southern upper classes had the habit of command. In prewar days their best youngsters had been trained at West Point, the US Military Academy. They dominated the senior posts in the old Union army; the general in chief, old Winfield Scott, was a Virginian, and so were several of his bureau chiefs and field commanders. About 30 per cent of the serving officers in the Union regular army joined the Confederacy—among them that superlative soldier Robert E. Lee, and several Northerners. The Confederate army benefited too from the talent of ex-West Pointers such as Thomas J. "Stonewall" Jackson who had resigned their commissions before the war began and who were in other occupations. Some of these were lawyers, engineers, planters; one, Leonidas Polk, was even an Episcopal bishop. A Charleston newspaper summed up a widespread feeling when it claimed in June 1861 that "our raw troops are far superior to the raw troops of the United States. Our people are used to arms. They are accustomed to the gun and the horse. The people of the North can neither shoot a rifle nor ride a horse, unless trained."

Courtesy Museum of Fine Arts, Boston. M. & M. Karolik Collection

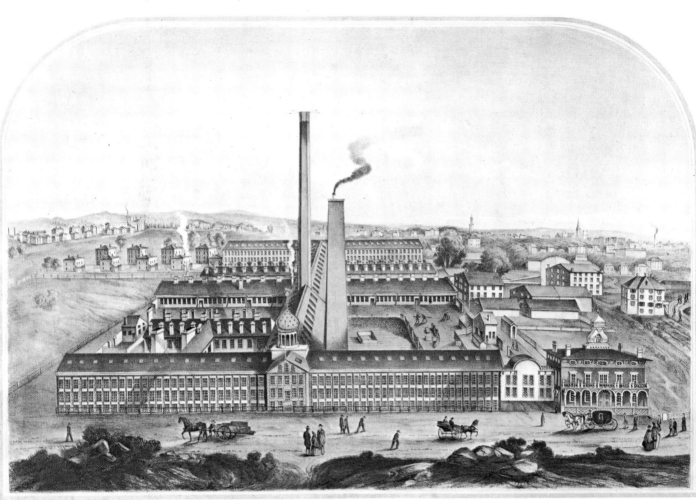

The towering smokestacks of the Colt gun factory at Hartford, Connecticut, symbolize the industrial might of the North. Could the South survive against an adversary vastly superior in wealth, men, and materials?

Fighting spirit, then, seemed higher in the South than in the North on the eve of the war. They had the cream of the old Union army, in the shape of the best officers. The enlisted men among the regulars remained loyal but did not count for much when the whole army numbered only 16,000. Northerners were ready to believe the South had been plotting the war for years, in part by secretly accumulating weapons and ammunition in militia armories. A common Southern claim was that Northern ''free society'' had gone soft, that it was concerned with nothing but swindling and rioting. The evidence suggests that the same criticism was voiced uneasily by Northerners, who were already half-willing to accept statements such as this from a North Carolina newspaper (April 1861): ''The army of the South will be composed of the best material that ever made up an army; whilst that of Lincoln will be gathered from the sewers of the cities—the degraded, beastly offscourings of all quarters of the world, who will serve for pay, and run away . . . when danger threatens them.''

An assessment of prospects in 1860–61 would thus put the material factors on the Northern side, and most of the non-material ones on the side of the South. There are some other considerations, including strategic ones. Even if the

''King Cotton'' dominated the South's economy, and at the outset of the war many considered this a source of strength rather than weakness. Could European nations dependent on cotton fail to support the Confederacy?

slave states were smaller than the free states in area, population, and resources, they were still a large block, far bigger than most European countries. The Confederacy could expand westward into the territories, and perhaps southward as well. Southerners had long grumbled about ''Southern wealth and Northern profits''—that is, about the exploitation of their section by Northern bankers, merchants, and shippers. But if they had control of their own wealth, above all of the profits from cotton production, they could prosper on their own account. Cotton was King not simply because it was easily the biggest single American export item in 1860 but also because the textile mills of the North and of Britain and France were dependent upon it. So, Southern spokesmen insisted, they held the whip hand. Without raw cotton, whole towns in the north of England would starve, and the British government, probably backed by France, would have every reason to try to bring the war to an end. Why should they not recognize the Confederacy as an independent nation?

And if it came to war, how could the North win? The Union had as hopeless and wrongheaded a task as Lord North, the British prime minister who had tried to coerce the colonies in the War of Independence. History provided the lesson that once a proud people came together as a nation, their final triumph was inevitable. The South would be fighting on interior lines, able to concentrate whenever necessary to hold off a thrust from the sprawling, overextended mass of Union formations. The North had some-

145

how to conquer: the South merely needed to resist to survive. That was how General Washington of Virginia had beaten the British in the War of Independence. It was how hopeful Southerners expected to beat "Lord North" in their similar struggle. And, sure enough, the balance sheet helps to explain why an apparently overmatched Confederacy held out for four long years against heavy odds.

The chapters that follow examine in detail the various aspects of the conflict of 1861–65. At this stage, without the benefit of hindsight, we must try to imagine the position as it looked to men on the spot, as they labored to understand what was happening and to decide what must be done. Above all, let us try to enter the mind of Abraham Lincoln, both because he was a representative American of the era and because he was the person on whom the terrible burden of responsibility weighed. And the point to grasp is that, in the nightmarish limbo of 1860–61, he was almost as much in the dark as his fellow citizens.

Hindsight makes us admire him even more for his honest bewilderment. To his contemporaries, though, bombarding him with a host of contradictory proposals, he often looked hopelessly lost. In February 1861, for example, the powerful New York *Herald* advised him not to go to Washington for his inauguration but to resign as president-elect in favor of "some national man who would be acceptable to both sections." The *Herald* added, ominously: "If he persists in his present position, in the teeth of such results as his election must produce, he will totter into a dishonored grave, driven there perhaps by the hands of an assassin. . . ."

Lincoln had been picked by the Republican party as an "available" figure from the middle-western state of Illinois, rather than as an outstanding national personality. On grounds of ability and national prestige some Republicans preferred William H. Seward of New York and continued to think of Seward as the party's real leader. "Honest Abe" won because the Democrats had split into two and because yet another party, the Constitutional Unionists, had come into being. In this four-way contest Lincoln had received not a single popular vote in ten Southern states, and only a sprinkling in the others. In the eyes of the South he was no true president-elect but a sectional, minority politician chosen by the "Black Republicans," who hated slavery and therefore hated the South.

The response from the Deep South was swift. The election was held on November 6. South Carolina's legislature unanimously called for a state convention. This met on December 20 and—again unanimously—agreed to take South Carolina out of the Union, one reason being the election of a president "whose opinions and purposes are hostile to slavery." In the next six weeks South Carolina's lead was followed by Mississippi, Florida, Alabama, Georgia, Louisiana, and Texas. Four other states in the upper South—Virginia, Arkansas, Tennessee, and North Carolina—waited upon events, with the warning that they would resist any attempt by the federal government to use force against any Southern state.

Lincoln's reactions to this dismaying sequence altered from week to week. Immediately before and after the election he cheerfully assured himself and the thickening stream of visitors who began to descend on his Springfield home that there was no serious risk of secession. The "fire-eaters" in South Carolina were bluffing, or else did not speak for the mass of people in the slave states. Then and later, he repeated his conviction that they had no reason to secede. He was no abolitionist; he and his party abided by the Constitution and the laws of the land. They conceded the legal right of slavery to exist in every state where it was already constitutionally approved. They were willing to uphold other laws, such as the one that compelled the return of fugitive slaves to their masters. Encouraged by a Unionist speech delivered in Georgia by Alexander H. Stephens in November 1860, Lincoln corresponded with him. "Do the people of the South," he asked, "really entertain fears that a Republican administration would, *directly*, or *indirectly*, interfere with their slaves? If they do, I wish to assure you, as once a friend, and still, I hope, not an enemy, that there is no cause for such fears."

The trouble was that Southerners *did* distrust the Republicans, and that Lincoln in these crucial weeks refused to make public statements of exactly where he stood. One reason was that until March 4, 1861 he was only president-elect; the federal government was still in the hands of the hesitant James Buchanan and his Democratic administration. In his final message to Congress on December 3, Buchanan said that secession would be unlawful, but that the federal government would be powerless to prevent it by force.

The Last Attempts at Compromise

In this feeble, lame-duck interlude Americans longed for guidance. For answer, there were oblique comments from Mr Lincoln referring his acquaintances to Republican party doctrine. The 1860 party platform, though, could be interpreted in different ways. One plank reaffirmed the Declaration of Independence's phrase that "all men are created equal"—and were not slaves men? Another plank said that each state had the right to control "its own domestic institutions"—and what could that mean but slavery? A third plank insisted that Congress was entitled to decide the conditions on which territories should come into the Union as states: in other words, could insist that they should come in as free and not slave states.

None of these issues was new. There had been angry debates and indeed miniature civil wars during the 1850s over the question of whether a territory such as Kansas should allow slavery. Nor was the instinct to compromise new: for forty years American politics had been built upon

Many in the North suspected that there was truth in the Southern assumption of martial superiority. Opposite: The untried but confident soldiers of the 1st Virginia Regiment pose in early 1861.

the notion of keeping both sides happy—especially the Southerners, since they were the ones who complained most. Faced with secession, many Northerners could only hope that the old scheme was the best: give the Southerners further assurances, and trust to the census returns to weaken the slaveholding component through peaceful evolution. "Let the erring sisters go in peace" was the recommendation of a famous article by Horace Greeley, editor of the New York *Tribune.* They would soon realize that secession was a mistake; or, if "Secessia" did become a viable separate country, then at least the vexed problem of slavery in the Union would have been solved: every remaining state would be free.

More specific moves were made within Congress during that winter. The House of Representatives set up a committee to discuss ideas for ending the crisis; the Senate voted another committee. Senator John J. Crittenden—whose two sons were both to become generals, but on opposite sides—came forward with a compromise formula. The main idea was to extend the old Missouri Compromise line across all the remaining territories. South of 36° 30' would automatically be slave soil; north of it would be free.

The Fundamental Issues

Possibly the formula might have worked. There was a case for insisting that it *must* work, to hold the Union together and avoid the growing risk of an armed clash between North and South. But here Lincoln privately began to stand firm; in sending his conciliatory letter to Alexander Stephens Lincoln added with apparent mildness: "You think slavery is *right* and ought to be extended; while we think it is *wrong* and ought to be restricted. That I suppose is the rub." The disagreement boiled down to whether slavery should be shut out of the huge but empty domain of public lands stretching between Kansas and California. Some thought the issue itself was empty: how could there be plantations in Colorado or New Mexico? But Lincoln believed slavery was liable to spread anywhere that it was not prevented. The South was expansionist, and desperate, and the ordinary white Northerner was threatened with a slave empire, hemming him in and degrading him.

So Lincoln instructed Republican members of the congressional committees that they must stand firm on the territories. Thus, behind the scenes, the president-elect worked to defeat the well-meaning Crittendens. He did not do so lightly. Journalists who watched him in Springfield saw how, little by little, his flow of jokes and genial stories dried up. With each week Lincoln looked paler, wearier, more preoccupied. The prairie lawyer was shut in between the mistakes of the past and the dilemmas of the future. Reasoning with himself, working out the logic of the

evidence, he had reached the first point: no yielding on the matter of the territories. So far as he was concerned, slavery was to go no further. How could he let it, believing slavery to be a moral wrong?

The second point involved secession. Had states dissatisfied with the Union the right to leave it? Here, like Buchanan, his answer was no. He devoted a good portion of his inaugural address to explaining why. The original Union of the States was, he said, meant to be perpetual. Even if it were simply a contract between the individual states, a contract could not be broken in law without the agreement of all the parties to it. Any state that tried to leave the Union was acting unlawfully; and "acts of violence . . . against the authority of the United States, are insurrectionary or revolutionary, according to circumstances." Pleading with Unionists everywhere, Lincoln appealed for the triumph of common sense. The nation belonged to the people. Within the nation the majority will must always prevail, for if it did not, anarchy would result. The people had not given him any authority as president to "fix terms for the separation of the states," though they could do so if they wished. His duty was "to administer the present government, as it came into his hands, and to transmit it, unimpaired by him, to his successor."

The third point, a necessary consequence, was that he would have to confront force with force if the deadlock were not broken. During the early weeks of 1861, as the tally of seceding states multiplied and the Confederacy formed its own constitution and government, he could only hope there would be no war. After all, the upper South had not seceded; there was as yet no fighting; in the state conventions of the lower South the vote against secession had been fairly impressive, considering the heated atmosphere. "Suppose you go to war," Lincoln reminded the South in his inaugural address, "you cannot fight always; and when, after much loss on both sides, and no gain on either, you cease fighting, the identical old questions, as to terms of intercourse, are again upon you." Since in his opinion war would be lunatic, he clung to the faith that his countrymen were not lunatics.

The fourth point in the Lincoln brief was that, while slavery might be the basic cause of secession, and while he and the Republican party thought it morally wrong, it was not the basic issue of the present dispute. He had neither the power nor the desire to force abolition on the South, even if Southern extremists misrepresented him on this. Of course, from where they stood there was precious little difference between a government that disapproved of slavery and one that would work to abolish it. Lincoln, however, argued not about the moral *wrongness* of slavery, but the moral *rightness* of the Union. His sole constitutional commitment as president would be to preserve the Union. All else was an irrelevance, no matter how important in every other context.

So Lincoln groped toward an understanding of his task.

After his ride up Pennsylvania Avenue, Lincoln's inauguration on March 4, 1861 took place beneath the hoists and scaffolding of the unfinished Capitol. Twenty-five thousand people listened as the new president, closely guarded by troops with fixed bayonets, reminded them of his oath ``to preserve, protect, and defend`` the Constitution. When war broke out, some argued that the construction work on the Capitol should be suspended, but Lincoln approved its continuation as a ``sign we intend the Union shall go on.`` Above: Edmund Ruffin, a long-standing and ardent secessionist, who fired the first shot on Fort Sumter. When the Confederacy was defeated, Ruffin committed suicide rather than swear allegiance to the Union.

Major Robert Anderson commanded the small force of Union troops at Fort Sumter. His refusal to obey the Confederate demand to surrender was answered by cannonfire.

For thirty-four hours Fort Sumter endured the bombardment. Then, after firing a ceremonial salute to the flag, Anderson and his men abandoned the fort and surrendered.

149

Yet none of these major principles was much use to him in deciding how to tackle day-to-day problems. Northern newspapers and politicians veered between fury and panic: insisting first that he should break his silence and give a lead; then that he should put the seceders in their place; or else that he should do a deal with them. The mail brought him obscene abuse and threats to kill him. His high-strung, petulant wife was on edge. In February 1861 he, too, seemed to have lost his grip. On February 11, the day before his fifty-second birthday, he set out by train on a zigzag course for Washington, stopping along the route to shake hands and make speeches. His audiences were on the whole disappointed. At first sight Lincoln was a gangling, ugly man with what one observer described as a "plain, plowed, furrowed face." Usually people forgot he was ugly when he began to speak because his intelligence and decency shone through, but on his pre-inaugural tour he hit the wrong note several times. In Columbus, Ohio, for example, his assurance that "there is nothing going wrong . . . there is nothing that really hurts anybody" was ridiculed. Nothing going wrong, when Jefferson Davis was being sworn in as president of the Confederate States of America, and an actress in a Montgomery theater danced upon the Stars and Stripes to wild applause!

Still more lamentable was Lincoln's arrival in Washington, twelve days after he set forth. The District of Columbia lay within slave territory and the presidential train had to pass through pro-Confederate Baltimore. Detectives assigned to Lincoln had picked up rumors of an assassination plot. So he was smuggled into the capital overnight, and taken to Willard's Hotel in the early morning clad in a grotesque outfit that was supposed to disguise him. The Lincoln family remained in the hotel until March 4, the day of the inauguration, besieged by callers. The inaugural ceremony impressed some spectators because of the high quality of Lincoln's speech. Others were depressed by the cold, gray sky, hanging low over the skeletal scaffolding on a Capitol that the builders had not yet finished—a symbol perhaps of a Union never destined to be complete? Congress was not in session, but if it had been seven states would have been conspicuous by their absence.

One of the new president's pressing problems was how to stop other Southern states from deserting to the Stars and Bars. Delaware and Maryland could be physically prevented, if the need came, and possibly one or two other border states including Kentucky—which by chance was the birthplace of both Lincoln and Jefferson Davis. If the Union "coerced" secessionists by trying to retake or even hold on to federal property (customhouses, mail depots, or military bases like Fort Sumter in Charleston harbor), there would be fighting. In the resultant uproar Virginia and the other slave states that had not yet seceded would almost certainly side with the Confederacy. But if Lincoln let these federal properties pass into the hands of the Confederacy he would have been false to his oath of office.

Immediately after Sumter, Lincoln called for 75,000 volunteers to serve for three months to restore order. The appeal to patriotism was strong —and in the first flush of war fever thousands flocked into the army. Left: A Union recruiting poster, capturing the spirit of the time, shows hundreds of smiling Uncle Sams marching across the Potomac into Dixie. Right: A contrast in styles as the gallant young Confederate soldier goes off to war. All the elements of the idealized Southern way of life seem to be on hand: the dignified, if heartbroken, family; the loyal retainers; even the officer's faithful dog. Below: A contemporary sketch by the German-born artist Lewis Miller of a parade of Pennsylvania recruits. Troops both North and South were encouraged to take special pride in their state units, some of which contained a wide variety of immigrants.

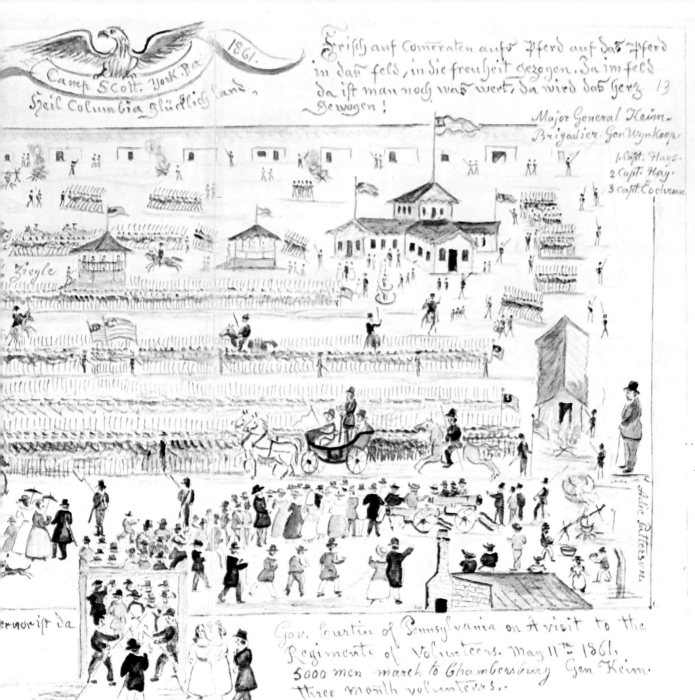

He would have let the victory go to ''Secessia'' by default.

On the other hand, an armed clash would drive much of the upper South away from the Union. The immediate test was Major Robert Anderson and his gun-crews, holed up inside Fort Sumter, within easy range of a formidable assembly of Confederate artillery. Anderson and his garrison would need supplies: should these be sent, or should the fort be surrendered, together with others, as Confederate commissioners were demanding? Most of the advice the president received from his senior chiefs, including General Winfield Scott and Secretary of State Seward, was to evacuate Sumter, or at any rate not to provoke the Confederates. He still seemed dazed by the responsibilities of his new office. But he was methodically, almost stubbornly, sorting out the pros and cons. When he finally acted he did so with a blend of wisdom and guile.

Lincoln's solution was to send ships to Sumter with food only, and to notify the governor of South Carolina in advance. If the supplies were allowed through and Fort Sumter was left alone, it could hold out indefinitely in the very heart of the Confederacy. The South, however, could not accept such a challenge to its presumed sovereignty. On the morning of April 12, before the relief ships could arrive, the guns of Charleston opened up on Sumter. Next day, almost out of ammunition, the battered little fort surrendered. ''You can have no conflict,'' Lincoln had told the South in his inaugural address, ''without being yourselves the aggressors.'' Now the Confederacy had fired the

General Burnside's Union troops attack equally inexperienced Confederates at the First Battle of Bull Run. Initially, it seemed as if the Northerners had the advantage, but then their lines broke. When rumors of disaster spread through the ranks, the troops panicked and fled toward Washington.

first shots. The onus was theirs, as Lincoln had almost certainly planned. He had lost a fort he could not in any case expect to retain for long. But he could now say that the decision for conflict had been taken by the South, in the knowledge that the news of the assault would electrify and unify the North.

Perhaps he still hoped there would be no general war. Perhaps he hoped against hope to bind all the border states to the Union. Instead, Virginia voted for secession on April 17, and Arkansas, Tennessee, and North Carolina a few weeks later. Delaware, Maryland, Kentucky, and Missouri were slave states that stayed loyal. Those that seceded could hardly have been held after Lincoln's swift move of April 15. Within two days of the fall of Sumter he was proclaiming that an ''insurrection'' existed, and calling for 75,000 volunteers, enlisted for three months, to restore order. He soon called for 42,000 additional volunteers to enlist for three years, and provided for increases that would more than double the regular army and navy.

Lincoln could quite possibly have avoided war by supporting Crittenden or other compromisers, but whether

152

Anne S. K. Brown Military Collection

The first obvious military necessity was to defend Washington, precariously placed with Virginia just across the Potomac. A motley collection of volunteer regiments poured into the city and was organized within a few weeks into an army of 30,000 men under General Irvin McDowell. Most of them had been recruited from volunteer militia units; they knew a little about drilling and target-practice but were novices in war. So for that matter were the majority of the 20,000 Confederates under General Pierre G. T. Beauregard who were encamped not far away to the southwest, around Manassas Junction. Off in western Virginia was another Union army of 20,000, commanded by George B. McClellan, an ex-regular soldier, while in between, protecting the Shenandoah Valley, were 15,000 men at Harper's Ferry, under an old militia general named Patterson. Against Patterson stood Joseph E. Johnston's Confederate army of about 10,000 men.

The Battle of Bull Run

As the spring wore into summer Lincoln was under pressure to take the initiative. It was known that the Union forces outnumbered their opponents. Why not have a battle, perhaps *the* battle to crush the rebellion, before the 90-day volunteers had to be sent home again? The Union regiments were in good spirits, and at least as well equipped as the enemy. If Washington was within easy reach of invaders, so after all was the Confederate capital, which had been shifted northward from Montgomery to Richmond, Virginia. Horace Greeley of the New York *Tribune*, recently so reluctant to offend the "erring sisters," had caught the war fever and was printing "FORWARD TO RICHMOND!" on his front page. A dangerous optimism seized the North.

Lincoln, possibly himself overconfident, ordered McDowell to advance. The plan was that Patterson should keep contact with Johnston, leaving McDowell free to attack Beauregard. The operation started with something of the make-believe mood of peacetime maneuvers: blistered feet, squabbles and jokes and boasts, swarms of spectators, music round campfires, officers conferring importantly over maps (except that there were no proper, detailed maps of this patchwork countryside of woods, clearings, and farmsteads linked by dusty lanes). By the evening of July 20 McDowell was within striking distance of Manassas. Before dawn of July 21, a Sunday, his advance columns were crossing the little stream called Bull Run.

What they did not know was that Johnston had given Patterson the slip and was bringing his army by rail to Manassas. There would be no significant advantage in numbers, or not when all of Beauregard's reinforcements had joined him. Even so the fight at first went well for the Union: well enough for newspaper correspondents to begin

that would have brought the Deep South back into the Union is problematical. If Lincoln had acted thus he would probably rank, along with Buchanan and various others, as a president judged guilty of caution verging on cowardice. He was certainly bewildered during the secession winter, but it is hard to see, given his points of principle, that he could have behaved very differently at any particular stage. What is undeniable is that he obeyed his own lawyerlike logic, and without flinching. Perhaps the news of Sumter, awful for what it implied in the way of future bloodshed, was nevertheless a relief to him. At least he could from that moment begin to move forward.

Of course a great deal was still unclear to him, as to nearly every other American. He had almost no idea of how to fight a war, let alone a civil war. His only experience of military affairs had been nearly thirty years earlier, as temporary captain of a comic opera company in the Black Hawk "War" against the Indians, in which he had done no shooting. Tactics and strategy were closed books to him. He had never been in contact with the regular army, and was not heartened by his first dealings with the elderly General Scott or the overworked, fussy desk-men in the War Department, who were suddenly required to organize a war machine bigger than any of them could imagine. He was pestered all day and every day in the White House by hords of handshakers, office-seekers, cranks, officers wanting commissions or promotions, and department heads who had lost their nerve, their temper, or both.

The battlefield and cannon at Manassas, Virginia, the site of the two clashes at Bull Run. For the first, many Washingtonians, in a holiday mood, packed picnic lunches and journeyed across the river in anticipation of an easy Union victory.

preparing their copy to announce a victory. Then the Confederate pressure increased. Here and there in the smoke and din mistakes were made, a line of Union men caved in, rumors spread of disaster elsewhere on the field. Gradually a kind of panic seized whole regiments. Men began withdrawing, then running, throwing away their weapons. The bridge across Bull Run was blocked by a wagon. McDowell's brigadiers lost control. By nightfall his weary, grimy, gloomy troops were in full retreat, pouring back toward Washington, leaving behind four hundred dead, a thousand wounded, and another thousand prisoners.

A few days afterward Greeley sent Lincoln a letter: ''This is my seventh sleepless night—yours too, doubtless. . . . Send me word what to do. I will live till I can hear it, at all events. If it is best for the country and for mankind that we make peace with the rebels at once, and on their own terms, do not shrink even from that. . . .'' Fortunately for the Union, Greeley's frantic reaction was not typical. After all, the First Battle of Bull Run was not a total disgrace: apart from prisoners, the Confederate losses were roughly the same in killed and wounded as those of the Union. Nevertheless it was a blow. It helped to reinforce the secret fears of many in the North that the free states were inferior in fighting capacity to the Southerners.

Lincoln had some hard thinking to do, not for the first or the last time. He had already, sheltering under the powers entrusted to him as commander in chief, asserted an

Crusty old Winfield Scott, a veteran of the War of 1812, was general in chief of the Union army when the war broke out. Scott had a keen grasp of strategy, but was shortly to retire because of poor health.

authority that went far beyond previous presidential claims. He was not entitled, for example, to increase the regular army and navy without the approval of Congress. When Congress came into session at the beginning of July it sanctioned what he had done. One of the many odd things in the career of that strange, humble, proud man was that he did not believe presidents should be allowed much power. All that he knew for sure, in the heartbreaking aftermath of Bull Run, was that he meant to preserve the Union, and must do so on the battlefield.

From Bull Run to Gettysburg

An American army had never suffered such humiliation as did the Federal army at Bull Run.

The battle fought near Manassas Junction, Virginia, was actually indecisive from a military standpoint. Psychologically, the engagement produced definite results. The newly established Confederacy viewed this first "major victory" with a confidence that led to lethargy. Reaction in the North was quite different—and more severe. Federal officials no longer saw this civil war as a momentary disagreement solvable by a single clash of arms. So Lincoln promptly ordered an immediate tightening of the naval blockade of the South, a firmer control of the strategically important border states, and a widespread expansion of all Federal armies. The last-named objective appeared to be the most critical. Accordingly, late in July, Lincoln summoned Major General George B. McClellan to Washington and placed him in charge of reconstructing the shattered remnants of the Bull Run army.

Controversy still swirls around the figure of McClellan. Some historians regard him as a farsighted general who wrought miracles with a demoralized command, only to have his strategy nullified by political meddling. Others view him as a man blinded by ambition—one who wanted the glory without the gore. No one will deny that McClellan was a brilliant organizer of troops. He alone perfected the Army of the Potomac, the most formidable fighting machine the Western Hemisphere had ever seen. Yet he took seven months to organize and polish it, while Lincoln and other Union leaders chafed with impatience.

Meanwhile, the US Navy reacted to war with commendable dispatch. In 1861, America's war fleet consisted of forty-two ships on active duty. The navy's first task was to blockade 3,500 miles of southern coastline. At the same time, the navy was expected to combat all Confederate privateers and blockade-runners while affording protec-

The demoralized troops who fled from Bull Run were reorganized by their new commander, George McClellan. They learned to carry out maneuvers in the field precisely and efficiently, while even the horses, it seems, learned to prance in step.

155

tion to American commercial vessels at sea. It seemed a hopeless task with the number of ships available. Yet Secretary of the Navy Gideon Welles proved to be one of the most unsung heroes of the Civil War. Welles impressed into service every type of vessel "from Captain Noah to Captain Cook." He approved such new warship designs as ironclads, monitors, and steel gunboats. As a result, the navy jumped from 42 vessels in March 1861, to 264 in December 1861, to 671 by the end of 1864. These Federal ships slowly locked the Atlantic and Gulf coasts while simultaneously securing the Mississippi and other strategic rivers. This systematic encirclement of the South was one of the main reasons for the ultimate collapse of the Confederacy.

Naval assaults on Southern seacoast targets further weakened Confederate resistance. They gave the North toeholds on the beaches and fueling stations for its blockading fleets, thereby enabling Federal forces to move easily to other coastal targets. Federal amphibious parties used such "hopscotch" tactics in 1862 to seize Fort Clark and Fort Hatteras plus Roanoke Island in North Carolina, Port Royal, Beaufort, and the vital sea islands of South Carolina, and Fort Pulaski on Georgia's important Savannah River. With the Federal recapture of Norfolk, Virginia also lost its major gateway to the sea.

The Union government could ill afford to ignore the western theater. By an accident of geography, the almost unbroken ranges of the Appalachian Mountains split the South into two areas: the country between the Atlantic and the mountains, and the region lying between the mountains and the Mississippi. In many respects, the western theater was the key to preservation of the Union. If the North could hold Kentucky and Missouri, gain control of the Mississippi, and then strike at the South by means of combined army and navy operations on the network of existing rivers, the western half of the Confederacy could be wrenched away.

Confederate forces in the West were in a dilemma even before the Federals struck. Jefferson Davis had unwisely insisted that every foot of territory be defended. His western commander, General Albert Sidney Johnston, had thus established a 600-mile defensive line that the 48,000 soldiers at his disposal could not adequately man.

Late in January, the Federals initiated their "river war."

THE WESTERN THEATER 1861-63
Railroads - - - - -

St Louis

INDIANA

ILLINOIS

Louisville

Ohio River

MISSOURI

KENTUCKY

Cairo

Island Number 10 April 8, 1862

Ft Henry
February 6, 1862

Ft Donelson February 16, 1862

Nashville

TENNESSEE

Murfreesboro
December 31-January 2, 1863

Memphis, occupied
June 6, 1862

Shiloh
April 6-7, 1862

Tennessee River

ARKANSAS

GEORGIA

Mississippi River

Arkansas River

MISSISSIPPI

Vicksburg
Surrendered July 4, 1863

Meridian

Selma

Jackson

Montgomery

LOUISIANA

ALABAMA

Mobile

FLORIDA

Baton Rouge, occupied
May 12, 1862

New Orleans
April 25-May 1, 1862

Ft St Philip

Ft Jackson
April 24, 1862

Map showing the western theater of operations until the fall of Vicksburg. The war here centered on control of the Mississippi and the river towns. While Grant and his men pushed slowly southward, Farragut's navy—after taking New Orleans—moved northward, clearing the river of Confederate shipping.

This version of the Battle of Shiloh comes from a manufacturer's advertisement. The reaper in the foreground stands unscathed in the midst of total carnage.

At the head of their principal striking force was General Ulysses S. Grant. An unassuming, unpretentious leader, Grant had been a prewar failure in both military and civilian careers. Now given a second chance in the army, Grant quickly discerned that the Cumberland and Tennessee rivers were natural avenues through Tennessee. The Confederates had shortsightedly constructed only a single fort on each stream. Grant's strategy called for a coordinated land and water operation against each stronghold. A flotilla of gunboats would assail a fort from the river while Grant's 15,000-man army struck by land.

For once, tactics equalled strategy. On February 6, 1862, Andrew H. Foote's fleet steamed up the Cumberland River and unleashed a bombardment so severe that Fort Henry surrendered before Grant could get his army into position. Taking Fort Donelson on the Tennessee River proved more difficult. Confederate batteries sent Foote's gunboats limping downriver. Grant was establishing his troop line when, on February 15, Confederates delivered a surprise assault on his right flank. Grant quickly reacted by counterattacking on the other flank. His onslaughts bottled up the Donelson defenders and sealed all escape routes. With Grant offering "no terms but unconditional surrender," the Confederate commander, on February 16, surrendered 12,000 men and 40 pieces of artillery.

The South shuddered in despair at the loss of the two forts. Grant's brief campaign had permanently cracked the great Confederate defense line. It had dashed Southern hopes of obtaining Kentucky. The subsequent fall of Nashville meant the loss of a vital state capital. Union armies could thenceforth utilize the rivers to overrun much of Tennessee. Moreover, the North had found a hero in U. S. Grant, a quiet, cigar-smoking officer who was thereafter called "Unconditional Surrender" Grant.

In the month that followed, Albert Sidney Johnston consolidated and strengthened Confederate forces at Corinth, Mississippi. Grant then started after Johnston via the Tennessee River. The Federal army was encamped at Pittsburg Landing, a few miles from the Mississippi state line, when Johnston daringly launched a heavy assault. The resultant Battle of Shiloh (April 6–7) marked the first time in America that as many as 100,000 men were engaged in combat on a single field. All Confederate hopes at the outset of the battle were based on the element of surprise. It almost worked. Johnston's green troops attacked on three fronts and caught the equally green Union army all but totally unprepared.

The first day's action was vicious and tragically confused. Units became detached and scattered; all semblance of a Union chain of command disintegrated; Johnston bled to death from a minor bullet wound which he overlooked in the heat of battle. The Confederates managed to bend Grant's lines almost to the breaking point, and by nightfall thousands of Federal soldiers were huddled panic-stricken along the riverbank while Southern generals tried to reconcentrate their broken ranks.

That night General Don Carlos Buell's Federal army providentially reached the field. Grant once again demonstrated boldness in the face of disaster. On the following day, the Confederates renewed their assaults; but midway through the ten-hour fight, Grant launched a general counterattack that ultimately broke the enemy's line and drove the Confederates through the rain back to Corinth. Casualties in the two-day holocaust exceeded 23,000 dead and wounded. In many respects, Shiloh was a battle of raw troops and numerous mistakes.

Elsewhere in the West, Federal forces tightened their hold through a series of isolated successes. On March 7–8 at Pea Ridge (or Elkhorn Tavern), Arkansas, Union forces won a sharp victory that gave the North firm control of Missouri and northern Arkansas. (This was one of the few engagements of the Civil War in which sizable numbers of Indians were used in combat.) From March 14 to April 7, an amphibious force under General John Pope secured the upper Mississippi by capturing the strategic posts of New Madrid, Missouri, and Island Number Ten. More than 5,000 Confederate prisoners were taken in these operations. On April 26, Admiral David G. Farragut's fleet captured New Orleans after fighting its way past the city's two river forts. The seizure of that vital port severely restricted Confederate use of the Mississippi River.

While these events were occurring, McClellan in the East had finally begun to move. Month after month had passed while he carefully perfected his Army of the Potomac. Congress, the press, and the public clamored for military action, not military pomp. Lincoln as commander in chief thereupon ordered McClellan to advance against Confederate General Joseph E. Johnston's smaller force at Manassas. McClellan countered with a grandiose proposal: a roundabout move on Richmond by way of Hampton Roads and the peninsula lying between the York and James rivers. This would necessitate transporting the Federal army and all of its equipment and supplies by boat to the Virginia coast. Nevertheless, McClellan was convinced that such a campaign would be less dangerous to execute and far more likely to succeed. Lincoln was unenthusiastic about the plan. Still, some kind of offense was better than none, so he gave reluctant approval.

One naval obstacle stood in McClellan's way. At Hampton Roads the Confederates had converted the former USS *Merrimack* into a revolutionary ironclad battleship which they renamed the *Virginia*. This awesome-looking vessel reigned supreme in the Norfolk harbor— until the Federals sent the *Monitor*, a new ironclad of their own, steaming into the bay. For three hours on March 9, 1862, the two iron monsters hammered at one another before the *Virginia* gave ground. This duel signalled the birth of modern steel navies.

McClellan's massive troop embarkation began a week later. It was the largest armada the world had ever seen.

Courtesy Chicago Historical Society

Island Number Ten in the Mississippi receives a pounding from Federal gun and mortar boats. When bombardment proved fruitless, Union General John Pope decided to bypass the island by digging a canal for his troop transports through swampland to the north.

Some 389 ships were required to transport 112,400 men, 14,600 animals, 1,200 wagons, 220 cannon, and tons of other supplies to the Yorktown area. To McClellan's surprise, Joseph E. Johnston's army had shifted from Manassas and was waiting for him on the tip of the Peninsula. Johnston, a nephew of Patrick Henry, had no peer in waging defensive warfare. He delayed McClellan's advance for a month before withdrawing from the York- town lines. McClellan started forward, but his march ground to a halt at Williamsburg. There, on May 5, Johnston turned and delivered a stunning check on the van of the Federal army before continuing his retreat. A cautious McClellan then moved at a snail's pace up the Peninsula. The countryside became a quagmire from heavy rains. A Federal fleet, protecting McClellan's left, steamed up the James toward Richmond. Confederate batteries atop Drewry's Bluff on a sharp curve below the city repulsed the naval threat.

Johnston retreated to within nine miles of Richmond. On May 31 and June 1, at the hamlet of Seven Pines, Con- federates struck viciously through the mud against McClellan's left flank. Disjointed assaults failed to penetrate the hastily improvised Federal works. Johnston fell seriously wounded in the action, and many among the 10,000 casualties were wounded men who drowned in seemingly depthless mud. Yet the Southern attacks melted McClellan's remaining optimism and brought the Federal advance to a permanent halt.

Forts Jackson and St Philip guarded the entrance to the Mississippi. Six days of bombardment failed to subdue them, so Farragut ordered his fleet to sail past the batteries in darkness. Running the gauntlet of heavy fire, one ship sank—but thirteen came safely through.

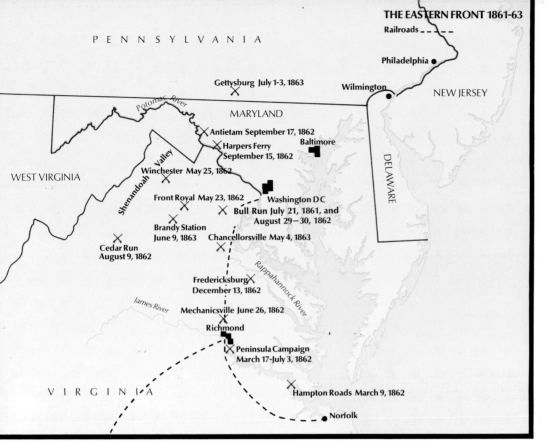

Railroads ‒ ‒ ‒

PENNSYLVANIA

Philadelphia ●

Gettysburg July 1-3, 1863 ✕
Wilmington ●
NEW JERSEY

Potomac River

MARYLAND

✕ Antietam September 17, 1862
✕ Harpers Ferry
September 15, 1862
Baltimore ■

Valley

WEST VIRGINIA

Shenandoah

Winchester May 25, 1862 ✕

DELAWARE

Front Royal May 23, 1862 ✕
Washington DC
✕ Bull Run July 21, 1861, and
August 29–30, 1862

Brandy Station
June 9, 1863 ✕
✕ Chancellorsville May 4, 1863

Cedar Run
August 9, 1862 ✕

Rappahannock River

Fredericksburg ✕
December 13, 1862

James River

Mechanicsville June 26, 1862 ✕

Richmond ■
✕ Peninsula Campaign
March 17-July 3, 1862

VIRGINIA

✕ Hampton Roads March 9, 1862

● Norfolk

Map showing the eastern theater during the early years of the war. Northern Virginia and Maryland bore the brunt of the fighting, which centered on the Union's obsession with capturing the Confederate capital, Richmond.

McClellan continued his anguished cries to Washington for more men. Lincoln was giving consideration to releasing General Irvin McDowell's 40,000 troops at Fredericksburg to McClellan when events in the Shenandoah Valley suddenly threw Washington into consternation.

No area was more strategically important to the eastern theater than a strip of land known variously as the Shenandoah Valley, the Valley of Virginia, and the Valley. It was a 170-mile storehouse of livestock herds, grain fields, and fruit orchards. It was also a natural avenue into both North and South. Any invading army had to have control of it in order to protect its western flank.

Accordingly, a Federal army under General Nathaniel P. Banks had moved into the Valley at the same time as McClellan's shift to the Peninsula. Banks heavily outnumbered the Confederate defenders, but they were under the command of a thirty-eight-year-old general about to achieve stardom. Thomas J. "Stonewall" Jackson was as eccentric in behavior as he was fanatical in religion. His men looked on him with a mixture of awe and affection. He sucked lemons constantly, counseled with none of his subordinates, behaved oddly, and was militarily unpredictable. "I never saw one of Jackson's couriers approach," stated one of his division commanders, "without expecting an order to assault the North Pole."

Late in March 1862, Jackson began a campaign in his beloved Valley that eclipsed all others for daring and ingenuity. His responsibilities were twofold: to protect the Shenandoah and to prevent Federals there from going to McClellan's aid. Thus, when Banks entered the Valley, Jackson went into action with the martial and religious fervor of a resurrected Cromwell. Secretive maneuverings,

hard marches, surprise attacks at unexpected points, unrelenting assaults when the time came to attack—these were the tools that the stern Confederate Calvinist employed.

Three Union armies dispatched to the Valley by Lincoln recoiled from Jackson's onslaughts. Beginning with a check at Kernstown (March 25), Jackson won victories at McDowell (May 7), Front Royal (May 23), Winchester (May 25), Cross Keys (June 8), and Port Republic (June 9). His famed "foot cavalry" tramped 676 miles over rough country in forty-eight marching days. The 16,000 Confederates inflicted 7,000 casualties among the 64,000 Federals campaigning against them. Jackson's 2,500 losses were slight in comparison to the harvests reaped. His troops seized 10,000 needed muskets and tons of supplies, prevented thousands of Federals from joining McClellan, secured the Valley for the Confederacy, and gave the South its first lasting hero.

The scene of action now shifted back to Richmond. President Jefferson Davis was a man of broad military experience. His critics charged that he too often neglected civilian affairs for military matters and that he played favorites with his generals. Both assertions were true. Davis surely evidenced the latter trait to a singular advantage when he bypassed all field commanders and named his military adviser, Robert E. Lee, to succeed the wounded Johnston as leader of the Army of Northern Virginia.

Lee was the son of Revolutionary War hero "Light Horse Harry" Lee and distantly related to George Washington. His distinguished prewar career included an outstanding record at West Point (where he never earned a

Gift of Anton T. and Phillip J. McCook, 1954. Collection of Chrysler Museum at Norfolk, Va

Merrimack Against Monitor

To counter McClellan's ponderous advance against Richmond from his bases on the Yorktown Peninsula the Confederacy had one trump card: the big, tough, steam frigate *Merrimack*, which the retreating Federals had abandoned and burned at her moorings in 1861. Confederate engineers and shipwrights had recovered *Merrimack* and transformed her into the first wonder-weapon of the Civil War: cut down to the waterline, sheathed in armor, and armed with a powerful broadside which would spell death to any fleet of transports which the North dare send within her reach. They also renamed her *Virginia*, but it is by her original name that the mighty ironclad is remembered.

The ship was based on Norfolk, Virginia, which was blockaded by frigates of the Union navy at the outset of the Peninsula campaign. But on March 8, 1862, this all-important blockade was shaken to its foundations. *Merrimack* came out to see what big guns and armor plate could do against the cannon broadsides and wooden hulls of the age of fighting sail.

Captain Franklin Buchanan steered past the frigate *Congress*, exchanging broadsides as he went. The shells from *Congress* bounced harmlessly off *Merri-*

mack's armor and she came surging in to ram the sloop *Cumberland*, ripping open a huge gash below the waterline. As *Cumberland* heeled over she fired three broadsides at *Merrimack*, but even at point-blank range the shells did no damage. *Merrimack* then turned on *Congress* and smashed her into a blazing wreck. By sunset *Merrimack* was in absolute control. It seemed that nothing could stop *Merrimack* from finishing off the two remaining Union ships, *Minnesota* and *Roanoke*, in the morning.

But at the last moment the Union flotilla was saved by the arrival of the North's first ironclad: John Ericsson's experimental *Monitor*. Smaller and more agile than *Merrimack*, *Monitor* had two 11-inch guns in a revolving turret instead of fixed broadsides. Like *Merrimack*, *Monitor* was completely untried. Her first battle was to be the world's first duel between ironclads.

When *Merrimack* came out again on the morning of the 9th she found *Monitor* shielding *Minnesota*. Battle was joined, and for over two hours the two ironclads hammered away at each other, neither able to hurt the other and both constantly in danger of running aground. During the fight *Merrimack* snatched the chance to bombard *Minnesota* and set her

Library of Congress

The Merrimack/Virginia *and the much smaller* Monitor *poured fire at each other for two hours in the world's first clash between ironclads. They fought to a standstill, and the* Merrimack *retired to her base. Above: sailors aboard the* Monitor.

on fire, but *Monitor* closed again and the duel was resumed. It ended about noon in complete stalemate. *Merrimack* returned to base; *Monitor* continued to cover *Minnesota*. The two ironclads never fought again. The Union blockade was restored, and the ironclad age had arrived.

On August 29-31, 1862 Confederate and Union armies clashed again at Bull Run. Lee outmaneuvered Pope's newly reorganized army and sent Federal troops back to the defenses of Washington. The Confederate victory rid Virginia of Northern troops and wiped out all Union advances in that state.

demerit), valorous service in the Mexican War, the superintendency of the US Military Academy, and command of the forces that suppressed John Brown's raid on Harper's Ferry. Lee had opposed both slavery and secession, yet he felt compelled to follow the destiny of his native Virginia. He exuded an aura of authority and leadership. His character was so exalted, his makeup so flawless, that the men in the Army of Northern Virginia openly viewed him with an adoration that became hero worship.

His assumption of army command at last gave Lee the opportunity to demonstrate one of the most brilliant military minds of the age. He was convinced that McClellan had lost all enthusiasm after the bitter clash at Seven Pines. Hence, and in spite of numerical odds against him, Lee decided to abandon defensive strategy and to take the initiative. McClellan's vulnerable point, Lee discovered after a spectacular reconnaissance sweep by Confederate cavalry chief "Jeb" Stuart, was the Federal right flank. It was dangling in the air north of the swollen Chickahominy River. Lee carefully laid plans to shift the Southern army away from McClellan's front and to assail his flank with everything he had. He ordered Jackson's forces to join him with all dispatch. Those reinforcements would give Lee 85,000 men with which to attack a third of McClellan's army. If the Confederates struck hard enough and long enough, the Federals could be routed by a flanking movement and driven southward into the James River.

The ensuing battles of June 25–July 1 are known as the Seven Days' campaign. The fighting began with a premature Confederate assault at Mechanicsville. Federal troops fought valiantly and dealt Lee a bloody repulse. Jackson's men arrived on the field the following day. After a severe engagement at Gaines's Mill, Lee and Jackson finally smashed the Federal lines. Then came desperate fighting at Savage Station and Frayser's Farm as McClellan struggled to get his army out of a death trap. At Malvern Hill, only a stone's throw from the James, McClellan managed to win a victory that marked the end of the Peninsula campaign. Heavy guns of the US Navy in the James now protected McClellan's army, but Lee's forces solidly blocked all further land movements.

The grand Federal effort to capture Richmond had failed. Lee had turned the tide—but at a horrible cost in human life. Richmond became a vast hospital as over 20,000 Confederates fell dead or wounded in the Seven Days. McClellan suffered 15,800 losses during the same period.

McClellan asserted that he had avoided complete defeat. Lincoln asserted that he had avoided complete victory. The president thereupon reshuffled military command in the East. McClellan was ordered to evacuate his army from the mud of the Peninsula to the defenses of Washington. General Henry W. Halleck, an old line officer and author of a well-known text on infantry tactics, came from the West as Lincoln's new general in chief. Also from the West journeyed General John Pope. He was given command of a new Union army composed in the main of Federal units from the Valley and around Washington. Pope's orders called for a new advance through central Virginia along the route followed by McDowell the previous year.

Lee and Jackson responded with teamwork unexcelled in the Civil War. It was obvious that Lee's whole army could not abandon the Peninsula so long as McClellan's forces remained. Yet Pope's advance had to be checked. Lee ordered Jackson's corps to march northward, circle behind Pope's army, and sever all communication and supply lines between Pope and Washington. This would almost certainly cause Pope to veer off in search of Jackson. By then, Lee could move to Jackson's support. Lee was confident that Pope's known cockiness would give way to uncertainty and mistakes once pressure was applied.

This was precisely what happened. On August 9, Jackson struck the van of Pope's army at Cedar Run (or Slaughter Mountain). For once the Confederates enjoyed superior numbers in battle. The engagement, though indecisive, did serve to shake Jackson from a lethargy that had impaired his effectiveness during the Seven Days. "Old Jack" then swung skillfully around Pope's forces. His troops slashed Union communications at Bristoe Station, destroyed Pope's major supply depot at Manassas, and took up position near the 1861 battlefield to await the arrival of Pope's army. The angry and bewildered Union general reversed his march and went in pursuit of Jackson. The search ended at Second Bull Run (August 29–30). On the

Virginia was momentarily free of Federal troops, and the Union high command was in a state of demoralization. A Confederate invasion would take the war away from Virginia and might induce Maryland to cast its lot with the South—thereby isolating Washington. Most importantly, a successful thrust by Lee's army might prove the last, needed element to gain recognition, and aid, from Britain and France.

On September 5, 1862, columns of Confederate soldiers splashed across the Potomac, entered Maryland, and soon occupied Frederick. Panic swept through the North. In desperation, Lincoln fell back on McClellan, whom he ordered with the Army of the Potomac to intercept Lee's invaders. The situation called for the promptest action. Yet McClellan still lacked the aggressiveness—the "killer instinct"—necessary for decisive victory. As the Union army moved cautiously toward western Maryland, Lee again divided his own forces. Jackson and 25,000 troops marched southward to secure Harper's Ferry and the gateway to the Shenandoah Valley. The rest of Lee's army crossed a mountain chain and stopped at Sharpsburg. Even though McClellan chanced accidentally upon a copy of

Library of Congress

first day, Federal soldiers gallantly executed several uncoordinated attacks ordered by Pope. Jackson's men—many of them hurling stones when ammunition ran out—held their ground. The arrival of Lee's army the following day produced a counterattack that drove Pope's forces from the field. The Federals beat off an attack at Chantilly on September 1, and retreated to the defenses of Washington. Pope's army of 73,000 men suffered 14,400 casualties. Lee's losses were 9,400 of 55,000 engaged.

Lee then made the momentous decision to invade the North. The opportunity might never again be so ideal.

The west side of Hagerston Pike is littered with the dead of the Battle of Antietam, September 17, 1862. The bloody standoff forced Lee to retreat, and marked the end of the first Southern invasion of the North.

Lee's orders for the division of the Southern army, the ever-wary Federal general would not exploit the good fortune. He methodically fought his way over South Mountain (September 14) and carefully deployed his army in Lee's front. By the time McClellan was ready for battle, the bulk of Jackson's corps had rejoined Lee.

Confederate Infantry Private: few Confederate infantrymen were able to maintain their regulation uniforms. The habit of wearing the blanket and cape across the body was much less cumbersome than the usual pack and was commended by Stonewall Jackson. The shoes are of undyed leather, with metal-shod wooden soles. His weapon is a British-made Enfield long rifle.

Captain in the Confederate Navy: dressed according to regulations, though the trousers could also be steel gray. **Trooper of Confederate Cavalry:** here shown in regulation uniform, though being well-armed was more important. He is armed with the regulation saber, a Sharp's carbine and twin Colt Army .44 M1860 revolvers.

Admiral D. G. Farragut: the first admiral in the US Navy, shown in full uniform but without the trimmings such as epaulets reserved for ''dress'' occasions.
Trooper of Union Cavalry: as the war progressed the Union cavalry became better equipped and better mounted than the enemy. The broad-brimmed hat could be pushed into a variety of shapes in imitation of popular senior officers. It was often replaced by the kepi.

Union Infantry Private: wearing full regulation equipment, including the ungainly pack. The kepi (often crushed in front) carries his brigade insignia. His weapon is the M1861 Springfield rifle.

US Signal Corps (Brady Collection) NA

Shortly after the Battle of Antietam, Lincoln paid a visit to McClellan (facing the president). His aim was "to try to get him to move." But the general, as usual, would not "stir an inch until fully ready."

Wednesday September 17, 1862 was the date of the bloodiest one-day battle of the war. Lee's army faced Antietam Creek. Yet his back was to the Potomac. Had McClellan hurled his 75,000 men in a widespread, full-scale assault against Lee's 40,000 troops, the Southern line would have snapped at some point and Lee would have been trapped. Instead, McClellan chose to launch a series of piecemeal attacks. This led one authority to state: "It does not seem possible to find any other battle ever fought in the conduct of which more errors were committed than are clearly attributable to the commander of the Army of the Potomac."

The sun was barely visible in the early morning mist when Federal divisions advanced through cornfields and pasture land and attacked the Confederate left flank. When these assaults met with bloody defeat, McClellan ordered other units to pound Lee's center. Lee adroitly used his inner lines of defense to beat back waves of charging Federals. Finally, McClellan sent forward a portion of his left wing to assail the Confederate right. The Union soldiers seemed on the verge of cracking Lee's line when, up through the cornfields from the south, dashed Confederate General A. P. Hill's "Light Division" from Harper's Ferry. Hill's men savagely charged the exposed Federal flank, drove the demoralized bluecoats down the hill and across the Antietam, thus bringing the conflict to a merciful end. Official records place the day's losses at 26,193 men killed, wounded, and missing. For days thereafter, Antietam Creek ran red with blood. A volunteer nurse named Clara Barton gave rise to the American Red Cross

by her ministrations to countless wounded men brought to the field hospitals.

With a third of his army casualties from the inconclusive battle, Lee withdrew to Virginia. Lincoln took advantage of the Antietam "victory" by issuing on September 22 the Emancipation Proclamation. This document promised freedom to Confederate slaves; but of more importance to the moment, it served as a diplomatic weapon to block European nations from granting aid to a section proclaimed to be perpetuating human slavery. Lincoln's already low spirits sagged even more in the weeks following Antietam. McClellan's failure to strike Lee's wounded army as it returned to Virginia seemed inexcusable. Then, during October 10–12, "Jeb" Stuart's Confederate cavalry made another, even more dramatic, raid around the Union army. All the while, McClellan continued to display a reluctance to strike with his army against Lee's inferior numbers.

On November 5, Lincoln's patience ended. He removed McClellan from command and sent him home to await further orders that never came. General Ambrose E. Burnside, affable but painfully aware of his own limited abilities, was named McClellan's successor. Burnside wasted little time in initiating another "On to Richmond" drive. His design was to sweep secretly around Lee's right flank, cross the Rappahannock River at Fredericksburg, and then to march southward on Richmond while Lee gave frantic pursuit. But what resulted was one of the colossal blunders of the war.

Hesitations, uncertainties, and Burnside's insistence on waiting for pontoon bridges so delayed the Federal advance that, by the time Burnside got his 130,000 men across the Rappahannock, Lee's 72,000 Confederates were waiting atop unassailable heights south of Fredericksburg. The situation demanded a reconsideration of Union plans. But

Burnside refused to alter his strategy. He divided the Federal army into two wings and issued vague orders for massive assaults against the Southern lines. The Battle of Fredericksburg occurred on December 13, a cold Saturday. Brigade after brigade of Federals charged across open ground and into the jaws of death. One wave after another rushed forward over the dead and dying, only to be ripped apart by concentrated artillery and musketry. When nightfall came, nearly 13,000 Federal soldiers lay sprawled on the plain. The dead were piled three deep in places. "It is well war is so terrible," Lee sadly noted, otherwise, "we should grow too fond of it."

A month later, Burnside attempted another movement around Lee's flank. This "mud march" accomplished nothing except the end of Burnside as an army commander. General Joseph Hooker was named to replace him and began the arduous task of revitalizing the Army of the Potomac during the inactive months of winter. Hooker's nickname of "Fighting Joe" promised renewed action in

The charge of Kimball's brigade at the Battle of Fredericksburg. Union troops unsuccessfully assaulted Confederate positions on the hills south of the town. The carnage prompted Lee to observe, "It is well war is so terrible—we should grow too fond of it."

the spring when armies could again take the field.

Military fortunes in the West throughout the latter half of 1862 had also fluctuated. After Shiloh, Grant took charge of Federal operations in western Tennessee and northern Mississippi, while General Don Carlos Buell had responsibility for middle Tennessee. Command of the Confederate Army of Tennessee passed after Shiloh to General Braxton Bragg. During July and August, Southern cavalry raids by Nathan Bedford Forrest and John Hunt Morgan created havoc throughout Tennessee and Kentucky. Bragg decided to exploit this chaos with a full-scale invasion of Kentucky. All went well, initially, and by mid-September the largest Confederate army ever to enter the state was threatening the important railroad center of Louisville, on the Ohio.

Then everything collapsed for the Southerners. Bragg proved to be much like McClellan—a good organizer but a poor fighter. At the critical moment in Kentucky he vacillated, and gave Buell's forces time to reinforce Louisville. Even though Bragg received additional troops, he refused to press forward. On October 8 the armies of Buell and Bragg collided at Perryville. Skillful generalship was lacking on both sides: almost 7,000 casualties were the only results of a battle of blunders. Bragg retreated to Tennessee. Buell relinquished command to General William S. Rosecrans, whose army in Mississippi had won successes at Iuka (September 19) and Corinth (October 3–4) over the

Confederate forces of Sterling Price and Earl Van Dorn.

Rosecrans chose the day after Christmas to begin a long-delayed advance from Nashville against Bragg's army, thirty miles south at Murfreesboro. The Federal army's 41,000 men opposed Bragg's 34,000 troops. Rosecrans's confidence was somewhat shaken on December 29, when General Joseph Wheeler's 2,500 Southern cavalry began a productive raid around the Union army. The Confederates took a thousand prisoners and captured so many Federal supply wagons that, in the battle which followed, many Union soldiers were forced to eat the meat of horses slain on the field.

The bloody contest between Rosecrans and Bragg began on December 31 at Stone's River and lasted three days. Most of the fighting was on open, level country. Heavy Confederate assaults dented the Federal lines in a number of places, but Federal generals managed bravely to keep the works intact. Bragg's troops finally forced an opening. But as Confederates rushed through the gap, they were raked end to end by Federal batteries that reduced the columns to fragments. A Kentucky officer viewed his hundreds of dead and moaned: ''My poor orphans.'' Thereafter his brave unit was known as the ''Orphan Brigade.'' Total casualties exceeded 23,000 men—losses hardly equal to the results,

Courtesy Chicago Historical Society   Inset: Valentine Museum, Richmond, Va

Fredericksburg (below) was little more than a shambles after the battle on December 13, 1862. ''Jeb'' Stuart (right), the South's glamorous cavalry commander, was moved to write, ''Fredericksburg is in ruins. It is the saddest sight I ever saw.'' Nevertheless he was enthusiastic about the result: ''The victory won by us here is one of the neatest and cheapest of the war''—with some 13,000 Federal dead on the slopes below him.

*Ulysses S. Grant had an unprepossessing appearance—
according to Dana he ''had no gait, no station, no
manner.'' But this unassuming soldier became the
country's first full general since George Washington and
a national hero. Above: General Logan's headquarters
during the siege of Vicksburg, surrounded by dugout
shelters.*

for Bragg retired from middle Tennessee and Rosecrans
did not resume the offensive for more than six months.

The Vicksburg Campaign

The major event in the West during this period was Grant's
Vicksburg campaign. The attempts to take the city
consumed a year of trial and error and the final success
stands as the general's greatest achievement.

Vicksburg stood on a high bluff overlooking a long hair-
pin curve in the Mississippi River. Confederate long-range
guns bristled from the heights and presented a deadly peril
to all unwanted traffic on the river. In May and June of
1862, a Federal naval expedition against the city gained
nothing and suffered heavily. Late in November, Grant
and his chief compatriot, General William T. Sherman,
embarked on a two-pronged land offensive against Vicksburg. Yet Grant's wing had to turn back when Confederate
cavalry on December 20 destroyed his supply base at Holly
Springs, Mississippi. Sherman then proceeded alone. His
assaults at Chickasaw Bayou on December 28–29 were
almost an attempt at the impossible and cost him 1,200 men.
Efforts by Sherman early in 1863 to construct a canal that
would divert the Mississippi from Vicksburg collapsed as
ingloriously as did Admiral David D. Porter's plan to launch
an amphibious attack through the stagnant swamps north
of the river fortress.

In the spring of 1863, Grant abandoned novel suggestions

as well as textbook tactics. He consolidated his army at Memphis and marched overland to Milliken's Bend, twenty miles above Vicksburg. There he met up with Porter's fleet of sixteen gunboats and transports. While this junction was taking place, Colonel Benjamin H. Grierson and 1,700 Federal cavalry left the vicinity of Memphis on one of the war's most daring raids. Grierson's troopers rode all the way across Mississippi and continued to Baton Rouge, Louisiana, in a two-week foray of little military consequence except for the destruction of railroad track, stations, and bridges. Yet the raid did serve to divert attention from Grant's next move.

Grant's army crossed the river at Milliken's Bend and marched eighty miles over Louisiana bottomland to Grand Gulf. At the same time, Porter's fleet stubbornly fought its way past the Vicksburg batteries with the loss of only two transports. The US Navy now controlled the river below Vicksburg; but on a more immediate note, it was in a position to cover Grant's crossing into Mississippi. Grant then started on the last, and most critical, stage of his strategy. The 40,000-man Union army would slash its way across the state. Marching rapidly, living off the country and unencumbered by baggage trains, the Federals would hammer unrelentingly at the enemy until Vicksburg was theirs.

The ensuing operation was brilliantly executed, to be sure, but Confederate ineptitude on the command level played a significant role in Grant's success. In charge of the Confederate defenses of Mississippi was General Joseph E. Johnston, who strongly advocated a concentration of all available forces against Grant's dangerously exposed army. Yet Jefferson Davis still insisted that all Confederate territory be stubbornly defended. Hence, General John C. Pemberton at Vicksburg found himself caught in a strategic argument between his commanding officer and his commander in chief. Consequently, historian Robert Selph Henry observed, Pemberton "at times attempted to follow both plans, finally followed neither—and lost everything."

Grant's army fought its way past Port Gibson, won another victory at Raymond, and concentrated between the now separated commands of Johnston and Pemberton. The Federals then neutralized Johnston's forces at Jackson, turned, and headed westward. Union victories at Champion's Hill and Big Black River drove Pemberton's disheartened army back into Vicksburg. Four Federal assaults against the city's defenses on May 22 could not break the Southern lines. Grant thereupon resorted to siege operations.

Shutting off all escape routes, Grant's men constructed fifteen miles of interlocked trenches and gun emplacements. Federal ships kept him regularly supplied and, at the same time, maintained a steady bombardment of Vicksburg from the river approaches. Grant's field pieces and siege guns rained shells night and day on the town.

Constant artillery barrages drove the inhabitants quite literally underground. For six weeks, Vicksburg's defenders lived in caves, subsisted on mules, dogs, and rats, and hoped for aid that never came.

On July 4, 1863, the Pennsylvania-born Pemberton accepted Grant's surrender terms. Included with the capitulation of the city were 30,000 troops, 60,000 muskets, and 172 cannon. Five days later, nearby Port Hudson, Louisiana, and its 6,000 emaciated defenders surrendered. Lincoln was able to exclaim joyfully: "The Father of Waters again goes unvexed to the sea!"

Grant's resounding success at Vicksburg did more than give the North control of the Mississippi. It also isolated all territory west of the river from the Confederacy, provided an unprecedented boost to Northern morale, and demonstrated more forcibly that Grant was one of the few Union generals capable of scoring a decisive victory.

It was also evident that Union fortunes in the war had finally swung upward in the East. On the day before Vicksburg fell, the Army of the Potomac won its first indisputable victory. However, this success came on the heels of another near disaster in Virginia.

General Joseph Hooker devoted the first months of 1863 to strengthening and rejuvenating the hardluck Federal army. It soon numbered 135,000 fully equipped men and was, in Hooker's words, "the finest army on the planet." The strategy that he devised for the spring campaign was almost faultless. Lee had depleted his Army of Northern Virginia to 60,000 men by sending James Longstreet's corps on an expedition to south Virginia. Hooker's plan was, in essence, a giant pincer movement in which Lee would be trapped and overwhelmed on two fronts by superior numbers. Two Federal corps under General "Uncle John" Sedgwick would hold Lee's attention in front of Fredericksburg. Hooker and three corps (about 75,000 men) would march up the Rappahannock, cross the river, and strike Lee's left flank and rear. Two other Federal corps would be held in readiness to give additional strength to either wing.

Hooker's strategy contained one weakness and one oversight. Its weakness was the assumption that Lee would do nothing while the Federal pincer closed; the oversight was the fact that Hooker's two wings would be thirteen miles apart—with the Army of Northern Virginia squarely in between.

The Federal offensive began smoothly and came very close to success. Hooker's wing crossed the Rappahannock and actually had flanked Lee's army before the Confederate general discerned the Federal strategy. "I have Lee in one hand and Richmond in the other," Hooker chortled.

Then Hooker inexplicably lost his confidence—at the worst possible moment. His portion of the army had marched deep into the Wilderness, a tangled mass of pine, oak, underbrush, creeks, swamps, and gullies. Only two miles from the exit into open country, Hooker abruptly stopped the advance and assumed the defensive. Lee promptly responded by taking the greatest gamble of his career. He divided his comparatively meager forces—not in two but into three separate components. Jubal Early's division was left at Fredericksburg to contain Sedgwick as long as possible. Jackson's corps was sent on a wide flanking movement to strike Hooker's exposed right flank. Lee and his 15,000 remaining troops would assail Hooker in front.

Bewildered and angry Federal troops began digging entrenchments near a road junction called Chancellorsville. While they shoveled, Jackson's column, six miles long, wound its way quietly across Hooker's front and into battle position on his flank. At 5 PM on May 2, many Union soldiers were cooking supper when 30,000 Confederates exploded from the woods with their chilling "rebel yell." The Federal XI Corps on the extreme right

battle. Because of—or in spite of—Hooker's mismanagement, those that did fight lost a total of more than 17,000 men. Lee's casualties amounted to almost 13,000 and included the irreplaceable "Stonewall" Jackson, mortally wounded by his own men in the confusion of battle. His death was the deepest personal loss the Confederacy would suffer. Thereafter, Lee never again undertook the daring flank movement that had brought the Army of Northern Virginia some of its most crushing victories.

Collision at Gettysburg

In mid-June, Lee resolved to make a second invasion of the North. His army could ill afford to continue winning defensive victories that thinned its ranks while accomplish-

American Antiquarian Society

broke apart as Jackson's men overran camps and earthworks while Hooker frantically tried to readjust his lines.

The Battle of Chancellorsville (May 2–6) raged back and forth amid burning timber and smoke-filled air as unsupported Federal units fought desperately to escape annihilation. Burning underbrush cremated men too wounded to move; command structure in the dense woods collapsed as pockets of men engaged in life and death struggles. The combined forces of Lee and Jackson battered Hooker's lines until Sedgwick pushed his way past Early and began to close the vice. Lee calmly shifted his section of the army eastward. He and Early assailed Sedgwick's wing at Salem Church and sent it reeling in confusion. Lee then returned for a final series of attacks on Hooker.

By nightfall of May 6, the Army of the Potomac was again moving northward in defeat. Little more than half of the regiments had been actively engaged in the five-day

The screaming headlines of a broadsheet issued in May 1863 warn the people of Pennsylvania of the impending invasion of their state by Confederate troops. The governor called for volunteers to face the "imminent" danger.

ing no strategic gains. His men were badly in need of supplies, especially shoes. Virginia had earned a respite after two years of ravaging by opposing forces. Moreover, particularly following Lee's victory at Chancellorsville, Emperor Napoleon III of France seemed favorably disposed toward the Confederacy. If Lee could win an offensive campaign, France might repeat history and come to the aid of her "American cousins." Should Lee win a smashing success on Union soil, war-weariness in the North might increase to the point of forcing Lincoln to end hostilities. Such an action would bring peace and still leave

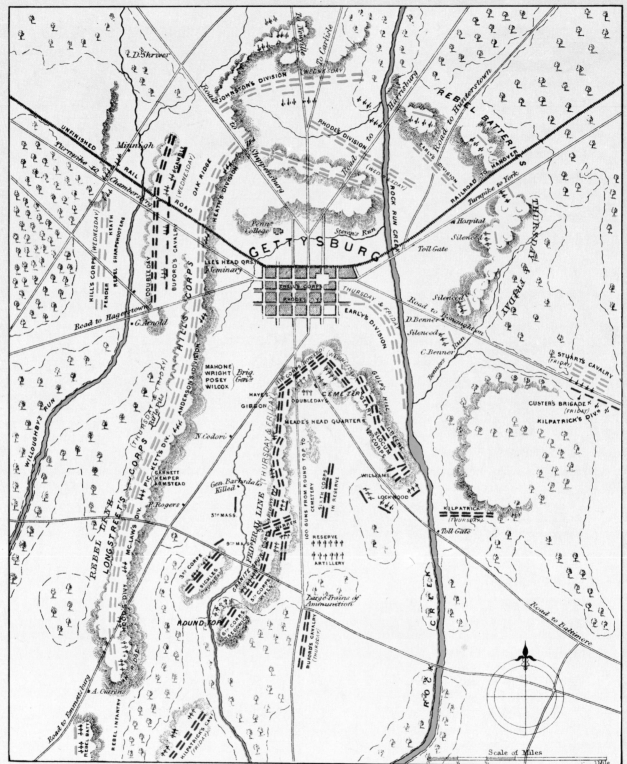

The Battle of Gettysburg, July 1-3, 1863, was the most significant engagement of the war. Fighting began when an advance Union column heading toward the town stumbled on a contingent of the dispersed Army of Northern Virginia, due to rendezvous nearby. Two pugnacious men— A. P. Hill for the South, John F. Reynolds for the North—threw all available troops into what might have been a skirmish, and called for reinforcements. Thus, both Lee and Meade were forced to take command of a battle already in progress. The map shows the Confederate positions in blue and points up the massed Union forces (in red) atop the strategically important Cemetery Ridge.

General Pickett's men formed a mile-wide line below the Union position on the last day of the battle. The clash, seen here from behind Union lines, was a disaster for the Confederates. Nearly half their troops perished, and Lee admitted, "All this has been my fault."

the South free and independent.

Invading the North a second time was a desperate risk, but for the embattled Confederacy the times called for desperate measures. It is true that Lee's move across the Potomac would leave Richmond virtually unprotected. Yet if Hooker advanced to seize the Confederate capital, Lee could just as easily do the same with the Northern capital. By 1863, such a "swapping of queens" had little value. Perseverance and the enemy's army had become the primary objectives in the East. These were aims that, after Chancellorsville, "Fighting Joe" Hooker displayed a reluctance to pursue.

The Army of Northern Virginia left Fredericksburg early in June and started westward to the Shenandoah Valley corridor. The long gray ranks, protected on the flank by Stuart's 10,000 horsemen, were passing Culpeper when one of the largest cavalry battles of the war occurred.

Hooker had dispatched 10,000 cavalry under General Alfred Pleasonton to ascertain Lee's movements. On June 9, near Brandy Station, this force met Stuart's men. The battle had a storybook atmosphere, with flashing sabers and lines of mounted soldiers charging back and forth across open ground. At day's end Stuart held the field, but Pleasonton retired with useful information on Lee's army. The fight at Brandy Station produced only 1,400 casualties, but it marked the first time in the war that Northern cavalry had held their own against the vaunted Southerners.

On June 14–15, Jackson's old corps (now under Richard S. Ewell) routed the Federal garrison at Winchester and took 4,000 prisoners, 23 guns, and 300 wagons loaded with badly needed supplies. Lee's army then crossed the Potomac and proceeded northward into Pennsylvania. Hooker's failure to press vigorously after Lee, plus his unrealistic insistence that the Federal army begin an offensive of its own in Virginia, proved his undoing.

On June 28, Lincoln relieved him from command and named General George G. Meade to lead the army. Meade was a steady, studious soldier, a Pennsylvanian who had displayed an occasional flash of brilliance in the field. His Federal army numbered 97,000 men as it marched into Pennsylvania in search of Lee's 75,000 Confederates. Meade's hope was to catch Lee before the Southern army crossed the Susquehanna River. Lee's plan to win a major victory on Northern soil was nearing fruition: he was confident that success was only a battle away.

Lee was concentrating his army at Cashtown, Pennsylvania, when, on July 1, Confederates met the van of Meade's approaching army northwest of Gettysburg. Both armies rapidly converged on the town. After hard fighting on the afternoon of July 1, Lee's men drove the Federals back through Gettysburg and onto a range of hills south of the town. Lee quickly deployed his army for battle while Meade's forces just as quickly took positions on a series of ridges shaped like an inverted fishhook. The three days of

In a steady downpour, Federal troops trudge after Lee's shattered army. Like McClellan, Meade allowed the enemy to retreat to safety—but with his men exhausted after ten days' marching followed by three days' fighting, there was little else he could do.

vicious combat in that rolling country ranks as Lee's worst mistake. He repeatedly assaulted a numerically superior army on ground of its own choosing. His army was "blind" for much of the campaign because Stuart's cavalry had embarked on a raid more flamboyant than wise and had been disastrously delayed. Ewell's failure on the first day to drive the few Federal brigades from the heights of Culp's Hill and Cemetery Ridge gave Meade both precious time and the strongest geographical position in the area.

The second day's fighting shifted to the Federal left flank. Longstreet's Confederates tried desperately to seize Little Round Top, the anchor of Meade's line. Bloody combat raged in such places as Devil's Den and the Peach Orchard. That day the 1st Minnesota lost 85 per cent of its strength while repulsing waves of attacking Confederates. One of the units involved in those assaults was the 1st Texas, which suffered 82 per cent losses.

Two days of valiant but futile attacks on the Federal flanks convinced Lee that Meade's weak point was the Union center. Thus, on the afternoon of July 3, occurred the climax of the battle. General George E. Pickett led 15,000 Confederates in an open-field charge that

Dead horses provide a grim reminder of the carnage at Trostle Farm, scene of heavy fighting on the second day of the battle. A Union artillery unit was captured by Mississippians leading the assault on the Peach Orchard.

Overleaf: An observation balloon hovers over Gettysburg, while in the foreground wounded soldiers receive attention. Medical treatment was rough and ready—with amputation on the spot and in full view of those going into action.

resembled a parade. Well-dressed lines of infantrymen surged forward, color-bearers proudly waving their flags, and mounted officers rode in front and shouted encouragement. Across the way, massed Federal infantry and artillery waited. Pickett's charge pitted gallant determination against heroic defiance. Concentrated Federal fire ripped Pickett's lines to shreds. No more than a hundred Confederates ever reached the Union works. Half of Pickett's division lay dead and dying in the wheatfield through which it had passed. Those bleeding fragments that struggled back to the Southern lines were consoled personally by Lee, who could only say, "All this has been my fault."

Gettysburg produced staggering casualties: 23,049 Federals, 20,451 Confederates. The battle was the most significant of the war.

The Gettysburg campaign marked the last major Confederate invasion of the North. Meade, like McClellan, threw away a golden opportunity to deliver a counterblow against Lee's crippled forces. The Southern army returned safely through torrential rain to Virginia. Yet Federal soldiers in the Army of the Potomac rejoiced understandably. Stunning defeats and indecisive but bloody battles had been their lot for two years. Now, for the first time, they had soundly defeated the elite of the Confederate armies. Lincoln would stand on the Gettysburg battlefield four months later and speak of "a new nation . . . dedicated here to the unfinished work which they who fought here have thus far so nobly advanced."

The victory at Gettysburg, coming simultaneously with Grant's triumph at Vicksburg, marked the dawn of a new day. The tide of war had swung to the North's favor.

Chapter 7

THE POLITICS OF WAR

Americans were so imbued with the idea of democracy that they could conceive of no other form of government—even in wartime. In the North, it was a case of ''politics as usual,'' and the hard-pressed Lincoln administration came under bitter attack from opposing politicians, dissidents, and an unrestrained press. The Confederacy for its part produced a constitution closely resembling that of 1787. Yet democracy and war make uneasy bedfellows, and if Abraham Lincoln found the war effort hampered by interminable squabbling, he could take comfort from Jefferson Davis's predicament in juggling the doctrine of states' rights against the needs of a war for survival.

Government by the People

Lincoln and the men close to him never forgot how dangerously weak the nation was during Buchanan's lame-duck months. The outgoing administration, which felt powerless to act, failed almost totally to oppose, much less to stop, the Southern states seceding.

At home and abroad commentators drew the conclusion that the lowering of the Stars and Stripes and the hoisting of the Stars and Bars over Fort Sumter signaled the end of the "old" Union. Since 1820 the United States had bowed to slave state pressures. It stood by helplessly while several states seceded. It was even unable to defend a solitary fort. How could such a nation govern a continental federation?

The general opinion in 1861 was that, though a great experiment in federalism, the American Constitution simply did not work. Champions of democracy answered that the fault was the cancerous element of slavery. Critics noted, however, that even the Latin American republics, the British Empire, and the Russian autocracy were managing to restrict or abolish their servile labor institutions. In sharp contrast the United States, the only western society to increase its slave territory during the century, was failing abjectly to cope with the problem.

Lincoln stretched his constitutional powers to the limit—and over the limit in the eyes of many. In this allegorical painting, New York's powerful Tammany Hall chains the president to the Constitution as he attacks the dragon of secession.

The timidity of the Buchanan administration in the face of secession seemed to be the final proof that federalism and democracy were fatal to a nation's survival. Odds were high that more states would soon secede, and there was little reason to expect that Lincoln would succeed where Buchanan had failed.

Some observers, including those sympathetic to popular government, felt that elections should be canceled (or at least delayed) until things were back to normal. But federal and state constitutions, laws, and customs set rigid election timetables. Faith in constitutional government, already at a low level, was unlikely to survive the overthrow of these commitments. Lincoln and his subordinates concentrated each day on winning one day more of survival. They had little time for, or interest in, proposals to suspend elections in order to avoid politics and muffle dissent. So, from Washington down to the most rural hamlets, open politics continued. During 1861, local elections took place as scheduled. Even under combat conditions neighborhood elections were interrupted only briefly. This continued throughout the war.

In 1862 regular congressional, state, and local contests were held—an unprecedented wartime phenomenon. Most Americans even took for granted the unique event in 1864 when their soldiers voted by absentee ballot. When states lacked such arrangements, the War Department ferried whole regiments to their homes. Either way, neither coercion nor corruption marred the proceedings. Expressing pleasure in this performance, Americans saw it as proof that their democracy worked in war as well as in peace.

However imperfectly, the political party apparatus—which many condemned as irrelevant—continued to express the majority will. Further, it joined the president, congressmen, and governors to their local constituents, many of whom were in the army. But in early 1861, before the party and administration showed vigor and resilience, both political parties labored under enormous weights. Both showed an unsuspected adaptability.

Democrats were tarred with the brush of secession and disloyalty, but the various Republican wartime measures allowed them to bypass these hazards. Among other things, they criticized disloyalty arrests, the Negro recruitment policies of 1862–63, and the president's retention of emancipation in his Reconstruction statement. They also attacked the Republicans' 1864 platform. Exploiting and perverting the party's Jeffersonian and Jacksonian traditions, the Democrats made themselves the protectors of ''whites-only'' civil liberties and of states' rights.

The militia muster of April 1861 seemed to stretch endlessly in time and incredibly in scale. Democrats capitalized on the growing war-weariness of Northern whites and preached defeatism—in other words, acceptance of Southern independence. Democratic leaders understood that the Confederacy enjoyed the large psychological advantage of needing only to resist and endure, rather than win outright victory. They believed that at every election deep policy divisions would find expression. No matter how local or trivial the office being contested, each election would test the conduct, cost, and aims of the war. Democratic party leaders looked longingly toward a military armistice with the rebels and, in some instances, toward a permanently separate, slave-owning Confederacy. General McClellan's departure from the army allowed his party to add an anti-military flavor to its rhetoric.

Republicans enjoyed the formidable asset of patriotism in their insistence on the Union's preservation. It proved lure enough to recruit ''War Democrats'' at least temporarily into a Union party coalition with the

Lincoln's cabinet included Secretary of the Treasury Salmon P. Chase (top), Secretary of War Edwin M. Stanton (center), and Secretary of the Navy Gideon Welles (bottom). Chase had tried for his party's nomination in 1860, and was involved in backstage maneuvering to replace Lincoln in 1864. At the same time he performed the arduous task of managing the Union's finances. Stanton, though ill-tempered and abusive, was an extremely able administrator. Welles was the architect of the formidable Union navy.

Republicans. The Republicans also enjoyed a second advantage derived from their belief that the existing political institutions were adequate in the Civil War emergency. The Republicans scooped into the Union party coalition all those who wanted reunion for whatever reason—from advocates of protective tariffs or homestead laws to abolitionists. Emancipation, the dream of a tiny minority for decades, was at last a realistic goal if abolitionists could persuade enough people to consider in political terms that freedom for Southern blacks would save Northern whites' lives. But first they had to convince the army's civilian overlords.

Slowly at first, then more rapidly, the public turned to consider emancipation. This was because Union victory and emancipation became joined. Only the Republican party could accommodate this opinion change. The Democrats remained immobile on race. Race relations and war aims were the principal issues in the 1862 elections and, in terms of postwar policies, in the 1864 presidential campaign. It was an enormous advance from 1860.

The Problems Facing Lincoln

The qualities of a president are all-important to his party, his Congresses, and his administration. Lincoln's qualities are definable in part by contrasts with those of his predecessor, Buchanan, and his 1860 opponent, Stephen A. Douglas. Both Democrats failed to hold their party together in Congress, in the nominating convention, or in the states. Lincoln, on the other hand, never let party lines break. He neither raced ahead nor lagged behind the majority of his party on such basic questions as emancipation.

Lincoln's capacity for growth made change possible. Politics was the lubricant for government operations that might introduce and establish acceptable changes. Race relations were the source of the Union's distresses, and the nation's war powers—with the army as primary instrument—must cope with this source. Lincoln's views on race and the war powers were of primary importance, therefore. Lincoln was no abolitionist in 1861, though he detested slavery. He insisted firmly that the Constitution allowed its containment, or even its abolition, if this was the will of the people. Only the Union's military perils and Lincoln's development moved his party to the conclusion that emancipation was an essential factor of military success.

Lincoln's capabilities and his grasp of the law are clearly shown by his unerring resort to a constitutional use of the president's war powers in the weeks after Sumter's fall. He insisted that these war powers were not mere implications, but derived from the Constitution's explicit injunction that the nation provide for the common defense.

Always in the forefront of popular attention, harried by the newspapers, and criticized by the Democrats, the executive establishment of 1861 was woefully unprepared to perform effectively. The presidency is always a complicated as well as difficult office and Lincoln assumed office at a time when its influence was at its lowest point. As a former Whig, Lincoln had shared that party's inclination toward a weak executive. As a devoted nationalist, he believed in a Union composed of strong states, subordinate in a limited way to the government in Washington. And as a firm Republican he advocated legislative aids to farmers, railroads, and other business enterprises. Beyond this, he had an almost mystical trust in political democracy which was to capture the imaginations of such disparate people as Frederick Douglass, Edwin Stanton, and Walt Whitman.

Ordinary citizens, including the soldiers, came to a remarkable understanding of the unique army that the war created, and Lincoln shared that insight. It was truly a citizen's army, and the soldiers never allowed themselves to be severed from party politics. So literate as to cause the administration to create the world's first military postal service, the bluecoats maintained close communications with their homes. Soldiers debated political speeches, wrote uncensored political comments to their families, legislators, and journalists, and advised home-town newspapers on all public issues. In addition, states' provisions for soldier-voting made politicians peculiarly aware of their bluecoated constituents' situations and aspirations. Union soldiers were "thinking bayonets," to use a phrase which met with Lincoln's approval. His responsibility to command the military involved earning and keeping the support and obedience of its citizens in the ranks. The Republican party could never outpace the army's willingness to continue fighting, to embrace emancipation, and to accept blacks as fellow soldiers. The greater danger came from party and government lagging behind the citizen-soldiers.

Lincoln compared the government and its army to a wagon with four teams of horses. The "Radical" Republicans, in the lead traces, were galloping hard toward emancipation as well as reunion. Next, moderate Republicans moved forward at a slower canter, responding occasionally to Radical tugs, but also to "stop" and "slow" signals from the teams behind them. Third, War Democrats plodded at a still-slower walk. They wanted primarily to restore the status quo, but were unwilling to stall progress toward reunion. At the rear, "regular" Democrats dug their heels in stubbornly, hoping to immobilize the national wagon and to reverse its course even at the risk of its further, total disruption. All reins led to the president's hands. The question was whether he could run these discordant pacers in sufficient concord so that Democratic lurches rearward could be withstood before Union soldiers and voters gave up striving, and the wagon fell apart.

The greatest danger to this motley team was the constant criticism by the extreme antiwar Democrats, a faction of whom were scathingly known as "Copperheads." The Copperheads advocated immediate peace on any terms.

Above: Order # 11, *an oil painting by George Caleb Bingham. In some areas the military exercised strict control over the civilian population. General Thomas Ewing issued the order on August 25, 1863, which brought about the evacuation of people who lived more than a mile from Union military posts in four counties of western Missouri. (This was a direct result of Quantrill's bloody raid on Lawrence.) Right: A particularly colorful poster calling for volunteers from New York. Below: Reporters from the New York* Herald *relax beside their mobile office. It was sometimes said that generals learned more about the enemy's movements from the newspapers than they did from their intelligence reports.*

They were particularly strong in Ohio, Indiana, and Illinois, and the government found it virtually impossible to suppress the movement. General Burnside, military commander in the area in 1863, issued a general order stating ''the habit of declaring sympathy for the enemy will not be allowed in this department.'' Nevertheless Clement Vallandingham, an Ohio congressman and a leading Copperhead, violated the order during his campaign speeches and was arrested. Tried by a military commission, he was sentenced to be confined for the duration of the war, a sentence which Lincoln ironically commuted to banishment. Vallandingham was escorted through the military lines to the Confederacy. He proved an embarrassment to his unwilling hosts, and subsequently went to Canada, returning to his country in 1864.

The Copperheads, meanwhile, continued to agitate for peace. They proved so strong that Vallandingham was able to draft a resolution which was adopted by the Democratic convention in 1864. This called for a cessation of hostilities ''after four years of failure to restore the Union.'' However, the culmination of military successes that fall, combined with Lincoln's victory in the election, finally took the wind out of the Copperheads' sails.

Soon after Sumter, all branches of the national government, so long moribund, sprang to life. White House vigor awakened all officialdom. Not since the days of Chief Justice John Marshall had federal judges asserted such review powers. United States Chief Justice Roger Brooke

Taney in *ex parte* Merryman asserted that the executive could not suspend the writ of habeas corpus. Lincoln chose to ignore Taney, who failed thereafter to enlist his fellow justices in concerted assaults on the White House or Congress. During the remainder of the war, as during Reconstruction, the federal courts were constructive partners with both president and Congress.

When the Thirty-seventh Congress convened in July 1861, it, too, exhibited the energy that was suddenly the Washington norm. There were important improvements in legislative operations. The obstructive southern delegations were gone, and Republican majorities were impressive.

Within two years of Sumter, the nation that had been unable to succor a single fort was maintaining without bankruptcy Napoleonic-size armies across a continental stage. In the East, the Army of the Potomac probed toward the Confederate capital. Westward, Union armies dominated the river systems and occupied New Orleans. Everywhere, the navy's offshore blockade tightened. The North's citizens had proved capable even of surmounting the reversals at Bull Run and the Peninsula, changes in army command, and political reshuffles. Northern morale and institutions even survived the large-scale Confederate invasions of the North. By mid-1862 the desperate measures of the previous year were beginning to have an effect. Even the question of the black man's legal status, which in early 1861 was as seemingly immovable as secession, was in the arena of open politics by 1863.

How was it possible for a government that had been so unresponsive in the secession crisis to perform so energetically even in the first weeks of the war? Once hostilities had begun, some executive departments took on responsibility for war-emergencies, and makeshift arrangements were made to deal with them. Later, Congress and the courts sustained these measures with budgets and judgments. After the war, they disappeared almost totally.

Lincoln restored party harmony and balanced the party factions by bringing into his cabinet all the leading Republican presidential aspirants. Their views on military leadership, internal security, and emancipation, as well as on all other issues, helped to shape Republican policy. Lincoln could not afford to alienate or ignore any member of his cabinet. He quickly learned that there was no government machinery to cope with a crisis situation—as the anti-disloyalty problem suggests.

In 1861 disloyalty was not a crime; treason was. Individual treason prosecutions, however, proved to be totally unrealistic for reasons that soon became clear. There were no government investigators. The attorney general had only a few clerks. Post Office and Treasury detectives, a tiny corps, were only used to chase thieves and counterfeiters. Army and navy professionals knew nothing about internal security matters or defining the limits of dissent. It was necessary to do something about disloyalty and national action of a limited sort was the sole alternative to local vigilantism or total centralization.

Lincoln assigned internal security responsibilities to Secretary of State William Seward, the powerful ex-governor of New York, who later became a personal friend. Seward recruited a mixture of local officials and volunteers into an anti-disloyalty force, but it was seriously defective because it sometimes went out of control. Yet many of those arrested admitted—without duress—disloyal acts or the intention to commit them. Seward ordered almost all of them to be released quickly. Many of the accused had lawyers—an unplanned "policy" that astonished foreigners though Americans took it for granted. No capital punishment for disloyalty was imposed, though death sentences were levied on saboteurs and spies in areas of military operations by military courts. These were mistakenly attributed (sometimes deliberately by Democrats) to Seward. No secret proceedings faced the

Horace Greeley, above, founded the penny daily New York Tribune *in 1841. Staunchly abolitionist, it was the most widely quoted newspaper in America while Greeley was editor from 1841 until his death in 1872. In January 1861 he was content to counsel "Wayward sisters, depart in peace!" but once hostilities began his tone changed. For months the* Tribune *carried on its masthead the nation's war cry "Forward to Richmond! Forward to Richmond!" Right: Rival presidents Lincoln and Davis engage each other in a game of badminton with Ohio's Clement Vallandingham as shuttlecock. The most outspoken of the Copperheads, Vallandingham was tried by a military court for uttering treasonable statements. After he was convicted, Lincoln banished him to the Confederacy—which did not want him either. Vallandingham abandoned the South for Canada and was nominated for governor of Ohio in absentia. Left: An 1861 propagandist cartoon showing the American eagle vigilantly protecting its nest of states against traitors.*

THE UNION
IT MUST AND SHALL BE PRESERVED.

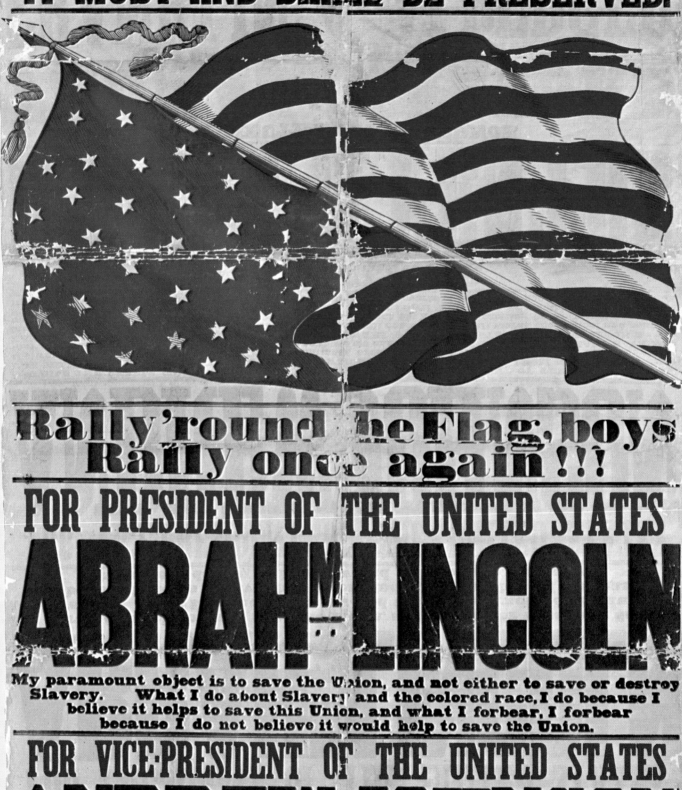

Rally 'round the Flag, boys Rally once again !!!

FOR PRESIDENT OF THE UNITED STATES
ABRAHᴹ LINCOLN

My paramount object is to save the Union, and not either to save or destroy Slavery. What I do about Slavery and the colored race, I do because I believe it helps to save this Union, and what I forbear, I forbear because I do not believe it would help to save the Union.

FOR VICE-PRESIDENT OF THE UNITED STATES
ANDREW JOHNSON

WHILE THE REBELS CONTINUE TO WAGE WAR AGAINST THE GOVERNMENT OF THE UNITED STATES "prisoners of state." Indeed, since one of the purposes of the arrests was to discourage others from risking evil, government officers publicized their operations.

Early in 1862, Democratic critics turned their attention to the new secretary of war, Edwin M. Stanton, who took on the anti-disloyalty burden. Under his predecessor so much corruption had attended the army's enormous growth that the officer corps openly sneered at their civilian overlords. Field commanders pursued independent and contradictory courses on such matters as fugitive slaves, and the ordinary soldiers and their families felt less confidence in their government. Stanton hustled the War Department into honest activity and the army command into obedience. Like McClellan, generals who refused to conform to policy decisions sooner or later were dismissed

Modernized War Department bureaus included the offices of the inspector general and the surgeon general. In the process they came to cooperate closely with such volunteer associations as the Sanitary Commission. Of the new bureaus, two deserve special note. The first was the office of provost marshal general, which Congress created in March 1863. The provost marshal general, James B. Fry, administered the nation's first draft law in relative harmony with local officials, party leaders, and public sentiment. This achievement is the more remarkable in that, conforming with Lincoln's emancipation order, the draft drew blacks into the army. The second innovation was the Freedmen's Bureau created early in 1865. This regularized many unofficial arrangements made since 1861, under either army or private sponsorship.

Among other matters, the bureau was to see to the Freedman's legal standing in his own state, rather than through any national formula. Freedmen's Bureau officials were to attend to the ex-slaves' physical and moral conditions as well as their education. Congress spelled out these activities as a result of information drawn from army field commanders, Unionist Southerners, and a variety of voluntary welfare and missionary associations. Since almost all bureau rank-and-file agents were to be volunteers, Congress provided virtually no funds.

The law stipulated that the bureau should last only for a year after hostilities ceased—an optimistic assumption for the task in hand. The bureau's creators assumed that the primary need was for the simple elimination of the slave status in state laws. Thereafter (with minimal and brief assistance) the freedmen would help themselves by the same means as white men. The Freedmen's Bureau set the tone for all subsequent Reconstruction policies.

As well as providing for war-emergency bureaus, Congress approved legislation dealing with a wide range of matters such as homesteads, railroads, and tariffs. Lincoln was committed to encouraging the conditions of freedom by removing government restraints, such as state slave codes. To the men on Capitol Hill, emancipation and the upsurge in communications and industry seemed to march together.

The general feeling was that the government should be kept as small as possible. As a result the war was run largely with the usual executive establishment. Only the War, Navy, and Treasury Departments were greatly expanded during the fighting. But even they returned virtually to prewar levels very soon after Appomattox.

Inevitably, this increased government vigor and strength had political repercussions. The Democrats insisted that the growth of wide-ranging powers was making the executive despotic. But though the railroad and telegraph companies were nominally in government hands during the war, no government ownership or even much policy control resulted. Corporation officers made money for their companies by meeting the government's needs.

In the 1862 elections, the Democrats, condemning all war measures, substantially increased their numbers in state capitals and in Washington. They cut the Republican majority in the House of Representatives from thirty-five to eighteen. Nevertheless Lincoln felt fairly confident that the North's citizens, including soldiers, wanted the war to go on to reunion, even if it meant declaring emancipation to reach that goal. Immediately after the 1862 elections, Lincoln dismissed McClellan from his command. He made it clear that he would hold to the two-phase Emancipation Proclamation schedule, which called on Southerners to abandon the Confederacy by January 1, 1863, or lose their slaves in the event of defeat.

With that deadline passed, Lincoln authorized recruitment of blacks into the army, and under the March 1863 Conscription Act the provost marshal general enrolled blacks as well as whites. Former slaves could not then be bartered back into slavery as a short-cut to reunion.

The Reelection of the President

As the 1864 election neared, it became clear that the Republicans, having unleashed the energies of the once-sleeping national government, had defined the basic war and Reconstruction policies. Early in 1864 Congress passed a bill sponsored by Senator Benjamin Wade of Ohio and Representative Henry Winter Davis of Maryland that would secure Reconstruction on a firmer basis than Lincoln's proclamation of 1863. Instead of employing his right to veto, Lincoln chose merely to "pocket" the bill. This use of the pocket veto allowed the retention of as much stability as possible in Louisiana and Arkansas, where the state governments were struggling to take root according to his 1863 Reconstruction formula. His pocket veto did not create a split in the party and Lincoln received a second term nomination from the Republican party convention. The platform nourished concord rather than acrimony and stressed the nation's need for unconditional reunion. Both

This 1864 campaign poster emphasizes the president's overriding concern with preserving the Union: it reprints his memorable argument about the relative importance of slavery to the larger question.

party and president were committed to emancipation as the basic element in any formula for Reconstruction.

Republican unity forced the Democrats to shy away from the Copperheads. Their convention nominated the dismissed McClellan for president, but even he felt it necessary to repudiate several points in the platform which had been forced in by the antiwar extremists. These were: that the war was an utter failure; that individuals' civil liberties and states' rights were permanently crushed by both the Negrophile Republicans and by the Union army; and that an immediate armistice was necessary.

Democratic exaggerations did not deceive the majority of voters, however. They gave Lincoln 55 per cent of the popular vote, a 15 per cent increase over his 1860 total. His electoral college edge was 212–21. The soldiers' particpation offered a dramatic counterpart to the civilian vote, for the bluecoats' huge Republican majorities meant that they were calling for the war to continue.

Lincoln's second inauguration was brightened by the obvious health of a Union about to be restored. Two-party politics was vigorous; the Constitution visibly worked. Even race relations seemed capable of peaceful solution now that slavery was eliminated. Constitutional law, the government, and party machineries had proved themselves in a way that allowed for future progress. Lincoln, now an experienced administrator and political leader, was the first president since Jackson to be reelected. He had until March 1869 to cope with Southern Reconstruction.

The 1864 election tested the Union's desire to continue the war. The Democrats chose McClellan (above) to run against Lincoln. McClellan disavowed the peace plank in the Democratic platform and refused to admit that the war was a failure. "Little Mac" proved as unsuccessful on the stump as he had been on the battlefield. He lost to Lincoln by an electoral college margin of 212 to 21.

Right: "With malice toward none; with charity for all," Lincoln begins his second term of office on March 4, 1865. The oath was administered by Chief Justice Salmon P. Chase. Among the many thousands watching and listening to Lincoln that day was the actor John Wilkes Booth, who was to strike the president down one month later.

LINCOLN'S GETTYSBURG ADDRESS

*Four score and seven years ago our
fathers brought forth on this continent a new nation, conceived in liberty,
and dedicated to the proposition that all men are created equal.
Now we are engaged in a great civil war, testing whether that nation, or
any nation so conceived and so dedicated, can long endure.
We are met on a great battlefield of that war. We have come to dedicate
a portion of that field, as a final resting place for those
who here gave their lives, that that nation might live. It is altogether
fitting and proper that we should do this.
But, in a larger sense, we can not dedicate — we can not consecrate — we can not
hallow — this ground. The brave men, living and dead,
who struggled here have consecrated it, far above our poor power to add or
detract. The world will little note, nor long remember
what we say here, but it can never forget what they did here. It is
for us the living, rather, to be dedicated here to the
unfinished work which they who fought here have thus far so nobly advanced.
It is rather for us to be here dedicated to the great
task remaining before us — that from these honored dead we take increased
devotion to that cause for which they gave the last
full measure of devotion — that we here highly resolve that these dead
shall not have died in vain — that this nation, under God,
shall have a new birth of freedom — and that government of the people,
by the people, for the people, shall not perish from the earth.*

November 19, 1863

The Confederate States of America

If the North entered the war in a state of some confusion, was the South in a very much clearer frame of mind? In a rare instance of plain rhetoric, Jefferson Davis expressed the prime—indeed sole—objective of the Confederate States of America. In his first formal address to the provisional Congress in Montgomery, Alabama, he spoke for his new nation the simple plea, "all we ask is to be let alone." Davis and the Confederates sought no visionary utopia. They believed they had the best of all possible worlds and merely desired to preserve that world. Confederate Southerners meant their nation to be nothing so much as a celebration of the status quo.

But Southerners possessed a rather well-defined ideology, though they spoke simply of their "way of life." With an intensity which seems self-evident, Southerners in 1861 were convinced that they were different from other Americans and that continued union with the North put them in peril. As a people, Confederates clung strongly enough to their "way of life" to create a separate nation and to fight a long and bloody war for its survival.

Southerners said something very significant about themselves by the very act of secession. They wrote no philosophical declarations of independence. Instead they relied on the right of revolution expressed in the great Declaration of 1776. But when the convention delegates in each of the eleven Confederate states dissolved the bonds between their state and the United States, these Southerners acted out a political theory.

Secession rested upon a conception of the Union as a compact of states. The theory was that in 1789 each state had entered into a contract with the other states to form a federal government, which existed to serve the best interests of its parts, the states. However, the argument continued, the states never surrendered their sovereignty. Thus, if the federal government took action which was unacceptable to a state, that state had the option to declare the original contract broken and void, and to reassume its independence. This, said the Confederates, was what had happened in 1860–61. The Southern states had found the Union intolerable. They therefore exercised their option and left it. Then they made a new compact among themselves to form a new nation called the Confederate States of America.

The tattered Stars and Bars flies bravely over Fort Sumter. Not until February 1865 did the Union regain control of the stronghold which saw the opening of hostilities and which, to the end, remained a symbol of Southern independence.

When delegates from Florida, South Carolina, Texas, Georgia, Louisiana, Mississippi, and Alabama met in Montgomery to frame the Confederate Constitution, they no doubt had in their minds all the complexities of the states' rights theory. Curiously, however, the Montgomery Convention was basically conservative. It produced a constitution that was quite nationalistic in tone. The preamble began with the assertion that each state was "acting in its sovereign and independent character." A few lines later, though, the Confederates stated that one purpose of their document was "to form a permanent government"—a strong implication that states could not secede from the Confederacy as they had just done from the United States.

On the whole, the Confederate charter was little different from the Constitution of the old Union. Southerners assumed that the work done in 1787 would stand well enough, if properly interpreted. What differences there were seemed to strengthen the national government rather than the individual states. The president, for example, served for six years instead of four, but he could not succeed himself. He could veto portions of bills sent to him by Congress and thereby foil the practice of legislative "riders." For all practical purposes, Congress could not appropriate money except in answer to a presidential request. Thus, after insuring that no president could establish a dynasty for himself, delegates at Montgomery created a stronger executive than had their counterparts at Philadelphia in 1787. They did not set up a supreme court. The conservative nature of the constitution makers led them to prohibit the foreign slave trade. Southerners in the United States Congress, led by Jefferson Davis, had very recently crusaded for reopening the trade. It would seem that Southern leaders had spent much of their radical enthusiasm by seceding. In terms of political doctrine, the Constitution represented an attempt to shore up the status quo—to conserve rather than create.

It would be a mistake, though, to think of the Confederates' early conservatism and nationalism as a retreat from states' rights. Southerners had thought too long in states' rights terms. The doctrine, whether it fit their current circumstances or not, was a part of them. States' rights was the political expression of the South's provincialism and this was underlined by the Confederacy's guarantees of state sovereignty. Southerners tended to distrust distant abstractions like "Union" and to give more attention to local interests. States' rights was a natural extension of this frame of mind. Their loyalties began with "hearth and home" and radiated outward to community, district, state section, and nation. Other Americans may have been provincial in the mid nineteenth century. But Southerners as a group seemed more comfortable in their provincialism, and had codified it into political doctrine.

If the Confederate Constitution was somewhat ambiguous on the matter of states' rights, it was crystal clear about slavery. Congress could pass no law "denying or impairing

the right of property in negro slaves." Slavery was the South's "peculiar institution," the feature which had seemed most threatened by continued union with the North. It is not surprising to find slavery sanctified in the Confederate Constitution. On March 21, 1861 Vice President Alexander H. Stephens went so far as to speak of slavery as the "cornerstone" of the new Confederacy.

Slavery and Southern Society

Slavery pervaded Southern life. Much more than simply a crude labor system, slavery was a form of racial subordination resting on the universal white presumption of black inferiority. Slavery made possible the Southern plantation and thus sustained the large-scale production of staple crops—the backbone of the South's economy. Slavery also sustained the planter class and its economic and social dominance. The slave-plantation system discouraged the growth of capitalism and industrialism. The Southern economy was suspended somewhere between feudalism and capitalism. Slavery was a source of brutality, paternalism, guilt, and self-righteousness in the Southern mind. The "peculiar institution" was, in short, an element of the Southern ideology and, at the same time, a factor in almost every other element.

This same sort of overlapping was true of the other features in the South. For example, commitment to agriculture formed a large portion of the Southern way of life. The Confederate Constitution specifically forbade protective tariffs, subsidies, and internal improvements. Traditionally these measures had enriched commercial and industrial interests at the expense of planters and farmers. Here again though, agriculture was more than an economic enterprise. It was a way of life. The fundamentally rural, pre-industrial Southerners developed and sustained cultural patterns which were somewhat different from those of the more diversified and industrialized North. A "folk culture"—with highly personal man-to-man and man-to-nature relationships—persisted in the South after other Americans had begun to adjust to a more industrial, anonymous society.

The South's leading agriculturalists—the planters— were an aristocratic economic and social class. Planters formed a tiny percentage of the South's population. Nevertheless, they functioned as an aristocracy and generally retained the deference of the non-planter majority. Planters and their class interests were clearly in the forefront of the secession movement. The Southern aristocracy rested upon ties of race, paternalism, kinship, ambition, and short-range economic cooperation among planters and other whites.

Supposedly, Southerners were proud, independent, violent, romantic, and provincial. The Confederacy

Top left: Jefferson Davis, the man who "looked like president." Above: Alexander H. Stephens, "The little pale star of Georgia" who weighed less than 100 lb, became vice president of the Confederacy. Left: Davis was inaugurated as president on February 18, 1861 at Montgomery, Alabama. The capital was later moved to Richmond, Virginia. Below: The Great Seal of the Confederacy was not authorized until the spring of 1863. It was made in Britain at a cost of some $700 and brought in through the blockade in September. The design features George Washington, a wreath of cotton, wheat, tobacco, rice, and sugarcane, and it bears the motto "With God as Defender."

certainly exhibited these qualities in corporate form. Only a proud, romantic, provincial people would have challenged the physical supremacy of the North with any hope of success.

The Confederacy existed solely to preserve the Southern way of life. So, when secession led to confrontation and confrontation to war, the Confederacy's war aim could be put in one word—independence. Very early in the war, however, it began to dawn upon Confederate leaders that independence and the Southern ideology might be inconsistent. The kind of war in which they were engaged demanded sacrifice and change. To achieve independence the South had to win; to win, the Confederacy had to slaughter some "sacred cows." Few men perceived this hard fact more clearly than Jefferson Davis. Perhaps no Confederate remained more committed to victory and independence at any cost than the president. The fundamental conflict between Confederate nationhood and the Southern way of life can be traced in his mind and actions.

Jefferson Davis was the president as a result of compromise. The Montgomery Convention passed over those secessionist radicals who had done the most to bring about the Confederacy and chose Davis, a strong "Southerner," but a moderate on the question of secession. Davis looked like a president. He was tall, lean, and carried himself with dignity. He was a graduate of West Point, minor hero of the Mexican War, Mississippi planter, congressman, secretary of war, and senator. In fact, Davis had near perfect credentials. He had been one of the leaders of the Southern-rights wing of the Democratic Party, and some looked upon him as the new Calhoun. To the infant nation he offered a posture of leadership, experience in the government and the military, and the correct blend of moderate Southernism.

His less attractive qualities were not immediately apparent. For one thing, the man worked too hard. It was difficult for him to delegate authority and consequently he found himself attending to petty details. Eventually his

health broke, and he had to carry on the intricate business of government while tired and sick. Under these conditions, the dignity and self-assurance which he had displayed turned into hauteur and stubbornness. In good health or bad, the president loved and hated too well. He had the knack of letting a disagreement become a quarrel and then a feud. On the other hand, he stood by his friends—even when they proved to be bunglers or political liabilities. In the delicate circumstances of Confederate politics and statecraft such flaws were fatal. Davis was a man of vision and character and a creative statesman. But in conflict or debate his policies, however well conceived, suffered from the limitations of his political personality. No one, however, could have predicted all this in 1861 when Davis was a popular choice. Although some of the radicals would have preferred one of their own or some other moderate, the convention made Davis's election unanimous and greeted him with enthusiasm.

As vice president, the Montgomery delegates selected Alexander H. Stephens of Georgia. Stephens and Davis shared a moderate position on secession but little else. The vice president was small and frail, an ex-Whig, and a doctrinaire states' rightist. In time Stephens became a foil to Davis as the two leaders responded to the demands of war in opposite extremes. Davis bent; Stephens stood with legalistic rigidity against compromise with the principles of the Old South's ideology.

Davis arrived in Montgomery for his inauguration amid a wave of Confederate patriotism. The fiery William Lowndes Yancey—who significantly was not a delegate to the Convention—greeted the president-elect's train and proclaimed, "The man and the hour have met!" The Montgomery Convention had acted with dispatch. Convened on February 4, it adopted a provisional constitution, elected a president and vice-president, resolved itself into a provisional congress, and inaugurated the new government—all within two weeks.

The Davis Administration

Davis chose his cabinet with equal speed. Robert Toombs of Georgia became secretary of state because Davis needed a secessionist Georgia Democrat in the government to balance Stephens. Christopher G. Memminger, from South Carolina, was secretary of the treasury. He was a successful lawyer and banker, as well as an active secessionist. Leroy Pope Walker as secretary of war represented a plum for Alabama. Stephen R. Mallory had been a member of the US Senate Committee on Naval Affairs. This and the fact that he was from Florida earned Mallory the navy secretaryship. The postmaster general was John H. Reagan of Texas, and the attorney general was Judah P. Benjamin of Louisiana. Both these men had talent, and their selection insured every original Confederate state of recognition at cabinet level. This cabinet did not remain together for long, however. Davis continued to use cabinet portfolios as political weapons and rewards. The president gradually built up an official circle of advisers both in and out of the cabinet, whose opinions (rightly and wrongly) he trusted.

The Davis administration began its political life in Montgomery, talking about peace and frantically preparing for war. When the war did come, it presented the new government with staggering problems. Fortunately for the Confederacy, Abraham Lincoln's government was almost equally unprepared for the conflict. Lincoln, however, had at least completed the political chores associated with a

Witte Museum, San Antonio

The farm of Julius Meyenberg, Fayette County, Texas. As with other trans-Mississippi states, Texas was far removed from the fighting and totally cut off from the rest of the Confederacy after Vicksburg. On the whole, life there was little affected by the distant war.

new administration. In the midst of mobilizing for war, the Confederacy added four more states—Virginia, Tennessee, North Carolina, and Arkansas. Even as the Confederate Congress debated moving the capital, three more states (Missouri, Kentucky, and Maryland) seemed likely allies. Davis faced the prospect not only of a war for his nation's existence, but also of broadening the political base of his administration to include these states. Congress solved one of Davis's problems and rewarded Virginia for her allegiance by moving the capital to Richmond. The president, the government, and the "placemongers" made the trip to Richmond in May 1861. Then, in the midst of patronage battles and conflicts of dignities, the real war intruded.

Americans believed that wars should be fought by volunteers. At first, the Confederacy had an abundance of volunteer warriors, more in fact than the War Department could equip. The problem was that Southern "minutemen" assumed that the war would last little longer than the "minute" it supposedly took them to get ready to fight. Consequently, Confederate soldiers volunteered for three months or a year at a time. In addition, the Confederacy's existing military structure, the militia, was under the control of the eleven state governors and a host of honorific appointees. Even as the Federal army prepared to cross the Potomac River and invade Virginia, that state's ordnance officer warred with the Confederate War Department over the control of some cannon which belonged to the state.

In time the Confederacy was able to manufacture its own guns and ammunition and did not have to bargain with state authorities to equip its armies. It could not manufacture soldiers however, and the Davis administration often had to beg, borrow, or steal troops from the states in order to bolster its major field armies. President Davis, whenever he could, mustered troops into the national service. Nevertheless, state militias, home guards, and like organizations kept many Southern soldiers beyond the control of the Confederacy and kept the Davis government dependent upon the good will of state governors. Some of these were indeed cooperative. Others, like Joseph Brown of Georgia and Zebulon Vance of North Carolina, were downright obstructive. The Confederacy was still very young when Davis learned the hard way about states' rights and the need for centralized leadership in wartime.

Patriotism and belief in a short war hid the conflict between theory and practice during most of 1861. The South's deceptively easy victory at Bull Run on July 21, 1861 fed Confederate illusions of invincibility and bolstered the government. In the long run, though, the Confederacy's early success made Davis's task as war leader more difficult. The North did not quit after Bull Run, and during the winter of 1861–62 the Confederacy suffered several reverses. These defeats, together with the normal

amount of friction associated with establishing a government, had the effect of bursting a pretty balloon. And the blame for dashed expectations and shattered illusions was laid on the head of Jefferson Davis.

By the time Davis took the oath of office as the first president on February 22, 1862, his administration had encountered more than its share of ill will. In the pouring rain Davis delivered his inaugural address and promised to do better for his country. Some of the administration's difficulties were beyond anyone's control. But others were clearly Davis's fault. The Confederacy had not mobilized enough soldiers, indeed *could not* mobilize enough soldiers, to defend its vast perimeters. Thus the commander in chief had to centralize military priorities and planning to make efficient use of the South's limited manpower and resources. Davis only learned this hard fact through error; states' rights and the national war effort were incompatible.

The First American Draft Law

In the spring of 1862 the Confederacy faced some hard issues. The "short war" had already become long. Volunteering had slowed, and the South's armies were too small. On every side, by land and water, the North threatened to invade. At this juncture, Davis asked his Congress for unprecedented power. He requested authority to suspend the writ of habeas corpus and declare martial law. He asked for money to stimulate and expand the government's war industries. He requested action "declaring that all persons residing within the Confederate States, between the ages of eighteen and thirty-five years, and rightfully subject to military duty, shall be held to be in the military service of the Confederate States, and that some plain and simple method be adopted for their prompt enrollment and organization . . ."—a draft law.

Surprisingly, Congress did what Davis wanted. The president got his appropriations and authority to suspend habeas corpus in areas threatened by invasion. Then on April 14 Congress passed the first conscription act ever imposed in America. Obviously, the Habeas Corpus and Conscription Acts were departures from the South's states' rights traditions. Suspension of habeas corpus could, and did, permit military commanders to make arbitrary arrests, fix prices, control the movement of people, and do all manner of other "un-Southern" things. The Conscription Act insured for a time at least adequate manpower for Southern armies (either by its enforcement or by the flood of volunteers who sought to avoid the odious label of "conscript"). It also increased the length of service for all troops to at least three years or the duration of the war. Because volunteers for state units were classed as conscripts, the law stimulated volunteering for national

For the South, inflation was a source of anxiety right from the beginning. Confederate paper money began to decline in value as soon as it was issued, and as more and more rolled off the printing presses inflation reached catastrophic proportions. By late 1864 a $500 bill was scarcely enough for a barrel of flour.

The bustling town of Atlanta became the hub of the Confederacy's internal communications, with several railroads converging on it. Sherman's destruction of both the city and the railroads in November 1864 was a crushing blow. Below: Locomotives in the ruins of the roundhouse.

service and enabled the Confederate military organization to circumvent state governors. Because the War Department made most of the crucial decisions about exemptions, the Conscription Act gave the government considerable control of the Confederate labor market. Those men employed in "vital occupations" did not have to serve, and the government defined "vital occupations."

There were, however, glaring flaws in both the idea and the execution of the Habeas Corpus and Conscription Acts. The president could suspend habeas corpus only in limited areas which lay in the enemy's path. Thus martial law existed in isolated pockets along the South's perimeter. Moreover, the military commanders involved used their expanded powers unevenly and often unsuccessfully.

Needless to say, the draft law was unpopular in the same way that draft laws usually are. The Confederates were wise enough to realize that drafting every able-bodied male into the army would leave no producers behind the battle lines to feed, clothe, and equip the army and nation. Therefore Congress wrote various classes of exemptions

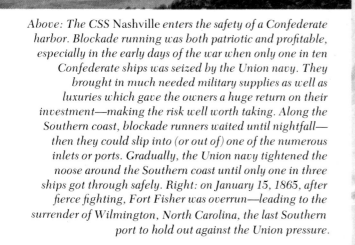

Above: The CSS Nashville *enters the safety of a Confederate harbor. Blockade running was both patriotic and profitable, especially in the early days of the war when only one in ten Confederate ships was seized by the Union navy. They brought in much needed military supplies as well as luxuries which gave the owners a huge return on their investment—making the risk well worth taking. Along the Southern coast, blockade runners waited until nightfall— then they could slip into (or out of) one of the numerous inlets or ports. Gradually, the Union navy tightened the noose around the Southern coast until only one in three ships got through safely. Right: on January 15, 1865, after fierce fighting, Fort Fisher was overrun—leading to the surrender of Wilmington, North Carolina, the last Southern port to hold out against the Union pressure.*

into the act, and in so doing made an unpopular law even more unpopular. Opportunities to avoid service were many. For example, anyone having charge of twenty (later reduced to fifteen) slaves was exempt from the draft. Rich men could hire substitutes to take their place. Because druggists were excused, anyone so inclined could buy a few bottles of patent medicine, offer them for sale at a country crossroads, and avoid conscription. Nor did the hard core states' rightists overlook the government's affront to them. Georgia's Governor Brown reportedly vented his resentment by taking advantage of the exemptions granted to officers of state militia and commissioning ten thousand lieutenants in the Georgia militia.

The Confederacy suffered because political parties never crystalized in Congress. Davis had no pro-administration organization to help him formulate legislative policy and to guide bills through Congress. He had no "loyal opposition" either. Those men opposed to one or another administration measure had little or no obligation to pose alternatives and no responsibility to speak or vote for anyone but themselves. As a consequence, each bill existed in a kind of political vacuum, and by default the already overworked executive branch bore almost sole responsibility for war legislation.

Most of the time Davis got his way with Congress, especially the First Congress. The administration's handling of war received criticism, and sometimes the president had to compromise with the legislative branch. But Davis was rare among American presidents in that sooner or later, in some form or another, he got what he asked for from his Congresses.

In the spring of 1862, after some wrangling about the military, appropriating the necessary funds, and passing the Conscription and Habeas Corpus Acts, Congress adjourned. As one member said, the people were looking "somewhere else than to this Congress for aid." He referred, of course, to the army—and he was correct. The war was going badly for the Confederacy. A Federal fleet had taken New Orleans. A large enemy army was loose in Tennessee. In addition, the Army of the Potomac was advancing steadily on Richmond. During the summer campaigns, however, the Confederates rallied. Robert E. Lee took command in the East, drove off McClellan, defeated John Pope, and invaded Maryland. In the West, Braxton Bragg invaded Kentucky, forcing the Federals onto the defensive in their own country. Even though both Lee and Bragg shortly had to retreat, the Confederacy seemed far more secure in the fall of 1862 than it had in the spring. Nevertheless the war persisted, and Southern independence became ever more costly.

The High Cost of Independence

During the winter of 1862–63, Southerners felt the full effects of a cruel economic irony of "modern" war. A "nation of farmers" could, and did, go hungry. No one factor can explain the failure of Southern agriculture to sustain the Confederacy. Planters who continued to plant cotton, tobacco, and other inedible staples did not help. Poor roads, fought-over farmland, and inadequate rail transportation were also factors. Cities, swelled by soldiers, refugees, and industrial workers, represented a

Southerners believed—and many Northerners agreed— that their way of life gave them a great advantage over the enemy. Their tradition of military service was strong; their country-style living meant that most men knew how to ride and shoot; while an air of command came naturally to anyone who had been served by slaves all his life. Left: David Meade of the Dinwiddie troop, 3rd Virginia Cavalry, exemplifies the "flower of Southern manhood" who gaily went off to war in 1861 to fight for an independent Confederacy. Right: "Our Heroes and Our Flags"—a patriotic picture which today is only a reminder of the "Lost Cause."

new and large body of consumers. So too did armies, whose members suffered from the general shortage of food. War emergencies brought about a sharp change in Southern economic thinking during the Confederate period.

First, planting cotton—which went unsold unless smuggled—suddenly became unpatriotic. State governments even went so far as to impose quotas on the number of acres which could legally be planted in cotton. The national government, state authorities, and army commanders impressed cotton for use in trade with Mexico and Europe. Other examples of government intervention in the economy were numerous. Military commanders attempted to fix prices on food and fodder. Municipalities often bought food in quantity and sold it to the poor at cost. Two state governors, William Smith of Virginia and Vance of North Carolina, sponsored blockade runners in an attempt to feed their constituents.

The Confederate War Department was the governmental agency by far the most deeply involved in these efforts to manage the South's economic resources. During 1862 and the early months of 1863, it used its authority over the draft to influence the Southern labor market and to commandeer the railroads. In the spring of 1863, however, Congress gave the War Department still another lever with which to organize the war effort.

In March 1863, Congress enacted a law allowing the impressment of private property. The military could thus seize not only food, but crucial raw materials and slave labor as well. Army agents gave the property owner the government's promise to pay for the impressed goods or services according to a scale of prices fixed by the War

Department. The law was unpopular—and so was its enforcement. Most Southerners, however, submitted to this one more compromise with the ideology they were supposedly fighting to protect.

Even more interesting was the Confederate effort to create industry, again led by the War Department. Having neither the time nor the inclination to raise up a class of industrial capitalists, the Confederates attempted to industrialize "from the top." Different departments established factories and works throughout the South to manufacture the tools of war, while the government fixed the profit margin of private suppliers by law. Using the exemption power of the conscription law, the impressment authority granted in 1863, and its control of railroads, the government stimulated and sustained enough war industry to supply Confederate armies to the end of the war. Significantly, the troops usually ran out of food before they ran out of ammunition. It was amazing that the South could achieve so much so quickly. Even more amazing, though, was the manner in which the Davis government achieved wartime industrialization. The thrust of the government's economic activity was in the direction of industry, not agriculture. This does not, of course, mean that the South became an industrial giant or that the government managed every facet of the South's wartime economy. But the Confederacy certainly generated sufficient industry to sustain the war, though with considerable chaos and inefficiency.

The tax legislation of 1863 called upon Southerners to sacrifice even more principles and possessions in the hope of independence. Soaring inflation and slackening bond sales convinced Congress that heavy taxation was the only solution to the problem of national solvency. Despite inefficiency in collecting the taxes, the best estimates indicate that the Southerners, per head, made more than twice the financial sacrifice of their enemies in the North.

As the 1863 tax legislation indicated, the Confederacy was in trouble after two years of war. Military events during the year confirmed that trouble, and following the disasters of Gettysburg and Vicksburg, Southern morale sank to new depths. The Davis administration had to look for new ways to sustain the "cause" during the usual break from fighting that winter.

The president had a new Congress to work with in 1864. The elections held during the fall of 1863 produced a group of legislators generally less eager to enact Davis's programs into law. By this time the Davis government had, perhaps unavoidably, made a lot of bitter enemies. In Georgia, for example, Vice President Stephens and Governor Brown became so vocal in their opposition to "King Jeff the First" that Union General William T. Sherman wrote to them proposing a separate peace between the United States and Georgia. Stephens and Brown were not willing to go that far.

But in the face of heightened opposition in Congress and in the country, Davis persevered. The government overhauled the Conscription Act, abolished many of the exemption categories, and provided for army units to serve vital industries. In an attempt to counter inflation, Congress passed an act which, essentially, repudiated one-third of the government's paper money. Congress also made blockade running, and thus all foreign trade, the exclusive province of the government. Consequently, the Confederacy existed for the last year of its life in a state socialist political economy. These were the desperate measures of a beleaguered government. They were also sacrifices consciously made for the sake of Southern independence. But Stephens and others asked, in so many words, "What good is independence, if the South must sell its very soul to secure it!"

The Final Sacrifice

The campaigns of 1864 only mocked the Confederacy's sacrifices. By the time cold weather temporarily ended major military action in 1864, Lee was besieged at Richmond and Petersburg. Joseph E. Johnston was retreating in the Carolinas, pursued by Sherman. By the fall of 1864 Davis realized that the Confederacy was all but bankrupt. The South had expended its substance and sacrificed its ideals. It had not been enough. One last resource remained, one final tenet of the Southern way of life—the slaves.

At some point during the summer and fall of 1864, Davis concluded that arming and emancipating the slaves was the Confederacy's last hope for victory. Others had advocated this policy in public and private for some time, but their voices were few and their words lost in the din of defeat and despair. The president realized that only with the aid of black Southerners could the Confederacy persist in its struggle for independence. With full appreciation of the difficulties he would encounter with Congress and the

Early in the war Confederate soldiers were at least as well equipped and supplied as the Union troops. Left: A warmly-clad sentry at his post in "Quarter Guard."

*President Davis and members of his administration fled
Richmond on April 3, 1865 and headed south. At Charlotte,
North Carolina, the Confederate government held its last
meeting; then (above) its members set out across the Georgia
Ridge. On May 10 Davis was captured at Irwinville, Georgia.
Imprisoned for two years, indicted for treason, he was
never brought to trial. Until his death in 1889, he spoke
and wrote in defense of the Southern cause.*

country, Davis moved circumspectly. On November 7 he
asked Congress for money with which to purchase 40,000
slaves for non-combatant duties with the army. He then
proposed that the government emancipate them so that
they might serve as free men. The president understated
the case when he said that this represented a "radical
modification in Southern law and theory."

During the final months of the Confederacy's life, debate
raged in Congress, the press, and elsewhere over the
wisdom of employing black troops. On the surface, the issue
was whether or not to arm the slaves. Thoughtful men
realized that the real issue was emancipation, for in the
hypothetical event that black Southerners should save the
Confederacy, they would never again be chattels. Ultimately Davis, Benjamin, Lee, and others convinced Congress to authorize black enlistments in the army. Congress
hedged about freedom for the slave-soldiers, but Davis and
the War Department wrote emancipation into the orders
implementing the law. Davis was prepared to sacrifice the
"peculiar institution" in the faint hope of victory. In
December 1864, he sent word by special envoy to Britain
and France that he would emancipate all Southern slaves in
exchange for recognition.

By the time Davis and Congress acted, of course, the
Confederacy was beyond military or diplomatic salvation.
Nevertheless the Confederacy went on record as willing to
place its "cornerstone" upon the altar of independence.
The record may have been confused. No referendum confirmed the decisions of Davis or the Congress. But yet the
fact remains that the Confederates themselves doomed
slavery in the South.

The attempt to arm the slaves was, of course, a last gasp.
Like many of the other Southern concessions to wartime
necessity, it came too late. Within a few weeks after Congress acted, the Confederacy collapsed. Indeed it had been
crumbling for some time. Jefferson Davis, however,
never gave up. He fled his capital on April 2, 1865 and kept
on fleeing in the wake of Lee's and Johnston's surrenders.
In those final days, the president exhorted his generals and
his countrymen to fight on, to continue the struggle as
guerrillas. The Confederacy could live, Davis believed, as
long as its people remained committed to the "cause." In
his last address to the people of the Confederacy, Davis
spoke of a "new phase" of the war and concluded, "let us
meet the foe with fresh defiance, with unconquered and
unconquerable hearts." But by the spring of 1865,
Southerners had neither the resources nor the will to
sacrifice further. For this reason, and because of his own
limitations, Davis could not inspire a new phase of the war,
a struggle of partisan bands.

On May 10, a small body of Federal cavalry captured
President Davis at Irwinville, Georgia. Thereafter, the
"cause" lived only in memory. Having forfeited their
ideology, Southerners chose finally to save themselves and
asked only to be left alone.

Chapter 8

BEHIND THE LINES

The industrial North and the agrarian South faced different problems in turning their resources to war. Yet their overriding concerns were identical: to equip and supply the armies in the field. And altogether these armies numbered over a million and a half men. How did this mighty war effort affect the lives of people at home? Was it, as many said, "a rich man's war, a poor man's fight"? All wars cause hardship, and civil wars the most anguish of all. But the essential difference between the two sides was that the North grew richer and stronger as the war progressed, while the South became poorer and weaker. The North emerged not only victorious but prosperous; the South suffered not only military defeat but near ruin.

Life on the Home Front

When William Howard Russell, the noted war correspondent for the London *Times*, visited New York City in March 1861, he marveled at the complacent attitude he found toward the prospect of civil war. No uniforms were to be seen in the streets, no evident signs of military preparation. The sprawling city of 800,000 went about its daily occupations as if no Confederacy existed. To be sure, business was dull and reflected uncertainty about the future. The newspapers carried stories about Sumter and other threatened Union outposts in the South, but they devoted far more space to metropolitan affairs—politics, fires, thefts, and murders. Even among leading figures of New York society, men of importance and education, Russell found an apparent indifference to the gathering crisis. At a breakfast with a group of editors, the chief topic of conversation had been prizefighting. Table talk about secession soon gave way to an earnest debate over the respective merits of the American bareknuckles champion, John C. Heenan, ''the Benicia boy,'' and his British opponent, Tom Sayers. When Russell returned to New York some months later after a trip to the South, he was astonished at the change. Uniformed men and recruiting posters seemed everywhere. Flags and bunting bedecked the fronts of factories, offices, warehouses, and private homes.

During his journey through the South just after the attack on Sumter, Russell had been impressed at the spontaneous, lighthearted enthusiasm for war. Along the rickety, one-track rail line between Goldsboro, North Carolina, and Charleston, South Carolina, he saw thousands of people, many barefooted, swept away with patriotic ardor. In Charleston itself the streets were crowded with armed men singing and cheering and drinking. ''Here was the true revolutionary furor in full sway . . . all was noise, dust and patriotism,'' he wrote. Had he been in New York or Chicago or Boston, or in any of the hundreds of small towns and cities throughout the North, he would have found the same mass hysteria.

Some 200,000 New Yorkers gathered in the Union Square area for the greatest rally in the city's history. From Bangor, Maine, to Racine, Wisconsin, the rallies went on. Volunteers by the thousands came forward, adding their numbers to those of the militia regiments which Lincoln

Northern newspapers in particular kept their readers fully informed of military events. Here, a soldier's wife studies details of one of the most important victories of the war, while her family celebrates the fall of Vicksburg in more childish fashion.

Above: New York's Seventh Regiment marches down Broadway before setting off for the front. Enthusiasm such as this was soon to decline as the first wave of patriotism sagged under the effect of the war.

Left: Designs for the "very elegant" uniforms of Ellsworth's Zouaves— representative of the somewhat fanciful dress of many of the volunteer regiments which answered President Lincoln's call for militia.

had called out. Massachusetts and New York led the van. Their governors, anticipating conflict, had four regiments fully equipped and ready to go. When secessionist groups in Maryland cut Washington's telegraph lines with the North, Governor John A. Andrew of Massachusetts, a man of energy and foresight, immediately dispatched the Sixth Massachusetts to the relief of the capital. As soon as it was learned in the North that these troops had to fight their way through mobs in Baltimore, a second wave of patriotism swept over the free states. On April 19, 1861, New York's Seventh marched down Broadway to the train that would carry it south, between two miles of cheering citizens who jammed the sidewalks and filled the windows and roofs of the buildings overlooking the street. Within a week of these stirring events there were enough troops in Washington to defend the capital.

Meanwhile, through the efforts of the governors and of hastily created Union Defense committees, the Northern states had gone on recruiting and organizing regiments far in excess of the 75,000 militia Lincoln had called for. But the War Department, without enough weapons to arm the troops and no facilities to feed and shelter the volunteers already in the capital, refused the frantic demands of the states that their quotas be enlarged.

Both sides were utterly unprepared for war. About 300,000 muskets, from forty to fifty years old, were stored in Union arsenals. Most were smooth bore which had been converted from flint lock to percussion cap, and only about 40,000 were rifles or rifled smooth bores. The federal government maintained two small gun factories—one at Harpers Ferry, Virginia, which the Confederates seized during the first few weeks of the war, and the other at Springfield, Massachusetts, its capacity a mere thousand muskets a month. Powder and shot, uniforms, knapsacks, harnesses, sabers, bayonets, and canteens were all in short supply. Had it not been for energetic state governors, who had foreseen conflict and had begun purchasing military equipment for the previous three months, the situation would have been far worse than it actually was.

But the governors themselves during those emotion-packed days after Sumter fast became victims of their own zeal and the volunteer efforts of their citizens. While they were still railing at the Lincoln and Davis administrations for not accepting more regiments, the governors were beginning to understand that there was more to organizing armies than accepting volunteers. If their regiments had to fend for themselves in Washington or in Richmond, the new troops that were constantly being raised fared little better at home. Fortunately patriotic civilian groups banded themselves into temporary Soldiers' Aid associations. They raised funds, collected supplies, and donated facilities, and saved the various states from

Even without its blockade on Southern ports, the North was better equipped to cope with the demands of war. Above: A forest of masts in New York harbor gives some idea of how busy the port was during the conflict. Below: An 1860 photograph of iron ore mining at the Jackson Mine, Marquette County, Michigan.

floundering in a morass of inexperience and confusion.

Uniforms, equipment, campsites, and rations could not be supplied through voluntary efforts alone; nor could any of these essentials be provided overnight. It took time and many mistakes before the totally inexperienced and completely inadequate staffs of the governors developed procedures that could clothe, feed, and house their volunteers, much less arm and drill them. The recruits themselves had as much to learn about drawing rations and keeping their makeshift camps clean and orderly as they did about mastering infantry drill or the use and maintenance of their muskets, if they were lucky enough to have been issued any.

A complete lack of coordination among the various states, with little or no direction from Washington, had created a chaotic market in military equipment where the speculator and the grafter flourished. On May 3, Lincoln called for 42,000 additional men to serve for three years. As the first call had emptied state arsenals, this second call and the prospect of further calls spurred the governors into purchasing equipment for their own levies. At the same time, the War Department began massive purchasing for an expanded regular army. Small arms, especially rifles and muskets, which were scarce and expensive when Lincoln made his first call for troops, rapidly became unobtainable. Though the Springfield armory and a score of private arms manufacturers in New England and New York were working to full capacity, they could produce fewer than 5,000 small arms a month; not one-tenth of the demand. Thus state and national governments both North and South rushed pell-mell into the European arms market, and fell prey to international speculators. Union and Confederate agents were able to purchase some new English and French rifles, but the majority acquired in the first months of the war were cast off Belgian, Austrian, and Prussian muskets in such poor repair that they were inaccurate, dangerous to fire, and short of range. By the spring of 1862, the Northern small arms industry had expanded enough to meet the demand. The Confederacy, however, would be dependent on imports and on captured Union arms until the end of the war.

Fewer problems were encountered in forming artillery batteries and cavalry regiments. Horses, harnesses, and saddles were plentiful even in the South, though sabers, carbines, and revolvers were difficult to obtain. Most of the states had light field pieces and both Union and Confederate governments had enough heavy field howitzers, at least for the first year of the war. Demand for cannon and munitions never exceeded supply except in the South, and then only during the closing months of the Confederacy.

When General Grant and Admiral Foote captured Forts Henry and Donelson early in 1862, supplies from Kentucky, particularly horses, were denied the Confederacy. From that point on, horse-drawn transport declined rapidly in quality and quantity as Arkansas, most of Tennessee, and southern Missouri fell to the Union. A Union prisoner of war, after the Battle of Chancellorsville, described the sorry state of the Confederate train. "Their artillery horses are poor starved frames of beasts, tied on to their carriage and caissons with odds and ends of rope and strips of raw hide. Their supply and ammunition trains look like a congregation of all the crippled California emigrant trains that ever escaped off the desert, out of the clutches of the rampaging Comanche Indians." Behind the lines, the situation was no better. The hacks and carriages in the streets of Richmond or of Charleston were few and shabby and harnesses and bridles were worn and patched.

The Inevitable Slide Toward Conscription

After the initial confusion over organizing and equipping the volunteer regiments, the Union and the Confederacy developed more systematic practices in the raising and the training of troops. Throughout the war, the Lincoln administration depended heavily upon the state governors for this vital function. And by liberal resort to state and federal bounties along with appeals to patriotism at mass rallies, their efforts were successful until the fall of 1862. Then, volunteers began to fall off.

The great war boom in the North was gaining momentum. With wages rising rapidly and plenty of jobs available, army life looked far less attractive than it had before. Prices for farm products were increasing sharply, too. A shortage of farm labor for hire made farmers more reluctant than ever to let their sons volunteer. The reverses of McClellan on the Peninsula, that of Pope at Second Bull Run, and the bloody conflict at Antietam put a final damper on conventional techniques of raising men. Congress, still reluctant to transfer recruitment from the states to the Federal government, had passed a law enabling state governors to draft men for not more than nine months service if they could not meet their quotas under the July 1862 call for 300,000 militia. This legislation inspired another intense recruiting drive. By underscoring the benefits a volunteer would have over a draftee, and by raising bounties substantially, most of the states met their quotas without a draft. Although the Confederate government relied on the states too, it moved far more vigorously toward centralizing recruitment than did the Union.

A year before the United States adopted a Federal draft, the Confederate Congress had enacted a conscription act. Marred by such class provisions as exemptions for college students and professional men, the law provided for the purchase of substitutes. When the Union government reluctantly adopted conscription in 1863, it also permitted the purchase of substitutes or exemption from the draft by the payment of $300.

Prisoners of both sides during the Civil War suffered through inexperience and bad management on the part of their captors. Southerners shivered in the bitter cold of an Illinois winter; Northerners sweltered in the oppressive heat of a Georgia summer. The Confederacy was hard pressed to feed its own soldiers and it is no wonder that prisoners fared so badly. There were, however, lighter moments—musical groups were organized, plays performed, and one group of imprisoned Northerners even ran an election to coincide with the real one in November 1864. Above: Union prisoners at Salisbury, North Carolina, playing baseball. Right: One of a series of wry sketches by John Omerhausse, a prisoner at Point Lookout, Maryland, shows inmates washing out the lice from their clothes. Below: Defiant Confederates captured at Gettysburg—note that their clothes bear little resemblance to any kind of uniform.

Supplying the Troops

Moving an army into position for attack or retreating in good order was not just a matter of getting the troops to the right place at the right time: both men and horses had to be fed and supplied. Right: the supply train of the Army of the Potomac in retreat over Bear Creek in the summer of 1862 with wagons stretching into the distance as far as the eye can see. Above: A humorous sketch of the Commissary Department of the 6th Massachusetts Regiment which shows an ample supply of food for the troops. In McClellan's army, at least, they could be sure of getting their rations. Engineers attached to the military assumed a greater importance during the Civil War than ever before. As artillery and other equipment increased in weight, rivers could no longer simply be forded. Pontoon bridges had to be constructed, like the two (below) over the Rappahannock, photographed in May 1863. The Confederates were generally more lightly equipped and supplied and often supplemented their rations with captured Union goods. Below right: A French engraving shows troops of the Army of Northern Virginia retreating from Maryland with supplies taken from the enemy.

Courtesy of Kennedy Galleries, Inc

The Maryland Historical Society, Baltimore

A certain amount of individual chicanery had been associated with recruiting as soon as state and federal governments offered bounties for three-year volunteers. So lax were administrative procedures that many crafty men enlisted, collected state and federal bounties, then deserted, repeating the performance in other states or even in other counties. Some of these "bounty jumpers," as they were called, made small fortunes before they were caught or fled the country. Yet bounty jumping was small business compared with the emergence of another special class of profiteers associated with conscription—the substitute broker. Taking advantage of the ignorance or the youth of a potential prospect, the broker would persuade him to enlist, usually for a fraction of what he could have received directly from the principal.

If substitute brokerage did a brisk business in the South, it did a roaring trade in the North, especially after blacks were permitted to enlist and be counted in state quotas. Northern substitute brokers found a rich harvest among fugitive slaves, whose military service could be purchased for next to nothing. Despite the strictures of radical Northern papers like the New York *Tribune* and the clamor of the labor unions, which denounced the hiring of substitutes, the practice continued throughout the war. With wages averaging about ten dollars a week, the hiring of substitutes and the purchase of exemptions provoked real unrest, as in the great four-day draft riot in New York.

Conscription in the North (as in the South) did promote volunteering; otherwise, it was a failure: a mere 36,000 men were actually drafted into the Union army. Most of the blue-clad hosts that followed Grant and Sherman had all enlisted by December 1862. Thereafter, repeated calls for men and resort to state and federal drafts brought few recruits. The only significant addition to the Union army came from the enlistment of blacks—some 170,000—most of them recruited in occupied Southern states. Conscription was better organized and far more successful in the Confederacy, an index of its desperate need for manpower.

The state of North Carolina alone furnished 21,343 draftees in addition to 8,000 volunteers who were forced to enlist or be conscripted.

The Wide Disparity in Resources

In manpower, as in every other essential for waging war except in spirit and leadership, the South was at a distinct disadvantage. The resources of the North were so much more extensive that it kept a well equipped army of nearly a million men constantly in the field for three years, while at the same time producing more consumer goods than ever before. The Southern population wore homespun clothes and drank a coffee substitute made of parched corn. Northern civilians on the other hand were dining better and wearing more and better clothes than they had before the war. With its established armaments industry, its thousands of factories, its extensive railroad network, and its unlimited access to European sources for raw materials and finished goods, the North faced but one major problem —that of organizing and allocating its resources—which was solved after the first year of the war.

Because the South had almost no industry and only one-fourth of the Union's railroad mileage, it was perilously dependent upon outside sources of supply. Necessity forced the blockaded South to interfere with property rights; by the spring of 1862 several of the states had passed laws that restricted acreage devoted to the cotton crop. Foodstuffs and forage were to be grown in its place, and where legislation was lacking, local vigilance committees brought community pressure to bear on planters who would not

The primitive state of medical services in the army meant untold added suffering for wounded on both sides. Dr Hurd of the Union army tends Confederate casualties under makeshift shelters after the Battle of Antietam.

comply. In 1863 the Army Quartermaster Corps was given authority to impress foodstuffs, and a tithing act compelled farmers to donate one-tenth of their crops. Most planters, large and small, resented these arbitrary measures. But the legislation that aroused the greatest uproar was the exemption from military service of overseers and planters who possessed more than twenty slaves. The law was denounced as a class measure, raising the cry of ''A rich man's war, a poor man's fight,'' a slogan that would be echoed in the North during the draft riots. So adverse was public opinion that the Davis administration shied away from enforcing it.

Draconian measures could not make up for shortages of draft animals, tilling and harvesting equipment, salt for curing meat, boxes and barrels for storage, and railroads to transport foodstuffs; but by 1863 the Confederacy was producing enough food to supply its armies and its civilian population. Ragged, ill-shod, and ill-fed as the Confederate armies were, there were usually sufficient rations until the very end.

The civilian population of the South, too, rarely suffered from actual want, though the standard of living declined dramatically. Coffee, tea, better grades of textiles, thread, paper, soap, boots, shoes, and indeed all manufactured items, became increasingly difficult to purchase as the Union blockade became more efficient. But the staples of the Southern diet for blacks and whites alike—beef, pork, bacon, molasses, and corn meal—were in adequate supply, barring areas of actual combat or of intense guerrilla

A volunteer refreshment saloon for troops passing through the railroad station. This lithograph commemorates the patriotic work which was ''supported gratuitously by the citizens of Philadelphia.''

activity. The primitive nature of the Southern agricultural economy made for unusual resilience under wartime conditions.

Of course the absence of so many young men placed a heavy burden of labor upon the old, the women, and the young children. But since a majority of the population lived and labored on small farms with few or no slaves, the transition from raising cotton to raising foodstuffs was not that difficult. It was more of a problem on larger plantations with larger slave populations, where gangs of field hands had to be retrained. But this task, too, was met successfully. What food shortages occurred were the direct result of inadequate transportation and faulty distribution, not of production.

Living conditions in the Confederate capital of Richmond were as bleak as anywhere in the country. The seat of government and a major center of industry, Richmond housed large numbers of workmen and white-collar workers. Food and clothing became so expensive that municipal authorities frequently had to requisition staples and fix their price, yet only once was there a serious disturbance over the cost of living. On April 2, 1863, a mob demanding ''bread'' looted clothing and jewelry stores, as well as food stores. Hoarding and speculation were the

211

major causes of the riot, not actual starvation.

Gold or silver in place of notes would do wonders. In 1864 a visiting Englishman, who was paying three shillings (thirty-five cents) a day in silver for room and board, declared that he had never lived so well, so cheaply. And Mrs Roger Pryor, who had been a famous belle during the Buchanan administration, found a ready market in Richmond for her prewar finery. Removing the costly French and Belgian lace which trimmed her evening dresses, she made them into collars and sleeves. Then, she cut the yards and yards of silk, fine muslin, and velvet of her crinolines and sold them by the piece to be made into the fashionable bonnets of the day. Before the war, Mrs Pryor had thought nothing of wearing only once an imported opera cloak that cost a hundred dollars in gold. Now, she labored long hours manufacturing "vanities," as she called them, for the luxury market in Richmond. From her earnings in December 1864, she paid $1,200 in Confederate money for a barrel of flour, and $50 for a piece of corned beef. The beef, some boiled peas, and a pie of sorghum molasses thickened with flour and garnished with walnuts made up the Pryors' Christmas dinner.

Like Mrs Pryor, the Confederate War Department clerk,

John B. Jones, counted himself lucky to dine on a piece of fat beef shoulder and a head of cabbage from his kitchen garden. While he bemoaned the exorbitant price of hard candy for his Christmas tree, a cluster of Kentucky generals and Confederate politicians sat down to a dinner of oyster soup, roast mutton, ham, boned turkey, wild duck, partridge, plum pudding, and the appropriate vintage wines. But even these grandees could afford few such splurges; daily life in the Confederacy had become a grim struggle for food and clothing, with precious little left over.

The scarcity of rags to manufacture newsprint, of paper mills to process it, of printers to set the type, and ink for printing, soon reduced Southern newspapers to a single folded page, often printed on wrapping paper or wallpaper. The publication of books was also restricted with serious consequences for the level of Southern education from the primary grades to the universities. Largely

dependent upon Northern and English publishing houses, new books for instruction or entertainment soon became luxury items too. By 1863, the Southern public was so starved for news that it became profitable to establish "Confederate reading rooms" in the larger cities where Northern newspapers and magazines could be read for a fee. Especially popular were the illustrated weeklies, *Frank Leslie's* and *Harpers'*, which through the lavish use of woodcuts gave visual reproduction to the events of the day.

Northern War Correspondents

If the war throttled, then all but destroyed, the Southern press, it stimulated the Northern press, widening its audience and increasing its revenues from circulation and advertising. The great metropolitan dailies devoted most of their content to war news. Corps of "special" correspondents followed the armies and the navy. Although they had no recognized status, and were always at the mercy of arbitrary military action, they provided volumes of information and vivid feature items. The New York *Herald* employed more war reporters than any other paper, and maintained its own mapmakers who drew unusually clear sketches of military dispositions. Almost every week, one of these maps would appear on the front page of the *Herald's* large "elephant" edition. The *Herald's* reporting may have been more colorful, but the New York

The fanciful dress of the early militia regiments gave way to more practical outfits as uniforms became more standardized. These three belt buckles were regulation issue for the Union army.

Quantrill's Raiders

Civil war brought not only battles between armies but atrocities and murders by guerrilla bands—the most notorious of which was led by William Clarke Quantrill. Quantrill was a former Kansas school teacher, born in Ohio, who had never lived a day of his life in the South. When war came, however, he emerged as a rabid ''Southerner,'' and he received a commission in the Confederate army.

Quantrill was totally unscrupulous. He could double-cross his own men, murder in cold blood, and affect the disguise of Union garb. Moreover his raiders were well suited to their grisly profession: they were mounted on the best horses in the area for they stole only the best; they were heavily armed; they were eager to follow their leader's injunction to ''kill every man big enough to carry a gun.'' His mob included four men who would later become infamous in their own right: Frank and Jesse James, and Cole and James Younger.

Quantrill's treachery matched his savagery. At one point he apparently pretended to go along with an attack aimed at freeing slaves. Quantrill had however told the plantation owner of the raid before it occurred and the men were gunned down while Quantrill watched.

Quantrill's most blood-chilling raid began before dawn on August 21, 1863. With about 450 men, he had ridden through the night from Missouri to Lawrence, Kansas, a center of abolitionism and, as such, a special target for Confederates. Men were gunned down on the streets in full view of their wives and children. Just out of town, some Union recruits, who were as yet unmustered, were murdered. Senator Jim Lane, an abolitionist spokesman, narrowly escaped death by removing the name from his house before the arrival of the raiders and hiding in a nearby cornfield. At nine o'clock in the morning, a lookout spotted an advance column of Union troops and gave the signal to abandon the town. They left in their wake many gutted build-

Lawrence, Kansas, in flames as Quantrill's men ride out after a raid, leaving 150 dead and 200 houses and barns destroyed. Inset: The notorious guerrilla leader.

ings and 150 corpses. Not one of the guerrilla band was killed—nor, as Quantrill made a point of boasting, were any women.

In October 1863, while on their way to Texas where they would spend the winter, Quantrill and his men, dressed in Union uniforms, drew across a line of Federal troops en route to the Union fort near Baxter Springs, Kansas. Quantrill and his men took them by surprise—the Federals thought they were being met by a welcoming party. While a few managed to escape, the bulk of the Northern column was slaughtered.

This trail of murder and mayhem was finally brought to a halt in May 1865 when the twenty-seven-year-old Quantrill was surprised by Union troops in Kentucky, shot in the melee, and died from his wounds the following month.

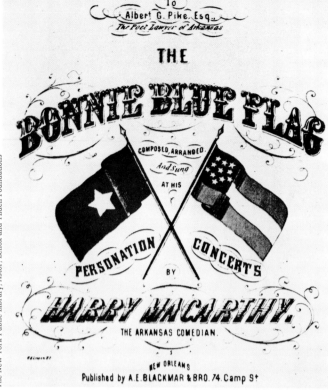

*Sheet music of "The Bonnie Blue Flag," a patriotic
Confederate song which enjoyed great popularity early
in the war. Such stirring numbers later gave way to
more plaintive ballads like "The Vacant Chair."*

sorrow of war. As the North had its humorous, mock-heroic characters like Charles G. Halpine's "Private Miles O'Reilly," Southerners chuckled at the antics of "Bill Arp," the creation of Charles H. Smith, a Confederate soldier with an ear for country dialect and rustic whimsy.

Threadbare planters and the hard-pressed professional classes in the cities could also gain a measure of entertainment from the legitimate stage. Here, as with all social activities in the Confederacy, the offering was pitifully meager. After Admiral Farragut captured New Orleans in April 1862, only Richmond and Charleston had theaters of any note, and only in those cities could one catch an occasional performance of a Shakespeare play. Since most of the actors had left for the North, performances ranged from indifferent to bad, but the theaters did a thriving business. Unlike the rich and more populous Union, the scattered small towns and county seats of the Confederacy were almost completely devoid of any professional entertainment. Few traveling troupes of actors, musicians, or humorists, found it profitable to venture into the countryside where even Confederate notes were scarce.

After two years of war, Hartford, Connecticut, a small city of 35,000 inhabitants, provided as much public entertainment and more varied cultural events than the entire Confederacy. During the week of March 11, 1863, the average citizen in Hartford could attend performances of a

Tribune's was more accurate, its editorial policy less eccentric, though every bit as opinionated. Through weekly editions of the New York, Chicago, Boston, and Philadelphia papers, not to mention scores of dailies and weeklies published in smaller cities, the people of the North were given wide coverage of the war. The press, of course, was supplemented by the illustrated weeklies and by the more stately periodicals, such as the *North American Review, Harper's New Monthly Magazine,* and the *Atlantic Monthly,* which offered, in addition, articles of broad cultural interest.

As the Union army sliced through large areas of the South, it reduced further the dwindling resources of the Confederacy, and drove thousands of non-combatants, white and black, from their homes. Refugees clogged the roads. The housing and care of these unfortunate people, many of whom were the very old and the very young, was beyond the scope of private charity or government relief. Yet the undoubted hardships they suffered could not compare with the plight of fugitive slaves. A contemporary witness said that "anything more helpless or wretched than their aspect I never saw. Miserably clothed, footsore and weary . . . they seemed to have no idea, no plan and no distinct purpose."

Although scenes like this bespoke grave social dislocation, the harried citizen of the Confederacy managed to enjoy some amusement and gain some relief from the

*The three Booth brothers pose in costumes from their
only joint appearance, in Shakespeare's Julius Caesar.
From left to right: John Wilkes as Mark Antony,
Edwin as Brutus, and Junius Brutus Jr as Cassius.*

The New York Draft Riot

As the war dragged on both sides were forced to come to terms with the problem of falling enlistments. The Confederacy moved first, enacting the first draft law in American history in the spring of 1862. The Union followed suit almost a full year later with the Conscription Act of 1863. The act was no more popular than draft laws ever are, and probably it was more unfair than most. It provided that a man could avoid military service if he paid $300 or hired a substitute. For the working man this was the better part of a year's wages and therefore beyond his reach. The injustice was blatant, and to the Irish of New York City it was not an injustice to submit to tamely.

On July 11, 1863 the first names were pulled from the lottery wheel at the provost-marshal's office on Third Avenue at Forty-sixth Street. To begin with there were no signs of trouble, but as the names of the first draftees were published in the Sunday papers, an angry crowd of Irish workers began to protest. By Monday, when more names were pulled from the wheel, the crowd's anger spilled over into violence.

The rioters first attacked and seized the provost-marshal's office. They poured camphene over the draft records and set the building on fire. In mid-town Manhattan shops were broken into, looted, and burned. The mob controlled the fire hydrants so fire fighting was severely hampered. The Colored Orphan Asylum at the corner of Fifth Avenue and Forty-sixth Street was burned to the ground. A black man was seized, beaten, hung from a tree, and burned to death.

On Tuesday the governor returned from New Jersey to find New York City in open rebellion. He declared the city and county of New York to be in a state of insurrection and called for troops. The city's police made a valiant effort to gain control of the city, but with the mob now numbering almost fifty thousand they were virtually powerless. Nor could they

The angry mob gives vent to its fury: after setting fire to the provost marshal's office, the rioters then prevented fire-fighting services from getting through.

call on the militia, which was away at Gettysburg.

The insurrection raged for four days. On July 16 several regiments of militia returned from Pennsylvania, and order was finally restored. Some estimates of deaths among the rioters go as high as a thousand; police deaths are estimated at about fifty. During the riot, the city's legislators passed a bill authorizing the payment of $300 for any drafted New Yorker who could not afford to pay the commutation fee for himself. The governor urged the president to suspend execution of the draft act until its constitutionality could be tested in the courts; Lincoln replied that he would abide by any court's decision on the matter but in the meantime the law would be enforced.

humorous adaption of the old fable, *The Seven Sisters*, Shakespeare's *Richard III*, or George Christy's minstrels including his "famous live pig." New York City, of course, had dozens of theaters, concert halls, and opera houses. At Niblo's Garden, one could see Edwin Forrest in his last great role, *King Lear*; during the same season of 1864, the Booths—Edwin, Junius Brutus, and John Wilkes—played in *Julius Caesar* to packed houses in the Winter Garden. If a New Yorker preferred lighter entertainment, he could choose a variety show at six large, well-established theaters, and at least twenty less pretentious ones. Grand Opera also enjoyed a vogue in New York and throughout Northern cities, and four European opera companies toured the North during the winter of 1863–64. Prima donnas like Adelina Patti, or the American soprano Clara Louise Kellogg, who played Margarita in Gounod's new opera *Faust*, always performed to capacity houses. Beethoven's symphonies, including the Ninth with its choral accompaniment, his concertos, and his sonatas were standard repertoire for New York's Philharmonic concerts at the Academy of Music on 14th Street.

There was also a great outpouring of popular music; the prolific Henry Clay Work, a Connecticut Yankee, easily headed a list of perhaps fifty composers in the North and the South who turned out scores of simple melodies that caught the public's fancy. Patriotic and martial airs were the most popular at first, but after the awful carnage of Murfreesboro in the west, of Gettysburg and Grant's Wilderness campaign in the east, a deep sadness, almost a sense of despair, marked the sentimental themes of the day. "The Vacant Chair," "When This Cruel War Is Over," "Tenting Tonight," replaced the stirring refrains of "The Union Forever," "Rally Round The Flag," even "Dixie," the jolly Confederate army marching song written by the Northern comedian Dan Emmett. Both publics shared many of the same sad songs—the plaintive air "Just Before the Battle Mother" being as much appreciated in the North as in the South.

The ballads of the day, especially those that were popular during 1864, show how deeply the war was affecting the lives of people. After every major battle, a doleful procession of parents or other loved ones journeyed from North and South to nurse their wounded or bring back their dead for burial. When Captain Oliver Wendell Holmes (later to become one of the nation's great jurists) was badly wounded at Antietam, his father, the distinguished Boston physician and poet, searched for days through rude field hospitals near the battlefield and lurching, springless ambulances until he finally found his son. The wife of a Connecticut captain nursed her wounded husband in a shabby farmhouse near Fredericksburg for sixteen days before he died. As the English journalist Edward Dicey said, "I suppose there is scarce a household in Massachusetts, which the war has not associated with some hope, or fear, or sorrow of its own."

The sorrow lay even heavier in the South where the death rate was proportionately higher than in the North. In all, the war claimed the lives of some 600,000 Americans—over 4 per cent of the entire male population.

Care and Comfort for the Wounded

This dreadful toll, great as it was, would have been greater had it not been for volunteer assistance in the North and South. Inadequate military medical facilities and ill-trained army doctors could never have coped with the wounded and the sick. Neither the Union nor the Confederacy had at first any organized corps of nurses. Both were desperately short of hospitals and medical supplies of all kinds. There was no lack of zeal in supplying many of these essentials, but a woeful lack of coordination. An example of the confusion that reigned in the early days of the war was the shipment of a thousand pillow cases, along with only a dozen sheets, to a United States regimental hospital.

Typically, the North responded more vigorously to the need for organized effort in this area than the poorer, less sophisticated South. The determined Dorothea Dix, every bit as forceful as Florence Nightingale, badgered the Lincoln administration into accepting women nurses. In the face of opposition from the army and from a society that thought women too delicate for this kind of work, she recruited and organized an able group of volunteer nurses who helped staff both field and general hospitals.

Influenced by British precedent in the Crimean War, a small group of private citizens in New York formed the United States Sanitary Commission. It aimed to centralize all voluntary contributions and to distribute them systematically. After winning reluctant acceptance from the War Department, the commission formed a highly effective, well-financed army relief organization providing care and comfort for the Union soldier. In the capable hands of its executive secretary, Frederick Law Olmsted, an able journalist and the nation's first professional landscape architect, the commission brought about much needed reforms in the archaic army medical corps. Through its efforts, the commission saved thousands of lives that would otherwise have been lost by neglect.

Regretably, this spirit of high-minded patriotism and personal sacrifice did not reflect predominant social attitudes. Pleasure-seeking, newly-rich war profiteers were more apt to set the style of living, at least in the cities. Speculators, who had suddenly grown rich dealing in government contracts or in cotton or gold, thought nothing of spending thousands of dollars on matched thoroughbred horses and costly, imported carriages. The great boom in the North, which reached its height in mid-1863, had

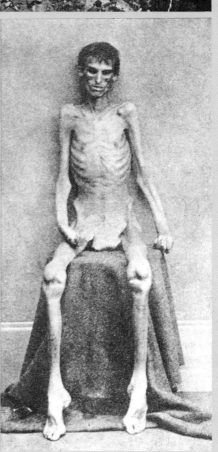

Both pictures: Library of Congress

The Andersonville Nightmare

The arrangements made between the two sides in July 1862 for exchanging prisoners on parole gradually collapsed, largely over the problem of former slaves, captured while serving with the Federal forces. General Grant's belief that "every man we hold when released on parole or otherwise, becomes an active soldier against us at once either directly or indirectly" meant that by 1864 the policy was dead. With the abandonment of prisoner exchanges, the numbers of prisoners held by both sides increased alarmingly. The North was hard pressed to house and feed them adequately. For the South—which could not even keep its own troops sufficiently supplied—it was an impossibility.

With the advance of Union armies toward the capital, Richmond prisons were abandoned, and in February 1864 the Confederate authorities hastily constructed a stockade near Andersonville, Georgia, to house the growing thousands of prisoners. It was simply a bare log enclosure, covering some twenty-six swampy acres, and though barracks were planned, they were never built. Intended to house 10,000 men, Camp Sumter was crammed with 32,000 prisoners by the summer of 1864.

The only water supply was a small, sluggish stream which ran through the camp, and sanitary conditions were abominable. Food was grossly inadequate—mostly unsifted cornmeal eaten raw. There were no drugs, and medical care of any kind was practically nonexistent. And there was very little shelter from the elements. As a result of these appalling conditions disease was rampant—dysentery, acute diarrhea, scurvy, and gangrene ran their course unchecked, and men weakened by near-starvation could not withstand them. Some prisoners did escape and the sight of them sickened and enraged the Union soldiers marching through the South. Almost 13,000 of the prisoners at Andersonville died, and were buried in

Holding three times as many prisoners as originally intended, with almost no shelter, no sanitation, and one source of water, it is not surprising that Andersonville meant death for thousands. This man somehow emerged alive—a human scarecrow.

a common grave outside the stockade.

In the postwar atmosphere of vengeance the commander of Andersonville, a Swiss immigrant named Henry Wirtz, was charged with "murder in violation of the laws and customs of war." Despite a spirited defense, Captain Wirtz was found guilty and hanged on November 10, 1865—the first soldier to be executed for atrocities against prisoners of war.

brought with it unparalleled prosperity. True, real income for the working classes was declining as inflation sapped earnings. But near full employment in the factory and on the farm gave a surface air of material well-being. And more often than not, the average standard of living was higher because all who were able to work within a family unit found ready employment. As life in the Confederacy was drab, deprived, and dull, so it was glittering, varied, and opulent in the boom atmosphere of the industrial and urban North.

A Flourishing Economy

Military purchasing had stimulated all aspects of the Northern economy. By 1862 the government was spending $2.5 million dollars a day for items ranging from carpet tacks to marine engines, from Colt revolvers weighing a few pounds to the giant Columbiad cannon weighing several tons. The great grain- and meat-producing states of the northwest were likewise responding to the impact of what was then massive government spending. They had suffered heavy losses when they lost the Southern trade, but government purchases of food stuffs soon took up the slack. These, together with crop failures in Europe during 1862 and 1863, put a premium on western farm products.

Four great east-west train systems—the Baltimore & Ohio, the Pennsylvania, the Erie, and the New York Central —together with the Great Lakes and the Erie Canal, easily absorbed the Mississippi River traffic, which the Confederacy had blocked. Labor may have been scarce, but markets were so strong and profitable that even small farmers could afford the newly developed mechanical reapers and threshers that substituted horsepower for manpower. The result was a spectacular rise in farm productivity, much of which was passed on to millers,

Above: The formidable women of the US Sanitary Commission with convalescent troops at Alexandria, Virginia. The commission was started by New Yorkers, shocked at the lack of army medical services.

owners of packing houses and grain elevators, railroads, and inland shipping lines. Northern railroads, debt-ridden after the depression of 1857, were able to pay off all their obligations and were declaring dividends as high as 20 per cent on the market value of a share of stock well before the war drew to a close.

New England's textile industry had experienced a similar upheaval when the war began. Owners of cotton mills not only lost their large Southern trade in coarse sheetings, shirtings, and denims, but also their supply of raw cotton. Anticipating trouble as early as the summer of 1860, mill owners had stockpiled a year's supply of cotton at normal demand. Despite sharp increases in retail prices, supplies of the staple soon ran out. Most of the mills had closed down early by 1862, displacing some 200,000 workers. Unemployment was temporary, however. The army absorbed many of these workers, while the woolen textile industry, which was undergoing a meteoric rise in production, employed most of the remainder.

Large scale purchase of raw wool for uniforms and military blankets had caused an immediate upward price spiral of that staple. Profiteering manufacturers of woolen cloth stretched their precious supplies of raw wool as far as they could by mixing it with processed woolen rags to produce an inferior material called "shoddy." Volunteer regiments early in the war were uniformed with shoddy, which after a few weeks in camp quite literally fell apart. Eventually the price of raw wool fell to reasonable levels when imports of British and Australian wool and an increased western wool clip reached the market during the winter of 1862–63.

At the same time increasing quantities of raw cotton were coming into New England from India and from those areas of the Confederacy that fell to Union arms. Both governments had prohibited trading between the lines, but by 1864 the Confederacy was in such dire straits that

Above: A Union field hospital at Savage Station, Virginia, June 30, 1862. The doctor is in the foreground.
Left: For the survivors, the pristine conditions of an army hospital tended by Dorothea Dix's corps of nurses.

CHRISTMAS EVE '62

it was willing to relax its restrictions on the export of raw cotton to the North. New England cotton interests, which had always lobbied for wider access to Southern supplies, stepped up pressure on the Lincoln administration. Worried about his political future in the summer of 1864, Lincoln bowed to their demands, authorizing limited trade under government regulation.

Inflation and the Currency Crisis

Northern capitalists had begun a rapid expansion of new mill capacity in anticipation of a strong peacetime demand for cotton textiles. That Northern businessmen had the means to make long-term investments for future markets was an indication of the intrinsic strength of the Union economy. Yet inflation promoted an economic imbalance in

which mass purchasing power lagged behind productivity. Inflation was a problem in the North, but it reached catastrophic proportions in the Confederacy where it wiped out the savings of the white population.

Both governments shied away from heavy taxation. The Union managed to stagger through the first year of the war primarily by borrowing from the banks. But as war expenditures continued to escalate, these sources of ready cash dried up. A much longer war was now anticipated, and Lincoln's secretary of the treasury, Salmon P. Chase, working closely with the finance committees of Congress, took the United States off the gold standard. On February 25, 1862, Congress authorized the issuance of $150 million in paper currency, not redeemable in gold or silver but made legal tender. These notes, promptly dubbed "greenbacks," put a premium on all metallic currency down to copper cents. For a brief period no coins could be found throughout the North as speculators bought

Though it may be over-sentimental for modern tastes, this contemporary painting is nevertheless touching. With the children tucked safely in bed, the wife prays for her husband's safe return while he, sitting by his lonely camp fire, looks fondly at pictures of his family and dreams of home. At top left, Santa Claus delivers presents by his traditional route and, top right, pays a visit to an army camp. The scenes at lower left and right are reminders that the war does not stop, even for Christmas. As a final touch, husband and wife are separated by an ominous row of snow-covered gravestones.

Although the Union did raise excise taxes and duties substantially, and adopted both an income tax and a direct tax apportioned among the states according to population, it financed the war primarily through inflating the currency and through large-scale borrowing.

With far scantier resources of capital, the Confederacy, was compelled to resort to the printing presses almost from the beginning of the conflict. It, too, levied direct taxes and raised excise rates, but it lagged behind the Union in imposing a comprehensive system of taxation. The Davis administration fought the entire war on about $36 million in specie. The result, of course, was predictable. Confederate paper money, which was not made legal tender, began to decline in value almost at once. When the Union greenback fell to its lowest point, it was still worth in gold eight times the amount of the Confederate dollar. The war cost the Southern people the equivalent of almost $600 million in gold. Emancipation wiped out another three billion gold dollars invested in slave property.

The Southern Revival

Though its economy was wrecked, its transportation system all but destroyed, and its moneyed classes beggared, ten years after Appomatox the South was producing far more goods and services than it had in 1860. The Confederate war effort, as fumbling as it was, had developed talents for organization, disclosed mineral wealth in coal and iron, and fostered the spirit of enterprise that had been hobbled so long by the institution of slavery and the complete dominance of the cotton culture. The North, whose war debt in gold was about three times that of the South, emerged from the conflict with a much stronger economy than it had in 1860. Enterprising men in the North had learned and were applying the arts of complex organisation. Vast material resources like coal, oil, and iron ore, which had been discovered and tapped during the war, would now be exploited on a grand scale. With peace came renewed immigration that stimulated industrial development and opened up new farming regions in the trans-Mississippi west. The wartime expansion and consolidation of eastern railroads made them far more efficient than they were before the war, and the rails would soon be pushing their way westward.

It is true that the slower recovery of the war-devastated South put a brake on the economic growth of the nation. And inflation in the North had cut down on capital investment during the war. Still, if the war-enhanced capital resources of the Union are taken into account, the total economy in 1865 was far stronger, far wealthier than in 1860. Even in the South, the abolition of slavery was in the long run an economic, psychological, and moral blessing of the first magnitude.

them up with greenbacks and shipped them abroad. Retail businessmen could not make change for their customers. Various expedients such as postage stamps came into use until the Treasury issued fractional currency, or "shin plasters," as they were named. Eventually the government circulated $450 million in greenbacks whose value fluctuated in terms of gold with the fortunes of the Union. They fell to their lowest point during Grant's Wilderness campaign, when a greenback dollar was worth thirty-five cents in gold.

In 1863, Chase secured passage of the National Banking Act, which authorized member banks to issue notes backed by government bonds that could be purchased with greenbacks but paid interest in gold. Besides providing a market for government bonds, the national banking system supplied a currency of uniform value throughout the nation, the first such currency since Andrew Jackson destroyed the Second Bank of the United States in 1834.

Chapter 9

THE WIDER VIEW

No matter what Northerners said about preserving the Union or Southerners about securing independence, at the heart of the conflict was the issue of Negro slavery. The "peculiar institution" was fundamental to that way of life the South was fighting to defend. For the North the Emancipation Proclamation elevated the struggle from a war of coercion to a crusade. For blacks it transformed a distant hope into a real and immediate promise. At the same time the slavery question profoundly influenced views on the other side of the Atlantic. And as both North and South realized, the issue of European involvement could be critical to the outcome of the war.

The Death of Slavery

The Civil War was the single most important event in the history of black people in America. Just as slavery was the basic cause of the Civil War, so also was emancipation one of its most important results. Not only did 4 million slaves achieve freedom, but the impetus of wartime change led to the passage of equal rights legislation and of the Fourteenth and Fifteenth Amendments to the Constitution after the war. These equalitarian measures were never fully carried out even during Reconstruction and became ineffectual for three generations after 1875. But they remained in the Constitution and helped to form the legal basis for the resurgence of civil rights progress that started in the 1950s.

The Negro question that had plagued the country since the Missouri Compromise was a central issue of the war. The South seceded to escape from what it looked on as a Northern threat to "Southern institutions." The foremost Southern institution was slavery. Confederate Vice President Alexander Stephens said in 1861 that the slavery controversy was the "immediate cause" of secession. "Our Confederacy," he continued, "is founded upon the great truth that slavery—subordination to the superior race—is [the Negro's] natural and normal condition. This, our new government, is the first in the history of the world based upon this great physical and moral truth."

While the South fought to preserve slavery, the North did not, at first, fight to destroy the "peculiar institution." President Lincoln's principal war aim was restoration of the Union. In the first year or more of the conflict this meant the Union "as it was"—with slavery still in it. Lincoln had no love for slavery. He once said that "if slavery is not wrong, nothing is wrong." But as president he was pledged to preserve the Constitution, and slavery was one of those institutions protected by the Constitution. Abolitionists and radical Republicans implored the president to use his

Newly picked cotton being cleaned by slaves on the Smith plantation, Beaufort, South Carolina—a photograph taken in 1862.

In the 1850s the artist Eyre Crow accompanied the English novelist William Makepeace Thackeray on a tour of the South. Their object was to study slavery. In Richmond, Virginia, Crow witnessed a slave auction which he later recorded on canvas.

war powers to seize enemy property as an instrument of emancipation. In the end, Lincoln did this, but he believed that an emancipation proclamation early in the war might fatally divide Northern public opinion. Anti-Negro racism pervaded the North. The Democratic party stood adamant against emancipation, while the old Whig element in the Republican party abhorred abolitionism. Four border slave states had remained loyal to the Union, and Lincoln feared that premature measures against slavery would drive them into the arms of the Confederacy. But he did hope that a demonstration of arms by the North would topple secessionist control of the South, reestablish Unionists in power there, and prepare the way for reunion by negotiation and compromise. Precipitate action against slavery, as Lincoln saw it, would only unite the South behind the Confederacy while dividing the North. So long as restoration of the Union was the chief war aim, any policy toward slavery would have to be a question of means subordinated to this larger objective rather than an end in itself. "My paramount object in this struggle is to save the Union, and is not either to save or to destroy slavery," wrote Lincoln to the antislavery editor Horace Greeley in

In the 1850s the artist Eyre Crow accompanied the English novelist William Makepeace Thackeray on a tour of the South. Their object was to study slavery. In Richmond, Virginia, Crow witnessed a slave auction which he later recorded on canvas.

August 1862. "If I could save the Union without freeing any slave I would do it; and if I could save it by freeing all the slaves I would do it; and if I could save it by freeing some and leaving others alone, I would also do that."

Actually, Lincoln had already decided to issue a proclamation of emancipation when he wrote to Greeley, but was waiting for the best time to do it. Developments in the war combined with pressure from radical Republicans and abolitionists had pushed the administration to an antislavery policy by the middle of 1862. The "military necessity" thesis became the most compelling argument for emancipation. The eleven Confederate states contained altogether 3.5 million slaves, two-fifths of their total population. These slaves were a vital military resource for the South. They raised much of its food and fiber, manned part of its transportation network, worked in

Collection of J. P. Altmayer

While military necessity furnished the main argument for emancipation, political and moral considerations were also important. An antislavery policy would strengthen the North's diplomatic efforts to keep Britain from helping the South, for liberal opinion there was strong enough to prevent British intervention on the side of slavery against freedom. The radicals also insisted that even if the Union could be restored by compromise, slavery would remain a source of future strife. There could be no permanent peace, they maintained, while 4 million people (including the half million in loyal slave states) were in bondage. Moreover, the North's tolerance of slavery made a mockery of its claim to be fighting for the preservation of republican government as the "last, best hope" of mankind. Radicals urged Lincoln to convert the war from a mere struggle for dominion into a crusade for freedom.

"Contraband of War"

As time went on, events made these arguments *for* emancipation more crucial than those *against* it. In the first place, there was the problem of what to do with fugitive slaves. As Union armies began to invade the South, a swelling volume of slaves straggled into Yankee camps hoping for freedom. Proslavery Northern generals returned these fugitives to their masters under provisions of the Fugitive Slave Law of 1850, even though the South had seceded from the government that had passed the law. Antislavery generals, on the other hand, searched for some legal justification to retain the fugitives. General Benjamin Butler of Massachusetts, commanding Union troops lodged on the coast of Virginia, provided that justification. When three fugitives entered his lines in May 1861, Butler labeled them "contraband of war," refused to return them to their masters, and put them to work for the North. The term "contraband" became immediately popular and was used for the rest of the war to describe escaped or freed slaves. Nine hundred contrabands followed the first three into Butler's camp within three months. By then, thousands of others had done the same elsewhere and Congress had sanctioned the contraband policy by passing, on August 6, 1861, a confiscation act providing for the seizure of all property, including slaves, used "in aid of the rebellion." Although this did not *emancipate* the contrabands it was an important step toward freedom.

Lincoln's final commitment to emancipation was still a year away, but in the months after passage of the confiscation act antislavery pressures continued to grow. One of these pressures was the disastrous military situation: the Confederacy won most of the major battles in the first two years of the war, and there was a constant danger of British intervention on the side of the South. War weariness and defeatism lowered Northern morale. Lincoln's cautious

Southern industries, and dug trenches, constructed military fortifications, and hauled supplies for the Confederate army. This freed a larger proportion of white males for military combat than any other society in history has been able to mobilize. The Confederate government began to conscript slaves and free Negroes for military and logistical labor well before it drafted white men for the army.

Antislavery Northerners were quick to point out the military importance of the black population to the South. A blow against slavery, they said, would cripple the Confederate war effort and attract thousands of freed slaves to the Northern side, where they could work and fight not only for their own freedom but for the Union as well. "Why? Oh! why does our Government allow its enemies this powerful advantage?" asked the black abolitionist Frederick Douglass. "The very stomach of this rebellion is the Negro in the condition of a slave. Arrest that hoe in the hands of the Negro, and you smite the rebellion in the very seat of its life. To fight against slaveholders, without fighting against slavery, is but a half-hearted business, and paralyzes the hands engaged in it."

"CÆSAR IMPERATOR!"
OR,
THE AMERICAN GLADIATORS.

Contemporary cartoon from the satirical London magazine Punch *showing the Union on the left and the Confederacy on the right. A black "Caesar" waits for the outcome of the gladiators' fight on a throne above them.*

policy toward slavery increasingly alienated his own party. It had become clear that the war was going to be a long, hard conflict, a *total* war requiring a total commitment of Northern resources to achieve victory. Thus the radical argument for emancipation as a blow to weaken the Confederacy and strengthen the Union cause began to win masses of converts. A series of antislavery measures issued from Congress in the spring and summer of 1862. A resolution forbade army officers to return fugitive slaves who entered Union lines. Slavery was abolished in the District of Columbia and prohibited in federal territories. A second confiscation act, passed on July 17, 1862, freed the slaves of all persons in rebellion against the United States.

The Proclamation of Emancipation

Amid these events, Lincoln drafted a preliminary proclamation of emancipation. Persuaded that publication of the proclamation while Northern troops were suffering defeats would be viewed as "our last *shriek* on the retreat," the president waited to issue it until September 22, 1862, following the Union victory at Antietam. The document proclaimed that all slaves in states still in rebellion on January 1, 1863, would be "forever free." Thus it decreed the freeing of slaves in all portions of the Con-

Right: A group of fieldhands in 1862 on the Hopkinson plantation in South Carolina. Slave labor was the backbone of the Southern economy and it freed able-bodied whites for military service.

226

Above: Lincoln reads a preliminary draft of the Emancipation Proclamation to his cabinet on July 22, 1862. The president decided to withhold it until the Union's military position was stronger.

federacy except Tennessee and a few enclaves elsewhere, which were under Union occupation. In one sense, the cliché is true, that the Proclamation did not free a single slave since it applied only in areas under Confederate control. But the Proclamation was a mighty promise; it proclaimed that the North was now fighting for freedom as well as Union. Actual physical emancipation could be achieved only as Union armies moved southward, but word of the Proclamation circulated quickly among slaves, who thenceforth knew that Yankee soldiers truly came as liberators.

The battle for freedom was far from over, however. Not only did more than two years of war lie ahead during which the prospects of Union victory were often bleak, but anti-Negro and anti-abolition sentiments in the North remained strong. The Democratic press screamed that emancipation would loose a horde of black men into the North to compete with white working men for jobs and "social equality." The small black population of Northern cities was augmented during the war by a handful of contrabands who found jobs on the docks and in factories. Fearful that this was only the beginning of a black invasion, whites rioted against Negroes in several cities in 1862–63, culminating in the New York draft riots of July 13–16, 1863.

Continuing Northern hostility toward blacks confirmed Lincoln's long-standing conviction that white racism would make racial harmony impossible if the 4 million slaves were freed. This had been one reason for his slow

steps toward emancipation. Once freedom became official Union policy, the president hoped to soften its impact by colonizing some of the freed slaves outside the United States. Emigration was also advocated by a small number of black nationalists who could see no future for their race in America and wanted to build a powerful black nation, led by expatriate black Americans, in Africa or the Caribbean. Black nationalist sentiment almost disappeared after the war broke out, however, as Negroes united behind the

Above: The 1st Tennessee (Colored) Battery. After Emancipation, freed and fugitive slaves joined the Union army in large numbers; how to use them to best advantage was a thorny problem for the North.

hope that emancipation and the incipient drive for equal civil and political rights heralded the dawn of a new era.

Lincoln feared that this new era would never come. He therefore sanctioned several colonization schemes during the war. In 1862 Congress appropriated $600,000 requested by the president to finance a pilot project for the voluntary emigration of Negroes freed by the war. Lincoln told a delegation of black leaders in August 1862 that racial differences would make it impossible for whites and blacks to live together as free men. "There is an unwillingness on the part of our people," said the president, "for you free colored people to remain with us. Whether it is right or wrong I do not propose to discuss, but to propose it as a fact with which we have to deal. It is better for us both, therefore, to be separated." The administration persuaded a group of 450 freed slaves to emigrate to Haiti, but the project collapsed in a shambles. White promoters of the colony funneled part of its funds into their own pockets, and smallpox and starvation decimated the ranks of the colonists. Lincoln finally admitted failure and sent a ship to bring the surviving Negroes home in February 1864. Even if this fiasco had not scotched the colonization program, the mobilization of the black community against the idea of getting rid of the race problem by getting rid of Negroes would have done so. "Sir," said a black leader to a white advocate of colonization, "this is our country as much as it is yours, and we will not leave it."

In addition to the 225,000 free Negroes in the North and the half million slaves and free blacks in loyal border states, at least another half million Confederate slaves

Above: A barred slave pen at Alexandria, Virginia. The Emancipation Proclamation dramatically changed the significance of the war to the blacks, holding out the hope of freedom and dignity in a new kind of world.

came within Union lines during the war. To be sure, freedom for some of them did not turn out to be all that they had hoped it would be—at least, not at first. They were often crowded into filthy contraband camps with poor food and worse medical care. They were promised wages for their labor, but somehow the wages arrived late or not at all. They found Billy Yank as ready as Johnny Reb to kick them around and curse them as "niggers." In cotton-growing areas occupied by Northern troops, the Union government leased captured plantations to white men (often Southerners who had taken an oath of allegiance) who worked them with black labor under conditions little different from slavery.

Despite hardships and oppression, freed slaves who came under Union control during the war constituted an important balance of power in the conflict. And not all their relations with Northern whites were characterized by exploitation or meanness. The government leased some of the occupied land directly to contrabands themselves, including the Mississippi plantations formerly owned by Jefferson Davis and his brother. Northern humanitarians did their best to improve conditions in contraband camps. In one of the major outpourings of idealism and missionary

zeal in American history, Northern abolitionists and churches organized freedmen's aid societies and sent thousands of teachers to the South to establish schools for the freedmen. 200,000 contrabands received some missionary schooling during the war. This was the forerunner of a larger postwar effort that established a network of elementary schools that became the basis of public education for blacks in the South. Northern missionaries also founded more than a hundred secondary schools and colleges that provided most of the higher education for southern Negroes until well into the twentieth century.

Ex-slaves in the Union Forces

While the freed slaves who worked as laborers for the North made a significant contribution, far more important in terms of both the Union war effort and of the impact on Northern public opinion were the 200,000 black men, four-fifths of them ex-slaves, who fought in the Union army and navy. More than any other single factor, black soldiers and sailors helped win the respect of the North for their race, made emancipation secure, and paved the way for the gains made in civil and political rights after 1865. They also helped win the war.

The United States Navy had never barred Negroes from its ranks. During the Civil War at least 20,000 black men served in the Union navy (the exact number is unknown since the navy did not keep records by race). They were confined for the most part to the lowest ranks and most menial jobs. Nevertheless some of them earned recognition and promotion, especially Captain Robert Smalls of the *Planter*, a Confederate steamer he had daringly sailed past Fort Sumter and the Charleston shore batteries to join the blockading Union fleet.

But the greatest amount of controversy, publicity, and glory was generated by the 176,000 black soldiers who fought in the Union army. At the outbreak of war, blacks in many parts of the North volunteered for the army, but the government rejected their services. An administration not yet ready to alienate conservatives or borderstate Unionists by declaring emancipation was not about to arm blacks to kill whites. As late as August 1862, Lincoln told a group from Indiana who proposed to raise two black regiments that "to arm the negroes would turn 50,000 bayonets from the loyal Border States against us that were for us."

Black leaders and radical Republicans, on the other hand, insisted that black men constituted the Union's greatest unused military resource. As the North continued to lose battles and to bewail its recruiting difficulties, radicals condemned the suicidal folly of rejecting black troops. "This is no time to fight only with your white hand," said Frederick Douglass, "and allow your black hand to remain tied." Douglass and his allies had another

reason for urging the arming of blacks. They knew that it would bury slavery beyond hope of revival and create a national debt to the black race that could be repaid only by granting full citizenship. "Once let the black man get upon his person the brass letters, *U.S.*," said Douglass, "let him get an eagle on his button, and a musket on his shoulder and bullets in his pocket, and there is no power on earth which can deny that he has earned the right to citizenship."

By the early fall of 1862 when the government had committed itself to emancipation, Lincoln was also on the verge of deciding to arm black soldiers. But still he hesitated, now because he and many others wondered whether black men, bred to fear and defer to whites, would fight or run when they met white men in arms. Many thought they would run. "Negroes—plantation negroes, at least—will never make soldiers in one generation," said one official. "Five white men could put a regiment to flight." Lincoln at first shared this view. "If we were to arm them," he said in September 1862, "I fear that in a few weeks the arms would be in the hands of the rebels."

By this time, however, the Northern situation was alarming. Morale had been shattered by repeated defeats in the summer of 1862. Lincoln had issued a call for 300,000 additional volunteers in July, but recruiting lagged badly. Finally the government decided to try organizing a few black regiments as an experiment. The first such regiment was mustered on November 7, 1862, on the sea islands off the coast of South Carolina and Georgia occupied by Union forces. Commanded by the Massachusetts abolitionist Thomas Wentworth Higginson, the enlisted men of the 1st South Carolina Volunteers were all freed slaves. After a number of successful skirmishes with rebel platoons, Higginson reported to the War Department in early 1863 that "no officer in this regiment now doubts that the key to the successful prosecution of this war lies in the unlimited employment of black troops." Lincoln was impressed by the success of the experiment, and ordered the War Department to proceed with a full-scale program of black enlistment. By August 1863 there were fourteen black regiments (approximately 14,000 men) in the field or ready for service, and twenty-four additional regiments being organized.

Already several of these regiments had proved themselves in battle. In May 1863 two Louisiana black regiments led an assault on the Confederate Mississippi River stronghold at Port Hudson, Louisiana. Although repulsed with heavy losses, the attack earned plaudits for the black men's courage and fighting ability. "You have no idea how my prejudices with regard to negro troops have been dispelled by the battle the other day," wrote one white officer. The New York *Tribune* stated flatly that the Port Hudson battle "settles the question that the negro race can fight." Two weeks later a raw regiment of freed-

The Bettmann Archive Inc

Courtesy Chicago Historical Society

*Above: Captain Robert Smalls, commander of the gunboat
Planter. He daringly sailed her out of Charleston harbor under the
noses of the Confederate batteries to join the blockading Union
ships. Above right: "Come and Join Us Brothers"—a recruiting
poster issued by the Supervisory Committee for Recruiting
Colored Regiments to induce more blacks to sign on for service in
the Union army. Blacks were rarely granted commissions, however.
When they were first formed, white officers were reluctant to
command these regiments, so various inducements were offered,
including (right) a free course at military school for those who
volunteered. Below: Frederick Douglass, lecturer and author, who
had escaped from slavery in 1838. He became a well-known figure
in the abolition movement, both in America and Europe, and
during the war he helped to organize two black regiments.*

The Bettmann Archive Inc

FREE MILITARY SCHOOL
FOR APPLICANTS FOR THE COMMAND
OF COLORED TROOPS

FREE MILITARY SCHOOL FOR APPLICANTS
COMMAND OF COLORED TROOPS

SUPERVISORY COMMITTEE
FOR RECRUITING COLORED TROOPS
AND FREE MILITARY SCHOOL
FOR APPLICANTS
FOR COMMAND OF COLORED TROOPS.

American Antiquarian Society

231

men garrisoning a Union outpost at Milliken's Bend on the Mississippi fought off a furious Confederate bayonet charge. "The bravery of the blacks," wrote the Assistant Secretary of War after viewing the battlefield, "completely revolutionized the sentiment of the army with regard to the employment of negro troops. I heard prominent officers who formerly in private had sneered at the idea of the negroes fighting express themselves after that as heartily in favor of it." On July 18 the 54th Massachusetts, the first black regiment recruited from the North, led an attack on Fort Wagner, which protected Charleston harbor. This assault was beaten back, but the black men fought with such bravery in the face of heavy odds that the 54th earned wide praise and became the most famous black regiment of the war. "It made Fort Wagner such a name to the colored race," commented the New York *Tribune*, "as Bunker Hill has been for ninety years to the white Yankees."

General Grant and President Lincoln were converted to this viewpoint by August 1863. Grant told Lincoln that the arming of blacks was "the heaviest blow yet given the Confederacy." The president repeated this assertion in a public statement on August 26, and added some caustic words to Northern opponents of emancipation. "You say you will not fight to free negroes. Some of them seem willing to fight for you." When the war was won, he continued, "there will be some black men who can remember that, with silent tongue, and clenched teeth, and steady eye, and well-poised bayonet, they have helped mankind on to this great consummation; while, I fear, there will be some white ones, unable to forget that, with malignant heart, and deceitful speech, they have strove to hinder it." Whatever Lincoln's private reservations about the future of race relations, from this time until his death he publicly moved ever closer to a commitment to equal rights.

As Union forces occupied more Southern territory, they gathered up able-bodied freedmen and enlisted them in the army. By October 20, 1864, there were 140 black regiments in service. Thirty-eight of them participated in the massive invasion of Virginia in 1864. Black men were the first soldiers to enter Charleston and Richmond when these two important Confederate cities fell in 1865. By the time the war was over, 176,000 blacks had fought in the Union army, about 9 per cent of the total enrollment. The black regiments fought in 449 engagements of which thirty-nine were major battles, most of them occurring in the last, decisive year of the conflict. More than 37,000 Negroes lost their lives fighting for the Union. Seventeen black soldiers and four sailors were awarded Congressional Medals of Honor. Some military analysts estimated that the black troops may have shortened the war by as much as a year.

But there was also a negative side to Northern policy on Negro soldiers. It was a Jim Crow army, and the separate regiments were seldom treated equally. Black troops were often given inferior arms, equipment, food, and medical care. They were assigned to far more than their share of labor and fatigue duty. Some black regiments were confined to garrison defense instead of being used in field operations because they were thought to be more acclimatized to the malarial lowlands in which many coastal and river garrisons were located. Black servicemen suffered a slightly higher death rate than white, but their rate of battle-related casualties was lower than for white troops while deaths from disease were higher. Nearly all commissioned officers in black regiments were white. Racial prejudice made promotion difficult for blacks, and fewer than one hundred black officers were commissioned during the war. While many of the white officers were abolitionists and racial egalitarians, others shared the army's pervasive racism and sometimes expressed openly their contempt for "niggers." And for more than a year, black enlisted men received less pay than whites. The Militia Act of July 17, 1862, authorizing the enlistment of blacks in the army, had envisaged their use primarily as laborers rather than soldiers and had set their pay at $7 per month. White soldiers received $13. Once blacks were organized in combat regiments this discrimination in pay made no sense, but Republican efforts to end it had to overcome the resistance of Democrats and conservatives who repudiated even this symbol of racial equality. Not until June 15, 1864, did Congress equalize the pay of black soldiers, and though this adjustment was made retroactive for most regiments, the families of many black soldiers had suffered hardship in the meantime.

A Great Step Forward

Despite these inequalities the enlistment of black troops was an enormous gain for black people as well as for the North. Colonel Higginson recorded in his journal the views of one corporal in the 1st South Carolina Volunteers: if the blacks had not become soldiers things might have slipped back as they were before, and Lincoln's four years would have come to nothing. And if freedom had been achieved, but without black soldiers, "it would have been always flung in dere faces—'Your fader never fought for his own freedom'—and what could dey answer? *Neber can say that to dis African race any more.*"

Even the Confederacy in the end was sufficiently impressed with the value of black troops to take the once-inconceivable step of recruiting its own. When the North first began to enlist black regiments, Southern leaders had screamed outrage, and the Confederate Congress had even authorized the execution of captured soldiers as slave insurrectionists. The South probably would never have actually carried out such a barbarous policy even if Lincoln had not threatened to retaliate by putting to death a Con-

Thomas Nast's painting of the entry of the 55th Massachusetts (Colored) Regiment into Charleston, South Carolina. The sight of Negro soldiers infuriated white Southerners, but their joyous reception by the freed slaves was repeated all over the South.

federate prisoner for each Unionist so treated. But there were scattered reports of inhumane treatment of black soldiers after capture. The worst such incident was the Fort Pillow massacre. On April 12, 1864, rebel troops under General Nathan Bedford Forrest murdered a large number of black troops after they had surrendered in a battle for Fort Pillow, Tennessee. The sight of an armed black man inspired rage in the hearts of most Southern whites. Thus the initial reaction of the Confederate government to a proposal by several of its army officers in January 1864 that the South raise its own black army as the only alternative to defeat was wholly negative. "If slaves will make good soldiers," said one official, "our whole theory of slavery is wrong." But the issue remained alive. As the Confederacy slid toward collapse early in 1865, General Robert E. Lee threw his support behind the idea of black troops. On March 13, 1865, Jefferson Davis signed a "Negro Soldier Law" providing for the enlistment of slaves, but this bill did not even promise definite freedom to those who served. It was a dying gasp in any case. A few companies were enrolled, but the war ended before the dubious theory that they would fight for the Confederacy could be tested.

The home-front record of slaves in the Confederacy was ambiguous. On the one hand, millions worked quietly on their plantations through the war. Southern whites in later years fondly recounted the faithfulness of their slaves, who did not rise in mass insurrection despite the absence of white men from home. Touching stories abound of slaves who helped the mistress bury the silver before the Yankees came. On the other hand, a few small insurrections took place during the war, and the stringent measures of Confederate home guards to prevent uprisings belie the stories of confidence in slave tractability. News of the Emancipation Proclamation traveled quickly via the slave grapevine, and while many thousands of slaves in isolated corners of the South probably remained ignorant of it, most bondsmen were well aware by 1863 or 1864 that Northern victory would bring them freedom. On many plantations, large numbers deserted when Northern troops came near, welcoming the Yankees as liberators.

Charles Beard described the Civil War as the Second American Revolution. For black people it was the first. It emancipated 4 million slaves and set in motion the forces that wrote their civil and political equality into the Constitution. The Thirteenth Amendment confirming emancipation as the major social revolution in American history was ratified in 1865. The Freedmen's Bureau and the Fourteenth and Fifteenth Amendments granting civil and political rights tried to complete this revolution after the war. Frustrated by the reaction of the 1870s, the revolution remained incomplete. But had it not been for the Civil War and especially the contribution of black troops to northern victory, it might never have begun.

Europe and the Civil War

Concern over slavery—and about the war in general—was not confined to America. The Civil War presented Europe with a dilemma. It was desirable, perhaps essential, to appease both North and South. But how was this possible when the North demanded neutrality and the South pleaded for recognition as a separate and sovereign nation? It could not be done, and since European statesmen dreaded the prospect of actual military involvement in the conflict, the diplomatic pattern was one of indecision and inactivity. In practical terms this meant that any decision would hinge on military success: if only one horse could be backed it was vital that it should be the winning horse. This sounds impartial—if coldblooded—but for the South it was a cruel paradox. It had to demonstrate its ability to survive in order to gain recognition, yet recognition might prove essential to that survival.

Both American powers were fully aware from the start of the war that Europe's actions would be determined by British attitudes. The diplomatic, naval, economic, and potential military strength of Great Britain was such that a natural leadership fell on her during the war. This leadership was not matched by arrogance because of the unambiguous statement made by the Federal government about the consequences of interference. Secretary of State William Seward made it perfectly clear that any attempt to provide the South with even moral support—in other words to recognize the Confederate States of America—would be taken as provocation. His tone was blunt and threatening. Lincoln was far more ambivalent about the possibility of war with Europe under such circumstances, but the president was not thought to be the prime mover in American foreign policy.

Lord John Russell, the British foreign minister, and Lord Palmerston, the prime minister, shared a common mistrust of Seward—a mistrust based on the conviction that he was personally anti-British. As for Lincoln, his presidential capacity was seriously doubted in British diplomatic circles, and few suspected that he had any real political acumen or the personality to enforce his policies. He was dismissed as a mere figurehead, with Seward the dangerous and slippery power in the shadows.

Not only was Seward supposedly anti-British, he was considered unscrupulous and unreliable, and too little concerned with accepted standards of international morality and law. This poor reputation was made all the more credible by his insistence that support for the Confederacy meant war. And as if to resolve any lingering doubt, Seward had sufficient arrogance to order the governments of Europe not to receive William Yancey, Pierre Rost, and Dudley Mann, the first Confederate commissioners. He was obeyed after only token receptions, which were no more than symbols of a shortlived defiance.

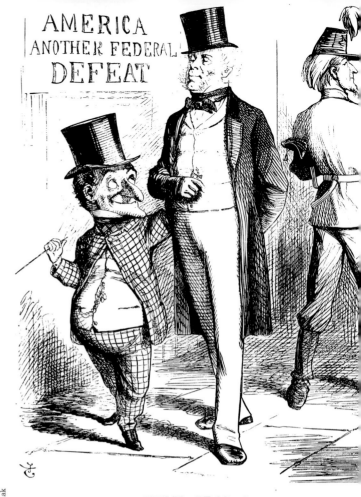

Angelo Hornak

VERY PROBABLE.

LORD PUNCH. "THAT WAS JEFF DAVIS, PAM! DON'T YOU RECOGNISE HIM?"
LORD PAM. "HM! WELL, NOT EXACTLY—MAY HAVE TO DO SO SOME OF THESE

The magazine character Punch chides Lord Pam (Lord Palmerston, the British prime minister) for his non-committal attitude toward the South. The Confederacy urgently needed British recognition; all it got was popular sympathy.

To counter this, the Union was most fortunate to have in Charles Francis Adams an extremely able minister in London. Adams, the son of John Quincy Adams and grandson of the second president, was a statesman of the first rank, and his personal attitudes and attributes made the Union's task of maintaining European neutrality very much easier. In times of crisis Adams could not only communicate easily with Russell, but he could also explain the integrity that underlay Seward's often bellicose statements. This was vital because most European powers, including Britain, were sympathetic toward the Confederate cause.

Why this sympathy? Why would so many Europeans who abhorred slavery look favorably on a nation established to protect "the peculiar institution"? The reasons are complex, but in the first place few Europeans believed that slavery was a crucial issue. Lincoln was taken at his word that this was a struggle to preserve the Union, not to destroy slavery. In that case it was quite natural to be on the side of those fighting for independence, much as continental Europeans had wished the American colonists well in their struggle with Britain nearly a century before.

And this support cut right across political, religious, and class divisions. In Britain, for example, Tories were joined by as many Liberals and Radicals, and a preponderance of newspaper editors, in backing Confederate independence. Quakers and Unitarians, Methodists and Baptists were as inclined to attack the Northern ''oppressors'' as were Anglicans and Roman Catholics. The spectrum of pro-Southern agitators ran through peers, middle class reformers, landowners, and businessmen, and included a solid body of working-class spokesmen. This may seem curious, and, as had been the case with the War of Independence, there was a certain amount of hypocrisy. Europeans of the ruling classes were happy to encourage movements for independence and liberty *abroad* which they would have rigorously suppressed *at home*, perhaps for no more exalted motive than the delight in seeing a rival discomfitted.

There was, however, a solid practical reason for supporting the Confederacy. The concern shown by European governments was closely related to the amount of cotton spun by each country. Britain was the first hope of the South not only because of its unique position as a world power, but because it possessed 30 million spindles. If cotton were ''King,'' an article of faith in the Confederacy,

United States Department of the Interior, National Park Service, Adams National Historic Site, Quincy, Mass.

Charles Francis Adams, the Union minister in London, was a masterly diplomat. He smoothed over difficulties between the British government and Washington.

then surely Britain must break the Union blockade.

Southern cotton was certainly essential to the economic health of Lancashire, Britain's most industrialized county. While support for the North might well have been the simplest way to help end the war and ensure a speedy renewal of the cotton supply, this argument found few adherents. Demands for the government to recognize the Confederacy spread through Lancashire in the winter of 1862–63 as the dearth of cotton became more acute. Well

The Northern blockade caused a dearth of cotton which threw thousands of English millhands out of work. Here, coal is doled out to the poor in hard-hit Manchester.

The Mansell Collection

over half of the county's 400,000 cotton operatives were out of work. Nearly one-half million people were destitute and dependent on official or charitable aid. The more severe the distress, the more extreme were the public meetings and parliamentary petitions seeking recognition or mediation. Set against this there was a famous meeting in Manchester on New Year's Eve 1862 at which working men pledged adherence to the Union cause. This was naturally seized upon by Lincoln and his supporters, at home and abroad, as an indication of the *real* British feeling. Here were men prepared to suffer through no fault of their own in the interests of justice and humanity. In fact the meeting was engineered and unrepresentative, and throughout the affected regions there was widespread and surprisingly articulate pro-Southern feeling. The clamor did, however, stop short of a cry for war.

France, like Britain, relied on the Confederacy for approximately 90 per cent of its raw cotton. While the consumption was only one-fifth of that in Britain, the cotton industry was still one of the largest in the country. By the end of 1861 factories were closing, but alternative sources of supply were opened up and greater use was made of other raw materials such as linen, silk, hemp, and wool. And a general decrease in trade with America was compensated for by an increase in trade with Britain. On the whole there were far fewer demands for intervention from the cotton-dependent regions of France than of Britain. And again, few Confederate sympathizers urged the sort of involvement that would result in war.

The "Hypocrisy" of Emancipation

Even the consciences of those in Britain and elsewhere who had supported the abolitionist movement in the United States were not troubled by making clear their preference for a Southern victory. In fact, strange as it sounds, the deep well of abolitionist feeling in Britain was tapped more effectively by the Confederacy than by the Union. For example, James Spence, the Liverpool-based financial agent of the Confederacy, genuinely believed that "slavery can never be abolished in the States except by the will of the Southern people." There was a widely based, if fantastic, belief that an independent South would both abolish slavery and achieve what the North could never attempt—the racial integration of Southern society. Few in Britain were weaned from Confederate allegiance by the Proclamation of Emancipation. It was dismissed as a strategic military move of blatant hypocrisy, freeing slaves in the Confederacy while leaving those of the loyal border states in bondage. It was thought to have either a slave insurrection or the duping of Europe as its aim. Britain refused to sanction the one or fall victim to the other.

Despite all this pro-Confederate feeling, Europe did not intervene in the Civil War. The reason is not difficult to find. As has been said earlier, only the losing side could safely be insulted, and increasingly the South looked like the losing side. The British desire not to antagonize the Union was influenced by a concern for the defense of Canada and an interest in the protection and furtherance of British foreign commerce. British commerce suffered little during the war. The decline in the cotton trade was to some extent offset by rising production in other industries favorably affected by the war, such as munitions and shipbuilding. For his part, the emperor of France, Napoleon III, was not inclined to step in without British support.

The Confederate cause was further undermined by inept or inadequate diplomacy. According to James Orr, who for a time chaired its House Committee on Foreign Affairs, the Confederacy "never had a foreign policy, nor did its government ever consent to attempt a high diplomacy with European powers." Jefferson Davis evidently overestimated the critical worth of cotton and underestimated the strength and intransigence of the Union. The Confederacy never got over the major hurdle of gaining recognition as an independent state.

In the spring of 1861 the prospects looked most promising. European statesmen saw immediately that by blockading Southern ports Lincoln was in effect granting the Confederacy belligerent status, since it is absurd to think of a nation blockading its own ports. Therefore first Britain, then France, and in their wake several other European states, accompanied their declarations of neutrality with recognition of the Confederacy as a belligerent. The term "belligerent" is important here because in international law it means party to a war, which is a far cry from a group of people in rebellion. This was progress indeed for the Confederacy. It might have been the first stage of a journey toward acknowledging Southern independence.

Seward was enraged by this, but to no avail. But for Adams's tact, his fury might have provoked the British government to war. As 1861 drew to a close the possibility of some form of British intervention seemed to increase. The young Henry Adams, working on his father's staff, was so impressed by the strength of Southern sympathy that he forecast British recognition of the Confederacy within a matter of months. More specifically, a crisis occurred that made British intervention seem imminent.

In November 1861, James Murray Mason and John Slidell were on their way to England in the hope of gaining immediate recognition for the Confederacy. They were prudent enough to be traveling on a British ship, the *Trent*, when to general consternation the ship was boarded by Captain Wilkes of the Union *San Jacinto* and the men forcibly seized. A flame of anger spread through Britain at this outrage on her maritime integrity, and war would have been a popular outcome. The British government demanded both an apology and the immediate release of

James Murray Mason and John Slidell (top right and top left respectively), sailing to London on the British ship Trent, were seized by Captain Wilkes of the San Jacinto (top center). The painting (above) shows the scene in the Bahama Channel in 1861 as the American warship forces the British merchantman to halt. The incident was greeted with enthusiasm in the North, and Wilkes became a national hero. The Confederacy, on the other hand, was convinced that Britain would not tolerate the outrage on her neutrality, and would declare war on the Union. In Britain itself, feeling ran high: in a letter to Seward one Englishman wrote:

"I fear that 999 men out of 1,000 would declare for immediate war." Lord John Russell, the British Foreign Minister, drafted a stiffly worded memorandum to be sent to Washington, demanding reparation, apology, and the instant release of the two prisoners. It was owing to the intervention of Queen Victoria's consort, Prince Albert (left), that the tone of this was modified. Thanks to this, Prince Albert's last official act before he died of typhoid two weeks later, Lincoln was able to get out of the affair with some grace. Mason and Slidell were released and while there was no apology, the action was disavowed.

237

Mason and Slidell—in terms that would brook no refusal. It was ironic that the traditional British and American roles were reversed here, with the British demanding precisely those neutral rights which they had flagrantly violated during the Napoleonic wars and would again ignore during the First World War. The Union, on the other hand, was in the awkward position of trying to defend the sort of action that had provoked an earlier generation of Americans to war in 1812. It was obvious from the beginning to Seward, and eventually became so to Lincoln, that the Union must find some way to back down over the issue or face a war that it could hardly afford. The action was disavowed—although there was no apology—and the men were released. The moment of greatest hope for the Confederacy was lost and the impulse to intervene would never again be as strong. Only with consistent success on the field of battle would the South be able to tilt the scales in its favour.

The smashing victory at Second Bull Run in August 1862 was the closest they got. Napoleon suggested mediation—which could only be to the Confederacy's advantage—but at this critical moment Britain and Russia hung back. A further French proposal of a six-month armistice met with a lukewarm reception in Britain and an icy one in Russia. Antietam and the Emancipation Proclamation (September 1862) had convinced the British government that, however the war eventually went, now was not the time for any sort of intervention at all. The Confederacy's high-water mark passed, and the great hopes placed in British initiative withered in the winter of 1862–63. They died with the disasters at Gettysburg and Vicksburg in the summer of 1863, and Mason was instructed to give up his post in London.

France's Mexican Adventure

From this point onward the Confederate government concentrated its efforts on France. Napoleon, imbued with the vision if not the genius of his illustrious uncle, had long harbored dreams of expanding French influence in the world. The American Civil War gave him his chance. Capitalizing on the political weakness of Mexico he persuaded the Austrian archduke Maximilian to accept the role of emperor of Mexico. It was an impressive title, but in fact Maximilian was to be no more than a French puppet. In 1864 the Austrian was duly installed. The Union was furious (did not the Monroe Doctrine expressly forbid such a move?), and the Confederacy was intrigued by the possibility of discord between France and the Union. In fact Slidell had already offered Napoleon Confederate support in return for recognition, but Napoleon had declined out of a well-founded fear of completely alienating the Union.

Napoleon's grandiose Mexican venture ended in disgrace for France and death for the unfortunate Maximilian. The

Emperor Napoleon III saw in the Civil War an opportunity to expand French influence. His Mexican adventure ended in a fiasco, and for the puppet ruler Maximilian it was a disaster.

artificially created empire attracted little support inside Mexico. The Union protests grew more heated, and as the Civil War drew to a close it was obvious that the French would soon face more than protests. Freed from the Civil War, and consequently from fears of French intervention on the side of the Confederacy, the American government would not hesitate to use force. Napoleon withdrew his French troops and in 1867 Mexican insurgents toppled Maximilian from power and shot him.

The Desperate Search for Friends

While the Confederacy's main diplomatic thrust throughout was aimed at Britain and France, it did not stop there. And as the possibilities of British recognition began to fade desperate efforts were made to win the allegiance of others. Overtures were made to Spain, a naturally interested power because of her Caribbean involvement. Moves were also made toward Sweden, where there was considerable popular support for the Confederacy; Belgium; even the Vatican. They all came to nothing. No one European country was prepared to jeopardize its position without a commitment from others, and particularly without a clear signal from Britain.

The one leading European nation that never seriously envisaged supporting Confederate independence was Russia. Quite apart from a solid determination to maintain

Above: The Old Dominion *being fitted out in the port of Bristol, England. British ports benefited greatly from equipping vessels for the Confederate navy. Below: At the end of 1862 Slidell negotiated a cotton-based loan with the French financier Erlanger. It provided for the selling of cotton bonds redeemable after Southern independence had been won. To begin with the bonds were eagerly snapped up by speculators. After Vicksburg and Gettysburg, however, sales fell off but the Confederacy did raise more than $8 million from the loan.*

SEVEN PER CENT. COTTON LOAN

OF THE

CONFEDERATE STATES OF AMERICA.

FOR

£3,000,000 STERLING, AT 90 PER CENT.

The Bonds to bear Interest at the rate of **7** per cent. per annum in Sterling, from 1st March, 1863, payable Half-yearly in London, Paris, Amsterdam, or Frankfort.
The Bonds exchangeable for Cotton on application, at the option of the Holder, or redeemable at par in Sterling in Twenty Years, by Half-yearly drawings, commencing 1st March, 1864.

Agents for the Contractors in Liverpool :— Messrs. FRASER TRENHOLM & Co., 10, Rumford Place.

This Loan has been contracted with Messrs. Emile Erlanger & Co., Bankers of Paris, by the Government of the Confederate States of America, and is specially secured by an undertaking of the Government to deliver Cotton to the holders of the Bonds, on application after sixty days' notice, on the footing aftermentioned.

The nature of the arrangement is fully set forth in Article IV. of the Contract made with Messrs. E. Erlanger & Co., which is as follows :—

a particularly friendly relationship with the United States, Russia had little need to aid the Confederacy. Her demand for cotton was slight in comparison with other raw materials, and economic links with the Confederacy were extremely tenuous. The Confederacy did eventually make overtures to Russia in December 1862 but Czar Alexander II refused even to see the Confederate envoy. Russia occasionally considered the possibility of mediation. But she always intended to be a sole mediator, the clear arbiter in a dispute that was ultimately to end in the retention of the United States. Joint mediation with the pro-Confederate British and French was never seriously contemplated. The balance of world power was seen by Russia to depend on the preservation of the Union. A strong United States was felt to be an insurance against British arrogance and aggression,

At the outset, Britain was most immediately concerned over the prospect of running head-on into a confrontation between the Northern determination to impose an effective blockade and the Southern decision to establish widespread privateering. Although the French government was advised by its ministers to Washington to break the blockade, Russell counseled against such precipitate action. At the same time Britain was accused by the North of demonstrating Southern sympathy by her toleration of privateering. The French were enthusiastic about a suggestion in 1861 that specific ports should be freed from the blockade to reopen the cotton trade with Europe, but the idea came to nothing. Many British politicians thought it was in the long-term British interest simply to do nothing. France was also aware that the precedents set by the

As well as carrying much-needed supplies from Britain to the South, Confederate ships scored many individual successes—here the Nashville *sets fire to the Union's* Harvey Birch *in the English Channel.*

and the Russian press assured the American people of their committed sympathy for the Union cause.

While Britain and France consistently held back from committing themselves to Southern recognition, they did find practical methods of demonstrating their sympathy. Although the two governments made no official move to break the Northern blockade of Southern ports, they were aware that a large number of British and French ships constantly ran the blockade. They also refrained from interfering with the building of warships for the Confederacy in their docks—until it was clear that such tolerance would be regarded by the North as a warlike act.

The career of the Liverpool-built Confederate raider Alabama *ended in the English Channel. The French painter Edouard Manet recorded her last battle with the Union ironclad sloop* Kearsarge *in 1864.*

Northern blockade of Southern ports could be of advantage in future international wars.

Britain did, however, give practical aid to the Confederacy in allowing ships to be built. The *Alabama* was only one of several laid down for the Confederates and the damage they did to Northern shipping almost provided sufficient cause for war. It certainly gave a reason for increasing bitterness directed against Britain. Had the two ironclad rams built for the Confederacy by the Laird Brothers been allowed to sail, Britain might have unwittingly found herself fighting for Southern independence.

Liverpool in particular found ways of actively intervening in the war on a unilateral basis. The number of ships built in the Mersey docks, the ships that ran the blockade from the port of Liverpool, and the provisioning of warships seemed to many almost a declaration of war on the North. At least seventy ships were built in Liverpool

of the rams be sold to Prussia instead of the Confederacy. The other ram was sold to Denmark and eventually purchased from that country by the Confederacy.

The Federal government, too, made determined efforts to supplement its own war effort. Least successful were its attempts to add to its naval superiority by using British technology and expertise. When Laird Brothers were asked to build ironclad rams, the request was refused. However, the search for troops to swell the Union ranks was far more productive. During the war years 90,000 people emigrated from Britain to the United States, of whom almost half became Union soldiers; while southern Germany sent 100,000 men into the Union ranks.

The Confederacy attempted to curtail the enlistment of Irishmen in the Federal army by sending envoys to counteract the incentives promised by Federal agents. However, they did no more than divert a small part of the flood that

Above left: A visible sign of Russian goodwill toward the North—sailors on board the frigate Osliaba *during a visit to the captured port at Alexandria, Virginia. Russia wanted the Union to be upheld, as she believed a powerful United States would keep British arrogance in check. Left: Many European military men took the opportunity presented by the Civil War to observe the latest techniques in warfare. This group of officers accompanied the staff of the Army of the Potomac. In the center, with a white moustache, is Count Ferdinand von Zeppelin, a young Prussian officer who later developed the famous airship that bore his name.*

between 1862 and 1865 specifically to run the blockade. Most of these were sold to the Confederacy, but others remained based in Liverpool with British crews. The Union was so incensed that after the war it felt justified in suing Britain for substantial compensation. After a lengthy legal battle $15.5 million was finally awarded in 1872 for the damage inflicted by the *Florida, Alabama,* and *Shenandoah.*

In October 1862 Napoleon III intimated to Slidell that ships could be built for the Confederacy in France, and that their safe departure would be arranged. A more concrete suggestion for building steamers for the South was made by the French in January 1863. In April 1863 Captain James D. Bulloch made a contract for the building in France of four clipper corvettes similar to the *Alabama.* In July a further contract was signed for the building of two ironclads. But when news of the destination of the ships leaked out, Napoleon insisted that the corvettes and one

flowed into the North during the war years. It was estimated at the time that 180,000 Irish had emigrated to the Union between 1861 and 1863 and that 100,000 of these had enlisted in the Union army. Europeans also enlisted in the Confederate army, and while it is more difficult to estimate their numbers accurately, it is certain that a large number of foreigners fought for the South.

In the final analysis, the policy of neutrality—pursued positively by Russia and negatively by the rest of Europe—worked to the advantage of the North. Federal agents and sympathizers in Britain and France agitated for no more than European noninterference. On the whole that is what they got. The Union did not win the battle for European sympathy. But this was more than compensated for by Europe's willingness—however reluctant—to stand aside while it got on with the painful job of restoring the United States of America.

Chapter 10

UNION AND VICTORY

After two years of bloodshed there was no end in sight. Although Confederate armies—and in particular Confederate generals—had proved more than a match for their adversaries, they had not gained a strategic advantage. Yet for the South, stalemate would mean victory: it had only to endure to achieve its aim. Then in mid summer 1863 the capture of Vicksburg and the victory at Gettysburg tipped the scales heavily—and in the end decisively—in favor of the North. Crippled by the blockade and squeezed between the armies of Grant and Sherman, the South still fought on for nearly two years. But its cause began to seem the "Lost Cause."

The Road to Appomattox

On July 18, 1863, William Nelson Pendleton, an Episcopal rector serving as an artillery general in Lee's army, penned a letter to his wife. "Our cause is, undoubtedly, at serious disadvantage just now," he wrote. "Our failure at Gettysburg and these events on the Mississippi will give us a vast deal of trouble. It is a case in which resort to God for help becomes doubly urgent, while we brace ourselves to the stern duties of the occasion."

Events in the eastern theater during the eight months after Gettysburg gave a measure of hope to the South. Meade warily pursued Lee back to Virginia. The two armies then parried like heavyweight boxers feeling out one another. In October, Lee feinted as if to move on Washington. Meade drew back his army to Centreville. When nothing materialized, Meade in November advanced to Culpeper. The two antagonists jockeyed for position in the Mine Run area, and a major battle seemed imminent. However, Meade soon withdrew across the Rapidan River. Separated only by that shallow stream, the two armies settled down to await the coming of spring.

While Lee and Meade were maneuvering, however, a full-scale action was developing in the West. It was to have major consequences.

The city of Chattanooga became a key Confederate stronghold during Grant's investment of Vicksburg. Nestled in the mountains of southeastern Tennessee, Chattanooga was the apex of the post–Vicksburg defense line. It was a vital railroad center and so strategically situated as to be the backdoor to the Confederacy. In the spring of 1863, Bragg's Southern army reinforced the town. Rosecrans and his Federal forces, apparently stunned by the Battle of Stone's River, showed no desire to renew the offensive. For almost nine months, and despite constant prodding from Washington, Rosecrans remained inactive at Murfreesboro. Finally, the Union army proceeded toward Chattanooga. Bragg became unduly alarmed that the Federals might flank the city and seize the indispensable railroad to Atlanta. Hence, on September 9, Bragg abandoned the town without a fight. His action further weakened the confidence of his officers and men. In their minds, he was continuing to display a lack of resoluteness and dash.

Confederate soldiers became more convinced of Bragg's deficiencies when he threw away a splendid opportunity to destroy Rosecrans's forces. Rosecrans commendably marched southward from Chattanooga in pursuit of Bragg, but he foolishly divided his 58,000 men and sent them through widely separated mountain passes. Instead of attacking the isolated segments, Bragg grumbled perplexingly about "the popping out of the rats from so many holes" and did nothing until Rosecrans reconsolidated his

The "Battle Above the Clouds" at Chattanooga in November 1863 was part of the two days' fighting that cracked the Confederate siege. In order to break through, the Army of the Cumberland had to climb the steep slopes of Lookout Mountain under heavy fire.

army. Then, to compound the error, Bragg attacked.

The Battle of Chickamauga Creek (September 19–20, 1863) was one of the largest engagements of the war. It occurred near a stream the Indians had named "River of Death." Bragg's army had swelled to 60,000 troops with reinforcements that included Longstreet's corps of 12,000 men sent westward from Lee's army. For once in the Civil War, the South enjoyed numerical superiority in a major battle.

Desperate fighting raged back and forth on the first day along the left of Rosecrans's three-mile battle line. Dense woods and underbrush turned the conflict into a soldier's battle, with little direction from the officers. Both sides fought and suffered severely, with neither side making appreciable headway. At noon on the second day, Longstreet's men broke through the Federal right-center and drove two whole corps in headlong retreat toward Chattanooga. Rosecrans himself left the field in the face of impending disaster. Yet the Union's left flank, under Virginia-born George H. Thomas, hurled back repeated attacks on two fronts. This gallant stand, which earned Thomas the nickname "Rock of Chickamauga," saved the day for the Federal army.

The fighting at Chickamauga was comparable in bloodshed to Antietam and Gettysburg. Rosecrans suffered 16,170 casualties; Bragg's losses were 18,454 men, including 44 per cent of Longstreet's corps. Appallingly costly in human life, Chickamauga was but a barren victory for the Confederates. Bragg failed to press after his demoralized foe, thereby fumbling away another opportunity to demolish Rosecrans's army. The Confederate general was content to secure the railroads, to ease back onto the mountains surrounding Chattanooga, and to lay siege to Rosecrans's forces inside the city.

Such a passive counterstroke prompted the Federals to take the offensive. Grant assumed supreme command of all Union operations in the West, while Thomas succeeded Rosecrans as commander of the Army of the Cumberland. Grant deftly opened a river supply route into Chattanooga to prevent the beleaguered army from starving. He next concentrated the armies of William T. Sherman and Joseph Hooker with Thomas's forces inside Chattanooga. In contrast, and at the same time, Bragg reduced his army to 40,000 men by sending Longstreet's infantry and Joseph Wheeler's cavalry to attack Burnside's army at Knoxville. This side campaign failed; even worse, it momentarily gave Grant a two-to-one superiority over the main body of Bragg's army. With characteristic aggressiveness, Grant then attacked the Confederate besiegers.

Three major actions comprised the Lookout Mountain-Missionary Ridge campaign (November 23–25). Sherman's men first assaulted the Confederate right on Missionary Ridge but made little gain. Hooker's two corps then assailed and broke the Confederate left on Lookout Mountain in what became known as the "battle above the clouds."

By late 1863, the Northern cavalry could easily match that of the South. Winslow Homer's painting shows two Union cavalry scouts, dressed as Confederates, about to go through the lines to gather information.

The climax of the battle came when two of Thomas's divisions moved on the afternoon of November 25 to assist Sherman. These forces were to make only a demonstration against the Southern rifle pits at the base of Missionary Ridge. Instead, and without orders, the Federals overran the pits, scaled the mountain, and stormed Bragg's main works.

A stunning disaster followed for the Confederacy. Massed Southern troops who could and should have handily repulsed the Federal thrust did the exact reverse. Low morale in the ranks and a complete lack of confidence in Bragg caused the Army of Tennessee to flee. Bragg himself stated: "A panic which I had never before witnessed seemed to have seized upon officers and men, and each seemed to be struggling for his personal safety, regardless of his duty or character."

Broken columns of Confederates raced all the way to Dalton in northern Georgia. There the impact of the colossal failure became fully known. Chattanooga and Tennessee were lost; the road to Georgia was at least partially open to Federal forces; and the major Confederate army in the West had suffered humiliation. The three days of fighting at Chattanooga cost Grant 5,616 men. Bragg's losses were 6,667, including 4,146 taken prisoner during the rout. Davis relieved the devoted but discredited Bragg and appointed Joseph E. Johnston to command. Johnston

Four Great Generals

Most of the leading generals involved in the Civil War had been to the same school—West Point—and gained their experience in the same field—the Mexican War of 1846–48. In the 1850s some of them left the army to pursue other careers, but as war approached both the Union and the Confederacy called on their services.

On the whole, the South was better served by her generals, but of all the men who came to prominence during four years of fighting, there are four who stand out above the rest: Robert E. Lee and Thomas "Stonewall" Jackson for the Confederacy; Ulysses S. Grant and William Tecumseh Sherman for the Union. Each had his own concept of war, and the Civil War in particular, and each had the opportunity to put his ideas to the test.

Of these four, only Lee was still serving in the regular army at the outbreak of war. Grant had been forced to resign because of his drinking, and had proved a failure in business; Jackson was teaching at the Virginia Military Institute; while Sherman had also left the army.

Immediately after Sumter, Lincoln offered Lee (though he only held a colonel's rank) overall command of the North's forces in the field. Lee's dilemma was acute: he abhorred slavery, and did not believe in secession. Yet he did not feel able to "raise my hand against my native state, my relatives, my children and my home." His duty to the Union was outweighed by his loyalty to his native state and, with sadness, he resigned his commission.

Jackson, too, followed Virginia into the Confederacy. Both men were made generals, but Lee was obliged to remain in Richmond as military adviser to President

Robert E. Lee

Collection of the Corcoran Gallery of Art

Thomas "Stonewall" Jackson

Davis while Jackson was given an immediate command in the field. Commanding a brigade at First Bull Run, his coolness helped to swing the balance in the South's favor. General Lee, attempting to rally his wavering men, pointed dramatically with his sword: "Look," he shouted, "There is Jackson standing like a stone wall! Rally behind the Virginians!"

Already known for his eccentricities, Jackson soon gained a reputation as a brilliant and aggressive strategist. The famous Valley campaign, when in the course of a month his army marched 400 miles, fought five battles, and defeated four larger armies, proved just how bold and skilful he was. He pushed his "foot cavalry" hard, but no harder than he pushed himself. At his best in independent command, Jackson could also perform lightning, crushing moves when in a supporting role.

Though he was rather sluggish during the Seven Days, Lee felt "such an executive officer the sun never shone on"—and Antietam, Fredericksburg, and Chancellorsville bear witness to this opinion. Jackson believed in keeping the enemy on the hop, never giving him a chance to settle down, and hitting him whenever possible. He raided supply bases, artillery posts, and wagon trains with the same efficiency that he mounted large-scale battles and—in the words of a fellow general—"he never knew defeat."

Despite his past experience and service, Grant had great difficulty being accepted by the army. Finally granted a commission as a colonel of volunteers, he was soon promoted to brigadier general after his first victory—an occasion when he realized that his enemy "had been as much afraid of me as I had been of him." The capture of Forts Henry and Donelson in a combined operation with the navy enhanced his reputation and gave him his nickname, "Unconditional Surrender"

National Portrait Gallery, Smithsonian Institution, Washington DC

Grant. But it was the Battle of Shiloh on April 6–7, 1862—the largest and bloodiest conflict so far—that hardened his attitude. From then on, he realized, it would have to be a war of attrition, a war to the finish, that would end only when the Confederacy was utterly crushed.

Grant believed that the best way to achieve this was to hit the enemy armies as hard as possible, with all the resources at his command. And with the industrial might of the North behind him, combined with the introduction of the draft to give him the soldiers he needed, he was able to hit the Southern armies harder and harder.

The huge casualty list at Shiloh caused a furore in the North, and despite the mounting numbers of dead and wounded during the following years, Grant was watched suspiciously by the newspapers. "Butcher" Grant they called him after Cold Harbor, when more than 6,000 Federals fell in half an hour, the culmination of a month's campaign resulting in some 50,000 casualties. But Grant achieved his object—the Confederate losses were almost as high, and they could not be replaced. Despite demands for Grant's dismissal after Shiloh, Lincoln refused, remarking "I can't spare this man—he fights."

Commanding a division at Shiloh had been Sherman—lanky, talkative, and resourceful. He had his own ideas on how to beat the South, and put them into effect when he broke free of his supply lines in the spring of 1864 on his imaginative and courageous march through Georgia and the Carolinas. His aim was the destruction of the Confederacy's supply bases—an aim he achieved brilliantly. The capture and burning of Atlanta—center of the South's communications—the ripping up of railroads and burning of vital crops, brought the war home to the civilian population of the Deep South with

Angelo Hornak

William Tecumseh Sherman

devastating and bitter effect. He demoralized an already disheartened population and destroyed the crops and railroads vital to the life of the armies in the field. In the words of one of his corps commanders, his campaign was "among the highest examples of the art of war."

The combination of Sherman's destructiveness in the rear, and the ruthless power of Grant facing him, proved too much even for a general of Lee's caliber. But for three years Lee—the greatest commander of the Civil War—had given the Confederacy hope. When he took command of the army defending Richmond in the summer of 1862 Lee knew that, although the Confederacy had only to survive to achieve independence, the army must do more than merely defend. He wrote to President Davis, "There is always hazard in military movements, but we must decide between the *positive* loss of inaction and the risk of action." It was a risk he was more than prepared to take. He had the knack of forcing the enemy to attack him on ground of his own choosing, and it was usually a strong defensive position which allowed him to detach a large force to carry out an audacious flanking movement.

Lee had a bold and imaginative concept of warfare, combined with an ability to take advantage of an opponent's mistakes which made him feared and respected by the Union generals. He retained the confidence of his political superiors as well as his military juniors—and while he listened to (and often followed) the suggestions of his corps commanders, he took the blame for disaster on himself. Lee possessed a rare—and genuine—humility, an air of simple dignity, and a compassion for the ordinary soldiers which was returned by their complete devotion. As one private put it: "His whole makeup of form and person, looks and manner, had a gentle and soothing magnetism about it. I fell in love with the old gentleman."

Ulysses S. Grant

National Portrait Gallery, Smithsonian Institution, Washington DC

247

spent the winter of 1863–64 in reconstructing the shattered ranks and spirit of the army.

The Chattanooga campaign had one other far-reaching consequence. It convinced Lincoln that Grant was the fighting general he had long sought. Accordingly, on March 9, 1864, Lincoln promoted Grant to the newly restored rank of lieutenant general and placed him in command of all Federal armies—except one then meeting embarrassing defeat.

Nathaniel P. Banks was another of several politicians appointed to military command by Lincoln. Like most men in that category, Banks was ill suited for the responsibilities thrust upon him. In March 1864, he started up Louisiana's Red River with 25,000 infantry and a fleet of gunboats and transports. His ultimate objective was an invasion of Texas; an intermediary target was the Confederate bastion of Shreveport, Louisiana.

Banks was nearing that city when General Richard Taylor's 13,000 Confederates dealt his army defeats at Sabine Cross Roads and Pleasant Hill. Banks began retreating; but the river fell rapidly, momentarily trapped his fleet, and subjected it to a deadly bombardment from Confederate batteries. For the Federals, who failed to achieve a single goal, the campaign was a fiasco. Banks suffered losses of 5,200 men, 1,007 draft animals, 187 wagonloads of supplies, 28 naval guns, and 8 ships.

Grant took scant notice of the Red River debacle. By the time it came to an inglorious end, he was unfolding the final grand strategy of the Civil War. The Confederacy had already suffered grievous military, economic, and geographical losses in the West. Its manpower had been depleted to a critical level. By the spring of 1864, the Federal navy had reduced outside supplies for the South to a dribble. Grant's strategy, simple but brutal, was to use Northern numerical superiority and to hammer relentlessly at the weakened Confederacy. There would be no letup until the South was brought to its knees. This "war of attrition" heralded the advent of modern warfare —and it ultimately brought triumph to the Union.

The grand Federal scheme devised by Grant called for multi-pronged, simultaneous offensives on all major fronts. Sherman was given command of the Union forces in the West. His main objectives were to march through Johnston's Army of Tennessee and to capture Atlanta, Georgia. While Sherman pushed southward from Chattanooga, Grant would oversee three separate invasions of Virginia. Franz Sigel's small Federal force would occupy the thinly defended Shenandoah Valley; Benjamin F. Butler's 36,000 troops would march up the Peninsula toward Richmond; the Army of the Potomac, 112,000 strong and still under Meade, would destroy Lee's army of 60,000 in central Virginia. Since Meade's actions would be the key to success in Virginia, Grant accompanied the Army of the Potomac on the frontal advance and called its signals throughout most of the campaign.

Library of Congress. Photos T. O'Sullivan

A remarkable set of photographs taken at Massaponax Church, Virginia, on May 21, 1864 by the war photographer T. H. O'Sullivan. The series shows a council of war in progress at Grant's headquarters in the field. In the large picture, Grant is leaning over Meade's shoulder to examine a map of the area. Next (top) he is seated, writing a dispatch. Finally (above) he is in discussion with Assistant Secretary of War Dana. Following his great success in the west, Grant early made his intentions clear in the east with the punishing Wilderness-Spotsylvania campaign which cost Lee his most precious asset—mobility. From then on Grant commanded the respect of both politicians and his fellow generals.

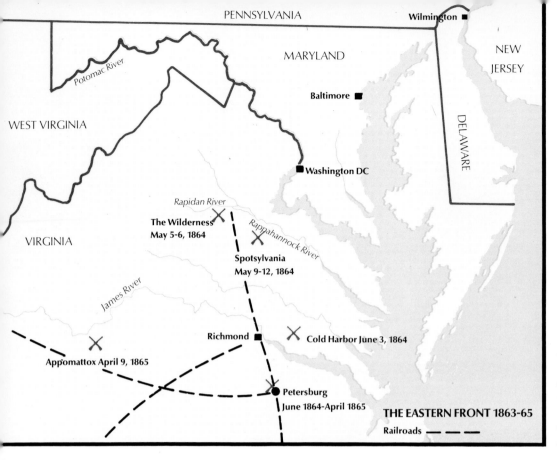

PENNSYLVANIA

Wilmington ■

NEW
JERSEY

MARYLAND

Potomac River

Baltimore ■

WEST VIRGINIA

DELAWARE

Washington DC ■

Rapidan River

VIRGINIA

The Wilderness
May 5-6, 1864 ✕

Rappahannock River

✕

Spotsylvania
May 9-12, 1864

James River

✕

Richmond ■ ✕ Cold Harbor June 3, 1864

✕
Appomattox April 9, 1865

● Petersburg
June 1864-April 1865

THE EASTERN FRONT 1863-65

Railroads ▬ ▬ ▬ ▬

Map showing the eastern theater during the latter part of the war. Grant's remorseless pursuit of Lee's army meant that the Southern general could no longer pick his spot for a battle and was forced to fight in an ever-decreasing area around the beleaguered Richmond.

Demoralizing failure initially marked every Union effort in Virginia. Meade's army crossed the Rapidan River and plunged once more into the darkness of the Wilderness. Lee's outnumbered, poorly equipped soldiers were waiting. Taking advantage of the confused terrain, Lee attacked with his entire army. The Battle of the Wilderness (May 5–6) was a disorganized, frightful contest. Battle lines broke into fragments as troops sought to maneuver in the wild country. Officers either lost sight of their commands or became confused as heavy musketry echoed from every direction. Two days of intense fighting left dead and wounded scattered throughout woods set afire by rifle and cannon balls. Tactically, the Battle of the Wilderness was a bloody standoff that cost Grant 15,000 men. Lee's losses numbered more than 11,000, which Grant

knew would be all but impossible to replace.

Hence, the Army of the Potomac did not retreat in defeat as it had done so often in the past. With Grant in the lead, the Federals veered to the southeast in an effort to get between Lee and Richmond. Lee adroitly shifted his army in the same direction.

During this maneuvering by the two great hosts, opposing cavalry were slashing at one another. General Philip H. Sheridan, a daring and relentless infantry commander, now led Grant's horsemen. Sheridan began a cavalry raid on Richmond to cut Lee's communications. The 10,000 Federal cavalry formed a column thirteen miles long. His outnumbered opponent, "Jeb" Stuart, could only harass the front and rear of the Federals as they pushed southward. On May 11, Stuart fell mortally

wounded in an engagement at Yellow Tavern, only a few miles from Richmond. Sheridan eventually abandoned the raid, but the death of the colorful Stuart cast a pall over the Confederacy.

Grant's army, meanwhile, reached Spotsylvania to find Lee's forces entrenched and ready for battle. The Federal general resolved to hammer again. Early on May 12, with rain steadily falling, deep ranks of Federals overran a salient and poured through Lee's works. Suddenly the fate of the Confederate army seemed to hang in the balance. Lee himself prepared to lead a counterattack. Yet his men, shouting "Lee to the rear," would not allow their beloved commander to endanger his life. Bitter fighting continued all day around the "Bloody Angle." Lee's army, minus 5,000 casualties, withdrew to a new line. Grant's sledgehammer assaults had cost him 6,800 Federals. With a grim determination to "fight it out . . . if it takes all summer," Grant pounded his way across the North Anna River and continued toward Richmond. Lee skillfully used his inner lines of defense to contest Grant's advance and to keep his forces always in front of the Federals.

Grant then lost his patience. At Cold Harbor, only ten miles from the Confederate capital, he ordered at least thirteen frontal assaults on Lee's entrenched army. The June 3 attacks rank as one of the greatest slaughters of the war. More than 7,200 Federals fell in the first half-hour's fighting as Confederates delivered a murderous fire into the advancing columns. Grant stubbornly refused after the battle to ask a truce for collecting his dead and wounded. For three days, Federal dead decomposed in the sun while hundreds of wounded soldiers perished in slow agony.

Northerners recoiled in horror at Grant's tactics. In less than a month, he had lost 55,000 men—almost the number in Lee's army. Moreover, Grant was no closer to Richmond than McClellan had been two years earlier. Grant seemed possessed of "callous indifference" and "reckless insanity," Northern newspapers screamed. Many Washington officials openly denounced him as "The Butcher." Yet Grant was undeterred by losses or public opinion. New recruits were reaching his army daily; his forces were well fed and supplied. Confederate casualties from the Wilderness to Cold Harbor had been proportionally larger than his own. Equally as important, Grant and Lee both knew that the Federal commander had by then eliminated the Army of Northern Virginia's chief asset: mobility. Lee was now on the defensive, and Grant intended to keep him there through constant pressure.

Cold Harbor proved the futility of seizing Richmond from the north. With Union navy gunboats protecting his left flank, Grant boldly transferred his army across the James to move on Richmond from the rear. This shift caught Lee by surprise. Before he could recover, Grant's army was hammering at Petersburg to the south. This new Federal offensive failed because of two factors: a stout defense waged at Petersburg by 30,000 makeshift Confederate

forces under P. G. T. Beauregard, and Butler's inept performance on the Peninsula.

Butler and his Army of the James had advanced westward from Fortress Monroe with commendable dispatch. However, when Beauregard's thin force lunged in his direction, Butler quickly withdrew and entrenched at Bermuda Hundred in a neck of land between the James and Appomattox rivers. Beauregard thereupon closed the little peninsula with manned earthworks of his own. Butler's army, snarled Grant, was "as completely shut off from further operations directly against Richmond as if it had been in a bottle strongly corked."

The Siege of Petersburg

Four days (June 15–18) of assaults by Grant could not break the Petersburg defenses. He then employed the siege tactics successfully executed at Fort Donelson and Vicksburg. His troops began digging trenches and earthworks that became an ever-widening arc in front of Lee's army. The Confederate general, hopelessly outnumbered, had no choice but to resist as staunchly as men and means would allow.

On July 30, Grant made a novel try at severing the Confederate defenses. Coal miners in a Pennsylvania regiment dug a 512-foot tunnel to a point beneath Lee's lines. About 8,000 pounds of gunpowder were placed at the end of the tunnel and detonated prior to an attack by two Federal divisions. The explosion hurled "men, guns, carriages, and timbers" into the air and blasted a hole 30 feet deep and 170 feet wide. Federal soldiers then charged through the area of the "crater." Confederates frantically regrouped and, further angered by the sight of Negro soldiers in the assault, struck back savagely. Hand-to-hand fighting occurred in many quarters as Lee's men slowly regained lost ground. The whole operation, which Grant termed a "stupendous failure," cost the Union 4,000 men.

Grant then resorted to standard tactics. Artillery bombardments, heavy skirmishes, and probes became daily events in the nine-month siege that followed. Casualties in Lee's army slowly mounted as Grant continued to exert unspectacular but effective pressure on Lee's defenses. One of Lee's soldiers best summed up the situation when he pointed to the Union lines and asked: "What's the use of killing those fellows? Kill one and a half a dozen take his place."

With Lee's army immobilized at Petersburg, Grant turned his attention to the Shenandoah Valley. Matters had not gone well there during the first months of Grant's Virginia strategy. General Franz Sigel and 6,000 Federal infantry moved leisurely into the Valley when Grant crossed the Rapidan. John C. Breckinridge gathered

Grant's headquarters at City Point, Virginia, from which he commanded the siege of Petersburg. For nine months the Federals steadily extended their lines until Lee's overstretched men could no longer defend the city.

251

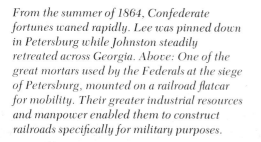

From the summer of 1864, Confederate fortunes waned rapidly. Lee was pinned down in Petersburg while Johnston steadily retreated across Georgia. Above: One of the great mortars used by the Federals at the siege of Petersburg, mounted on a railroad flatcar for mobility. Their greater industrial resources and manpower enabled them to construct railroads specifically for military purposes.

Right: General Philip Sheridan commanded 50,000 men in the Shenandoah Valley. They completely devastated the region so that no more food from it would reach the Southern armies. Below: Sherman's men rip up railroad tracks in Georgia—a work of destruction at which they were expert. The rails were torn up, heated, and then bent and twisted round a tree to ensure that they could never be relaid.

together a mixed force of 5,000 Confederates and, on May 15, attacked Sigel at New Market. The climax of the engagement came when 225 teenage cadets from Virginia Military Institute charged with other units through the mud and penetrated Sigel's lines in front and flank. Sigel retired from the field with 831 casualties. This relatively minor victory gave the Confederates time enough to gather a harvest needed for Lee's army.

Grant promptly replaced Sigel with General David Hunter, a stern, humorless soldier with no compassion for the South. Hunter's 8,500 troops lunged southward. On June 5, they encountered 5,600 Confederates under W. E. "Grumble" Jones at Piedmont. Ten hours of fighting resulted before Hunter routed the Southerners. Jones was killed early in the action. Federal casualties were 780 men; Confederate losses were more than twice that number. The Federals then burned their way through Staunton and Lexington before veering eastward toward the railroad junction at Lynchburg.

Lee quickly detached Jubal A. Early's 8,000-man corps from the besieged Army of Northern Virginia and sent it westward to combat Hunter's thrust. Early's men (many of whom were residents of the Shenandoah Valley) angrily assailed Hunter's lines at Lynchburg and drove the Federals into the mountains of West Virginia. Hunter lost a thousand men during the westward flight. The Valley was momentarily clear of Federal invaders.

Early, a gruff and salty Virginia bachelor, seized this opportunity to launch a counterattack on Washington. Half of his Confederates were barefooted; yet they jubilantly swung down the Valley, crossed the Potomac, and turned eastward toward the Northern capital. On July 9, hastily collected Federals under General Lew Wallace contested Early's crossing of the Monocacy River. The Confederates soon outflanked the Union line, but the delay enabled Grant to rush a corps from Petersburg to the defense of Washington. Early advanced to within sight of the capital. He studied elaborate earthworks "as far as the eye could see," took note of Federal reinforcements streaming into the trenches, and abruptly retreated back to the Valley. A raid seemingly promising for the South accomplished little more than to throw Washington residents into temporary panic.

Grant sent Hunter back into the Valley with brutal orders. Hunter was to "eat up" the Shenandoah "clear and clean, so that crows flying over it for the balance of the season will have to carry their provender with them." When Hunter subsequently displayed more doubt than determination, Grant made sweeping changes in the Valley forces. He reinforced the army there to 50,000 men and assigned his most dependable general, the thirty-three-year-old Sheridan, to dispose of both Early's army and the Valley's agricultural output. The 18,000 Confederates under Early were little match for Sheridan's horde. The Federals drove Early up the Valley after sharp fighting at Opequon Creek (September 19) and Fisher's Hill (September 22). Early's troops contested every mile of Sheridan's advance as casualties mounted on both sides.

While Sheridan was in Washington for quick consultations, Early came miraculously close to achieving a decisive success. His little army unleashed a surprise assault on the encamped Federal army at Cedar Creek (October 19). The Confederates stormed through the Union flank and sent two of the three corps of Sheridan's army fleeing down the Valley in widespread panic. One more hard blow by Early would have clinched victory, but hungry Confederates stopped to plunder abandoned camps and wagon trains. Officers were powerless in attempts to get their men to resume the pursuit. Meanwhile, Sheridan arrived at Winchester. Hearing the roar of battle in the distance, he made a dramatic twenty-mile ride to the front, rallied his troops, and delivered a heavy counterstroke. Early grudgingly fell back with 1,500 Federal prisoners. His own losses included 3,000 soldiers, as well as most of his artillery and supply wagons. The Cedar Creek defeat eliminated the Confederate army as an effective block to Sheridan's subsequent movements.

The Federal general then destroyed the Valley with systematic precision. His men burned houses, outbuildings, mills, and machinery. They applied the torch to haystacks, corncribs, and foodstuffs of every variety. They drove off Negroes and livestock needed for crop cultivation. The Valley became the scene of widespread waste and devastation. Its residents were left destitute as Sheridan completely stripped the "breadbasket of the Confederacy" and secured it permanently in Union hands.

Sherman Moves On Georgia

The deterioration of Confederate strength in Virginia, severe as it was, could in no way match the catastrophe that befell the South on the other major front. One Federal general, in one campaign, completed the conquest of the western theater and broke the will of the South to resist further. William Sherman was not a striking figure: red-headed, begrizzled, and slightly built, he disliked Negroes, newspapermen, and war. He felt that only by carrying the war to the Southern people could peace ever come. Like Grant he was willing to take chances—and to set new standards of war—for the accomplishment of that end.

Almost at the precise hour that Grant moved into the Wilderness of Virginia, "Uncle Billy" Sherman started southward from Chattanooga with 98,000 men. His immediate target was Atlanta, the "nerve center of Southern communication." Blocking his advance were 53,000 seasoned Confederates under Joseph E. Johnston. The Confederate general saw no hope in trying to thwart Sherman's forces in open combat. Instead, using his great

Library of Congress photo by G. N. Barnard. Inset: Cook Collection, Valentine Museum, Richmond, Va

Above: Confederate defensive lines around Atlanta. The trenches were dug in advance by slaves, ready for the army to take up position. The palisades and fearsome chevaux-de-frise were refinements, added when a long siege was expected. Sherman's men discovered during the Georgia campaign that it was impossible to take a well-entrenched position by frontal assault and so would dig their own interconnecting trenches in order to outflank the Confederates. When the army reached Atlanta President Davis removed Johnston from command. Right: General John Hood of Texas, who replaced Johnston. His savage attacks on the Federal lines around Atlanta resulted only in heavy casualties. In the end, he too was forced to retreat to save his army— and left Atlanta to the mercies of Sherman.

defensive skills, Johnston retreated in slow and orderly fashion. He destroyed bridges and railroads as he went, made painful stabs at segments of the Union army, and delivered an occasional heavy blow from behind strong entrenchments. He always retired to another position before Sherman could outflank him and maneuver the huge Federal army into position for a full-scale attack.

Sharp fighting at Resaca (May 13–15), Adairsville (May 17), and Pine Mountain (June 14) further slowed Sherman's advance and cost him heavy losses. At Kennesaw Mountain (June 27), Sherman tried to overrun Johnston's lines in a series of direct frontal assaults. The attempts failed and added 6,000 casualties to the Federal lists. By mid-July, Johnston's troops were safely in the trenches of Atlanta. Sherman had spent a bloody and frustrating two months in marching 160 miles while trying to destroy the one military obstacle in his path.

Johnston's movements from Dalton to Atlanta can be compared favorably with Lee's maneuvers in the face of Grant's advance. Yet popular and official dissatisfaction with Johnston's retreat was widespread in Georgia.

President Davis, who disliked Johnston personally, was convinced that the general should have done more than merely delay Sherman. On July 17, 1864, Johnston was relieved from command. His successor was General John B. Hood, a battle-proven soldier who had already lost a leg and the use of an arm in combat. Hood's gallantry was unimpeachable; what he lacked were skill and experience in independent command. Hood demonstrated this all too quickly. On July 20, he ordered Confederates from their trenches in an attack on Sherman's right flank. His battle plans were badly mismanaged. Confusion marked the Southern assaults, and the Battle of Peach Tree Creek proved a sharp defeat. Undeterred, Hood launched a series of attacks two days later against Sherman's left in east Atlanta. These, too, met with bloody repulse.

Sherman slowly extended his lines around Atlanta. Inside the city, morale sagged as Hood tried vainly to keep the railroad lines open to the south. When it became obvious that Sherman's forces were about to isolate Atlanta, Hood sent a portion of his army to attack the Federals at Jonesboro. It was the same pathetic story of

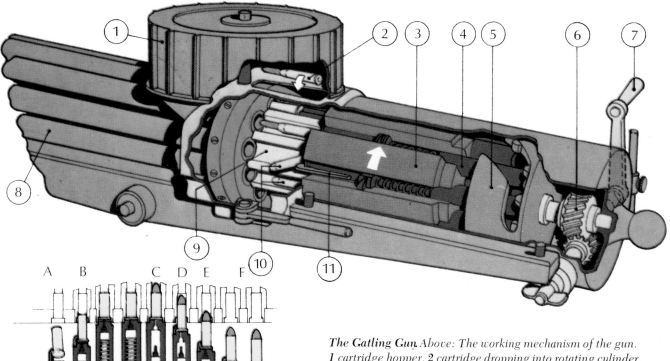

The Gatling Gun. *Above: The working mechanism of the gun.*
1 cartridge hopper. 2 cartridge dropping into rotating cylinder.
3 lock cylinder. 4 tappets. 5 cam. 6 worm gear. 7 operating handle.
8 barrels. 9 rotating cylinder. 10 spent cartridges. 11 ejector claw.
Left: The Gatling's firing cycle. A ejection. B unlocking and
extraction. C locking and firing. D cocking. E chambering.
F feeding. Below: The Gatling gun was patented by Richard
Jordan Gatling in 1862. It was first used by Federal troops at the
siege of Petersburg in 1864-65.

Peter Sarson

inferior numbers attempting to carry strong earthworks. The August 31 battle was a complete failure and Hood then abandoned Atlanta in order to save his army.

On September 2, 1864, Sherman's troops marched triumphantly into the city. The Union occupation of Atlanta had both immediate and long-range effects. Its fall meant the loss of the Confederacy's chief commercial center in the lower South, as well as a disruption of every railroad that previously had passed into the city. On the Union side, Sherman's victory restored confidence among the Northern people. It came during a barren period when the chances of Lincoln's reelection looked remote. The capture of Atlanta went far toward sparking Republican success in the autumn elections—and that in turn ensured that the war would be waged to a decisive conclusion.

The military picture now assumed a curious twist. Two opposing armies that had faced and fought from Shiloh to Atlanta turned their backs on one another. Sherman began gazing eastward toward the Atlantic Ocean. Hood infused new spirit in his 40,000 soldiers by marching northwest toward Tennessee. His objectives were to cut Sherman's communications with Nashville, brush aside all Federal resistance, and strike for the Ohio River. Both Hood and Davis believed that this would force Sherman to retire from Georgia in order to protect his rear.

Sherman refused to be intimidated. He did not feel that one army could catch Hood. Moreover, Sherman was more interested in marching across Georgia to the sea. Such a daring act would cut the South in two both geographically

and psychologically. It would also subject the lower South to the full horror of invasion and, said Sherman, "make Georgia howl." Both Grant and Lincoln had reservations about this proposal, but both gave their approval.

To keep Hood occupied, Sherman transferred John M. Schofield and 30,000 men to Nashville as reinforcements for Thomas's forces. Schofield would have arrived too late had Hood moved rapidly on Nashville. Instead, the Confederate general procrastinated for three weeks, marched in a dilatory and roundabout way, and ended up pursuing Schofield's reinforcing army. Late in the afternoon of November 30, Hood struck Schofield at Franklin, eighteen miles south of Nashville. Hood sent his poorly clad soldiers charging across a mile of open ground without benefit of artillery support. Schofield's men were strongly entrenched. The Confederates assaulted bravely but without coordination. Southern brigades charged singly and in piecemeal fashion as Hood sought frantically to gain victory before sundown. The Federals repulsed at least thirteen separate attacks before withdrawing at midnight to Nashville. Schofield suffered 2,326 casualties. Hood's losses were 6,252 men, including 6 generals killed and 53 regimental commanders lost.

Hood then resumed the advance. Nashville had been strongly fortified during three years of Federal occupation, and Thomas's 60,000 troops now manned the works. Hood nevertheless laid siege to the city with less than half Thomas's numbers. Washington authorities, as well as Grant, became increasingly impatient when Thomas made

Hood launched a series of bitter attacks on the Federal lines round Atlanta in an attempt to break Sherman's grip on the city. Above: Desperate hand-to-hand fighting as the Southerners capture an enemy battery while trying to keep the Georgia Railroad open. This scene is a section of the Atlanta Cyclorama, depicting the entire battle, which is said to be the largest painting in the world.

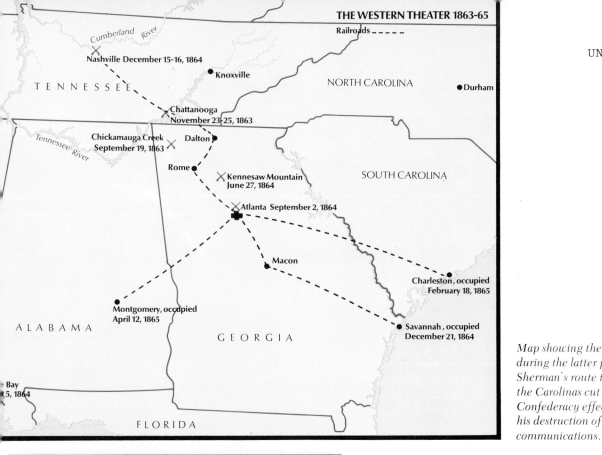

THE WESTERN THEATER 1863-65

Railroads ----

Cumberland River

Nashville December 15-16, 1864

Knoxville

TENNESSEE

NORTH CAROLINA

Durham

Chattanooga
November 23-25, 1863

Chickamauga Creek
September 19, 1863

Dalton

Tennessee River

Rome

SOUTH CAROLINA

Kennesaw Mountain
June 27, 1864

Atlanta September 2, 1864

Macon

Charleston, occupied
February 18, 1865

Montgomery, occupied
April 12, 1865

ALABAMA

GEORGIA

Savannah, occupied
December 21, 1864

Bay
5, 1864

FLORIDA

*Map showing the western theater
during the latter part of the war.
Sherman's route through Georgia and
the Carolinas cut the remnants of the
Confederacy effectively in half, while
his destruction of Atlanta crippled its
communications.*

*Mobile, Alabama, was one of the last Southern
ports to be closed by the Union navy. On August 5,
1864 a fleet of eighteen warships commanded by
Admiral Farragut (left) steamed into Mobile Bay.
Below: CSS Tennessee surrenders after the failure
of her engines. The city of Mobile held out for
another eight months, until the end of the war.*

no counteroffensive. After all, Hood's forces were too weak to attack and too exposed to risk retreat. Yet Thomas took his time in devising a battle plan. Everything must be in its rightful place when he struck.

Another general was en route westward to succeed Thomas when the "Rock of Chickamauga" assaulted Hood's lines with precise execution. The Battle of Nashville (December 15–16) matched gallant charges against grim resistance. In the second day's fighting, the Federals broke Hood's lines in several places, took prisoners by the score, and sent a shattered Confederate army stumbling southward in disastrous defeat. Hood lost 6,000 men in the battle. The proud Army of Tennessee had been reduced to a skeleton force that Thomas described sadly as "ragged, bloody, without food and without hope."

Meanwhile, Sherman had embarked on his memorable "March to the Sea." His army numbered about 62,000 soldiers. Ostensibly, they were carefully picked because of the risks involved in the campaign. In reality, however, Sherman's units included a large proportion of conscripts, drifters, and even some criminals who had joined the army to escape the sheriff. Sherman's plan was to abandon all communication and supply lines. His men would live off the country as they advanced. The field orders called for his forces to march fifteen miles a day by four parallel roads. Foraging as they went, the men were also ordered to demolish mills, cotton gins, and all other facilities for production. Any resistance encountered was to be met with "devastation more or less relentless." Yet his men were warned to treat non-combatants with civility.

Since Atlanta could not be left as a rallying point for the Confederates, Sherman's first act was to apply the torch to the city. Entire blocks of Atlanta were in flames when the Federal army started eastward on November 15. The subsequent conduct of the Federal soldiers went beyond the justifiable needs of war. Because it was impossible for Sherman to supervise the behavior of every one of his regiments, vandalism and wanton waste characterized the march. The confiscation of horses and mules and the indiscriminate slaughter of other livestock were common practices. The looting of homes and the stealing of family heirlooms became daily occurrences. Every public building along the way felt the heavy hand of the Federal invaders. The destruction of war-sustaining industries was carried out with methodical thoroughness. More than 200 miles of railroad were demolished, critically impairing the transportation of food and supplies to Confederate armies. Smoke and ruin were left in the wake of each Federal line of march.

Small Confederate detachments sniped at the Federal columns, but they were regarded as more of a nuisance than a threat. No major obstacle stood in Sherman's way. As a result, on December 22, Sherman presented the city of Savannah to Lincoln as a "Christmas gift." His campaign, even at that midway point, painfully demonstrated to the

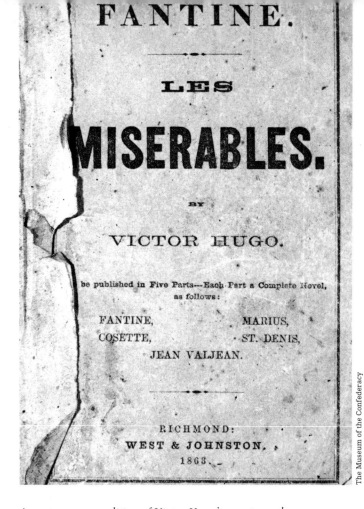

A contemporary edition of Victor Hugo's great novel, Les Misérables, *published in Richmond. This book enjoyed considerable popularity among the men of the Army of Northern Virginia, who cynically referred to themselves as* "Lee's Miserables."

Southern people the hopelessness of their situation. In bisecting the Confederacy, Sherman utilized the modern concept that military success comes only after the morale of the enemy's civilian population has been shattered. Thousands of Southerners thereafter regarded Sherman as an inhuman devil and all Yankees as fiendish barbarians. This detestation lasted for years and immeasurably delayed reconciliation between North and South.

At this time, the two sides were engaged in the final struggles at sea. The South was never able to match the growing might of the Federal navy, which goes far in explaining the short life of the Confederacy.

To the credit of Confederate Secretary of the Navy Stephen R. Mallory, every effort was made to create a fleet of warships. But successful Northern diplomacy and Southern lack of funds blocked all attempts to obtain vessels in quantity from Europe, and a shortage of raw materials and manufacturing facilities hampered large-scale production in the South. The Confederacy thus had to rely upon experiments and improvisations in its efforts to achieve a degree of naval power.

One such innovation was the widespread use of mines (or "torpedoes," as they were called). Matthew Fontaine

Maury was in charge of developing these weapons, which often were crude affairs made of demijohns or beer kegs filled with gunpowder. Scores of small boats with torpedoes affixed to the prows attacked Union ships with surprising success, for ironclad vessels of that day had wooden hulls and were quite vulnerable below the water line. Union authorities admitted after the war that torpedoes accounted for more destruction of Federal warships than all other Confederate weapons combined.

Another experiment undertaken by the Confederate naval department was the tactical use of submarines. The most famous of these vessels was the *H. L. Hunley*, a fish-shaped, sixty-foot boat propelled by the muscle power of a crew of eight. It proved to be a deathtrap for its volunteer crews. Five times it sank on trial runs. Finally, on the night of February 17, 1864, the semi-submersible *Hunley* attacked the Union sloop *Housatonic* in Charleston harbor. The *Hunley*'s torpedo struck the Federal ship and sent it to the bottom, but in the explosion the *Hunley* and all hands disappeared—victims of their lone success.

Sealing the Blockade

Sleek Confederate blockade-runners continued throughout the war to funnel limited quantities of supplies into the beleaguered South. Federal warships inflicted heavy destruction on such shipping, but the Federal navy simply could not match the speed of the "runners" or the daring of their skippers. The Lincoln government soon deduced that the only way to neutralize the blockade-runners was to close the Southern ports to which they traveled. Hence, Federal forces continued the "hopscotch" tactics of conquest begun early along the Atlantic coast. Yet three of the South's principal ports—Mobile, Alabama, Wilmington, North Carolina, and Charleston, South Carolina—maintained defiant resistance until the last months of the war.

Mobile served for three years as the Confederacy's chief port in the Gulf of Mexico. Its elaborate defenses included forts, a line of torpedoes across the harbor's mouth and a small fleet. On August 5, 1864 eighteen Federal warships under Admiral Farragut attacked Mobile Bay. The vessels first fought their way past the heavy guns of Fort Morgan. When the lead ship then stopped short of the torpedo line, Farragut (lashed to the rigging of his flag ship) reputedly shouted: "Damn the torpedoes! Full speed ahead!" A torpedo sank the warship *Tecumseh*, but the remainder of Farragut's fleet steamed into the harbor. The Confederates dispatched a lone ironclad ram, the *Tennessee*, against Farragut's ships. It was a hopeless duel. The *Tennessee*'s weak engines failed as gunboats converged on her, and after a series of point-blank broadsides the proud vessel was left dead in the water. Farragut's ironclads and wooden frigates thereupon closed

Mobile Bay to blockade-runners. Mobile itself did not surrender until eight months later.

Wilmington, North Carolina, by 1864 had become the most important port on the Atlantic for the supply of Lee's army. Blockade-runners regularly "ran the gauntlet" of Federal warships to reach safety in Wilmington's Cape Fear River. The port's major defense was Fort Fisher which stood on the peninsula where the river emptied into the sea. Late in December 1864, the most powerful American fleet up to that time concentrated on the fort. Admiral David Porter's 60 ships mounted over 600 guns. But even with assistance from infantry under Benjamin F. Butler, Porter's attacks failed to dislodge the fort's 1,900 defenders and 44 guns.

In mid-January 1865, Porter tried again. His ships bombarded the fort for two days and nights. Federal General Alfred H. Terry's 8,000 infantry then stormed the beaches and attacked the fort from front and rear. The small garrison waged a desperate hand-to-hand struggle, but sheer weight of numbers soon proved overwhelming. The loss of Fort Fisher doomed Wilmington and dealt the Confederacy a severely crippling blow.

It is ironic that Charleston, where the Civil War began, was the last major port to fall. Its defenders valiantly withstood one of the most protracted sieges of the entire conflict. The first major effort to take the city came in April 1863, when Flag Officer Samuel DuPont's nine ironclads assaulted the harbor. Confederate batteries skillfully trained by Beauregard fired over 2,200 shells at DuPont's flotilla. Five Federal ships were disabled by gunfire. On July 18, 1863, masses of blueclad infantry—including Negro troops of the 54th Massachusetts—attacked Fort Wagner but fell back with heavy losses. The final effort came six weeks later. Federal monitors unleashed a terrific bombardment on every section of the city. Yet the Confederates refused to abandon the port. Not until the approach of Sherman's army in February 1865, did the defenders of Charleston finally strike their colors.

Confederate naval efforts met with more spectacular success on the high seas, thanks to eighteen commerce raiders that roamed the oceans in search of Northern merchant marine. One of the first such raiders was the *Florida*, built in England, armed in the Bahamas, and captained by John N. Maffitt. She seized thirty-four vessels before her own destruction in 1864 in a Brazilian port. The attack on the *Florida* by the USS *Wachusett* was a flagrant violation of neutral hospitality. The Federal government subsequently apologized to Brazil and court-martialed the skipper.

The most famous of all Confederate raiders was the *Alabama*, commanded by swashbuckling "sea devil" Raphael Semmes. For two years the *Alabama* cruised the Atlantic and so effectively eluded Federal gunboats that she was regarded as a ghost ship. She captured sixty-two merchantmen worth $6,750,000 before her dramatic end

On the night of April 2, 1865, the Confederate
government abandoned its capital city. Above:
The citizens of Richmond flee across the river,
leaving the city in flames behind them.

off the coast of France. On June 19, 1864, the *Alabama*
rashly attacked the powerful USS *Kearsarge*. Semmes's
ship was too worn out to match the armorplate and
heavier guns of the *Kearsarge*. The *Alabama* sank after
a gallant fight and an unmatched career.

The saga of Confederate commerce raiders ended with
the *Shenandoah*, which specialized in attacking whaling
fleets in the Pacific and Arctic oceans. This ship did over
$1 million worth of damage to Federal commerce. On
June 8, 1865, it captured eight vessels in the Bering
Strait. Not until the autumn did Captain James I. Waddell
learn of the Confederacy's end. He then sailed to Liverpool
where, on November 6, 1865, he furled the last Confederate
flag. This act rang down the curtain on the Confederate
navy. Its history was a fatal combination of shortsighted-
ness, short supply, unpreparedness, and misfortune.

Sherman rested his army for a month at Savannah before
striking northward into the Carolinas toward Virginia and
Grant. The glee and fury of Sherman's men now
accelerated. In their eyes, South Carolina was the cradle
of secession and deserved no mercy. As Sherman stated
in a telegram to Washington: ''The truth is the whole army

A romantic painting of the North's victorious
generals. Grant is in the center with his chief
lieutenants, Sherman on the left and Meade to the
right. Sheridan rides the black horse, left.

is burning with an insatiable desire to wreak vengeance upon South Carolina."

Federal soldiers shortly enacted that "burning desire." Thirteen towns felt the torch as Sherman advanced on Columbia, the state capital. With its seizure on February 17, 1865, came the worst destruction of all. Fires suddenly erupted and swept through more than eighty blocks of the city. Sherman denied responsibility for the disaster and claimed that it began when retreating Confederates set fire to bales of unremovable cotton. However, lax discipline and widespread drunkenness in Sherman's army certainly played major roles in the wanton leveling of Columbia.

A month later, Sherman reached Fayetteville, North Carolina, at the head of the Cape Fear River. He then deviated from his northward march toward Raleigh and turned eastward for Goldsboro and the Confederacy's one remaining north-south railroad. By then, Johnston had taken command of the scattered Confederate forces in the Carolinas. His responsibility once more was to block Sherman's advance with inferior numbers. On March 19–20, Johnston's 15,000 men attacked one of Sherman's wings at Bentonville. The Southerners actually held their own in two days of sharp fighting, but the arrival of the remainder of Sherman's army forced Johnston to withdraw. Sherman seized Goldsboro and the railroad, then bivouacked to await news from Grant's now active army in Virginia.

The South's great hero, Robert E. Lee, is cheered by his troops. The affection that the men had for their general was undiminished by their ultimate defeat and surrender "to overwhelming numbers and resources."

The long winter months in the trenches around Petersburg took a deadly toll from Lee's besieged army. Near-starvation persisted as food supplies shrank to a trickle. Bitterly cold weather played havoc with emaciated men in rags and without overcoats or tents. The Southern poet-soldier Sidney Lanier wrote that his uniform blouse "afforded no protection to anything but the insects congregated in the seams of the same." Pneumonia, scurvy, fever, and infection constantly plagued "Lee's Miserables." The Army of Northern Virginia dwindled to 28,000 men as Grant continued a slow extension of the Union lines to the left and right. Lee had no choice but to do likewise.

On March 25, 1865, Lee made a last-ditch effort to break Grant's hold. Confederates en masse struck the Union lines and seized Fort Stedman. If they could hold this focal point in the Federal defenses, Lee reasoned, they could threaten Grant's main artery—the railroad to his supply base at City Point—and thus force Grant on the defensive. The Confederate attack caught Grant by surprise, but Federals quickly delivered a heavy counterassault and recaptured the fort. Grant then dispatched Sheridan to the far left to take control of the South Side Railroad, Lee's only remaining supply line. Sheridan's attack at Five Forks on April 1 was so unexpected that it came when the two Confederate generals in that sector were behind the lines at a shadbake. The Confederates resisted valiantly, but Sheridan's overwhelming numbers drove them from the trenches with heavy casualties. Grant then ordered attacks all along the Petersburg line. Lee's thin defenses could no

longer withstand the pressure. Federals in force poured through the works.

Lee abandoned Petersburg and Richmond the following afternoon. His half-naked, half-starved men slowly retreated west toward the Richmond & Danville Railroad. Lee's only hope was to use that railroad as a supply line and to follow it to Danville, where he would combine with Johnston's forces in a united stand against Grant and Sherman. The plan was a forlorn hope. Grant's better-fed men moved faster in pursuit and seized the Richmond & Danville line. Weary but dauntless Confederates turned to the northwest and fought from hilltop to hilltop as the Federal army pressed vigorously against Lee's disintegrating units.

On April 6, Federal forces captured a third of Lee's army after a bitterly contested fight at Sayler's Creek. What was left of the Southern army subsisted on grains of parched corn as it plodded toward Lynchburg. Federal infantry and cavalry quickly encircled the Confederates, cutting off all remaining avenues of escape. On April 9—Palm Sunday—a heavy-hearted Lee surrendered 13,000 survivors to Grant at Appomattox.

The death of the Army of Northern Virginia triggered capitulations by all other Confederate forces. On April 26, Johnston surrendered to Sherman near Durham, North Carolina. General Richard Taylor on May 4 surrendered his large army at Citronelle, Alabama. Three weeks later, on May 26, the Confederacy's last major army (under E. Kirby Smith) laid down its arms at New Orleans. The world's largest, most costly civil war had come to an end.

The conflagration in Richmond continued until the following morning when invading Union troops put out the fires. Below: A photograph of the ruined city taken shortly after its occupation. Such total desolation was not uncommon in the South, and Reconstruction was to be long and tormenting.

On Palm Sunday 1865, Lee surrendered his army of 13,000 men. The war was practically over—but too late for this Confederate soldier, dead in the lines at Petersburg, April 2, 1865. The 600,000 who died in the war bear witness to Sherman's comment that "war, at best, is barbarism."

Why Did the North Win?

The war was not quite over, though the end seemed near, when Abraham Lincoln was inaugurated for his second term in office on March 4, 1865. His speech, printed in two columns on a single large sheet of paper, was short but beautifully eloquent. The Union was on the brink of victory, yet Lincoln stressed the tragedy of the conflict rather than the success he was presiding over. "Neither party," he said, "expected for the war, the magnitude, or the duration, which it has already attained . . . Each looked for an easier triumph, and a result less fundamental and astounding. Both read the same Bible, and pray to the same God; and each invokes His aid against the other . . . The prayers of both could not be answered; that of neither has been answered fully. The Almighty has His own purposes." It was, Lincoln went on, a "terrible war." He ended with a magnanimous plea. "With malice toward none; with charity for all; with firmness in the right, as God gives us to see the right, let us strive on to finish the work we are in; to bind up the nation's wounds; to care for him who shall have borne the battle, and for his widow, and his orphan— to do all which may achieve and cherish a just, and a lasting peace, among ourselves, and with all nations."

A few weeks later, in Ford's Theater, the president's death at the hands of John Wilkes Booth added to the nation's wounds and made still harder the task of reconciling North and South to "this terrible war." During the middle of the war Lincoln had pointed out that the cost in money, let alone in human life, was far higher than the amount needed to end slavery on cash terms, as had been done thirty years earlier in the British West Indies. The slaveholders in the West Indies had been compensated for the loss of their slave property at a certain sum per head. Lincoln's suggestion was not followed up by either side.

In April-May 1865, as the men in Union blue and Confederate gray began to make their way home, these survivors may well have reviewed the sacrifice that had been called for. The true war, according to the poet Walt Whitman, would never get into the books. He was thinking mainly of the weariness, the horror, and muddle of actual battle. But this confusion extends too to the records of the war. Not that it was left undocumented. The *Official Records* of the Union and Confederate armies, which began publication in 1880, stretched to 128 volumes: those of the two navies filled another 26 volumes. Even so, the numbers involved and the casualties incurred are hard to state with any precision. At the beginning of the war in particular a good many men on both sides enlisted for only ninety days; in fact one Northern regiment at First Bull Run refused to remain in the field because its ninety-day engagement had expired. Many other soldiers joined up for three years; some fought for as long as four years.

Winslow Homer's expressive painting Prisoners from the Front, *emphasizes the disparity between the two sides that was obvious by the end of the war. Well-fed, well-equipped, and smartly-dressed young Northerners face a trio of defiant Confederates in ragbag uniforms.*

The Metropolitan Museum of Art, Gift of Mrs Frank B. Porter

North and South, as we might expect, the size of the armies steadily increased, and the weight of numbers lay more and more in the Union's favor. In July 1861, at the time of Bull Run, the Union army rolls totaled 187,000, those of the Confederacy 112,000. By the beginning of 1865 there were about a million men enrolled in the Union services, including 40–50,000 in the navy, as against a Confederate total of around 450,000. In most of the big battles the North might have 100,000 men under arms, facing Southern columns that numbered 60,000 or more. These figures were immensely larger than anything Americans had known in previous wars. In the Mexican War of 1846–48, for example, neither of the two main American armies under Zachary Taylor and Winfield Scott had ever got beyond an effective total of 15,000 troops; Scott marched on Mexico City with only 10,000.

The casualties also were on an unprecedented scale. On the Union side 110,000 men were killed in action or died of wounds. The Confederacy's battle-deaths probably amounted to about 90,000. So we have 200,000 men mowed down in combat, as compared with 1,720 Americans killed in action in the Mexican War. In addition, at least twice as many men died away from the battlefields— sometimes from the effect of wounds and the primitive surgery of the day, more often from diseases such as typhoid, malaria, and dysentery. Altogether from one cause or another the war took a toll of perhaps 360,000 men from the North and another 260,000 from the South. Many thousands more were maimed or broken in health.

Whitman devoted his spare time to visiting the army hospitals in Washington, DC, and was deeply moved by what he saw. He made notes of the soldiers he spoke to. Tom Haley "came over to this country from Ireland to enlist—has not a single friend or acquaintance here— is sleeping soundly at this moment, (but it is the sleep of death)—has a bullet-hole straight through the lung." W. H. E. was a New Jersey soldier sick with pneumonia, "an elderly, sallow-faced, rather gaunt, gray-hair'd man, a widower, with children." A New Hampshire farmer had "gangrene of the feet; a pretty bad case; will surely have to lose three toes." A youngster from Maine was "sick with dysentery and typhoid fever—pretty critical case— I talk with him often—he thinks he will die—looks like it indeed." An artilleryman, "shot in the head . . .—from hips down paralyzed" whose invalid mother sat at the bedside and watched him die. Of all these thousands, Whitman asked "aye, thousands, north and south, of unwrit heroes, . . . incredible . . . desperations—who tells?" The material cost was enormous, but any figure—$20 billion is one—is only a statistic compared with the anguish of the casualties and their families. Not even the White House was spared the suffering, or the special torment of divided loyalties produced by a civil war. Mrs Lincoln had three brothers killed fighting for the Confederacy. The president's sister-in-law was married to a Confederate brigadier, Benjamin

Many of the volunteers on both sides during the war were little more than boys, drawn by the glamor and excitement of army life. This young soldier seems almost lost in a uniform coat several sizes too large for him.

The Assassination of Lincoln

With the coming of peace five days before, the spring weather of April 14, 1865 was all the more enjoyable for the inhabitants of Washington. People along Pennsylvania Avenue gossiped about General Grant, who was in town to attend the usual Friday cabinet meeting. To celebrate the first week of peace, President and Mrs Lincoln planned to attend a performance of the English comedy, *Our American Cousin,* at Ford's Theater.

John Wilkes Booth, an actor and Southern fanatic, decided that here was his opportunity to strike down the man who symbolized everything he hated. Because Booth was well known at Ford's Theater he had easy access to places which were normally closed to the public. Counting on this advantage, Booth entered the theater that afternoon, bored a hole in the door to the president's box, and chipped away some plaster so that he could insert a bar to the corridor entrance. He planned to shoot Lincoln when an actor said, "Well, I guess I know enough to turn you inside out, old gal—you sock-dologizing old man trap," for at that point the shot would be muffled by laughter.

Lincoln, Mrs Lincoln, and their guests for the evening, Major Henry Rathbone and Miss Clara Harris, arrived at Ford's Theater shortly after half-past eight; the band played "Hail to the Chief," the actors on stage ad-libbed about the president's arrival, and the delighted audience broke into applause. Just after ten o'clock, midway through the third and final act, Booth slipped into the corridor behind the president's box; his entry had been unexpectedly easy because the one man assigned to guard the president had gone out for a drink. Through the hole he had bored earlier in the day, Booth watched his quarry and waited for his cue. The line was delivered and, while the audience was laughing, Booth quietly opened the door, pointed the derringer at the back of the president's head, and fired. In keeping with his flair for drama, Booth leaped to the stage and left the theater through the wings; a horse waited in the alley to carry him across the Potomac to the South and hoped-for safety. But Booth did not escape; he was hunted down in a barn in Virginia by Federal troops, the barn was set ablaze, and Booth was shot dead.

Lincoln was mortally wounded. Across

Above: A contemporary photograph of Ford's Theater, situated on 10th Street. Inset: Lincoln commemorated on a visiting card. Left: An engraving showing all those believed to be involved in the conspiracy, with an extract from a reward notice calling for information about "The Murderer of our late beloved President."

the street from the theater, in a boarding house, a bed was prepared for the dying president. There throughout the night his distraught family and members of the cabinet kept vigil. The next morning he suffered a final hemorrhage and died at 7:22 AM. At the president's deathbed, Secretary of War Edwin Stanton uttered the memorable epitaph, "Now he belongs to the ages."

Helm of Kentucky. After Helm's death at Chickamauga the widow lived for several months with the Lincolns.

Why did the war have to last so long? This question was posed again and again while the struggle was in progress, and it has been debated endlessly since then. One common answer in the North was that the whole affair was a gigantic Southern conspiracy. The slaveholders were alleged to have prepared for secession, and the battles that must inevitably follow, long before the break came. It was said that the South had trained its men to fight, wormed its leaders into key positions in the prewar army and administrations, and managed to implant disloyalty in high places. Believers in a Southern conspiracy pointed out that John C. Breckinridge, vice president under James Buchanan, went over to the Confederacy, as did several men who in peacetime had been secretary of the army or of the navy in Washington. The US Military Academy at West Point, which furnished most of the senior officers on both sides, was said to have been dominated by Southerners. A considerable number of Union generals were accused— especially by radical Republican members of the congressional Committee on the Conduct of the War—of being sympathetic to slavery, and therefore of being unwilling to fight battles, let alone win them. If they were Democrats with Southern family ties, like McClellan or Meade, suspicion was all the greater. A cousin of McClellan was chief of staff to the Confederate generals Jeb Stuart and Wade Hampton; Meade's brother-in-law was the Con-

Northern grief and fear were followed by a call for vengeance, directed against Booth's associates. On July 7, 1865, after trial by a military tribunal, four of them were hanged—Mary Surratt, George Atzerodt, Lewis Paine, and David Harold.

federate general Henry A. Wise, former governor of Virginia. Peace moves by Northern Democrats were denounced as Copperhead treason, in league with Confederate agents. Mrs Helm's presence in the White House, dressed in black in memory of her "Reb" husband, aroused criticism from people already disposed to attack Lincoln. What sort of example was this for the nation?

Such suspicions of President and Mrs Lincoln—both born in the slave state of Kentucky—were stilled only when Lincoln himself was assassinated. The fear of a widespread conspiracy was, however, understandably reawakened. Alarmed Northerners stressed that Booth had had several accomplices. They wondered how he had contrived to get past the president's bodyguard, and then to escape from the theater. They stressed that while Booth was carrying out his part of the plot, others tried to kill Secretary of State Seward, and nearly succeeded. Booth was tracked down and shot dead. Several men and a woman thought to be implicated in his scheme were tried, condemned, and hanged—one or two, including the woman, a boardinghouse keeper named Mrs Surratt, perhaps unjustly—in an atmosphere of intense alarm. In such a mood Americans were ready to take seriously a book like *The Adder's Den: or, Secrets of the Great Conspiracy to Overthrow Liberty in America* (1864). The author, John Smith Dye, asserted that the South had poisoned President Harrison in 1841 and President Zachary Taylor in 1850, and had tried to kill President-elect Buchanan in 1857 as well as President-elect Lincoln early in 1861. As late as 1886 a popular history of the war and the events leading up to it could still be entitled *The Great Conspiracy*.

Was War Inevitable?

In fact there was no conspiracy before secession, or during the war years. The Southern way of life may have put more emphasis on semimilitary practices than was true of life in the North, but there had been no concerted plan to smash the Union and arm the Confederacy. There had been a lot of wild talk by Southern "fire-eaters," but the average Southerner was taken by surprise when the war actually came. The conflict could be called inevitable, given the situation as Lincoln summed things up in his second inaugural: one side "would *make* war rather than let the nation survive; and the other would *accept* war rather than let it perish." But to say that the clash was bound to come, and that the South was stubborn, was very different from proving that the clash was premeditated by Southern plotters. The assassination of Lincoln *was* a conspiracy in the sense that Booth persuaded others to join him in his mad enterprise. If he had managed to carry out the idea at some previous stage, when the North was still far from sure of winning, the act might have severely shaken the Union. Coming in April 1865, the assassination was sheer folly. The Confederate leaders knew nothing of the scheme. If they had, common sense alone would have led them to veto it, since Lincoln was obviously much more willing to treat the South generously than were the radical Republicans in Congress.

Why then the widespread Northern belief in a Southern conspiracy, persisting long after the war was over? One reason is that the notion helped to explain away an otherwise embarrassing fact. According to calculations of relative strength in manpower and industrial output, the North ought to have been able to defeat the Confederacy with ease. Instead the effort had required four whole years. It was tempting to put forward the theory that this was because the Union had been thrust into the struggle at a disadvantage, and subsequently hampered by Southern and Copperhead intrigue.

A less palatable but more plausible interpretation, already touched upon, was that the white inhabitants of the slave states simply made better soldiers. The dread of slave risings led them to carry out systematic armed patrols in prewar days. Farmers were accustomed to horse and gun.

Library of Congress

Black children photographed among the ruins of Charleston, South Carolina, in 1865. Sherman's men were "burning with an insatiable desire" to ravage the state where the secession movement had started.

ARMY OF THE CUMBERLAND.

ROLL OF HONOR.

This Certifies That _____ has served as a Volunteer in Comp.?

FOR GOD AND MY COUNTRY.

WE'LL RALLY ROUND THE FLAG BOYS.

VICTORY OR DEATH.

THE WAY T. PEACE.

NEVER SURRENDER.

HONOR TO THE BRAVE.

Name
DESCRIPTION.	WHERE BORN.	ENLISTED.
Years of Age		When
Eyes		Where
Hair		By Whom
Complexion	OCCUPATION.	Period
Feet		
In.		

I Certify, *That the above is a correct transcript from the records.*
Date
Station

Entered according to act of congress in the year 1863 by W.R.Ve. Agent, in the Clerks Office of the District Court of the Southern District of Ohio.

Commemorative certificate issued to men who fought with the Army of the Cumberland in the western theater. On the field at Murfreesboro the soldiers of this army had resolved to "maintain the honor and integrity of our government from the St Lawrence to the Gulf, and between the Oceans"—with their blood.

The planter aristocracy, equally used to riding and shooting, had a natural habit of command. Hence the familiar picture of the Confederate army: the ordinary "Johnny Reb," wilder and tougher than his Northern counterpart "Billy Yank," led by brilliant officers such as Lee and Jackson, the cream of the old regular army. There were other explanations more or less along the same lines.

After the failure of McClellan's Peninsula campaign, the Union general John Sedgwick wrote gloomily to his sister: "The army are now around Washington, occupying nearly the same positions they did last winter. The enemy have outgeneraled us . . . On our part it has been a war of politicians; on theirs it has been one conducted by a despot and carried out by able Generals." Sedgwick's complaint was that the North was badly led. Lincoln was a good-natured but inexperienced civilian, whereas the "despot" Jefferson Davis, a one-time regular officer who had also been secretary of war, was thoroughly in command. The Union war effort was mishandled by interfering politicians who tried to dictate strategy and to wangle generalships for themselves and their cronies. The Confederacy, however, was thought to be run on proper military principles.

Another theory was that the Confederacy had been able to start out with a clean sheet, creating an army from scratch. The Union by contrast was held to be hampered by having retained the structure of the old regular army, minus the best officers who had gone south. The hidebound old regulars, in this view, sat tight in their Washington offices, offering ultracautious advice to Lincoln and refusing to let bright young West Point officers rise from lowly positions in regular regiments to take command of the new regiments and brigades of volunteers, which badly needed them. Promotion certainly appeared to be swifter in the Confederacy. In part this may have been because of the Confederacy's different system of grades. Until Grant became a lieutenant general in 1864, no Union general stood above the rank of major general. The Confederacy by the end of the war had not only appointed seventeen lieutenant generals, but eight other men to the still higher grade of full general.

Whatever the exact causes, worried and exasperated Union men emphasized the outcome. Jefferson Davis seemed to trust his generals, retaining them even when a campaign went badly. Abraham Lincoln, either bullied by politicians or through his own misguided decisions, appointed and then dismissed general after general—McDowell, McClellan, Pope, McClellan again, Burnside, Hooker, Meade . . . The Army of the Potomac lost confidence in itself. Commanders alternated between rashness and timidity. Only in the West, where Union forces were out of the clutches of Washington, did they act like winners instead of losers.

There is some truth in these contentions. A majority of military historians would probably insist that Robert E. Lee was the finest general on either side, and would no doubt rate "Stonewall" Jackson as an extraordinarily able secondary figure. How to assess the Union's outstanding pair, U. S. Grant and William T. Sherman, with their superiority in resources, is a matter of opinion. One might argue that both Lee and Grant fought as circumstances dictated. Lee, with an inferiority in numbers, had to take risks and build upon audacity. Grant, it could be maintained, was right to use his superiority by being methodical and building upon tenacity.

Taking the picture as a whole, though, we ought to question the soundness of some of the military evidence cited during the war and afterwards. The South was in fact not notably more "military" than the North on the eve of the war, except perhaps in having a rather greater aptitude for fighting on horseback. The Confederate cavalry was better than the North's for the first half of the war. But this was, after all, in essence an infantry war. Man for man Billy Yank and Johnny Reb proved about on a par—both of them hard fighters who could hang on under heavy fire, and also surge forward on their own initiative. If the South had a slight edge at the beginning, this was offset by the growing professionalism of the Union armies. The same might be said of the respective senior officers. Below Lee and Grant came a large group of corps and division commanders ranging from very good to mediocre. Each side could claim admirable strokes and be held responsible for regrettable blunders.

At the very top, historians have tended to rate Lincoln well above Davis, while admitting that in some ways Davis had the harder job. Lincoln learned from his mistakes where Davis was apt to deny self-righteously that he had made any. The Confederacy was not immune to politics, but to the extent that politics was more conspicuous in Union affairs, it is reasonable to believe that the free discussion it promoted was actually healthy. Lincoln had to worry about reelection in 1864 where Davis was still secure in his six year tenure. It was a considerable worry for Lincoln, who at one period felt he was likely to lose the election to the Democratic candidate, General McClellan. But the main factor in 1864 was the bad news from the fighting front, where "Butcher" Grant was unable to break through Lee's nimble formations. Politics was shaped by the war in this instance, not vice versa. As for Davis, he had plenty of home front anxieties. Lincoln enjoyed a great deal of executive authority, and on most occasions was well supported by state governors. Davis might look like a despot: in reality his authority was restricted, and he was often at odds with state governors.

The Sapping of Morale

In neither section was morale uniformly high. In both, war weariness increased. Voluntary enlistments fell away. Thousands evaded conscription; many thousands deserted. The punishment for desertion in face of the enemy was death. One of Lincoln's worst tasks was confirming the death sentences, or whenever possible commuting them, on what he called his "leg-cases"—the cases of soldiers who had lost their nerve in a battle and run away. Most soldiers, North and South, responded with remarkable bravery, especially when they trusted their commanders. Here perhaps lies the unique importance of Lee, revered as no other general was through campaign after campaign. Yet in broad perspective the sectional differences level out. Both Union and Confederate fighting men resented the comforts, or the profiteering, or the indifference, of civilians behind the lines. Possibly Union morale suffered more from the contrast between their hardship and civilian ease, while Confederate morale suffered increasingly from the knowledge that the South was being invaded and ground down by the Union war machine, including the blockade by sea. It has been estimated that the Union navy, never able to control the entire Confederate coastline, was intercepting a good half of the blockade runners in the last year of the war, as against only a quarter in the first year.

The Union situation was paradoxical. Billy Yank could usually feel his home was safe from the enemy. Even so, he could well be angered by the complacency of prosperous citizens of military age whom the war hardly touched. The caustic journalist H. L. Mencken has reminded us that America's three foremost authors of the postwar era, Mark Twain, William Dean Howells, and Henry James, could all be called "draft-dodgers." James had a suspect back; Howells spent the war in Venice, Italy, where Lincoln had appointed him consul in return for writing a campaign biography of the president; and Twain, having joined a makeshift Confederate company in Missouri, soon changed his mind and went off to try his luck in Nevada. The point is not that the trio were cowards, but that the terrible war was not terrible for everyone.

There is still the question: why did the North need four

In the end, Northern superiority in materials (as well as men) was decisive. Left: Repairing telegraph wires that speeded communication between generals in the field and Washington. Above: Observation of enemy lines on the Peninsula from a hot-air balloon.

The importance of railroads for troop movements was recognized early on. The US Military Railroad Construction Corps, here repairing a bridge over Bull Run, was commanded by the energetic General Haupt.

years to crush the Confederacy? If we concede that various presumed advantages and disadvantages canceled one another out, why did not the Union's preponderance in men and material have a swifter effect? It would be hard to gainsay the view of several thoughtful historians that, at least in the first half of the war, the South deployed its resources more intelligently, and through better generalship gained the upper hand in most of the battles from First Bull Run to Fredericksburg. One might speculate about the element of luck. Suppose for instance McClellan had been as good a fighting general as he was a training general? Or that Grant had come to the fore earlier in the war? These are intriguing possibilities. But they can be countered—suppose Pickett had broken through at Gettysburg?—and they deflect us from more fundamental considerations.

The main question could be turned round: why did the South fail to survive long enough to secure independence for the Confederacy? Two main types of evidence need to be examined. There is the problem of the *conduct* of the war—strategy, tactics, logistics. And, second, there is the problem of the *aim* of the war—what the two sides thought they were fighting for.

As a military problem, the war was arguably more perplexing for the Union than for the Confederacy. The Union had to take the offensive. Its armies had to strike deep into the enemy's country, which would mean ever-lengthening lines of communication and supply among a hostile population. The Union must hold the ground it had gained, which would mean installing garrisons in more and more places. The more of these, the fewer troops available for front line fighting. Lincoln's armies must carve the Confederacy into pieces. But this was what the British had done in the Revolutionary War; and they had found that the mere occupation of territory, even of America's main cities, was not enough, so long as General Washington's armies remained in being. The Confederate strategy, as with General Washington, was chiefly defensive—tempered by large scale raids like Lee's into Maryland and Pennsylvania. Jefferson Davis could afford to yield ground, on the assumption that he would sooner or later regain it. Operating on interior lines, the Confederacy did not need to maintain lengthy lines of supply. Self-sufficient in food and fodder, it could not be starved out, and could hope to make up what was lacking—weapons and ammunition, boots, items such as salt—by means of blockade runners, captures from Union dumps, and improvisation.

Union strategy has been criticized for becoming obsessed with seizing the Confederate capital, Richmond, instead of getting to grips with the main Confederate army. It is probably true that this happened, if we accept that some of the Union's most costly and futile battles were fought in the debatable ground between Washington and Richmond. Once or twice McClellan and other Union commanders had reason to grumble that, scared of a Confederate descent on Washington, Lincoln diverted too many troops to protect the city. Possibly he ought at an earlier stage to have concentrated more men in the West, where the spectacular war-winning thrusts were developed. The argument, however, cuts both ways. Both sides were determined to hold their capitals at all costs. Believing so fanatically in this necessity, and in the corresponding importance of seizing the enemy's capital, each bolstered its belief by putting large armies into the field along the Potomac front. A move on Richmond or on Washington thus became for each a move against the enemy's main military force. The symbolic goal of Richmond or Washington became inseparable from the classic military aim of destruction of the enemy's army.

New Concepts of War

In other respects Union strategy and Confederate strategy evolved along broadly sensible lines, each doing what it had to. The evolution was gradual. The lessons taught at West Point had largely to be unlearned. For example, nothing in the textbooks gave guidance on the strategic use of railroads to switch large bodies of men from front to front. While Sherman's march into Georgia and then north through the Carolinas—a 2,000-mile tramp for some of his men—was an amazingly bold concept. Looking back on the grand plan one might feel that the South's fate was settled once Union superiority began to count in the Mississippi Valley. The near stalemate in the East, however frustrating to Washington's horde of armchair warriors, could be seen as an essential holding operation while Grant and Sherman scythed through the Deep South, and the Union navy shut off port after port.

Tactically, however, the war was a cumbersome, bloody business. The tangled terrain, the deadly firepower of rifle and artillery, and the quickness of infantry to dig in, gave a distinct advantage to the defenders of a position. Big battles usually disintegrated into a series of isolated engagements. Since generals were often unable to control the battle in detail, or even bring the whole army into action, the North's numerical superiority was much less decisive than might have been expected. The attacker was liable to incur extremely heavy casualties, as happened to Lee at Gettysburg or Grant in the Wilderness. The Union was usually on the attack, and therefore more usually appeared to bear the brunt of an engagement. Only a handful of battles ended in clear victory. The great majority were hammering matches, not because of the stupidity of the commanders but because of the nature of the combat. Warfare was more mobile in the West, but also somewhat inconclusive until Sherman's bummers were able to cut loose. Gradually, set piece battles tended to be replaced by small clashes between armies in continuous contact. In this respect, perhaps, tactical brilliance gave way to strategic considerations. The war became one of attrition: a wearing-down of resistance by the side that could afford to lose more men. The Southern hope of a smashing success faded away under such remorseless rules.

Yet, turning to the question of war aims, it is clear that the Confederacy had at least a sporting chance of ultimate success until Vicksburg and Gettysburg in July 1863, and perhaps some chance even up to the autumn of 1864. Confederate war aims were simple and definite. First, to preserve the *idea* of the South, including slavery. Then, to stave off invasion where possible and to make the North pay dearly for ground gained. Thirdly, to offer so firm a demonstration of Southern solidity that the government in Washington would lose the capacity to keep the war going. The North's war aims were far harder to define. Preservation of the Union was a fairly powerful motive. But to a good many people in the North it sounded either impossible or dangerously close to coercion. From the outset it was mixed up with a second aim, difficult to put into terms generally acceptable to Northerners. This aim was to restrict the Southern slave interest. "All knew," Lincoln said in his second inaugural address, "that this interest was, somehow, the cause of the war." But if the war was ultimately about slavery, should not the Union avow the intent to *end* slavery?

The issue was immensely complicated. For one thing, there were several slave states still inside the Union. Abolition of slavery might alienate them beyond retrieval. Then, the Republicans had pledged themselves to recognize slavery where it existed. Again, property was a sacred institution. Many Northerners who were uneasy about slavery would be still more uneasy at the wholesale breaking of contracts that abolition would entail. In the first stages of the war abolitionists were regarded as trouble-makers. A little later, as Northern troops began to penetrate into slave territory, some confessed that they were now inclined to agree with Southerners: Negroes were backward, even primeval, and perhaps needed to be treated as such. When Lincoln finally announced that emancipation was a basic Union war aim, the result seemed to confuse and antagonize as many people as it pleased. Both his wisdom and his sincerity were queried. An optimistic Southerner, reading Northern newspapers, might be forgiven for deciding that the North was hopelessly at odds with itself. Assassination made Lincoln a martyr in Union eyes, and those of Europe. But until the end of 1864 he continued to be widely portrayed as an idiot, a callous murderer, a clown, a tyrant, a man without principles. The very inconsistency of these assaults indicated the deep divisions in Northern sentiment. Indeed, the Emancipation Proclamation opened up furious controversy over the way to treat the South when it was defeated. As the war dragged on, some Americans began

Silent guns command the fields which once rang with the deafening noise of war: the battlefield at Antietam as it is today. In September 1862, for three days, the creek ran red with blood.

to sense that a blind instinct of retaliation might for both sides have become the only real war aim: killing in response to killing, an eye for an eye and a tooth for a tooth, mere marauding in the name of vengeance.

Most of the histories of the war up to the early twentieth century were by Northerners. With lessening zeal they labored the notion that the Union cause was righteous. In the aftermath of the First World War, looking back on the appalling slaughter of that conflict, they began to argue that the Civil War had been a "needless conflict," brought on by a "blundering generation" of politicians who had been misled by the extremists of both sides. This new generation of historians usually commented that the war had ruined and embittered the South. They claimed that postwar Reconstruction had not solved, but only inflamed, the race question. Another argument was that the North's foremost war aim was economic, much as Southern spokesmen had alleged in the years before Secession. That is, the North wanted to bring the South within its commercial empire, treating it as a colony. An associated theory is that the 1860s was the decade of nationalism in which Germany, Italy, and the United States all became unified. Until then they were collections of separate states. Unification was carried out through war, which made any future dreams of secession unthinkable.

Was the war worth fighting? On the positive side, we can say that it dispelled forever the theory that any state could leave the Union. Lincoln's most cherished war aim was vindicated. A majority of Americans, including Southerners, probably today accepts that the United States has been more powerful and more prosperous as one nation than it would have been if split into two nations. The war also ended slavery more quickly than would otherwise have happened. Slavery lay heavy on the nation's conscience, North and South. Even if they did not like Reconstruction, Southerners rapidly agreed that slavery was, in more ways than one, gone for good. A third feature is that the nation as a whole recovered materially from the dislocations of war within an astonishingly short space of time. This was true even of the South, though the North got richer more rapidly. By 1871, for instance, Britain was importing more raw cotton from the South than before the war, in spite of having come in 1861–65 to depend on supplies from other countries. Outwardly, the wounds of war healed over faster than anyone could have expected. Fourthly, the ultimate triumph of the Union convinced the world that—to quote Lincoln's Gettysburg Address—a nation "dedicated to the proposition that all men are created equal" could in fact endure, and emerge from the ordeal stronger than ever.

The negative aspects? Many dead, for causes that might have been attained by peaceful means, with more lasting harmony. How we weigh these is conditioned by whether we feel that wars merely destroy, or that they may bring forth good. Lincoln himself was sickened by this "brothers' war." There is no sign that he thought it futile, if only his countrymen could learn to regard the war as an unavoidable precondition for "a just, and a lasting peace."

Bibliography

GENERAL

*Barker, Alan, *The Civil War in America* (Garden City, N.Y., 1961)

Boatner, Mark M., *The Civil War Dictionary* (New York, 1959)

*Brock, William R., ed., *The Civil War* (New York, 1969)

*Brock, William R., *Conflict and Transformation: The United States, 1844–1877* (Baltimore, 1973)

*Catton, Bruce, *The American Heritage Book of the Civil War* (New York, 1960)

*Catton, Bruce, *The Centennial History of the Civil War* (3 vols., Garden City, N.Y., 1961–65)

*Cole, Arthur C., *The Irrepressible Conflict, 1850–1865* (New York, 1934)

*Commager, Henry S., ed., *The Blue and the Gray: The Story of the Civil War as Told by Participants* (2 vols., Indianapolis, 1950; also 1-vol. edn.)

Coulter, E. Merton, *The Confederate States of America, 1861–1865* (Baton Rouge, 1950)

Craven, Avery O., *Civil War in the Making, 1815–1860* (Baton Rouge, 1959)

Craven, Avery O., *The Coming of the Civil War* (New York, 1942)

*Cruden, Robert, *The War that Never Ended* (Englewood Cliffs, N.J., 1973)

Donald, David, *Charles Sumner and the Coming of the Civil War* (New York, 1960)

*Donald, David, *Lincoln Reconsidered: Essays on the Civil War Era* (2nd edn., New York, 1961)

*Eaton, Clement, *A History of the Southern Confederacy* (New York, 1954)

Freidel, Frank, ed., *Union Pamphlets of the Civil War* (2 vols., Cambridge, Mass., 1967)

Meredith, Roy, *Mr Lincoln's Contemporaries: An Album of Portraits by Mathew B. Brady* (New York, 1951)

*Nevins, Allan, *The Statesmanship of the Civil War* (enlarged edn., New York, 1962)

Nevins, Allan, *The War for the Union* (4 vols., New York, 1959–71)

Nevins, Allan, *The Ordeal of the Union* (2 vols., New York, 1947)

Nevins, Allan, *The Emergence of Lincoln* (2 vols., New York, 1950)

*Nichols, Roy F., *The Disruption of the American Democracy* (New York, 1948)

*Nichols, Roy F., *The Stakes of Power, 1845–1877* (New York, 1961)

Parish, Peter J., *The American Civil War* (London, 1975)

Randall, James G., & Donald, David, *The Civil War and Reconstruction* (rev. 2nd edn., Boston, 1973)

*Rawley, James A., *Turning Points of the Civil War* (Lincoln, Neb., 1966)

*Roland, Charles P., *The Confederacy* (Chicago, 1960)

*Silbey, Joel H., *The Shrine of Party: Congressional Voting Behavior, 1841–1852* (Pittsburgh, 1967)

Simms, Henry H., *A Decade of Sectional Controversy, 1851–1861* (Chapel Hill, N.C., 1942)

*Unger, Irwin, ed., *Essays on the Civil War and Reconstruction* (New York, 1970)

Van Deusen, Glyndon G., *William Henry Seward* (New York, 1967)

*Wilson, Edmund, *Patriotic Gore: Studies in the Literature of the American Civil War* (New York, 1962)

Chapter 1: THE PECULIAR INSTITUTION

Bancroft, Frederic, *Slave-Trading in the Old South* (Baltimore, 1931)

*Blassingame, John W., *The Slave Community: Plantation Life in the Antebellum South* (New York, 1972)

*Degler, Carl N., *Neither Black Nor White: Slavery and Race Relations in Brazil and the United States* (New York, 1971)

*Elkins, Stanley M., *Slavery: A Problem in American Institutional and Intellectual Life* (2nd edn., Chicago, 1968)

*Fogel, Robert W., & Engerman, Stanley L., *Time on the Cross* (2 vols., Boston, 1974)

*indicates paperback

Gara, Larry, *The Liberty Line: The Legend of the Underground Railroad* (Lexington, Ky., 1961)

*Genovese, Eugene D., *The Political Economy of Slavery* (New York, 1965)

*Genovese, Eugene D., *In Red and Black: Marxian Explorations in Southern and Afro-American History* (New York, 1968)

Genovese, Eugene D., *Roll, Jordan, Roll: The World the Slaves Made* (New York, 1974)

*Genovese, Eugene D., *The World the Slaveholders Made* (New York, 1969)

Jenkins, William S., *Pro-Slavery Thought in the Old South* (Chapel Hill, N.C., 1935)

Meyer, John R., & Conrad, Alfred H., *The Economics of Slavery and Other Studies in Econometric History* (Chicago, 1964)

*Phillips, Ulrich B., *American Negro Slavery* (New York, 1928)

*Phillips, Ulrich B., *Life and Labor in the Old South* (Boston, 1929)

*Stampp, Kenneth M., *The Peculiar Institution* (New York, 1956)

*Starobin, Robert S., *Industrial Slavery in the Old South* (New York, 1970)

Staudenraus, Philip J., *The African Colonization Movement, 1816–1865* (New York, 1961)

*Wade, Richard C., *Slavery in the Cities: The South, 1820–1860* (New York, 1964)

Chapter 2: THE OLD SOUTH

Bagley, William C., *Soil Exhaustion and the Civil War* (Washington, D.C., 1942)

Bertelson, David, *The Lazy South* (New York, 1967)

*Cash, Wilbur J., *The Mind of the South* (New York, 1941)

Cotterill, Robert S., *The Old South* (2nd rev. edn., Glendale, Cal., 1939)

*Craven, Avery O., *The Growth of Southern Nationalism, 1848–1861* (Baton Rouge, 1953)

Eaton, Clement, *A History of the Old South* (2nd edn., New York, 1966)

Eaton, Clement, *The Civilization of the Old South* (Lexington, Ky., 1968)

*Eaton, Clement, *The Freedom-of-Thought Struggle in the Old South* (rev. edn., New York, 1964)

*Eaton, Clement, *The Growth of Southern Civilization, 1790–1860* (New York, 1961)

*Franklin, John Hope, *The Militant South, 1800–1861* (Cambridge, Mass., 1956)

*Osterweis, Rollin G., *Romanticism and Nationalism in the Old South* (New Haven, 1949)

*Owsley, Frank L., *Plain Folk of the Old South* (Baton Rouge, 1949)

Potter, David M., *The South and the Sectional Conflict* (Baton Rouge, 1968)

Robert, Joseph C., *The Road from Monticello: A Study of the Virginia Slavery Debate of 1832* (Durham, N.C., 1941)

*Sellers, Charles G., ed., *The Southerner as American* (Chapel Hill, N.C., 1960)

*Sydnor, Charles S., *The Development of Southern Sectionalism, 1819–1848* (Baton Rouge, 1948)

*Taylor, William R., *Cavalier and Yankee: The Old South and the American National Character* (New York, 1961)

Chapter 3: "I WILL BE HEARD"

*Barnes, Gilbert H., *The Antislavery Impulse* (New York, 1933)

*Duberman, Martin, ed., *The Antislavery Vanguard: New Essays on the Abolitionists* (Princeton, 1965)

Dumond, Dwight L., *Anti-Slavery: The Crusade for Freedom in America* (Ann Arbor, 1967)

*Filler, Louis, *The Crusade Against Slavery, 1830–1860* (New York, 1960)

Fladeland, Betty, *James Gillespie Birney: Slaveholder to Abolitionist* (Ithaca, N.Y., 1955)

Fladeland, Betty, *Men and Brothers: Anglo-American Antislavery Co-operation* (Urbana, Ill., 1972)

Kraditor, Aileen S., *Means and Ends in American Abolitionism: Garrison and his critics on Strategy and Tactics, 1834–1850* (New York, 1969)

Merrill, Walter M., *Against Wind and Tide: A Biography of William Lloyd Garrison* (Cambridge, 1963)

Nye, Russel B., *Fettered Freedom: Civil Liberties and the Slavery*

Controversy, 1830–1860 (East Lansing, Mich., 1949)

Pease, Jane H. & William H., *Bound With Them In Chains: A Biographical History of the Antislavery Movement* (Westport, Conn., 1972)

*Quarles, Benjamin, *Black Abolitionists* (New York, 1969)

Quarles, Benjamin, *Frederick Douglass* (Washington, D.C., 1948)

Ratner, Lorman, *Powder Keg: Northern Opposition to the Antislavery Movement, 1831–1840* (New York, 1968)

*Richards, Leonard L., *'Gentlemen of Property and Standing': Anti-Abolition Mobs in Jacksonian America* (New York, 1970)

*Smith, Elbert B., *The Death of Slavery, 1837–1865* (Chicago, 1967)

Thomas, John L., *The Liberator: William Lloyd Garrison, A Biography* (Boston, 1963)

Wyatt-Brown, Bertram, *Lewis Tappan and the Evangelical War Against Slavery* (Cleveland, 1969)

*Zilversmit, Arthur, *The First Emancipation: The Abolition of Slavery in the North* (Chicago, 1967)

Chapter 4: THE GREAT ISSUE OF THE AGE

Slavery and Politics

Blue, Frederick J., *The Free Soilers: Third Party Politics, 1848–1854* (Urbana, Ill., 1973)

Campbell, Stanley W., *The Slave-Catchers: Enforcement of the Fugitive Slave Law, 1850–1860* (Chapel Hill, N.C., 1970)

*Foner, Eric, *Free Soil, Free Labor, Free Men: The Ideology of the Republican Party Before the Civil War* (New York, 1970)

*Hamilton, Holman, *Prologue to Conflict: The Crisis and Compromise of 1850* (Lexington, Ky., 1964)

Holt, Michael G., *Forging a Majority: The Formation of the Republican Party in Pittsburgh, 1848–1860* (New Haven, 1969)

Johannsen, Robert W., *Stephen A. Douglas* (New York, 1973)

Malin, James C., *The Nebraska Question, 1852–1854* (Lawrence, Kan., 1953)

Nichols, Roy F., *Franklin Pierce: Young Hickory of the Granite Hills* (Philadelphia, 1931)

Rayback, Joseph G., *Free Soil: The Election of 1848* (Lexington, Ky., 1970)

Sewell, Richard H., *John P. Hale and the Politics of Abolition* (Cambridge, Mass., 1965)

To the Brink of the Abyss

*Berwanger, Eugene H., *The Frontier Against Slavery: Western Anti-Negro Prejudice and the Slavery Extension Controversy* (Urbana, 1967)

Beveridge, Albert J., *Abraham Lincoln, 1809–1858* (2 vols., Boston, 1928)

*Fehrenbacher, Don E., *Prelude to Greatness: Lincoln in the 1850's* (Stanford, 1962)

Foner, Philip S., *Business and Slavery* (Chapel Hill, N.C., 1941)

Furnas, J. C., *The Road to Harper's Ferry* (New York, 1959)

*Jaffa, Harry V., *Crisis of the House Divided: An Interpretation of the Issues in the Lincoln-Douglas Debates* (New York, 1959)

Kutler, Stanley I., *The Dred Scott Decision: Law or Politics?* (Boston, 1967)

*Litwack, Leon F., *North of Slavery: The Negro in the Free States, 1790–1860* (Chicago, 1961)

Malin, James C., *John Brown and the Legend of Fifty Six* (Philadelphia, 1942)

Milton, George F., *Eve of Conflict: Stephen A. Douglas and the Needless War* (Boston, 1934)

Oates, Stephen B., *To Purge this Land with Blood: A Biography of John Brown* (New York, 1970)

Rawley, James A., *Race and Politics: 'Bleeding Kansas' and the Coming of the Civil War* (Philadelphia, 1970)

Russel, Robert R., *Economic Aspects of Southern Sectionalism, 1840–1861* (Urbana, Ill., 1924)

Thomas, Benjamin P., *Abraham Lincoln: A Biography* (New York, 1952)

Wells, Damon, *Stephen Douglas: The Last Years, 1857–1861* (Austin, 1971)

Wender, Herbert, *Southern Commercial Conventions, 1837–1859* (Baltimore, 1930)

Chapter 5: THE SOUTH SECEDES

Baringer, William E., *A House Dividing: Lincoln as President-Elect* (Springfield, Ill., 1945)

Barney, William L., *The Secessionist Impulse* (Princeton, 1974)

Channing, Steven A., *A Crisis of Fear: Secession in South Carolina* (New York, 1970)

Crenshaw, Ollinger, *The Slave States in the Presidential Election of 1860* (Baltimore, 1945)

Dumond, Dwight L., *The Secession Movement, 1860–1861* (New York, 1931)

Fite, Emerson D., *The Presidential Campaign of 1860* (New York, 1911)

Gunderson, Robert G., *Old Gentlemen's Convention: The Washington Peace Conference of 1861* (Madison, Wis., 1961)

Keene, Jesse L., *The Peace Convention of 1861* (Tuscaloosa, Ala., 1961)

Klein, Philip S., *President James Buchanan: A Biography* (University Park, Pa., 1962)

*Knoles, George H., ed., *The Crisis of the Union, 1860–1861* (Baton Rouge, 1965)

*Potter, David M., *Lincoln and his Party in the Secession Crisis* (New Haven, 1942)

Rainwater, Percy L., *Mississippi, Storm-Center of Secession, 1856–1861* (Baton Rouge, 1938)

Scrugham, Mary, *The Peaceable Americans of 1860–61: A Study in Public Opinion* (New York, 1921)

*Stampp, Kenneth M., *And the War Came: The North and the Secession Crisis, 1860–61* (Baton Rouge, 1950)

Stern, Philip Van Doren, ed., *Prologue to Sumter* (Greenwich, Conn., 1961)

Strode, Hudson, *Jefferson Davis, American Patriot, 1808–1861* (New York, 1955)

Wooster, Ralph A., *The Secession Conventions of the South* (Princeton, 1962)

Chapter 6: BROTHER AGAINST BROTHER

The Struggle in Prospect

*Capers, Gerald M., *Stephen A. Douglas, Defender of the Union* (Boston, 1959)

*Current, Richard N., *Lincoln and the First Shot* (Philadelphia, 1963)

Donald, David, *Charles Sumner and the Coming of the Civil War* (New York, 1960)

*Fehrenbacher, Don E., *Prelude to Greatness: Lincoln in the 1850's* (Stanford, Cal., 1962)

*Foner, Eric, *Free Soil, Free Labor, Free Men: The Ideology of the Republican Party Before the Civil War* (New York, 1970)

Graebner, Norman A., ed., *Politics and the Crisis of 1860* (Urbana, Ill., 1961)

Klein, Philip S., *President James Buchanan* (University Park, Pa., 1962)

*Knoles, George H., ed., *The Crisis of the Union, 1860–1861* (Baton Rouge, 1965)

*Potter, David M., *Lincoln and His Party in the Secession Crisis* (New Haven, 1942)

*Stampp, Kenneth M., *And the War Came: The North and the Secession Crisis* (Baton Rouge, 1950)

Wooster, Ralph A., *The Secession Conventions in the South* (Princeton, N.J., 1962)

From Bull Run to Gettysburg
(see also list for Chapter 10, The Road to Appomattox)

Ambrose, Stephen E., *Halleck: Lincoln's Chief of Staff* (Baton Rouge, 1962)

Anderson, Bern, *By Sea and By River: The Naval History of the Civil War* (New York, 1962)

*Catton, Bruce, *This Hallowed Ground: The Story of the Union Side of the Civil War* (New York, 1956)

Catton, Bruce, *Grant Moves South* (Boston, 1960)

Connelly, Thomas L., & Jones, Archer, *The Politics of Command: Factions and Ideas in Confederate Strategy* (Baton Rouge, 1973)

Freeman, Douglas S., *Robert E. Lee: A Biography* (4 vols., New York,

1934–35; 1 vol. abridgment by Richard Harwell, New York, 1961)

Freeman, Douglas S., *Lee's Lieutenants: A Study in Command* (3 vols., New York, 1942–44)

Hassler, Warren W., Jr., *General George B. McClellan: Shield of the Union* (Baton Rouge, 1957)

Hassler, Warren W., Jr., *Commanders of the Army of the Potomac* (Baton Rouge, 1962)

Jones, Virgil C., *The Civil War at Sea* (3 vols., New York, 1960–62)

Lewis, Lloyd, *Captain Sam Grant* (Boston, 1950)

*Pullen, John J., *The Twentieth Maine: A Volunteer Regiment in the Civil War* (Philadelphia, 1957)

Thomason, John W., *Jeb Stuart* (New York, 1930)

Tucker, Glenn, *High Tide at Gettysburg: The Campaign in Pennsylvania* (Indianapolis, 1958)

Vandiver, Frank E., *Mighty Stonewall* (New York, 1957)

Warner, Ezra J., *Generals in Gray: Lives of the Confederate Commanders* (Baton Rouge, 1959)

Warner, Ezra J., *Generals in Blue: Lives of the Union Commanders* (Baton Rouge, 1964)

*Wiley, Bell I., *The Life of Johnny Reb: The Common Soldier of the Confederacy* (Indianapolis, 1943)

*Wiley, Bell I., *The Life of Billy Yank: The Common Soldier of the Union* (Indianapolis, 1952)

*Williams, T. Harry, *Lincoln and His Generals* (New York, 1952)

*Williams, T. Harry, *P.G.T. Beauregard: Napoleon in Gray* (Baton Rouge, 1955)

Chapter 7: THE POLITICS OF WAR

Government by the People

Belz, Herman, *Reconstructing the Union: Theory and Practice During the Civil War* (Ithaca, N.Y., 1969)

Carman, Harry J., & Luthin, Reinhard H., *Lincoln and the Patronage* (New York, 1943)

*Current, Richard N., *The Lincoln Nobody Knows* (New York, 1958)

Donald, David, *Charles Sumner and the Rights of Man* (New York, 1970)

Donald, David, ed., *Inside Lincoln's Cabinet: The Civil War Diaries of Salmon P. Chase* (New York, 1954)

*Fehrenbacher, Don E., ed., *The Leadership of Abraham Lincoln* (New York, 1970)

Hyman, Harold M., *A More Perfect Union: The Impact of the Civil War and Reconstruction on the Constitution* (New York, 1973)

Luthin, Reinhard H., *The Real Abraham Lincoln* (Englewood Cliffs, N.J., 1960)

*McWhiney, Grady, ed., *Grant, Lee, Lincoln and the Radicals* (Evanston, Ill., 1964)

Rawley, James A., ed., *Lincoln and Civil War Politics* (New York, 1969)

*Silver, David M., *Lincoln's Supreme Court* (Urbana, Ill., 1956)

Thomas, Benjamin P., & Hyman, Harold M., *Stanton: The Life and Times of Lincoln's Secretary of War* (New York, 1962)

Trefousse, Hans, *The Radical Republicans* (New York, 1969)

Van Deusen, Glyndon G., *William Henry Seward* (New York, 1967)

*Williams, T. Harry, *Lincoln and the Radicals* (Madison, Wis., 1941)

The Confederate States of America
(see also list for Chapter 8)

Amlund, Curtis A., *Federalism in the Southern Confederacy* (Washington, D.C., 1966)

*Davis, Jefferson, *The Rise and Fall of the Confederate Government* (2 vols., 1881; repr. New York, 1958)

Hill, Louise B., *Joseph E. Brown and the Confederacy* (Chapel Hill, N.C., 1939)

Lee, Charles R., *The Confederate Constitutions* (Chapel Hill, N.C., 1963)

Meade, Robert D., *Judah P. Benjamin: Confederate Statesman* (New York, 1943)

Owsley, Frank L., *State Rights in the Confederacy* (Chicago, 1925)

Patrick, Rembert W., *Jefferson Davis and His Cabinet* (Baton Rouge, 1944)

Ringold, May S., *The Role of the State Legislatures in the Confederacy* (Athens, Ga., 1966)

Strode, Hudson, *Jefferson Davis* (3 vols., New York, 1955–64)

Tatum, Georgia L., *Disloyalty in the Confederacy* (Chapel Hill, N.C., 1934)

*Thomas, Emory M., *The Confederacy as a Revolutionary Experience* (Englewood Cliffs, N.J., 1971)

Thompson, William Y., *Robert Toombs of Georgia* (Baton Rouge, 1966)

Yates, Richard E., *The Confederacy and Zeb Vance* (Tuscaloose, Ala., 1958)

Yearns, Wilfred B., *The Confederate Congress* (Athens, Ga., 1960)

Chapter 8: BEHIND THE LINES

(see also list for Chapter 7,
The Confederate States of America)

Black, Robert C., *The Railroads of the Confederacy* (Chapel Hill, N.C., 1952)

Dusinberre, William, *Civil War Issues in Philadelphia, 1856–1865* (Philadelphia, 1965)

Goff, Richard D., *Confederate Supply* (Durham, N.C., 1969)

*Gray, Wood, *The Hidden Civil War: The Story of the Copperheads* (New York, 1942)

Hesseltine, William B., *Lincoln and the War Governors* (New York, 1948)

*Kirwan, Albert D., ed., *The Confederacy* (New York, 1959)

Klement, Frank L., *The Copperheads in the Middle West* (Chicago, 1960)

*Leech, Margaret, *Reveillé in Washington* (New York, 1941)

Massey, Mary E., *Bonnet Brigades: American Women and the Civil War* (New York, 1966)

Moore, Albert B., *Conscription and Conflict in the Confederacy* (New York, 1924)

Murdock, Eugene C., *One Million Men: The Civil War Draft in the North* (Madison, Wis., 1971)

Myers, Robert M., ed., *The Children of Pride: A True Story of Georgia and the Civil War* (New Haven, 1972)

Niven, John, *Connecticut for the Union: The Role of the State in the Civil War* (New Haven, 1965)

Parrish, William E., *A History of Missouri*, vol. 3, *1860–1875* (Columbia, Mo., 1973)

Ramsdell, Charles W., *Behind the Lines in the Southern Confederacy* (Baton Rouge, 1944)

Smith, George W., & Judah, Charles, eds., *Life in the North During the Civil War: A Source History* (Albuquerque, 1966)

Thomas, Emory M., *The Confederate State of Richmond: A Biography of the Capital* (Athens, Ga., 1971)

Todd, Richard C., *Confederate Finance* (Athens, Ga., 1954)

Weber, Thomas, *The Northern Railroads in the Civil War, 1861–1865* (New York, 1952)

*Wiley, Bell I., *The Plain People of the Confederacy* (Baton Rouge, 1943)

Chapter 9: THE WIDER VIEW

The Death of Slavery

Blassingame, John W., *Black New Orleans, 1860–1880* (Chicago, 1973)

Brewer, James H., *The Confederate Negro: Virginia's Craftsmen and Military Laborers, 1861–1865* (Durham, N.C., 1969)

Cornish, Dudley T., *The Sable Arm: Negro Troops in the Union Army, 1861–1865* (New York, 1956)

Durden, Robert F., *The Gray and the Black: The Confederate Debate on Emancipation* (Baton Rouge, 1972)

*Franklin, John H., *The Emancipation Proclamation* (New York, 1963)

Gerteis, Louis S., *From Contraband to Freedom: Federal Policy Towards Southern Blacks, 1861–1865* (Westport, Conn., 1973)

McPherson, James, *The Struggle for Equality: Abolitionists and the Negro in the Civil War and Reconstruction* (Princeton, N.J., 1964)

*McPherson, James, ed., *The Negro's Civil War: How American Negroes Felt and Acted During the War for the Union* (New York, 1965)

*Quarles, Benjamin, *The Negro in the Civil War* (Boston, 1953)

Quarles, Benjamin, *Lincoln and the Negro* (New York, 1962)

*Voegeli, V. Jacque, *Free But Not Equal: The Midwest and the Negro During the Civil War* (Chicago, 1967)

*Wiley, Bell I., *Southern Negroes, 1861–1865* (New Haven, 1938)

*indicates paperback

Europe and the Civil War

Adams, Ephraim D., ed., *Great Britain and the American Civil War* (2 vols., London, 1925; 1 vol. edn., New York, 1958)

Case, Lynn M., & Spencer, Warren F., *The United States and France: Civil War Diplomacy* (Philadelphia, 1970)

Cochran, Hamilton, *Blockade Runners of the Confederacy* (New York, 1958)

Crook, D. P., *The North, the South and the Powers, 1861–1865* (New York, 1974)

Cullop, Charles P., *Confederate Propaganda in Europe, 1861–1865* (Coral Gables, Fla., 1969)

Ellison, Mary, *Support for Secession: Lancashire and the American Civil War* (Chicago, 1972)

Hyman, Harold, ed., *Heard Round the World: The Impact of the Civil War Abroad* (New York, 1969)

Jordan, Donaldson, & Pratt, Edwin J., *Europe and the Civil War* (Cambridge, Mass., 1931)

Owsley, Frank L., *King Cotton Diplomacy* (Chicago, 1931; rev. edn., 1959)

Sideman, Belle B., & Friedman, Lillian, eds., *Europe Looks at the Civil War* (New York, 1960)

Chapter 10: UNION AND VICTORY

The Road to Appomattox (see also list for Chapter 6, From Bull Run to Gettysburg)

Barrett, John G., *Sherman's March Through the Carolinas* (Chapel Hill, N.C., 1956)

Burne, Alfred H., *Lee, Grant and Sherman: A Study in Leadership in 1864–65* (London, 1938)

*Catton, Bruce, *A Stillness at Appomattox* (Garden City, N.Y., 1953)

Catton, Bruce, *Grant Takes Command* (Boston, 1969)

Cleaves, Freeman, *Rock of Chickamauga: The Life of General George H. Thomas* (Norman, Okla., 1948)

*Davis, Burke, *To Appomattox: Nine April Days, 1865* (New York, 1959)

Kerby, Robert L., *Kirby Smith's Confederacy: The Trans-Mississippi, 1863–1865* (New York, 1972)

Lewis, Lloyd, *Sherman, Fighting Prophet* (New York, 1932)

O'Connor, Richard, *Sheridan the Inevitable* (Indianapolis, 1953)

Stern, Philip Van Doren, *An End to Valor: The Last Days of the Civil War* (Boston, 1958)

Why Did the North Win?

Aaron, Daniel, *The Unwritten War: American Writers and the Civil War* (New York, 1973)

*Benét, Stephen V., *John Brown's Body* (New York, 1928)

*Bishop, Jim, *The Day Lincoln Was Shot* (New York, 1955)

*Commager, Henry S., ed., *The Defeat of the Confederacy: A Documentary Survey* (Princeton, 1964)

*Cunliffe, Marcus, *Soldiers and Civilians: The Martial Spirit in America, 1775–1865* (Boston, 1968)

*Donald, David, ed., *Why the North Won the Civil War* (Baton Rouge, 1960)

*Eisenschiml, Otto, *Why Was Lincoln Murdered?* (Boston, 1937)

*Lewis, Lloyd, *Myths After Lincoln* (New York, 1929)

Livermore, Thomas L., *Numbers and Losses in the Civil War in America, 1861–1865* (Boston, 1901)

*Pressly, Thomas J., *Americans Interpret Their Civil War* (Princeton, N.J., 1962)

*Stampp, Kenneth M., ed., *The Causes of the Civil War* (Englewood Cliffs, N.J., 1959)

*Warren, Robert P., *The Legacy of the Civil War: Meditations on the Centennial* (New York, 1961)

*Whitman, Walt, *Complete Poetry and Selected Prose*, ed. James E. Miller, Jr. (Boston, 1959)

Index

Page numbers in italics refer to captions

A

Abolition movement, 24, 26, 28, 35, 54, 55; W. L.
Garrison, 61, 68, 70–71; and Christianity, 62;
Enlightenment, 62; Quakers, 62–63; Methodists, *62*,
63; abolition of northern slavery, 63–64; Thomas
Jefferson, 65; weakening of, 65; ''gradualism'', 65;
aided by communications revolution, 68, 72, *73*;
B. Lundy, 68, 70; Tappan brothers, 71–72; abolition
in British West Indies, 71; American Anti-Slavery
Society, 71–72; organization of, 72; petition
campaign, 72, 74, *76*, 77; confrontation tactics,
74–75, 81; reaction against, 77–78, *79*; racial
equality, 78; radical party of, 81; ecclesiastical
party of, 81; political party of, 81; Afro-American
party, 81, 82–83; respectable element in politics, 91;
see also Negroes; Slavery
Adairsville, Battle of (1864), 254
Adams, Charles Francis, 89, 234, *235*, 236
Adams, Henry, 236
Adams, John Quincy (president), defense of J.
Cinque, *35*; attack on ''gag rule'', 76; Missouri
debates, 86, 104
Adder's Den, 269
Address of the Southern Delegates in Congress, 91
Address to the Slaveholding States, 134
Africa, 28, 30
African Methodist Episcopal Church, 68, *69*
Agnew, Samuel, 34
Agriculture, in the South, 40, 45–46, *46*, 48;
specialization, 42; effect of westward movement
on, 46
Alabama, plantation owners, 40; cotton, 43;
secession convention, 125, 132, 134; secession
ordinance, 134
Alabama (ship), 241–242, *241*, 259–260
''Alabama Arbitration'', 241–242
Albert, Prince Consort (Britain), *237*
Alexander II (Russia), 241
Allen, Richard, 68
Amalgamation (miscegenation), 78
American and Foreign Anti-Slavery Society, 82
American Anti-Slavery Society, 71–72, 82
American Colonization Society, 65, 68, 70
American Missionary Association, 81
American Red Cross, 166
American Slavery As It Is, 26, 72
Amistad (ship), 35
Anderson, Robert, 134, 136, 137, *149*, 152
Andersonville, Georgia, 217, *217*
Andrew, John A., 204
Antietam, Battle of (1862), *163*, 166, 206, *210*,
238, *274*
Appeal of the Independent Democrats, The, 101
Appomattox, Virginia, 262
Arkansas, cotton, 44; secession, 152; Confederate
state, 194
Army of Northern Virginia (Civil War), 160, 162,
170, 171, 173, *208*, 251, 253, 262
Army of Tennessee, 245, 249, 258
Army of the Cumberland, *244*, 245, *270*
Army of the Potomac, 155, 158, 163, 167, 170,
171, 175, *208*, 242, 249, 250, 271
Atlanta, Georgia, *195*, 247, 253, 254, *254*, 255,
255, 258
Atlanta Cyclorama, *256*

B

Atlantic Monthly, 214
Atzerodt, George, *266*, *268*
Augusta, Florida, 42

Bahia slave rebellion, 38
Baltimore, Maryland, population growth, 42, 51
Baltimore and Ohio Railroad, 218
Banks, Nathaniel P., 126, 128, 160, 249
Baptists, and slavery, 74
''Barnburners'', 88, 89, 90, 97, 104
Barton, Clara, 166
Bates, Edward, 126, 128
''Battle Above the Clouds'', *244*, 245
Beard, Charles A., 233
Beaufort, South Carolina, 156
Beauregard, Pierre G. T., 153, 251, 259
Beecher, Lyman, 98
Bell, John, *128*, 129, 131
Benjamin, Judah P., 193
Bentonville, Battle of (1865), 261
Bible Argument, The, 72
Big Black River, Battle of (1863), 170
''Billy Yank'', 270, 271
Bingham, George Caleb, *181*
Birney, James G., 72, 77–78, *77*, 82
Black Hawk War (1832), 153
Bledsoe, Albert Taylor, 57
Blockades, Civil War, 155, *196*, 198, 200, 211, 235,
236, 241, 242, 259
''Bonnie Blue Flag, The'', *214*
Booth, Edwin, *214*, 216
Booth, John Wilkes, *214*, 216, 264, *266*, 267, 268,
269
Booth, Junius Brutus, Jr., *214*, 216
Bounty jumping, 210
Bragg, Braxton, 167, 168–169, 197, 244–245
Brandy Station, Battle of (1863), 173
Brazil, slavery, 10, 12, 24, *26*, 28, 30, 35, 38
Breckinridge, John C., 125, *126*, 129, 131, 132,
251, 253, 268
Bristoe Station, Battle of (1862), 163
Bristol, England, *239*
Brooklyn (ship), 136
Brooks, Preston S., 107, *107*
Brown, John, 106, 107, 120, 122, *122*, 125, 132;
see also Slavery
Brown, Joseph, 194, 197, 200
Buchanan, Franklin, 161
Buchanan, James (president), presidential candidate,
108; 1856 elections, 110; Dred Scott case, 112,
112, 113, *113*; Kansas problem, 112; Lecompton
constitution, 114, 116; Lincoln's challenge, 116,
117, 118, 120, 180; John Brown's Raid, 122; and
Stephen Douglas, 125, *126*; 1860 presidential
campaign, 129; secession, 132, 134, 136, 137,
146, 178
Buell, Don Carlos, 158, 167
Buffalo, New York, 51
Bulloch, James D., 242
Bull Run, First Battle of (1861), *152*, 153–154,
154, 155, 194
Bull Run, Second Battle of (1862), *162*, 163, 206,
238
Burns, Anthony, 96
Burnside, Ambrose E., *152*, 166–167, 182

C

Butler, Andrew P., 107
Butler, Benjamin F., 225, 249, 251, 259
Butler, Pierce, 27

Calhoun, John C. (vice-president), 43; abolitionism,
76; slavery, *86*, 87, 88, 91, 93–94
California, Compromise of 1850, 92; statehood, 91;
proslavery, 94
Cameron, Simon, 126, 128
Canals, 48
Capitol, *93*, *149*, 150
Cass, Lewis, 88, *90*
Castle Pinckney, South Carolina, 134
Cedar Creek, Battle of (1864), 253
Cedar Run, Battle of (1862), 163
Champion's Hill, Battle of (1863), 170
Chancellorsville, Battle of (1863), 171
Channing, William Ellery, 27
Chantilly, Battle of (1862), 163
Charleston, South Carolina, 42, 51, *51*, 125, 259
Charleston Mercury, 129
Chase, Salmon P., Liberty party, 89, 96; on Kansas
Nebraska Act, 101, 102; Republican candidate,
126, 128; secretary of the Treasury, *179*, 220–221;
chief justice, *186*
Chattanooga, Tennessee, 244–245
Chicago, Illinois, 51, 125
Chickahominy River, 162
Chickamauga Creek, Battle of (1863), 245
Chickasaw Bayou, 169
Christy, E. P., 47
Christy, George, 216
Cinque, Joseph, *35*
Civil rights, 223
Civil War (1861–65), balance of forces at outset,
144–146; Union volunteers, *151*; Confederate
Soldier, *151*; Fort Sumter, *149*, 152; disposition
of troops at outbreak, 153; First Bull Run, *152*,
153–154, *154*; Union navy, 155–156, *257*, 258–260;
Western theater, 156, *156*, 158, 167–170, 253–254,
256, 258; ''river war'', 156, 158; Shiloh, *157*, 158;
Pea Ridge, 158; Ulysses S. Grant, 158, 246–247,
247; fall of New Orleans, 158; *Merrimack v Monitor*,
158, 161, *161*; Peninsula campaign, 159; eastern
theater, 160, *160*, 162–163, 166, *250*; Valley
campaigns, 160, 253; Robert E. Lee, 160, 162,
246, *246*; Seven days' campaign, 162; Second Bull
Run, *162*, 163; first invasion of North, 163, *163*,
166; Antietam, *163*, 166; Fredericksburg, 167, *167*;
Perryville, 167; Vicksburg, 169–170, *169*;
Chancellorsville, 171; second invasion of North,
171, 173–174; Union politics, 178–180; Confederate
army, 194, 196–197; conscription,
185, 194, 206, 210; prisoners of war, *207*, 217,
217; logistics, 208; reportage, 212, 214;
entertainment, 214, *214*, 216; medical facilities,
216, *218*–*219*; profiteering, 216, 219; Negro
troops, 185, 201, 210, *228*, 230, *231*, 232–233,
233; European reaction, 234–236, *234*–*235*,
238–239, 241–242; English cotton famine,
235–236, *236*; Chickamauga Creek, 245; Lookout
Mountain Missionary Ridge campaign, *244*, 245;
Cold Harbor, 251; Sherman's advance, *252*,
253–254, *254*, 256, *256*, 258; siege of Petersburg,
251, 262; Appomattox, 262; armies' size, 265;

Missouri Compromise (1820), 78, 85, 100, 101, 112, 113, 116, 223
Missouri debates, 65, 85–86, *85*, 91, 121
Missouri River, 42
Mobile, Alabama, 42, 51 *257*, 259
Monitor (ship), 158, 161, *161*
Monroe, James (president), slavery issue, 86
Monroe Doctrine, 238
Montgomery, Alabama, 140, 153, 189, 190, *191*
Montgomery, Convention, 140, 190, 192, 193
Moran, Thomas, *20*
Morgan, John Hunt, 167
Morris, George P., 47
Mouton, Alexander, 139
Mulattoes, 19, 26

N

Napoleon III, 171, 236, 238, *238*, 242
Nashville, Tennessee, 158, 256, 258
Nashville (ship), *241*
Nashville, Battle of (1864), 258
Nashville Convention (1850), 94
Natchez, Mississippi, 41, *49*
National Anti-Slavery Standard, 72
National Banking Act (1863), 221
National Era, 96
Nationalism, American, 43, 78
Nativism, 97, 110
Nebraska, Platte territory, 100; Kansas-Nebraska Act (1854), 100–102
Negro Convention Movement, 68
Negroes, slavery, 10, 13–38 *passim*; American Colonization Society, 65, 68; Negro Convention Movement, 68; in Union Army, 185, 210, *228*, 230, *231*, 232, 233, *233*; in Confederate Army, 201, 233; civil rights, 223; Northern hostility to, 228; nationalism of, 228
"Negro Soldier Law", 233
New England, industry, 48, 219; desegregation, 83
New England Anti-Slavery Society, 71
New England Emigrant Aid Society, 105
New Hampshire, slavery, 63
New Jersey, slavery, 10, 64; industry, 48
New Madrid, Mississippi, 158
New Market, Battle of (1864), 253
New Mexico, Compromise of 1850, 92
New Orleans, Louisiana, 42, *42*, 43, 51, 177
New Orleans Daily True Delta, 129
Newspapers, 203, *203*, 212, 214
New York, slavery, 10, 64; Know-Nothings, 102; Civil War, 204
New York Central Railroad, 218
New York City, trade, 51; Civil War, 203, *204*, *205*, 216; draft riot, 210, 211, 215, *215*, 228
New York draft riot, 210, 211, 215, *215*, 228
New York Herald, 146, *181*, 212
New York's Seventh Regiment, 204, *204*
New York Tribune, *183*, 210, 214, 230, 232
Nisbet, Eugenius, 138
Norfolk, Virginia, 156
North, the, hostility to the South, 86, 88, 91, 101, 116, 120; Republican strength, 103; expansionists, 120; Civil War industrial might, 144, 210; economic boom, 216, 218–221; Civil War aims, 274
North American Review, 214
North Carolina, tobacco, 44; secession, 152; Confederate state, 194, 210
North Star (abolitionist paper), *83*
Northwest Ordinance (1787), 65, 113, 118
Northwest Territory (US), 105
Nullification, doctrine of, 132

O

Oakland House, Louisville, *58*
Ohio River, 42, 45

"Oh! Susanna", 47
Old Dominion (ship), *239*
"Old Folks at Home", 47
Old Kentucky Home, The, 33
Old Plantation, The, 31
"Old Uncle Ned", 47
Olmsted, Frederick Law, 24, 216
Omerhausse, John, *207*
"Open Thy Lattice, Love", 47
Opequon Creek, Battle of (1864), 253
Oregon, American expansion into, 87
"Orphan Brigade", 168
Orr, James, 236
Osawotomie raid, 107, 122
Osliaba (ship), *242*
Ostend manifesto (1854), 101–102
O'Sullivan, T. H., *249*
Our American Cousin, 267

P

Paine, Lewis, 266, 268
Palmares, Brazil, 38
Palmerston, Henry John Temple, 3rd Viscount, 234, *234*
Panics, 1857, *114*, 116
Patterson, General, 153
Patti, Adelina, 216
Peace Convention (1860), 140
Peach Orchard, Gettysburg, 174
Peach Tree Creek, Battle of (1864), 254
Pea Ridge, Battle of (1862), 158
Pemberton, John C., 170
Pendleton, William Nelson, 244
Peninsula campaign (1862), 159, 162
Pennsylvania, slavery, 10, 64; Know-Nothings, 102
Pennsylvania Railroad, 218
Perryville, Battle of (1862), 167
Petersburg, Siege of (1864–65), 251, *251*, *252*, 262, *262*
Philadelphia, Pennsylvania, 51
Philanthropist, 72, 77
Phillips, Wendell, 81
Phipps, Benjamin, 37
Pickens, Francis, 137
Pickett, George E., *173*, 174–175
Piedmont, Battle of (1864), 253
Pierce, Franklin (president), *96*, 97, 100, 101, 107, 108, 118
Pine Mountain, Battle of (1864), 254
Plantations, 12, *12*, 13, *13*, 21–22, 27–38 *passim*, *40*, 40–59 *passim*
Platte, Territory of, 100
Pleasant Hill, Battle of (1864), 249
Pleasonton, Alfred, 173
Polk, James K. (president), 87, *87*, 88
Polk, Leonidas, 144
Pope, John, 158, *159*, 162–163, *162*, 197, 206
"Popular Sovereignty", 88, 100, 108, 116, 117, 118
Population, 1860, 144
Porter, David D., 169, 170, 259
Port Hudson, Louisiana, 170
Port Hudson, Battle of (1863), 230
Port Republic, Battle of (1862), 160
Potomac River, 153, 173
Pottawotomie Massacre, 107, 120
Potter, David, 59
Power of Congress over the District of Columbia, The, 72
Presbyterians, 74
Presidency, powers of, 154, *178*, 185; and Lincoln, 180
Price, Sterling, 168
Profiteering, 216, 219
Prosser, Gabriel, 38
Provost marshall general, office created, 185
Pryor, Mrs Roger, 212
Public Works, 91, 121, 128
Puerto Rico, 10
Pugh, George, 125

QR

Quantrill, William Clark, 213, *213*
Quantrill's Raiders, 213, *213*
Quilombo, 38

Racism, toward blacks, 34, 56, 57, 65, 68, 71, 78, 83, 90, 118, 191, 224, 228–229, 232
Railroads, 14, 48, 218, 219, *272*, 273
"Rally Round the Flag", 216
Randolph, Peyton, 86
Rankin, John, 66
Rapidan River, 244, 250
Rappahannock River, 166, 170, *208*
Reagan, John H., 193
Reconstruction, Freedmen's Bureau, 185; 1863 formula, 185
Red River, 249
Religion, slave, 34; unifier, 43; and reform movements, 68
Republican party, founding of, 102–104, *102*, 107, 108; 1856 election, 110–112; Illinois elections 1858, 117–118, *118*; Lincoln, 117–118; policy, 120; 1860 convention, 125–126, 128; 1860 election, 129, 131–132; Crittenden proposals, 135; Civil War, 179–180; 1866 elections, 160
Resaca, Battle of (1864), 254
Rhett, R. Barnwell, 129, 134, *134*
Rhode Island, abolition of slavery, 64
Rice, David, 63, 65
Rice, 11, *12*, 21–22, 42, 44, 45, *53*
Richmond, Virginia, 13, *13*, 153, 158, *160*, 166, 194, 211, 251, *260*, 262, *262*, 273
Richmond and Danville Railroad, 262
Ride for Liberty, A, 67
"Ring Shout", 34
"River War" (Civil War), 156, *156*, 158
Roanoke Island, North Carolina, 156
Roman Catholic Church, 110
Root, Robert Marshall, *118*
Rosecrans, William S., 167, 168–169, 244–245
Rost, Pierre, 234
Ruffin, Edmund, 125, *149*
Russell, John Russell, 1st Earl of, 234, *237*, 241
Russell, William Howard, 203
Russia, and US Civil War, 238, 239, 241, *242*

S

Sabine Cross Roads, Battle of (1864), 249
St Louis, Missouri, 51, *51*
San Jacinto (ship), 236, *237*
Savage station, Battle of (1862), 162
Savannah, Georgia, 42, 51, 258
Savannah River, 156
Sayers, Tom, 203
Sayler's Creek, Battle of (1865), 262
Schofield, John M., 256
Scott, Orange, 81, *81*
Scott, Winfield, *96*, 97, 136, 137, 144, 152, 153, *154*, 265
Secession, 132, *133*, 134, 135, 136, 138, 139–140, *139*, *140*, 146, 148, 152–153, 178, 189, 223
Second Bank of the United States, 221
Sectionalism, 86, 87, 88, 91, 94, 101, 102, 104, 105, 110–112, 116, 118, 120
Sedgwick, John, 170, 171, 270
Semmes, Raphael, 259, 260
Senate, response to abolition petition campaign, 76; debate on Compromise of 1850, 93–94
Settlers, and slavery issue, 105–107, *114*
Seven Days' campaign (1862), 162
Seven Pines, Battle of (1861), 159, 162
Seward, William H., 91, 93, 94, 96, 102, 105, 126, 128, 129, 132, 135, 146, 152, 183, 234, 236, 238, 268